GOOD GOVERNAN
GROWTH

Governance has been incorporated into the development models of many countries because of its role in ameliorating inequalities in society. This book explores whether good governance boosts or hinders economic growth with perspectives from countries like India, the USA, Nigeria, Turkey, Pakistan, Bangladesh, Nepal, and others, and on groups of developing nations like BRICS and ASEAN.

Governance has twin roles within economic systems. The first is where it guides administrators and the second is the normative role where it may act as a stimulus to economic growth and development. With the help of empirical investigations, this book analyses the interrelationships between good governance and inclusive and sustainable economic growth, productive employment, political stability, and decent work for all. It assesses the impact of various governance indicators and policy strategies on the economy and the GDP of countries in the Global North and South. The book also focuses on roadblocks to good governance such as violent conflicts, corruption, international threats, and crises and its implication on economic growth.

This volume will be of interest to students and researchers of economics, political science, social science, international relations, public administration, and sociology.

Ramesh Chandra Das, PhD, is a professor at the Department of Economics, Vidyasagar University, India, with 25 years of teaching and research experience in the fields of theoretical and applied economics, environmental economics, and political economics.

GOOD GOVERNANCE AND ECONOMIC GROWTH

Complimentary or Problematic?

Edited by Ramesh Chandra Das

Routledge
Taylor & Francis Group

LONDON AND NEW YORK

Designed cover image: Getty Images

First published 2025
by Routledge
4 Park Square, Milton Park, Abingdon, Oxon OX14 4RN

and by Routledge
605 Third Avenue, New York, NY 10158

Routledge is an imprint of the Taylor & Francis Group, an informa business

British Library Cataloguing-in-Publication Data
A catalogue record for this book is available from the British Library

Library of Congress Cataloging-in-Publication Data
Names: Das, Ramesh Chandra, editor.
Title: Good governance and economic growth: complimentary or problematic? / edited by Ramesh Chandra Das.
Description: Abingdon, Oxon ; New York, NY : Routledge, 2025. | Includes bibliographical references and index.
Identifiers: LCCN 2024026691 (print) | LCCN 2024026692 (ebook) | ISBN 9781032697567 (hardback) | ISBN 9781032870519 (paperback) | ISBN 9781003530688 (ebook)
Subjects: LCSH: Economic development--Political aspects--Developing countries. | Economic development--Political aspects--Developed countries.
Classification: LCC HD87 .G6463 2025 (print) | LCC HD87 (ebook) | DDC 338.9--dc23/eng/20240614
LC record available at https://lccn.loc.gov/2024026691
LC ebook record available at https://lccn.loc.gov/2024026692

ISBN: 978-1-032-69756-7 (hbk)
ISBN: 978-1-032-87051-9 (pbk)
ISBN: 978-1-003-53068-8 (ebk)

DOI: 10.4324/9781003530688

Typeset in Sabon
by SPi Technologies India Pvt Ltd (Straive)

To my teachers in the early age of my education
Pulin Bihari Mondal
Late Rajkumar Sahoo
Late Murarimohan Kanjilal
Thakurdas Mahapatra
Late Srihari Pattanayek
Nanigopal Mahapatra
Kumudendu Mahapatra
Late Ashutosh Jana
Late Gourisankar Jana
Kalipada Giri
Bisweswar Bera
Nabakumar Jana
Sirshendu Das
Bijon Kumar Panda

CONTENTS

FIGURES

TABLES

CONTRIBUTORS

Kishan Agarwalla is currently working as Assistant Professor of Economics at the Indian Institute of Legal Studies, Siliguri, India. He has completed his master's degree and MPhil degree in Economics from the University of North Bengal. His area of research interests includes Resource Economics, Environmental Economics, Mathematical Economics, Statistics, and International Economics. He has published articles in several peer-reviewed journals and various chapters in books.

Md. Saifullah Akon, PhD, is Assistant Professor in Japanese Studies at the University of Dhaka. He is also the Executive Director of Indo-Pacific Network (INPANET), a network of leading researchers that aims to exchange and enhance knowledge related to the Indo-Pacific. His areas of specialization are Indo-Pacific, FOIP, Security, Japan-South Asia Relations, Aid Diplomacy, Disaster Diplomacy, Foreign Policy, and Human Rights.

Joshua Kodjo Asiedu completed his master's in Economics from Jain (Deemed-to-be) University, Bangalore, India, and is an aspiring researcher currently living in Ghana, Africa. His research interests include econometrics, development economics, and public policy.

Olumide A. Ayetigbo is currently a lecturer and doctoral student in the Department of Business Administration, National Open University of Nigeria, Jabi, Abuja, Nigeria. His research interests lie on organizational behaviour, entrepreneurship development, and financial development.

Alemu Tulu Chala, PhD, is Lecturer in Economics at Dalarna University (Sweden). His PhD degree is from Lund University (Sweden). His research interests lie in the area of financial economics, with a focus on corporate finance, household finance, small business finance, and macro-finance.

Tonmoy Chatterjee, PhD, is an assistant professor in the Department of Economics at Bhairab Ganguly College, West Bengal, India. He has research interests in International Trade Theory, General Equilibrium, Health Economics, and Development Economics. He has published a number of research articles in several international journals of economics.

Catia Cialani, PhD, is an associate professor in Economics at Dalarna University (Sweden). She obtained her PhD in Economics from Umeå University (Sweden). Formerly, Dr. Cialani was an economist at the Italian National Agency for New Technologies, Energy and Sustainable Economic Development (ENEA) and at the National Council of Economy and Labor (CNEL). Her research interests include environmental and energy economics, economic growth, health economics, applied econometrics, and circular economy.

Akash Dandapat is an assistant professor, Dukhulal Nibaran Chandra College, Murshidabad, India, and a former ICSSR Doctoral fellow at the Department of Economics, Vidyasagar University, West Bengal, India. He worked as a JRF at the Indian Institute of Technology Kharagpur. He received MPhil in Economics from Vidyasagar University. He was a gold medallist in BSc and MSc for first position.

Dipankar Das, PhD, is an assistant teacher in Economics at the Ranghat Anchal High School, North 24 Parganas, West Bengal, India. He has earned his MPhil and PhD degrees from the West Bengal State University, India. His research areas are financial flows in emerging economies and the economics of education.

Pinaki Das, PhD, is Professor of Economics at Vidyasagar University in India. He was awarded the Gold Medal for first position in MSc in Economics. He has performed the role of Project Director of three major research projects funded by the University Grants Commission of India and the Indian Council of Social Science Research. He has over 50 research papers published in internationally reputed journals and guided 14 research scholars and published six books.

Promila Das, PhD, is an assistant professor at the School of Business, UIM, Karnavati University Gandhinagar. Her teaching interests include Micro

Economics, Macro Economics, Development Economics, and Econometrics. She is an active researcher in the areas of Behavioural Economics, Development Economics, Macro Economics, and Gender Economics and her research focuses on developing econometric and behavioral economic models to understand Development Economics.

Ramesh Chandra Das, PhD, is a professor at the Department of Economics, Vidyasagar University, India with 25 years of teaching and research experience in the fields of theoretical and applied economics, environmental economics, public finance, and political economics.

Soumita Dasgupta is pursuing PhD at the Department of Economics, Vidyasagar University, West Bengal, India. She worked as Research Assistant at the Indian Institute of Technology Kharagpur. She has completed an MPhil in Economics from Vidyasagar University. She was awarded a silver medal in MSc for second position. She has published some papers in peer-reviewed journals.

Maitree Dey is presently a doctoral research scholar at the Department of Economics, Vidyasagar University, India. She did her Masters in Economics at the same university; besides, she has cracked in national level entrance tests such as UGC-NET (with JRF), SET, GATE, etc. Her areas of research are public finance and economic growth. She has published some articles in Scopus-indexed books.

Manohar Giri, PhD, is an assistant professor at the School of Management, Graphic Era Hill University, Bhimtal, Uttarakhand, India. His research interests lie in development economics, quantitative economics, and political economics. Previously, he was associated with the Indian Institute of Technology, Kanpur, India. He has several publications in reputed journals.

Adem Gök, PhD, is currently employed in the Department of Economics at Kırklareli University, Turkey, as an associate professor. He received his bachelor's degree in Economics from Boğaziçi University in 2008 and master's degree in Economics (English) from Marmara University in 2012. He holds a PhD in Economics (English) from Marmara University since 2016. His research area includes foreign direct investment, growth and development, economics of governance, environmental economics, the economics of education, and financial crises.

Tanushree Gupta, PhD, is currently working an assistant professor at the School of Commerce and Management Sciences, Sandip University, Nashik, Maharashtra. Finance, Microfinance, Stock Market, and International

Business are some of her primary academic interests. She has in her credit many research papers/publications of national and international repute, and many of her book chapters have been published in international and Scopus-indexed journals.

Debashruti Jana, is pursuing PhD at the Department of Economics, Vidyasagar University, West Bengal, India. She has completed MPhil in Economics from the Department of Economics, Vidyasagar University, West Bengal, India. She has a deep research interest in the MSME sector of India.

Eyasin Khan, PhD, is presently an assistant professor in the Department of Political Science at Vidyasagar University, West Bengal, India. Previously, he served as Assistant Professor at Bankura Christian College, Bankura. He stood first class first at the UG and PG levels for which he was awarded gold medals. He has 18 books to his credit and published 55 research articles in various national and international journals and books.

Susobhan Maiti, PhD, is an assistant professor in the Department of Economics, School of Humanities and Social Sciences (SHSS), Jain (Deemed-to-be) University, Bangalore, India. He has published many research papers in the area of industry, efficiency, and productivity in international and Scopus-indexed journals.

Poulami Maity has completed her master's and bachelor's degree in Economics from Vidyasagar University, India. She is now pursuing her Bachelor's in Education in the Vidyasagar Teachers' Training College, Midnapore. Her areas of research interest lie in the social sector and development economics.

Sagnik Maity is a Doctoral Research Scholar (UGC-JRF) in the Department of Commerce of the University of Calcutta. His research mainly revolves around the area of finance. He holds a keen interest in the area of financial inclusion and financial technology. He has presented research papers in several national and international conferences and published articles and papers in various reputed journals.

Amit Majumder, PhD, is presently working as Associate Professor of Commerce and PG Coordinator of Bijoy Krishna Girls' College, India. He is also a visiting faculty, Department of Commerce, University of Calcutta. Dr. Majumder has authored three books from international publishers and contributed to 60 edited volumes and 50 nationally and internationally acclaimed peer-reviewed and referred journals. His areas of interests are Strategic Management, Corporate Governance, etc.

Surendranath Mandi, is an assistant professor in the Department of Economics, Midnapore College (Autonomous), Midnapore, India. Currently, he is pursuing his PhD from Vidyasagar University. He has published many research papers in the area of social sector in national and international journals.

Md. Juel Mia is working as an assistant professor at the Institute of Disaster Management and Vulnerability Studies, University of Dhaka. Prior to his career at University, Mia served as a newsroom editor at Somoy News (television channel). His research interests are disaster communication, disaster governance, and spatial analysis.

Abhishek Mitra, PhD, is presently Assistant Professor at the Department of Political Science, Acharya Sukumar Sen Mahavidyalaya, West Bengal (India). He received his PhD from the University of Kalyani in Political Science. Dr. Mitra received a merit certificate for holding 1st class 1st position in BA (Hons.) examination and received a Gold Medal & merit certificate for first class first position in MA in Political Science from the University of Burdwan. He has a list of publications in reputed journals to his credit.

Reza Mortazavi, PhD, is Associate Professor of Economics at Dalarna University (Sweden). His research is mostly in empirical and applied economics within the fields of transport, tourism, and energy demand.

Debabrata Mukhopadhyay, PhD, is a professor in the Department of Economics at the West Bengal State University, India. He has published a number of papers in scholarly national and international journals. He has obtained his PhD degree in Quantitative Economics from the Indian Statistical Institute in 2008.

Debasish Nandy, PhD, is an associate professor in the Department of Political Science at Kazi Nazrul University, West Bengal, India. Dr. Nandy is the Coordinator of the Centre for Studies of South and South-East Asian Societies at the same university. He is a visiting faculty member in the Department of Foreign Area Studies at Tajik National University, Dushanbe (Tajikistan), and the Indian Cultural Ambassador to Tajikistan. In 2022, Dr. Nandy served the Department of Japanese Studies at the University of Dhaka, Bangladesh, as the Visiting Faculty. He was the visiting faculty at the Frankfurt University of Applied Sciences, Frankfurt, Germany.

Okunlola Olalekan Charles, PhD, is a senior research fellow at the Institute for Peace and Conflict Resolution, Nigeria. His research area is focused on development economics, institutional economics, and defence economics. He has published in both local and international journals. He has published several articles on topics such as conflict, poverty, economic freedom, human development, and export promotion in Africa.

S. M. Rabby Raj is a former student of the Department of Japanese Studies, University of Dhaka. He obtained his Bachelor's and Master's degrees in Japanese Studies at the University of Dhaka. His fields of interest are international relations, foreign policy, security and strategic issues, development, political economy, and Japanology.

Imran Usman Sani is a researcher in the Peace Zonal Office, Plateau State, Institute for Peace and Conflict Resolution, Abuja, Nigeria, and currently a Doctor of Philosophy student in the Department of Economics, Nasarawa State University, Keffi. His research areas focus on international economics, development economics, and peace and defence economics.

Begum Sertyesilisik, PhD, is working in the Faculty of Architecture at the Istanbul University, Turkey. She has received her PhD degree from the Middle East Technical University and her MSc, MBA, and BSC degrees from the Istanbul Technical University. Her specialisation areas include green marketing, sustainability, sustainable development, and sustainable built environment.

Nausheen Sodhi is currently employed at Plaksha University, India, as Teaching Fellow in Data Science, Economics and Business (DSEB). She submitted her PhD thesis (Economics) at Panjab University, India, in August 2023. Her research area includes good governance, sub-national economic analysis, and contemporary issues in public policy. She has over seven years of teaching and research experience.

M. C. Omar C. Vargas-González is Professor and Head of the Department of Systems and Computing at the Technological National of Mexico Campus Ciudad Guzmán, Mexico. His areas of research interests lie in Business Administration, Entrepreneurial Economics, Computing in Social science, Arts and Humanities, and Mathematics Education.

José G. Vargas-Hernández, PhD, is presently a research professor at the National Technology of Mexico, Fresnillo/Budapest Center for Long-Term Sustainability, Mexico. He has a long career in Administrative and Management Sciences. He has published more than 200 articles in different journals and books, and reports.

PREFACE

The ups and downs of world economic events in the recent past have demanded the urgency of the incorporation of the factor "Governance" into the economic modelling so as to establish a coherent relation between this with the overall growth of an economy, although the term governance has assumed new importance in the shifting of economic paradigms in the seventies of the literature of public administration. But the traditional command and control-based economic positions of different countries have now been replaced by the new term of governance where it is defined as the tool of overseeing different networks of economic and political exchanges among different agents. Economies must go through the primary goal of attaining growth of their incomes and after persistent trends in the good magnitudes of the growth rates, they achieve the stage of development by means of so many economic, social, political, and environmental factors. One of such factors is the good governance practice, which works as a catalyst of economic development through good institutional supports. The endogenous growth theory in line with the approach of Robert Barro confirms this claim. The relation between good governance and economic growth can be explained in terms of supply leading and demand following approaches as has been done by Patrick (1966) in case of the relationships between financial and real sectors. According to the supply leading approach, good governance works as an indicator of growth, while in case of the demand following approach, economic growth influences good governance. In the first scenario, good governance is the means and in the second, it is the end.

Under this ambiance, the edited book titled *Good Governance and Economic Growth: Complimentary or Problematic?*, through its collection of different studies from different researchers, aims to examine broadly two hypotheses: (i) whether good governance is a necessary precondition to growth for all or the reverse and (ii) do all the well-known governance indicators need to play simultaneous roles in explaining the growth and development of nations? The studies therein cover countries and groups all around the world to find a common inference about whether they are complements or substitutes. The said book has the coverage of chapters on the impact of good governance on economic growth of the countries like India, the USA, Nigeria, Turkey, Pakistan, Bangladesh, Nepal, etc., the groups like BRICS, ASEAN, a panel of developing and panel of developed countries, etc. The particular focus of the book is to see whether good governance is complimentary or problematic to economic growth.

The final shape of the book contains 15 main chapters which deal with the main themes of the book and one introductory chapter, leading it to a volume of 16 chapters. The book has two broad parts: Part I deals with the growth and governance relationships for groups and regions in the world and it contains seven chapters. On the other hand, Part II comprehends the studies on the growth and governance linkages for the selected countries of the world and it contains eight chapters. The essences of the book are that good governance is the cause to as well as being caused by economic growth in different forms justifying the relationships between the two as complementary in some economies and problematic in some others.

In the stages of finishing the book project, the teamwork and ropes of several organizations and academicians are highly documented. I first recognise the prodigious support and cooperation of Routledge, the publisher, for their interminable efforts from processing the project to its final acceptance. Second, I am highly appreciative to Professor Kenneth M. Chilton for writing the valuable foreword for this volume and the contributing authors for their treasured research articles and maintaining fortitude for the project taking such a long duration. Finally, I am beholden to my family members for sharing strain and sacrificing the households' time for consociate. Of course, no one other than me, as the editor, disclose to remain completely responsible for any errors that still remain in the book.

Ramesh Chandra Das
Editor

FOREWORD

Across the globe, countries are trying to address a host of wicked problems that defy simple solution. In addition to challenges of funding, leaders are grappling with interdependent problems such as climate change, pandemics, war, famine, and immigration. The concept of 'good governance' is central to managing all these issues and more. In fact, good governance is a feature desired by global funding organisations, NGOs, and philanthropists who are trying to maximise their return on investment. However, what is good governance? How do we measure it? How can it be nurtured in an environment of finite resources? Organisations such as the World Bank focus on factors such as government stability, effectiveness, regulatory quality, the rule of law, corruption, and popular voice and accountability as pillars of good governance. Each indicator includes a subset of variables that enable researchers to quantify individual country performance. It is not perfect, but such models are testament to the important role good governance plays in promoting growth and change.

This book titled *Good Governance and Economic Growth: Complimentary or Problematic?* by Professor Ramesh Chandra Das of Vidyasagar University adds to our knowledge of good governance and its impact on economic growth through a variety of articles that focus primarily on the developing world with some focuses upon the developed countries too. The articles bring the concept of good governance to life by providing real-world analyses and case studies. The book also includes topical chapters that include a chapter on the Ukraine-Russia war and lessons drawn from Japan about good governance and the knowledge economy.

The strength of this book lies in the focus on developing nations. In this context, Western values often impose governance standards on countries in exchange for funding. The chapters in this book can help policymakers think through these assumptions. From multiple perspectives, the lens of good governance is not so clear. Different cultures, traditions, and regimes cannot easily shift gears and adopt standards that, in the short term, are not always realistic. Perhaps the transition to newer governance models is marginal and transpires over generations.

This collection of articles adds value to the existing literature on the linkages between good governance and economic growth. As the studies show, the linkages do not always manifest in accord with economic theory. That is, there is no cookie cutter approach to building a better government structure that will yield strong economic growth. However, the book demonstrates how some countries are experimenting with new models and concepts to promote economic growth and change. Some of the programmes are innovative and demonstrate resiliency in the face of extreme hardships.

NGOs and practitioners can learn how different countries are experimenting with new growth models under different types of political regimes. This is especially useful because international development rarely comports with theoretical models of what 'should' happen. The chapters in this book provide real-world examples of how government actors respond to economic development demands. Practitioners can use this knowledge to build programmatic linkages across different regimes and cultures.

In general, the book highlights the role of good governance in economic growth and development. It matters. Through a variety of statistical models and case studies, the chapters reinforce the central message that governance matters. The chapters in the book reinforce one another. Across different contexts, regulatory structures, strengthening highly functioning governance models is a central key to promoting greater global prosperity.

Finally, the book is especially useful for global scholars in economics, political science, public administration, and other social sciences. It provides a template for how to analyse good government. Both quantitative and qualitative researchers can benefit from how the international authors access and analyse governance and economic data. Many scholars who operate in the USA or Europe lack familiarity with robust international datasets.

Finally, the real-world analyses used by the authors in this book fill gaps in the contemporary literature. The book is a timely one that is valuable to international scholars who seek to better understand the relationship between governance and economic growth and development across the globe.

Kenneth M. Chilton
Professor
Tennessee State University
Nashville, TN, USA

ABBREVIATIONS

DFID	Department for International Development
EQS	Environmental Quality Standards
ESD	Education for Sustainable Development
GDP	Gross Domestic Product
HDI	Human Development Index
MDGs	Millennium Development Goals
NMS	New Member States
UNDP	United Nations Development Program
VAR	Vector Autoregression
WGI	Worldwide Governance Indicators
WHO	World Health Organization
2SLS	Two-Stage Least Squares
ADF	Augmented Dickey Fuller
BRIC	Brazil, Russian Federation, India, China
BRICS	Brazil, Russian Federation, India, China, South Africa
ECM	Error Correction Mechanism
FDI	Foreign Direct Investment
FEs	Fixed Effects
GDP	Gross Domestic Product
GMM	Generalized Method of Moments
OLS	Ordinary Least Squares
REs	Random Effects
ADB	African Development Bank
ADF	Dickey and Fuller

CONF	Conflict
COR	Corruption
DOLS	Dynamic Ordinary Least Square
ECOWAS	Economic Community of West African States
FMOLS	Fully Modified Ordinary Least Square
POLS	Panel Ordinary Least Square
RGDP	Real Gross Domestic Product
RMAFC	Revenue Mobilization Allocation and Fiscal Commission
SIC	Schwarz Information Criterion
TGE	Total Government Expenditure
EU	European Union
IMF	International Monetary Fund
NATO	North Atlantic Treaty Organizations
NGOs	Non-Governmental Organizations
OECD	The Organization for Economic cooperation and Development
OPEC	Organization of the Petroliam Exporting Countries
UN	United Nations
UNDP	United Nations Development Program
US	United States
AM	Arithmetic Mean
BCC	Banker–Charnes–Cooper
BRICS	Brazil, Russia, India, China and South Africa
CC	Consistency Coefficient
DEA	Data Envelopment Analysis
DMU	Decision Making Unit
FDI	Foreign Direct Investment
GDP	Gross Domestic product
MPI	Malmquist Productivity Index
OECD	The Organization for Economic cooperation and Development
OTE	Overall Technical Efficiency
PTE	Pure Technical Efficiency
SD	Standard Deviation
TFP	Total Factor Productivity
ARDL	Auto Regressive Distribution Lag
BRICS	Brazil, Russian Federation, India, China, South Africa
CPI	Consumers Price Index
EU	European Union
GDP	Gross Domestic Product
GE	Governments Effectiveness
GMM	Generalized Method of Moments
GNP	Gross National Product
IMF	International Monetary Fund

PS	Political Stability
RQ	Regulatory Quality
UNDP	United Nations Development Program
WGI	Worldwide Governance Indicators
WPI	Wholesale Price Index

AR	Auto-regression
FDI	Foreign direct investment
GDP	Gross Domestic Product
GMM	Generalized Method of Moments
OLS	Ordinary Least Square
PCA	Principal Component Analysis
PPP	Purchasing Power Parity
WGI	World Governmental Indicators
WB	World Bank

GDP	Gross Domestic Product
IT	Information and Telecommunication
KBE	Knowledge-Based Economy
KE	Knowledge Economy
MFAJ	Ministry of Foreign Affairs of Japan
R&D	Research & Development
TFP	Total Factor Productivity
WTO	World Trade Organization

EGPP	Employment Generation Program for the Poorest
FFW	Food for Works
FYP	Five Year Plan
GDP	Gross Domestic Product
GR	Gratuitous Relief
MP	Member of Parliaments
SDG	Sustainable Development Goals
TR	Test Relief
UP	Union Parishad
VGF	Vulnerable Group Feeding

AC	Assets Creation
ARI	Anganwadi/other Rural Infrastructure
CC	Control of Corruption
DP	Drought Proofing
FCP	Flood Control and Protection
GE	Government Effectiveness
LD	Land Development

MGNREGA	Mahatma Gandhi National Rural Employment Guarantee Act
MIW	Micro Irrigation Works
PAI	Public Affairs Index
RC	Rural Connectivity
RQ	Regulatory Quality
RS	Rural Sanitation
RTWB	Renovation of Traditional Water Bodies
SD	Standard Deviation
UTs	Union Territories
WCWH	Water Conservation and Water Harvesting
WGI	Worldwide Governance Indicators
WIL	Works on Individual Land
EEZ	Exclusive Economic Zone
FFDA	Fish Farmer Development Agency
MGNREGA	Mahatma Gandhi National Rural Employment Guarantee Act
ADF	Augmented-Dickey-Fuller
CC	Control of Corruption
GDP	Gross Domestic Product
GE	Government Effectiveness
GG	Good Governance
PV	Political Stability and Absence of Violence/Terrorism
RL	Rule of Law
RQ	Regulatory Quality
SSRUR	Sum square residual unrestricted
VA	Voice and Accountability
WDI	World Development Indicators
COE	Council of Europe
GG	Good Governance
MENA	Middle East North Africa
OHCHR	Office of the United Nations High Commissioner for Human Rights
SD	Sustainable Development
SDG	Sustainable Development Goals
SED	Sustainable Economic Development
SEG	Sustainable Economic Growth
UN	United Nations
UNDP	United Nations Development Programme

| UNESCAP | United Nations Economic and Social Commission for Asia and the Pacific |
| WGIs | Worldwide Governance Indicators |

CGTMSE	Credit Guarantee Fund Scheme for Micro and Small Enterprises
DPIIT	Department for Promotion of Industry and Internal Trade
NCEUS	National Commission for Enterprises in the Unorganised Sector
NSSO	National Statistical Organisation
PMMY	Pradhan Mantri Mudra Yojana
PSB	Public Sector Bank
UREs	Unorganised Retail Trading Enterprises
VAT	Value Added Tax

| HDI | Human Development Index |
| UNDP | United Nations Development Program |

INTRODUCTION

Ramesh Chandra Das

The importance of good governance by the state, or by private organizations or both, in influencing economic growth and development has been felt by the World Bank as unavoidable so far as the understanding of African countries in the recent past is concerned. According to the World Bank, good governance is a necessary precondition to growth for all types of countries. The critics of this claim show that good governance can be the result of growth, not the reverse. The relation between good governance and economic growth can be explained in terms of supply leading and demand following approaches as has been done by Patrick (1966) in the case of the relationships between financial and real sectors. According to the supply leading approach, good governance works as an indicator of growth while in the case of the demand following approach, economic growth influences good governance. In the first scenario, good governance is the means and in the second, it is the end.

The ups and downs of world economic events in the recent past have demanded the urgency of the incorporation of the factor 'Governance' into the economic modeling so as to establish a coherent relation between this with the overall growth of an economy, although the term governance has assumed new importance in the shifting of economic paradigms in the 1970s of the literature of public administration. But the traditional command and control based economic positions of different countries have now been replaced by the new term of governance where it is defined as the tool of overseeing different networks of economic and political exchanges among different agents. The importance of governance has been felt significantly after the phase of globalization that most of the world economies took part in. To quote Kofi Annan, former Secretary General of the UN, 'good

DOI: 10.4324/9781003530688-1

governance is perhaps the single most important factor in eradicating poverty and promoting development'. Governance has twin roles in economic systems. The first is the positive role where it guides administrators in an organized manner to shift the administrative practices from the bureaucratic state to third party government. The second is the normative role where it is assumed that good governance can be a precondition to economic growth and development. This particular concept of good governance was propounded by the World Bank in 1992 under the backdrop of its failure to revive the African economies despite a handful of foreign assistance.

The United Nations' 17-point sustainable development goals (SDGs) encompass how different components of growth should work in order to achieve a true sense of development in the long run (UN, 2017). Goal 8 focuses upon promotion of sustained inclusive and sustainable economic growth, full and productive employment, and decent work for all. The important indicators for this goal include economic growth in least developed countries and the rate of real per capita GDP, increase in the rates of youth employment, and the number of women engaged in the labor force compared to the men. This goal has 12 targets in total, some of which were proposed to be achieved by 2020 and some others by 2030. As we have already passed 2020 and the achievements are now subject to empirical investigations, the focus of the policy makers of the countries are now upon those which are to be fulfilled by 2030. The first nine are 'outcome targets' which are 'sustainable economic growth; diversify, innovate and upgrade for economic productivity', 'promoting policies to support job creation and growing enterprises', 'improving resource efficiency in consumption and production', 'ensuring full employment and decent work with equal pay', 'progressing youth employment, education and training', 'ending modern slavery, trafficking, and child labour', 'protecting labour rights and promote safe working environments', 'endorsing beneficial and sustainable tourism', and 'universal access to banking, insurance, and financial services'. The remaining two targets are for *means of implementation* which are increases in the aid for trade support and development of a global youth employment strategy (Bali Swain & Yang-Wallentin, 2020).

On the other hand, Agenda 16 of the SDGs focuses upon promoting peaceful and inclusive societies for sustainable development, providing access to justice for all and building effective, accountable, and inclusive institutions at all levels. All these heads are related to good governance practices which can be achieved through good institutional support. This goal has nine *outcome targets which are* reducing violence; protecting children from abuse, exploitation, trafficking, and violence; endorsing the rule of law and ensuring equal access to justice; contending organized crime and illicit financial and arms flows, substantially reducing magnitudes of corruption and bribery; developing effective, accountable, and transparent institutions; guaranteeing responsive, inclusive, and representative decision-making; strengthening the participation in global governance; providing universal legal identity; and warranting public access to information and securing fundamental freedoms. The two *means of implementation targets are* strengthening national institutions to prevent violence and combat crime and terrorism; endorsing and implementing non-discriminatory laws and policies. Thus, the good governance factor has been one of the most important indicators of achieving long-run growth of the economies (Bartram et al., 2018).

Governance is now utilized in various fields of studies, disciplines, and authorities. Governance was introduced on the agenda by the PlaNet Bank in 1989 because it needed to elucidate why a variety of nations did not develop despite the very fact that they need proper adoption (Frederickson & Smith, 2003; Kaufmann & Kraay, 2002; Kauffman, 2005, 2008; Kaufmann et al., 2010). The neo-liberal adjustment policies were forced on them by the IMF and therefore the International Bank for Reconstruction and Development. The solution was 'bad' or 'weak' governance. If it is now questioned: what can explain the differences in the level of development between Argentina and France while both were at an equivalent level of development and among the richest countries in the world at one time? The solution is bad governance for Argentina and good governance for France. The practice of good governance in the countries in the global north differs from that of the global south. While the former use it as the important input for development, the latter use it as the crucial input for growth in the primary stage. In the long run, good governance should promote the countries and regions to reap the developmental benefits in terms of good quality education and health services, low income inequality, low gender disparity, low level of crimes, good human development, and sustainable environmental practices, among others (Das et al. 2021; Das 2023; Maity & Das 2023).

Under this juncture, this edited book titled *Good Governance and Economic Growth: Complimentary or Problematic?*, through its collection of different studies from different researchers, aims to examine broadly two hypotheses – (i) whether good governance is a necessary precondition to growth for all or the reverse and (ii) do all the well-known governance indicators need to play simultaneous roles in explaining the growth and development of nations? The studies therein cover countries and groups all around the world to find a common inference about whether they are complements or substitutes. The book has chapters covering the impact of good governance on the economic growth of countries like India, the United States, Nigeria, Turkey, Pakistan, Bangladesh, Nepal, etc., groups like BRICS, ASEAN, panels of developing and developed countries, etc. The particular focus of the book will be to see whether good governance is complimentary or problematic to economic growth.

The final shape of the book contains 15 main chapters which deal with the main themes of the book and one introductory chapter, leading it to a volume of 16 chapters. The book has two broad parts: Part I deals with the growth and governance relationships for groups and regions in the world and it contains seven chapters. On the other hand, Part II comprehends the studies on the growth and governance linkages for the selected countries of the world and it contains eight chapters. The essences of the individual chapters in the two broad sections are given below.

Part I: Growth and Governance Relationships for Groups and Regions in the World

Chapter 1 is based on the examination of whether governance performance and sustainable governance are related in a panel of 115 countries in different income groups by hypothesizing sustainable governance as that which positively contributes to environment quality, health quality, or economic well-being and adapts positively to improvements in any one of them. Results of the panel vector auto regression analysis show that only high performer countries have sustainable governance since there is a bidirectional positive significant relationship between governance and sustainability. In the middle performer countries, governance does not adapt positively to improvements in sustainability. Lastly, in the low performer countries, governance negatively impacts sustainability.

Chapter 2 investigates the relationship between economic growth and governance indicators in the BRICS countries during the period 2000–2020 following a static panel data model based on the database of the World Bank. The study includes some control variables such as the role of infrastructure variables like physical capital, human capital, and some other relevant variables on economic growth at the individual country level. The results show that improving the effectiveness of governance and political stability positively and significantly promotes economic growth in the selected countries. Similarly, the control of corruption has a positive influence on economic growth. Moreover, in China and the Russian Federation, only the control of corruption is statistically significant.

Chapter 3 analyzes the effects of the cost of governance, measured by government spending, on real income growth in ECOWAS countries using the Fully Modified Ordinary Least Square and Dynamic Ordinary Least Square techniques. The results support the view that the cost of governance positively affects real growth in ECOWAS countries. However, the study finds that corruption and violent conflict reduce the impact of the cost of governance on real economic growth in ECOWAS countries and thereby suggests that a well-managed government can contribute positively to economic growth. The implication is that the cost of governance may not necessarily translate to real growth when ECOWAS countries experience poor institutional quality.

Chapter 4 discusses the history and evolution of good governance in relation to governability and focuses upon the future possibilities and problems of good governance as a practice in the context of the Russia-Ukraine war. It is true that Russia–Ukraine war has managed to change many ways of thinking. The war has shown that even when governance is an internal matter of a state, international threats and crises may affect it. It has been seen earlier in history that a democratic government has changed its mode of administration in the context of war. The Russia–Ukraine crisis has proven this. War is one such thing that forces the state to revert to its old traditional way of thinking.

Chapter 5, opening its discussion with respect to foreign aid and investments and the associated governance factors in smoothening the process, aims to analyze the effects of IBRD (International Bank for Reconstruction and Development) loans and IDA (International Development Association) credit, and Foreign Direct Investment on the country's Gross Domestic Product, Employment, and Export using Data Envelopment Analysis (DEA) for the BRICS nations for the period 2011–2021. The findings show that countries with higher scores in efficiency, an indicator of good governance practices, have more efficiently allocated their foreign resources. In the final efficiency result, India came out at the top, followed by Brazil, China, South Africa, and Russia.

Chapter 6 seeks to investigate the impact of governance indicators on economic growth using World Bank estimates for selected Asian countries from the year 2002 to 2021 and to determine which of the governance indicators contributes the most to economic growth. The results show that China is the most politically stable country, while Afghanistan has the most chaotic political situation. Of the selected Asian nations, China has the greatest gross domestic product, followed by India, Sri Lanka, Bangladesh, Pakistan, and Afghanistan. Findings show that political stability, government effectiveness, and regulatory quality all have positive and statistically significant effects on gross domestic product. The findings also show that, within a small group of Asian countries, political stability and governmental performance and regulatory quality play significant roles in determining economic growth.

Chapter 7 investigates the impact of governance quality on per capita GDP growth for 45 African countries using World Bank data. Governance is expressed by six different proxy indicators worldwide governance indicators. In addition to governance indicators, other variables such as measures of primary school enrollment, degree of openness to trade, capital, foreign direct investment, and government expenditure are used for a relatively long period of time, from 2002 to 2021, as the control variables using Generalized Method of Moments as an econometric method to estimate the model. The findings suggest that government effectiveness, rule of law and regulatory quality, and corruption are governance measures that influence economic growth.

Part II: Growth and Governance Linkages for the Selected Countries of the World

Chapter 8 investigates the relationship between good governance and knowledge-based economic growth in Japan. The basic argument of this chapter is that without ensuring good governance, economic development is quite difficult. The outlook of government, structural adjustment, and policy framework of the government are also equally essential for economic growth. Applying the content analysis method, the major finding of the chapter is that Japan has experienced enhancement of a knowledge-based economy with the support of a knowledge economy. This chapter also finds the viability of the knowledge economy in Japan.

Chapter 9 tries to search for the answers to the question of what the stumbling blocks are to ensure good governance in the local government of Bangladesh and whether this governing system affects the economic growth in the local areas or not under the backdrop that a strong local government is a prerequisite of people-centered and development-oriented local government where good governance at the local government level involves the grass root people in the development process. It observes that the local government institutions in Bangladesh are making a pivotal contribution to the social and economic development of the rural areas of the country. However, compared to the investment for the rural areas, the development is not observed in a similar manner due to corruption, poor governance, lack of good political will, and interference of central government, ruling political party, and local bureaucracy.

Chapter 10 analyzes the trends in the different heads of asset generations across the major states and all India levels under the popular MGNREGA scheme and relates the governance performance as measured by the Public Affairs Index (PAI) for the former and the World Banks good governance indicators for the latter with the asset generations for the period 2014–2022. Results show that asset creations in the heads of Anganwadi, micro irrigation works, works on individual land, land development, etc. are rising across the states over the period. For the pooled data in Indian states, the correlation and regression coefficients show striking negative signs in the case of PAI and asset creation, which means poor governance quality of local authority is associated with an increase in asset creation in the states. However, the correlation and regression coefficients for the entire country are positive for most of the heads justifying good governance is associated with larger numbers of asset creations.

Chapter 11 aims to evaluate the fish production function in five selected states of India over a 15-year period, with unevenly spaced intervals, for an aggregated analysis of production function determinants and to conduct a comparative analysis of selected factors determining the production function across different states over the period to investigate whether the impact of each factor on the production function varies across states. The study employs alternative models, including Pooled regression, Fixed Effect, and Random Effect, for comparison and evaluation. The estimated regression results reveal statistical significance for all explanatory variables in the case of Bihar with mixed results in other states. The outcomes suggest variations in the factors influencing technical efficiency across states, emphasizing the need for tailored approaches to fisheries management and development.

Chapter 12 seeks to analyze why some nations have seen rapid economic expansion, while others have had difficulties; the possible cause that it supposes is the differences in the operations of good governance practices. The first objective of the study is to establish a causal relationship between countries' economic growth and good governance and the second objective is to show how the six indicators are important in predicting economic growth in the panel of selected countries for the period 2002–2022. It is found that in China, Japan, and the United Kingdom the growth of GDP has a significant influence upon good governance, while no causality is found from GDP to good governance in the United Kingdom and Germany. The panel regression results show that political stability and absence of violence, regulatory quality, control of corruption, rule of law, voice and accountability, and square of government effectiveness have a positive impact on economic growth.

Chapter 13 tries to explore the roles of indicators and inhibitors of good governance (GG) in sustainable development (SD) and economic growth. With this aim, the relationship among GG, SD, and sustainable economic growth, the relationship between United Nations SDGs and GG, and the construction industry's roles in SD and GG have been examined. Furthermore, the study emphasized the construction industry, its contribution to and roles in SD from the GG perspective, and highlighted the importance of compliance with GG principles and elimination of inhibitors of GG at the company, industry, and country levels. It is revealed that effective and strategic compliance to GG principles and indicators at the company level can contribute to the company's competitiveness leading to contribute to its industry's competitiveness which can support SD and sustainable economic growth of the country.

Chapter 14 intervenes into a sensitive sector, the unorganized retail enterprises (UREs), contributing about 80 per cent of the nations' income in the developing world by examining the determinants of growth status of the sector, categorized as expanding, stagnating, or contracting using a multinomial logit regression model. In addition, it explores regional disparities and the types of government assistance received by the UREs. The findings indicate that government assistance plays a pivotal role in fostering the expansion and modernization of UREs, positively influencing their growth trajectory. However, it is noteworthy that only a fraction of UREs in India have benefited from such assistance which raises concerns about the aware-ness, accessibility, and accountability of UREs and government agencies. Financial loans and subsidies are the most common forms of government aid received by UREs. Notably, there is a decline in the proportion of UREs receiving financial assistance over time, suggesting the need for more effective and inclusive credit policies. Regional disparities are also evident, with the southern region of India outperforming others in increasing the share of UREs receiving government assistance.

The final chapter, that is, Chapter 15, analyzes the insinuations of policies and strategies for institutional participatory governance framework and empirically investigates the association between participatory governance and human development in a set of countries. It begins assuming the rele-vance of the policy analysis leading to the design and implementation of policies and strategies which have an effect on institutional participatory gov-ernance. Applying the analytical, descriptive, and statistical methods to develop reflective thinking based on the theoretical, conceptual, and empiri-cal literature, the study concludes that the design and implementation of pol-icies and strategies are critical to develop an institutional participatory governance framework. The empirical analysis across three groups of coun-tries from high, upper middle, and lower middle income levels shows that participatory governance and human development are positively associated.

Concluding Observations

The chapters under the coverage of the book have good concluding observa-tions. From Part I of the book consisting of seven chapters, it is observed that good governance practices work well for many groups of economies such as BRICS and ECOWAS, and regions like Asia and developed and less devel-oped economies. Sustainable governance practices work well for the world's so-called high-income countries, whereas the low-income countries do face lax governance as well as low income levels. In BRICS and ECOWAS, good governance practices in terms of political stability, control of corruption, and regulatory quality work as a panacea to income growth of the member coun-tries. On the other hand, the chapter covered in Part II lead us to conclude that good governance practices in Japan lead to knowledge-based economic growth, while good governance is a cause of economic growth for the panel of countries including China, Germany, the United Kingdom, Japan, etc. In Indian states, the popular MGNREGA project has close associations with governance practices. The Russia–Ukraine war has also been pointed out by one study as being the cause of governance failure. Therefore, the overall summary of the book is that good governance and income growth go hand in hand across countries and groups and this usual phenomenon can be a good input for the long-run developmental milestones. The essence of the book in particular is that good governance is the cause of, as well as being caused by, economic growth in different forms justifying the relationships between the two as complementary in some economies and problematic in others.

Therefore, it may be recommended in general form that countries and regions from all around the world should focus on practicing good governance at home and abroad to achieve sustainable development. The contents of the book will be beneficial to readers in Economics, Political Science, International Relations, and Public Finance, among others.

References

Bali Swain, R. & Yang-Wallentin, F. (2020). Achieving sustainable development goals: predicaments and strategies, *International Journal of Sustainable Development & World Ecology*, 27(2), 96–106.

Bartram, J., Brocklehurst, C., Bradley, D., Muller, M. & Evans, B. (2018). Policy review of the means of implementation targets and indicators for the sustainable development goal for water and sanitation, *Clean Water*, 1(1), 3, doi:10.1038/s41545-018-0003-08

Das, R. C. (Ed). (2023). *Social Sector Spending, Governance and Economic Development: Perspectives from Across the World*, Routledge, London, ISBN 9781032669496.

Das, R. C., Mandal, C. & Patra, A. K. (2021). Linkage between social sector's spending and HDI: study on individual as well as panel data of Indian states, *Review of Social Economy*, 79(2), 357–379.

Frederickson, H. G. & Smith, K. B. (2003). *The Public Administration Theory Primer*, West View Press, Boulder, Colorado.

Kauffman, D. (2005). Back to basics-10 myths about governance and corruption, *Finance and Development*, 42(3), 1–19.

Kauffman, D., Krray, A. & Mastruzzi, M. (2010). *The worldwide governance indicators: Methodological and analytical issues, World Bank Policy Research Working Paper*, Washington DC

Kaufmann, D. (2008). *Irrational Exuberance vs. 'Afro-Pessimism': Lessons from an empirical perspective on governance in Africa*, World Bank, Washington, DC.

Kaufmann, D. & Kraay, A. (2002). *Growth without Governance*, World Bank, Washington, DC.

Maity, N. & Das, R. C. (2023). Crimes against women during pre and post Nirbhaya incidence – A study of different states in India in Das, R. C. (ed) *Social Sector Development and Governance: Empirical Investigations for Countries and Groups*, Routledge, London.

Patrick, H. T. (1966). Financial development and economic growth in UDCs, *Economic Development and Cultural Change*, 14, 174–189.

United Nations. (2017). Resolution adopted by the General Assembly on 6 July 2017, Work of the Statistical Commission pertaining to the 2030 Agenda for Sustainable Development.

Growth and Governance Relationships for Groups and Regions in the World

PART 1

Growth and Governance:
Relationships for Groups
and Regions in the World

1

GOVERNANCE, SUSTAINABILITY AND SUSTAINABLE GOVERNANCE

A Panel Vector Auto Regression Analysis

Nausheen Sodhi and Adem Gök

Introduction

Governance issues have been widely discussed in forums of national and international significance, in various reports and publications and even in political campaigns. In 2006 and 2007, the United Kingdom's Department for International Development (DFID) and United Nations Development Programme (UNDP) included governance as one of their focal areas. Despite growing concerns, consensus on conceptualizing governance is lacking because of its wide applicability. This is evident from the various definitions of governance that range from"what governments (ought to) do" (Grindle, 2012) to "various rethinking processes that can enhance governance outcomes" (Lopez-Calva, Luis-Felipe et al., 2017). "Governance refers to the exercise of political and administrative authority at all levels to manage a country's affairs. It includes the processes and institutions through which decisions are made and authority in a country is exercised" (UNDESA & UNDP, 2012). Linking governance to the functions of governments brings out government effectiveness most closely, but does not serve an operational definition for governance. The World Development Report 2017 on "Governance and the Law" highlights how rethinking about governance can enhance the implementation and outcome of policies for development (Lopez-Calva, Luis-Felipe et al., 2017).

In this chapter, governance is defined as the functioning and capabilities of actors (policy and lawmakers, administrators, bureaucrats) to govern within a framework of institutions and structures to yield generally accepted outcomes. Governance depends on the structural designs for continuous implementation (that can house sustainability). Sustainability in governance is

DOI: 10.4324/9781003530688-3

broadly subjective, depending on how governance is defined. Sustainability as a concept itself is subjective but is mostly used to denote outcomes without negative externalities in the long run. (Brundtl et al., 1987). The three pillars of sustainability as pointed out first by Edward B. Barbier (1987) include the biological and resource system (BS), social system (SS) and economic system (ES). This chapter measures sustainability by constructing an index of environmental quality, health quality and economic well-being that pertain to these pillars, respectively. The relevance of sustainability for governance relates both to the outcomes and structures of governance. Governance is sustainable if it contributes positively to any of the three pillars of sustainability while ensuring resilience in its structures over time. When governance actors can help improve environmental quality, health quality or economic well-being of their nations without letting a deterioration in these negatively impact the governance quality itself, sustainable governance prevails.

The aim of the study is to develop a hypothesis for the theory of sustainable governance and to test it for 115 countries clustered into high, middle and low performers by panel vector auto-regression [panel VAR] analysis over the years 2000 to 2015 and to devise policy implications for countries to attain sustainable governance. This chapter contributes to the literature on sustainable governance in several ways. First, it builds a hypothesis for sustainable governance based on two criteria. Second, it divides countries into three clusters based on their governance scores by K-means clustering as an alternative to the old classifications such as developed, developing and least developed countries. Third, it employs panel VAR analysis to test the hypothesis of sustainable governance for three clusters and to determine the effect of control variables on sustainability and governance. Finally, it gives policy implications to countries in three clusters to attain sustainable governance.

The chapter is structured in four sections. The next section presents the theoretical perspective and a brief literature review. The third section presents the empirical analysis and the last section concludes.

Theoretical Perspective and Literature Review

Sustainable Governance

Governance can be defined as the capacity to implement and promote policy goals within the structures in which governance actors operate. These capacities are linked to functioning of the actors, but whether they are limited to their capabilities or not depends on the efficiency of governance structures. Efficiency can be linked to sustainability and further to dynamism of governance structures in which the actors implement pre-determined policy goals. The responsiveness of governance structures to changes in policy goals is the idea behind sustainable governance in this chapter.

Sustainable governance relates to the capability of governance structures to identify policy goals and their implications while ensuring responsiveness in the dynamic environment in which they operate (Türke, 2012). Governance goes far and beyond how and when actors participate and interact. However, governance structures are limited in their ability to sustain effective, efficient and dynamic delivery. The farther the boundaries, the higher the sustainability, as measured by structural adaptability for dynamic delivery.

It follows from the discussion how sustainable governance is defined depends on how governance is defined. First, if governance is defined with regard to the way that the actors govern the systems for pre-determined generally accepted outcomes, sustainable governance relates to how effectively, efficiently and dynamically those actors could bring about those outcomes. Mere (efficient) delivery of goals would not suffice for sustainability. That is, best governance practices leading to the best possible outcomes would not make governance sustainable. Efficient delivery of outcomes sustained in the long run via dynamic governance structures that respond to the changing environment is one criterion for sustainable governance. This definition can be said to be the outcome definition of sustainable governance.

Second, if governance is defined with regard to the institutions and structures that govern the functioning and capabilities of factors and actors in the governance arena, then sustainable governance relates to the dynamism and adaptability of those governance institutions and structures. Further, governance depends on the structural designs for continuous implementation that can house sustainability. When these designs nurture policy goals and implementation process(es), sustainable governance prevails. It is, hence, a continuous process of identifying and adapting while at the same time ensuring resilience. The mere existence of well-built structures and institutions of governance does not promise sustainability. Dynamic governance structures that are adaptive to changes in the environment and that ensure efficient governance outcomes in the long run are another criterion for sustainable governance. This definition can be said to be the dynamic structures definition of sustainable governance.

To hypothesize sustainable governance, the two definitions given earlier have been used. The former identifies sustainable governance outcomes as the positive and significant impact that governance has on sustainability (comprising environmental quality, health quality and economic well-being). The latter identifies sustainable governance structures (that are adaptive to changes in sustainability) as a positive significant impact of sustainability on governance. Hence, when changes in governance scores bring about significant changes in the sustainability index and when changes in the sustainability index bring about significant changes in governance scores, governance is said to be sustainable. The two criteria and the hypothesis derived from them are mentioned below.

Criterion 1: Sustainable Governance Outcomes

Governance improves or positively contributes to sustainability by increasing at least one of the sub-indices of sustainability.

Criterion 2: Sustainable Governance Structures

Governance positively adapts to improvements in at least one of the sub-indices of sustainability.

Hypothesis: Sustainable Governance

H_0: Governance is sustainable only when both criteria are satisfied, which requires that governance should positively contribute to environment quality, health quality or economic well-being and it should adapt positively to improvement in any one of them. This is represented in Figure 1.1.

Determinants of Sustainability

Sustainability as measured by an index comprising its three pillars can be also analyzed by certain other variables/determinants. The first such determinant is that of governance and its sub-dimensions. Literature on governance highlights a significant relationship between governance levels and sustainability. Fredriksson and Mani (2002) test the theory that an increase in the rule of law has two effects on environmental policies, i.e., higher policy implementation as per law and higher bribes in the industry because more is at stake.

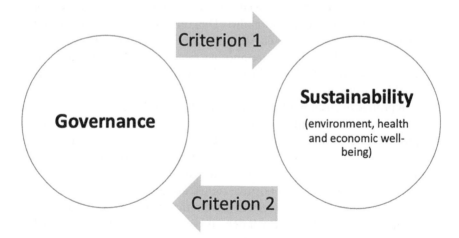

FIGURE 1.1   Criteria of governance and sustainability.

Source: Sketched by the authors.

Their results find that increased corruptibility of policy makers lowers the stringency of environmental policies and a greater degree of rule of law strengthens stringency of environmental policies, except when corruptibility is high. Ewers and Smith (2007) compare the results of the Ecological Sustainability Index and Ecological Footprint for the years 2002 and 2000, respectively, in governance analyses at the global scale and find that these two measures contradict each other and also that poor governance is likely to affect a range of environmental issues. Klomp and De Haan (2008) analyze the role of governance in improving the health of individuals using a cross-sectional analysis for 101 countries for 2000–2005 using 18 health indicators and WGI. Using structural equation modeling, they find that governance influences health via a positive impact on income and quality of the health care sector. Azam and Emirullah (2014) analyze the relationship between various governance indicators on GDP per capita for nine nations in Asia and the Pacific for 1985–2012 and find that corruption and inflation rates are negatively related to GDP per capita. Naimur (2010) studies the linkages between governance and extent of success of MDGs (Millennium Development Goals) in India for the period 2000–2008 and finds that there is an indirect linkage between governance and MDGs via growth and a direct link between each MDG and certain elements of governance.

The following studies investigated the effect of sub-dimensions of WGI (Worldwide Governance Indicators) on sustainability. Radu (2015) studied the influence of political stability on sustainable growth in Romania for 1990–2011 using multivariate regression and found that a stable political environment helps in building a coherent and continuous path for sustainability. An interesting conclusion given by Safaei (2006) is that democracies have a positive impact on public health. The author included data from Polity IV for 2003 for country identifications and applied multiple regression analysis for a cross-section of 118 countries and clubbed countries into three- autocratic, incoherent and democratic. These findings have important implications for health policy as they highlight the need to design policies that promote democracy, redistribute political power and enhance full participation of the masses. Franco, Álvarez-Dardet and Ruiz (2004) also studied the effect of democracy on health by taking data on life expectancy for 158 countries, on infant mortality for 162 countries and on maternal mortality for 140 countries. They find that democracy showed a stronger and more significant association with indicators of health (life expectancy, infant and maternal mortality) than economic indicators (GNP, total government expenditure or income inequality).

This chapter identifies certain other determinants of sustainability – physical capital, human capital and infrastructure. Xiaoqing (2005) explains the growth of China considering the effects of investment in physical capital and investment in health using annual data for 1978–2002 to estimate a regressive model of economic growth. The results show that increasing investment in physical capital by 1% increases GDP by 0.38% and increasing investment in health by 1% increases GDP by 0.368% per year. An important observation in this regard is that "in countries with low level of governance, human capital does not affect economic growth" (Muhammad, Egbetokun & Memon, 2015). Haider and Sharif (2016) analyze the impact of tele density on economic growth of South Asian countries from 1994 to 2014 using pooled regression analysis. Their study shows that tele density is the driving force for the economic growth of South Asian countries. Boeve-de Pauw et al. (2015) study the effectiveness of education for sustainable development (ESD) using data from 2413 students in grades 6, 9 and 12 from 51 schools across Sweden through a series of descriptive analyses and structural equation models. Their results indicate that ESD impacts student outcomes in terms of their sustainability consciousness which plays a key role in paving the way for a more sustainable future. Burja and Burja (2013) estimate the relationship between some indicators of education and GDP within 12 EU new member states (NMS) (with special reference to Romania) using regression analysis for panel data of 180 country-year observations, for the period 1997–2011. Their study identifies important education indicators that help GDP's sustainable growth in these nations and recommends the necessity to increase human capital value to boost sustainable development.

Determinants of Governance

The dynamic structures definition of governance as explained in this chapter highlights the impact that determinants of governance have on its levels. The more responsive governance levels are to such determinants (positively), the more dynamic will be the structures. This chapter considers the three pillars of sustainability as well as physical capital, human capital and infrastructure as important determinants of governance. As regards environmental quality, Burkhardt et al. (2019) studied the impact of air pollution on certain categories of crime, particularly those involving aggressive behavior. Using data for the years 2006–2013 for 397 counties in the United States, the study finds a positive effect of increased air pollution on violent crimes, specifically assaults, but not so in cases of property crimes. They suggest that a 10% reduction in daily PM2.5 and ozone could save $1.4 billion in crime costs annually. Emmelin and Lerman (2008) identify different kinds of EQS (environmental quality standards) as important tools of governance in Sweden. The study highlights importance of acceptability of development proposals, programs and industrial projects for environmental quality rather than emissions. It accords a prominent role to standards (National Environmental Objectives) and structure for quantified targets in policy making. Numerous studies highlight the importance of health quality for governance (Rontos, Syrmali & Vavouras, 2015; Barro, 1999). WHO declared violence as a leading worldwide public health problem and urged member states to assess the problem on their own territory and communicate their approach for the same to WHO. All social classes experience violence but research shows that those belonging to the lowest socioeconomic status are at greatest risk (Krug, Mercy, Dahlberg & Zwi, 2002). On the significance of economic well-being on governance, literature suggests a positive impact at all levels of development for nations. In a cross-sectional OLS estimation for 86 countries, Al-Marhubi (2004) find a positive significant impact of GDP per capita on overall governance of countries. He concluded that the significance of income per capita does not necessarily imply that politics and culture do not matter to governance, but the economic factors are the result of other factors, many of them cultural and political in origin. In a cross-sectional OLS estimation of 173 countries for 2012, Rontos, Syrmali and Vavouras (2015) found that GNI per capita has a positive significant effect on all six governance dimensions and HDI has a positive significant impact on two governance dimensions. They concluded that social structures that are captured by HDI are related to the quality of public services provided and the credibility of the government's commitment to such policies. Hence, human capital building is closely connected with increased governance capacities. Rontos, Syrmali and Vavouras (2015) argue that investing in basic social infrastructure, including education and health, emerges as a driver of sustainable human development, which is critical for promoting an adaptive governance structure. By conducting a panel data analysis of over 100 countries for the period 1960–1995, Barro (1999) found that the propensity for democracy significantly rises with an increase in per capita GDP, primary schooling and life expectancy and a decrease in infant mortality. He confirmed the Lipset/Aristotle hypothesis, which says that a higher standard of living (measured by the variables stated) promotes democracy.

The other determinants have also been widely researched in governance studies, with the exception of physical capital on which there is no study that directly links it to governance or any of its indicators. Against that backdrop, an attempt has been made to empirically test the relationship between physical capital and governance in this chapter. On the role of human capital (as measured by the education index) on governance, a well-educated population is expected to have a significant positive effect on governance. While Busse and Gröning (2009) argued that higher educational levels should promote governance (since a better educated population is more likely to participate in public decision-making and demand better governance), but on employing System GMM analysis for 106 countries for 1984–2004, they found that literacy rate has no significant effect on governance. In another study by Garcia-Sanchez, Cuadrado-Ballesteros and Frias-Aceituno (2013), a GMM analysis of 202 countries over the period of 2002–2008 found that GDP per capita and literacy rates had a positive significant effect on government effectiveness. They concluded that for countries with lower economic development, attention to political constraints is necessary and for economies that are in transition, the educational status is the most important determinant in densely populated areas. Lastly, the infrastructure determinant taken in this study highlights the impact on governance, with studies mostly highlighting it as a precondition to governance (structures). In a panel dynamic logit regression analysis of 171 countries over the period of 1960–2015, Rød, Knutsen and Hegre (2020) used various measures of communication technology and found that they have a positive significant effect on democracy. Bhatnagar (2014) studies the role of ICT in improving governance and development via improved delivery of services to the poor. Using case studies and a systematic review of literature, this study concludes that "well-designed e-governance projects with process reforms that target enhanced transparency and accountability reduce discretion vested with civil servants, enhance efficiency, and can lower corruption". But the impact of ICTs on governance is limited in developing countries due to slow trickle-down effects on the poor belonging to remote areas, owing to the current state of ICTs in those regions.

Empirical Analysis

Data and Variables

The study analyzes 115 countries for the period 2000–2015 due to the data availability. Since there is multicollinearity between indicators and sub-indices, principal component analysis (PCA) was used to generate indices and sub-indices.

Since CO_2 emissions per capita, infant mortality, unemployment rate and inflation rate are negative variables, i.e., a higher value of these variables indicates worse performance, they were converted such that a higher value indicates better performance (as in the case for the rest of the indicators and variables) by using the following formula:

$$\text{Converted Value} = \text{Max Value} + \text{Min Value} - \text{Actual Value} \qquad (1.1)$$

See Appendix 1 for the list of variables and Appendix 1.2 for descriptive statistics. Less than 1% of data is either interpolated or extrapolated. A simple average is used for interpolation and a 5-year moving average of growth rates is used for extrapolation.

To decide between first- and second-generation unit-root tests, cross-sectional dependency (CSD) test was applied. CSD test indicated cross-sectional dependency, and hence Pesaran panel unit-root test was used as a second-generation unit-root test. The results show that sustainability (sust) is $I(0)$, and governance (gov), physical capital (phycap), human capital (humcap) and infrastructure (infra) are $I(1)$. Instead of taking the first differences of $I(1)$ variables, first-differencing was used in panel VAR, which takes the first difference of all endogenous variables in the transformed equation. See Appendix 1.3 for the results of CSD-test and see Appendix 1.4 for results of the Pesaran panel unit-root test.

Clustering Countries: K-Means Clustering

The countries in the dataset have been divided into three clusters based on their governance scores using K-means cluster analysis so that overall differences are analyzed for meaningful conclusions based on similar governance levels. Cluster analysis objectively segregates data into groups and items in each group have a high resemblance with each other and a low resemblance with items of other groups (Mainfort Jr, 2005). K-means cluster analysis is one of the oldest and most reliable clustering methods (Baxter, 1994; Milligan, 1980) and can be applied when no hierarchical relationships exist among the units, i.e., countries in this study. The K-means clustering process is as follows. First, the desired number of clusters is specified, i.e., K. In this study, $K = 3$ (high, middle and low performer countries). Next, every data point is then assigned to the closest centroids and each collection of points assigned to a centroid forms a cluster. The centroid of each cluster is then updated based on the points assigned to that cluster. This process is repeated until no point changes clusters (Wu, 2012).

$D = \{x_1...x_n\}$ is the dataset to be clustered, x_i being the governance score of the i-th country for the year 2015 ($n = 115$). K-means can be expressed as an objective function that depends on the proximities of the data points to the cluster centroids as follows:

$$\min_{\{m_k\}, 1 \leq k \leq K} \sum_{k=1}^{K} \sum_{x \in C_k} \pi_x \text{dist}(x, m_k) \tag{1.2}$$

where π_x is the weight of x, n_k is the number of countries assigned to the cluster C_k, $m_k = \sum_{x \in C_k} \dfrac{\pi_x x}{n_k}$ is the centroid of the cluster C_k, $K = 3$ is the number of clusters chosen, and the function "dist" computes the distance between object x and centroid m_k, $1 \leq k \leq K$. While the selection of the distance function is optional, the squared Euclidean distance, i.e. $\|x - m\|^2$, has been most widely used in both research and practice (Wu, 2012).

See Appendix 1.5 for a list of countries in each cluster. Table 1.1 shows a number of counties in each cluster, based on governance scores of 2015. Tables 1.2 and 1.3 show that the results of ANOVA are significant for the overall and between cluster differences.

TABLE 1.1 Number of Countries in Each Cluster

Cluster	Panel A: High	Panel B: Middle	Panel C: Low	Total
No. of countries	39	49	27	115

Source: Authors' calculations.

TABLE 1.2 ANOVA Significance Test

ANOVA

	Cluster		Error		F	Sig.
	Mean Square	df	Mean Square	df		
GOV_2015	249.757	2	0.614	112	406.973	0

Source: Authors' calculations.

TABLE 1.3 Post-hoc Tests

Multiple Comparisons

	(I) Cluster Number of Case	(J) Cluster Number of Case	Mean Difference (I – J)	Sig.
Tukey HSD	1	2	5.04216316	0.000
		3	3.21961605	0.000
	2	1	–5.04216316	0.000
		3	–1.82254711	0.000
	3	1	–3.21961605	0.000
		2	1.82254711	0.000

Source: Authors' calculations.

Panel VAR Methodology

All variables in panel vector auto-regression (panel VAR) are taken as endogenous, allowing for unobserved individual heterogeneity (Love & Zicchino, 2006). Governments invest in physical capital, human capital or infrastructure to directly or indirectly increase governance and sustainability, and hence they are used as control variables. Other than governance and sustainability, these variables are also endogenous as there exists bivariate causal relationships between them (according to the Granger causality tests in the following sections), and hence panel VAR was employed by building a system of five simultaneous equations.

The optimal lag length for the panel VAR model is found one. Hence, a first-order panel VAR model is specified as follows:

$$y_{it} = \Gamma_0 + \Gamma_1 y_{it-1} + f_i + d_{c,t} + e_t \tag{1.3}$$

where y_{it} is a vector of five variables comprising infrastructure, physical capital, human capital, governance and sustainability (Love & Zicchino, 2006).

Fixed effects f_i and country-specific time dummies $d_{c,t}$ were introduced to allow for individual heterogeneity and to capture aggregate, country-specific macro shocks, respectively (Love & Zicchino, 2006). Since panel data is balanced, first-differencing was used instead of forward orthogonal deviation (Helmert procedure) to eliminate fixed effects. The model in first differences may be estimated consistently for each equation through instrumenting lagged differences with differences and levels of the dependent variable vector from earlier periods by the Generalized Method of Moments (GMM), which requires small T and large N (Abrigo & Love, 2016).

Panel VAR utilizes five different tools, viz., impulse response functions, stability test, Granger causality test, panel vector auto-regression and forecast-error variance decomposition. If all the eigenvalues lie inside the unit circle, then panel VAR satisfies the stability condition according to the stability test. The Granger causality test is used both for detecting the unilateral or bilateral causal relationship between variables and for justifying taking a variable as endogenous. Since first-order panel VAR was used, panel vector auto-regression presents the effects of the first lag of each independent variable on each of the five-variable dependent vectors. The impulse response functions show the reaction of one variable to shocks given to another variable while holding all other shocks equal to zero in the system. To calculate the standard errors of the impulse response functions, confidence intervals have been generated using Monte Carlo simulations. Finally, variance decompositions which show the magnitude of the total effect have been presented. They show the percent of variation in one variable explained by shocks to another variable, accumulated over time. Lastly, the total effect accumulated over 10 years by variance decomposition has been reported (Love & Zicchino, 2006).

Estimation Results

Since all the eigenvalues lie inside the unit circle, panel VAR satisfies the stability condition for all three models, according to the results in Table 1.4.

According to the Granger causality test in Table 1.5, there are at least two bidirectional causal relationships between variables, and it is concluded that the variables are endogenous, which justifies using panel VAR. Since there is a bidirectional causality between governance quality and sustainability index in all three panels, it is also concluded that a necessary but not sufficient condition is met for our hypothesis in all three clusters.

Since the first-order panel VAR model was defined for all three clusters, the results of Table 1.6 and Figures 1.2–1.4 are interpreted together for each cluster.

TABLE 1.4 Stability Test

Eigenvalue		
Real	Imaginary	Modulus
Panel A: High		
0.898	0	0.898
0.657	0	0.657
0.440	0	0.440
−0.337	0	0.337
0.096	0	0.096
Panel B: Middle		
0.917	0	0.917
0.592	0.189	0.621
0.592	−0.189	0.621
0.405	−0.082	0.414
0.405	0.082	0.414
Panel C: Low		
0.897	0	0.897
0.590	0	0.590
0.083	−0.470	0.477
0.083	0.470	0.477
−0.360	0	0.360

Source: Authors' calculations.

TABLE 1.5 Granger Causality Test

	sust	*gov*	*phycap*	*humcap*	*infra*
Panel A: High					
sust		0.000	0.000	0.597	0.171
gov	0.000		0.005	0.043	0.061
phycap	0.000	0.000		0.241	0.000
humcap	0.000	0.426	0.000		0.013
infra	0.000	0.035	0.003	0.000	
Panel B: Middle					
sust		0.000	0.602	0.363	0.000
gov	0.000		0.007	0.032	0.000
phycap	0.001	0.000		0.663	0.006
humcap	0.000	0.000	0.017		0.027
infra	0.006	0.000	0.025	0.000	

(*Continued*)

TABLE 1.5 (Continued)

	sust	gov	phycap	humcap	infra
Panel C: Low					
sust		0.000	0.000	0.000	0.000
gov	0.000		0.395	0.000	0.000
phycap	0.674	0.028		0.013	0.734
humcap	0.000	0.000	0.000		0.000
infra	0.002	0.009	0.082	0.000	

Source: Authors' calculations.

Notes: The numbers are the Prob > χ^2 values. Null hypothesis is that the row variable does not Granger-cause column variable.

TABLE 1.6 Panel Vector auto-regression Results

	Dependent Variables				
	sust(t)	gov(t)	phycap(t)	humcap(t)	infra(t)
Panel A: High					
sust(t − 1)	0.116***	0.267***	−2.743***	−0.001	−0.035
	(0.039)	(0.020)	(0.454)	(0.002)	(0.026)
gov(t − 1)	0.911***	−0.064*	1.668***	0.009**	0.095*
	(0.064)	(0.033)	(0.594)	(0.005)	(0.051)
phycap(t − 1)	0.029***	−0.008***	0.206***	0.0002	−0.007***
	(0.002)	(0.001)	(0.027)	(0.0002)	(0.001)
humcap(t − 1)	2.759***	0.335	57.882***	0.670***	1.012**
	(0.545)	(0.421)	(6.122)	(0.045)	(0.406)
infra(t − 1)	0.303***	0.042**	−1.198***	0.018***	0.826***
	(0.037)	(0.020)	(0.403)	(0.003)	(0.030)
No. of countries/obs	40/240				
Panel B: Middle					
sust(t − 1)	0.155***	−0.451***	−0.365	0.010	0.691***
	(0.058)	(0.086)	(0.701)	(0.011)	(0.084)
gov(t − 1)	0.216***	0.790***	−1.392***	−0.013**	−0.255***
	(0.036)	(0.062)	(0.513)	(0.006)	(0.056)
phycap(t − 1)	−0.007***	−0.016***	0.494***	0.0001	0.011***
	(0.002)	(0.004)	(0.055)	(0.0003)	(0.004)
humcap(t − 1)	4.209***	4.755***	−21.512**	0.634***	−1.512**
	(0.724)	(0.971)	(8.976)	(0.077)	(0.684)
infra(t − 1)	−0.088***	−0.246***	0.950**	0.016***	0.838***
	(0.032)	(0.040)	(0.424)	(0.004)	(0.035)
No. of countries/obs	39/156				

(Continued)

TABLE 1.6 (Continued)

	Dependent Variables				
	sust(t)	gov(t)	phycap(t)	humcap(t)	infra(t)
Panel C: Low					
sust(t − 1)	−0.030	0.426***	−50.056***	0.017***	0.392***
	(0.096)	(0.077)	(3.965)	(0.005)	(0.062)
gov(t − 1)	−0.504***	0.468***	3.128	0.032***	−0.215***
	(0.080)	(0.070)	(3.681)	(0.006)	(0.040)
phycap(t − 1)	0.002	0.008**	0.401*	0.0009**	−0.001
	(0.005)	(0.004)	(0.224)	(0.0004)	(0.003)
humcap(t − 1)	7.527***	−4.173***	317.161***	0.009	7.288***
	(1.174)	(0.911)	(67.120)	(0.072)	(0.847)
infra(t − 1)	−0.209***	0.133***	−4.153*	0.034***	0.446***
	(0.067)	(0.051)	(2.390)	(0.004)	(0.043)
No. of countries/obs	36/180				

Notes: Five variable VAR model is estimated by GMM. Country, time and fixed effects are removed prior to estimation. Countries are split into three groups based on their governance performance by K-means clustering. Reported numbers show the coefficients of regressing the column variables on lags of the row variables. Heteroskedasticity adjusted z-statistics are in parentheses. ***, ** and * denote significance levels at 1%, 5% and 10%, respectively.

For Testing the Hypothesis

Results show that the response of the sustainability index to governance is positive significant in the estimated coefficient for high performers in Panel A of Table 1.6 and in the impulse response function in the 2nd row – 1st column of Figure 1.2. The result confirms the first criterion that governance improves overall sustainability by increasing at least one of its three sub-indices. The result supports Fredriksson and Mani (2002) for the effect of governance on environmental quality; Klomp and De Haan (2008), Safaei (2006) and Franco, Álvarez-Dardet and Ruiz (2004) for the effect of governance on health quality; Azam and Emirullah (2014) and Radu (2015) for the effect of governance on economic well-being. The response of governance to the sustainability index is positive significant in the estimated coefficient for high performers in Panel A of Table 1.6 and in the impulse response function in the 1st row – 2nd column of Figure 1.2. The result confirms the second criterion that governance adapts to changes in overall sustainability with changes in at least one of its three sub-indices. The result supports Burkhardt et al. (2019) for the effect of environmental quality on governance and Al-Marhubi (2004), Rontos, Syrmali and Vavouras (2015) and Barro (1999) for the effect of economic well-being on governance. Both results confirm the hypothesis of sustainable governance for high performer countries.

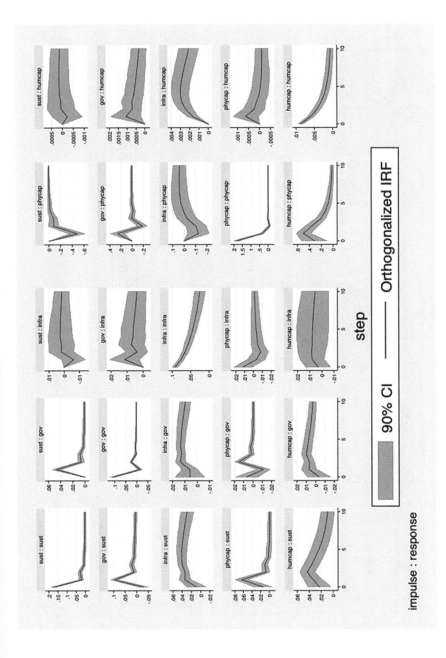

FIGURE 1.2 Impulse response function for high performers.

Source: Authors' calculations.

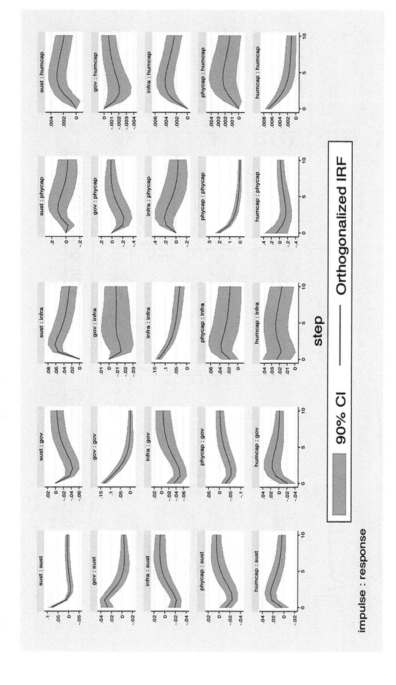

FIGURE 1.3 Impulse response function for middle performers.

Source: Authors' calculations.

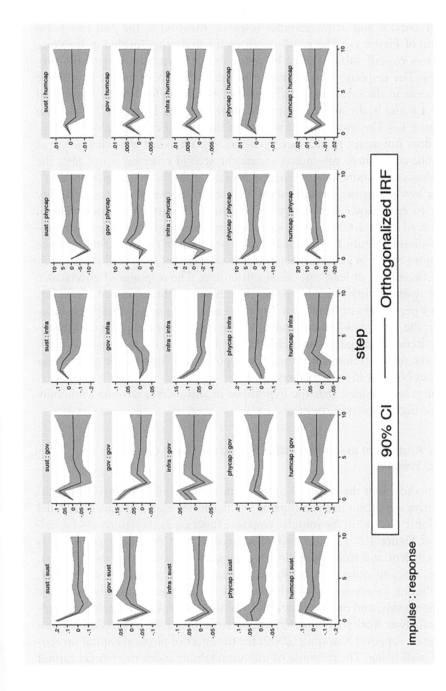

FIGURE 1.4   Impulse response function for low performers.

Source: Authors' calculations.

For middle performers results show that the response of the sustainability index to governance is positive significant in the estimated coefficient in Panel B of Table 1.6 and in the impulse response function in the 2nd row – 1st column of Figure 1.3 The result confirms the first criterion that governance improves overall sustainability by increasing at least one of its three sub-indices. The response of governance to the sustainability index is negative significant in the estimated coefficient for middle performers in Panel B of Table 1.6 and in the impulse response function in the 1st row – 2nd column of Figure 1.3 The result does not confirm the second criterion since governance does not adapt to changes in overall sustainability with changes in at least one of its three sub-indices. Since the second criterion is not met, the hypothesis of sustainable governance does not hold for middle performers.

For low performers, results show that the response of the sustainability index to governance is negative significant in the estimated coefficient in Panel C of Table 1.6 and in the impulse response function in the 2nd row – 1st column of Figure 1.4. The result does not confirm the first criterion since an improvement in governance negatively contributes to overall sustainability by decreasing at least one of its sub-indices. The response of governance to the sustainability index is positive significant in the estimated coefficient for low performers in Panel C of Table 1.6 and in the impulse response function in the 1st row – 2nd column of Figure 1.4. The result confirms the second criterion that governance adapts to changes in overall sustainability. Since the first criterion is not met, the hypothesis of sustainable governance does not hold for low performers.

The results suggest that the hypothesis of sustainable governance is only met for high performer countries.

For the Response of the Sustainability Index to the Shocks Given to Control Variables

Results show that the response of the sustainability index to physical capital is positive significant in the estimated coefficient for high performers in Panel A of Table 1.6 and in the impulse response function in the 4th row – 1st column of Figure 1.2. Physical capital utilized in high performer countries is most efficient and technology driven compared with the other two clusters. Hence, efficient utilization of physical capital leads to positive economies, contributing to economic well-being, and environmental quality by lesser emission levels, and improves health by positive spillovers to health technology and lesser working hours with the efficient utilization of physical capital. The result supports Xiaoqing (2005) for the effect of physical capital on economic well-being. The response of the sustainability index to physical capital is negative significant in the estimated coefficient for middle performers in Panel B of Table 1.6 and in the impulse response function in the 4th row – 1st

column of Figure 1.3. Physical capital utilization in middle performer countries is not efficient and technology driven. It is generally over employed leading to negative economies, deteriorating economic well-being, environmental
quality and health quality due to higher emission levels and increased working hours with repairs and maintenance. The response of the sustainability
index to physical capital is insignificant in the estimated coefficient for low
performers in Panel C of Table 1.6 and in the impulse response function in
the 4th row – 1st column of Figure 1.4. Physical capital utilization in low
performer countries is insufficient qualitatively and quantitatively compared
to the size of their population or country. Hence, any improvement in physical capital is not reflected as a positive impact on economic well-being, environmental quality or health quality.

Results show that the response of the sustainability index to human capital is positive significant for the estimated coefficient for high performers in
Panel A of Table 1.6 and in the impulse response function in the 5th row – 1st
column of Figure 1.2; for the estimated coefficient for middle performers in
Panel B of Table 1.6 and in the impulse response function in the 5th row – 1st
column of Figure 1.3; for the estimated coefficient for low performers in
Panel C of Table 1.6 and in the impulse response function in the 5th row – 1st
column of Figure 1.4. An improvement in human capital positively contributes to economic well-being by providing better paid jobs, to environmental
quality by sensitizing the public toward environmental issues and to health
quality by improving the efficiency of physicians and health officers and
increased awareness among the public toward medical issues. The results
support Boeve-de Pauw et al. (2015) and Burja and Burja (2013) on the effect
of education on sustainability. The result found for low performers contradict Muhammad, Egbetokun and Memon (2015) who argued that human
capital does not affect economic growth in countries with low governance.

Results show that the response of the sustainability index to infrastructure
is positive significant in the estimated coefficient for high performers in Panel
A of Table 1.6 and in the impulse response function in the 3rd row – 1st column of Figure 1.2. The infrastructure in high performer countries has positive spillovers on at least one of the sub-indices of sustainability. An
improvement in infrastructure positively contributes to economic well-being
by decreasing transportation and communication costs; to environmental
quality especially via low emission levels in transportation; and to health
quality by improving access to electricity and clean water. The result supports
Haider and Sharif (2016) for the effect of infrastructure on economic well-
being. The response of the sustainability index to infrastructure is negative
significant for the estimated coefficient for middle performers in Panel B
of Table 1.6 and in the impulse response function in 3rd row–1st column of
Figure 1.3 and for the estimated coefficient for low performers in Panel C
of Table 1.6 and in the impulse response function in 3rd row – 1st column of

Figure 1.4. The infrastructure in these countries is underdeveloped since it has negative spillovers on at least one of the sub-indices of sustainability. For these countries, improvement in infrastructure means exceeding beyond capacity since it is inefficient, and improvements are quantitative rather than qualitative. Improving infrastructure negatively contributes to economic well-being by increasing costs of transportation and communication, to environmental quality via allowing higher emission levels in transportation and to health quality by decreasing access to electricity and clean water via power and water cuts.

For the Response of Governance to the Shocks Given to Control Variables

Results show that the response of governance to physical capital is negative significant for the estimated coefficient for high performers in Panel A of Table 1.6 and in the impulse response function in 4th row – 2nd column of Figure 1.2 and for the estimated coefficient for middle performers in Panel B of Table 1.6 and in the impulse response function in 4th row – 2nd column of Figure 1.3. Increase in physical capital means increase in investments (domestic or foreign). The only meaningful explanation is that domestic or foreign firms pay bribes to obtain government contracts or trade licenses or to evade red tape and to forestall bureaucratic complications (Hines, 1995). Hence, an increase in physical capital deteriorates governance with higher corruption. The response of governance to physical capital is positive significant for the estimated coefficient for low performers in Panel C of Table 1.6 and in the impulse response function in 4th row – 2nd column of Figure 1.4. Since physical capital accumulation in these countries is low, any incremental increase positively contributes to governance via better rule of law with better equipped police cars and surveillance systems.

Results show that the response of governance to human capital is insignificant for the estimated coefficient for high performers in Panel A of Table 1.6 and in the impulse response function in 5th row – 2nd column of Figure 1.2. The reason may be because human capital (education) and governance are already developed in these countries and any incremental improvement in education is not reflected in improvements in governance. The result supports Busse and Gröning (2009) who found that education has no significant effect on governance. The response of governance to human capital is positive significant for the estimated coefficient for middle performers in Panel B of Table 1.6 and in the impulse response function in 5th row – 2nd column of Figure 1.3. The result support the argument of Busse and Gröning (2009) that higher educational levels promote governance since better educated population is more likely to participate in public decision-making and demand better governance. The response of governance to human capital is negative significant for the estimated coefficient for low performers in Panel C of

Table 1.6 and in the impulse response function in 5th row – 2nd column of Figure 1.4. The only meaningful explanation is that higher educational attainment grants better jobs with high potential corruption rents (Eicher, García-Peñalosa and Van Ypersele, 2009). Hence, increase in educational attainment increases the potential corruption rents, which increases corruptibility and deteriorates governance in low performer countries.

Results show that the response of governance to infrastructure is positive significant for the estimated coefficient for high performers in Panel A of Table 1.6 and in the impulse response function in 3rd row – 2nd column of Figure 1.2 and for the estimated coefficient for low performers in Panel C of Table 1.6 and in the impulse response function in 3rd row – 2nd column of Figure 1.4. The result supports Rød, Knutsen and Hegre (2020) who found that communication infrastructure has positive significant effect on democracy. The only meaningful explanation is that improvement in infrastructure, especially communication and transportation, leads to better rule of law and democracy via better surveillance systems, lesser response time of the police and higher freedom of information due to the prevalence of free media. The main difference between high and low performers is that high performers have efficient infrastructures with existing smart cities, and low performers have underutilized infrastructure. The response of governance to infrastructure is negative significant for the estimated coefficient for middle performers in Panel B of Table 1.6 and in the impulse response function in 3rd row – 2nd column of Figure 1.3. The only meaningful explanation is that the communication and transportation systems are overutilized in these countries and any quantity-based increase in these systems, i.e., additional telephone subscriptions and additional bus lines, would lead to inefficient outcomes like system-wide disconnections and heavy traffic which distort government effectiveness and rule of law, leading to decrease in governance performance.

According to variance decomposition at a horizon of ten years in Table 1.7, sustainability and governance forecast error variances are explained mostly by their own shocks. Governance explains forecast error variance of sustainability by 16.3% for high performers, 17.2% for middle performers and 9.7% for low performers and sustainability explains forecast error variance of governance by 13.4% for high performers, 10.6% for middle performers and 15.5% for low performers. Since they are all within the acceptable limits, the results justify using the panel VAR model to test our hypothesis. For the control variables, sustainability forecast error variance is explained second most by infrastructure (18.3%) for high performers and by human capital (30.8%) for low performers, and governance forecast error variance is explained second mostly by physical capital (17.6%) for middle performers and by human capital (32.2%) for low performers. These results justify using panel VAR by treating these control variables as endogenous rather than exogenous.

TABLE 1.7 Variance Decomposition

	sust	*gov*	*phycap*	*humcap*	*infra*
Panel A: High					
sust	0.480	0.134	0.055	0.001	0.002
gov	0.163	0.742	0.023	0.017	0.012
phycap	0.068	0.024	0.792	0.002	0.009
humcap	0.106	0.025	0.122	0.695	0.016
infra	0.183	0.075	0.008	0.285	0.961
Panel B: Middle					
sust	0.460	0.106	0.006	0.171	0.215
gov	0.172	0.540	0.019	0.061	0.012
phycap	0.115	0.176	0.940	0.099	0.086
humcap	0.153	0.021	0.015	0.335	0.057
infra	0.100	0.157	0.020	0.334	0.630
Panel C: Low					
sust	0.508	0.155	0.331	0.114	0.178
gov	0.097	0.394	0.105	0.140	0.072
phycap	0.045	0.089	0.172	0.149	0.173
humcap	0.308	0.322	0.350	0.464	0.078
infra	0.042	0.040	0.042	0.133	0.499

Source: Authors' calculations.

Notes: Percent of variation in the column variable (10 periods ahead) is explained by row variable.

Conclusion

According to the empirical analysis, results show that high performer countries have sustainable governance since there is a bidirectional positive significant relationship between governance and sustainability, which adheres to both criteria 1 and 2 and, hence, our hypothesis of sustainable governance. These countries are doing well, but we recommend them to bring in innovative governance practices for sustained economic well-being, environmental quality and health quality for sustainable governance, without any radical measures as that might change their governance structures altogether. The effect of control variables on sustainability for high performer countries is also positive significant. Any improvement in physical capital, human capital and infrastructure directly improves sustainability and indirectly improves sustainable governance. But since high performer countries witness deterioration in governance due to increases in physical capital, they should closely monitor the corrupt acts of domestic and foreign firms.

For middle performer countries, the study did not find prevalence of sustainable governance as per the hypothesis. Even though these countries meet the first criterion of a positive significant impact of governance on sustainability, their governance itself does not adapt positively to improvements in sustainability, which violates the second criterion. Since the increase in sustainability deteriorates their governance, we recommend them to bring in structural changes to economic, environment and health issues, i.e., have fiscal and taxation policies that increase per capita income without increasing income inequalities; have policies in the form of concessions and subsidies that encourage the use of renewable energy and stringent environment laws that discourage the use of old and purchase of new vehicles that increase CO_2 emissions; and have stimulus package in budgets (for boosting education and employment) for a relative increase in number of physicians than the increase in number of patients. As for the adaptability of governance structures, the governments in these countries should introduce administrative reforms that enhance participation (through decentralization) or do away with bureaucratic delays due to red-tapism (through transparent e-governance measures).

Since physical capital in middle performer countries deteriorates sustainability, they should try to renew their obsolescent physical capitals (equipment, plant and building) by building them with indigenous technologies or imported technologies with embedded know-how to turn negative economies of scale into positive economies of scale. Since infrastructure in these countries deteriorates sustainability, middle performer countries should invest in enhancing the quality of infrastructure instead of the quantity to overcome overcapacity problems, i.e., by building renewable energy resources instead of planting extra transducers, by building electricity propelled vehicles instead of vehicles consuming fossil fuels and by investing in 5G instead of installing extra cell towers. Physical capital that deteriorates the governance performance of middle performer countries could also signify corrupt practices by domestic and foreign firms and the same must be monitored.

Low performer countries also do not have sustainable governance as per our hypothesis. Even though they meet the second criterion, governance in these countries negatively contributes to sustainability, which violates the first criterion. We recommend that these countries should introduce structural reforms in governance as they have mostly inherited those structures from colonial times since any improvement in their governance structures justifies the validity of their inefficient governance structures and do not produce positive environmental, health or economic outcomes; i.e., they self-reinforce their own existence. It is time for them to reform their governance structures as those of their colonizers for sustainable outcomes. The same conclusion and recommendation for the effect of infrastructure on sustainability for middle performers apply to the same effect for low performers. And since human capital in the low performer countries negatively affects governance, they should check for possible corruption effects of higher education levels, as that provides an incentive to corruption due to the potential of higher rents with better positioned profiles.

References

Abrigo, M. R., & Love, I. (2016). Estimation of panel vector autoregression in Stata. *The Stata Journal*, 16(3), 778–804. DOI:10.1177/1536867X1601600314

Al-Marhubi, F. (2004). The determinants of governance: A cross-country analysis. *Contemporary Economic Policy*, 22(3), 394–406. DOI:10.1093/cep/byh029

Azam, M., & Emirullah, C. (2014). The role of governance in economic development: Evidence from some selected countries in Asia and the Pacific. *International Journal of Social Economics*, 41(12), 1265–1278. DOI:10.1108/IJSE-11-2013-0262

Barbier, E. B. (1987). The concept of sustainable economic development. *Environmental Conservation*, 14(2): 101–110. DOI:10.1017/S0376892900011449

Barro, R. J. (1999). Determinants of democracy. *Journal of Political Economy*, 107(S6), S158–S183.

Baxter, M. J. (1994). *Exploratory Multivariate Analysis in Archaeology*. Edinburgh University Press, Edinburgh, Scotland.

Bhatnagar, S. C. (2014). Public service delivery: Role of information and communication technology in improving governance and development impact. Asian Development Bank Economics Working Paper Series 391.

Brundtland, G. H., Khalid, M., Agnelli, S., Al-Athel, S. A., Chidzero, B. J. N. Y., Fadika, L. M., ... & Singh, N. (1987). *Our Common Future*, United Nations, Report of the World Commission on Environment and Development, New York.

Burja, C., & Burja, V. (2013). Education's contribution to sustainable economic growth in Romania. *Procedia-Social and Behavioral Sciences*, 81, 147–151. DOI:10.1016/j.sbspro.2013.06.403

Burkhardt, J., Bayham, J., Wilson, A., Carter, E., Berman, J. D., O'Dell, K., ... & Pierce, J. R. (2019). The effect of pollution on crime: Evidence from data on particulate matter and ozone. *Journal of Environmental Economics and Management*, 98, 102267. DOI:10.1016/j.jeem.2019.102267

Busse, M., & Gröning, S. (2009). Does foreign aid improve governance?. *Economics Letters*, 104(2), 76–78. DOI:10.1016/j.econlet.2009.04.002

Eicher, T., García-Peñalosa, C., & Van Ypersele, T. (2009). Education, corruption, and the distribution of income. *Journal of Economic Growth*, 14, 205–231. DOI:10.1007/s10887-009-9043-0

Emmelin, L., & Lerman, P. (2008). Environmental quality standards as a tool in environmental governance—The case of Sweden. In *Standards and Thresholds for Impact Assessment* (pp. 463–486). Springer Berlin Heidelberg, Berlin, Heidelberg. DOI:10.1007/978-3-540-31141-6_36

Ewers, R. M., & Smith, R. J. (2007). Choice of index determines the relationship between corruption and environmental sustainability. *Ecology and Society*, 12(1), r2.

Franco, Á., Álvarez-Dardet, C., & Ruiz, M. T. (2004). Effect of democracy on health: Ecological study. *Bmj*, 329(7480), 1421–1423. DOI:10.1136/bmj.329.7480.1421

Fredriksson, P. G., & Mani, M. (2002). *The Rule of Law and the Pattern of Environmental Protection*. IMF Working Paper No. 02/49, Available at SSRN: https://ssrn.com/abstract=879448

Garcia-Sanchez, I. M., Cuadrado-Ballesteros, B., & Frias-Aceituno, J. (2013). Determinants of government effectiveness. *International Journal of Public Administration*, 36(8), 567–577. DOI:10.1080/01900692.2013.772630

Grindle, M. (2012). Good governance: The inflation of an idea. *Planning Ideas That Matter* (pp. 259–282). The MIT Press, Cambridge, MA.

Haider, H. & Sharif, A. A. (2016). "Impact of teledensity on economic growth: A comparative analysis of south Asian countries." *International Journal of Economics and Empirical Research*, 4(11), 571–581.

Hines, J. R. (1995). Forbidden payment: Foreign bribery and American business after 1977 (No. 5266). National Bureau of Economic Research, Inc.

Klomp, J., & De Haan, J. (2008). Effects of governance on health: A cross-national analysis of 101 countries. *Kyklos*, 61(4), 599–614. DOI:10.1111/j.1467-6435.2008.00415

Krug, E. G., Mercy, J. A., Dahlberg, L. L., & Zwi, A. B. (2002). The world report on violence and health. *The Lancet*, 360(9339), 1083–1088. DOI:10.1016/S0140-6736(02)11133-0

Lopez-Calva, L. F., Zhou, Y., Al-Dahdah, E., Bulman, D. J., Isser, D. H., Larizza, M., ... & Sharma, S. (2017). *World development report 2017: Governance and the law*. World Bank Group. United States of America. Retrieved from https://policycommons.net/artifacts/1523583/world-development-report-2017/2208632/ on 06 Jun 2024. CID: 20.500.12592/c5tfcw.

Love, I. & Zicchino, L. (2006). Financial development and dynamic investment behavior: Evidence from panel VAR. *The Quarterly Review of Economics and Finance*, 46(2): 190–210. DOI:10.1016/j.qref.2005.11.007

Mainfort Jr, R. C. (2005). A k-means analysis of late period ceramic variation in the central Mississippi Valley. *Southeastern Archaeology*, 24(1), 59–69.

Milligan, G. W. (1980). An examination of the effect of six types of error perturbation on fifteen clustering algorithms. *Psychometrika*, 45(3), 325–342.

Muhammad, A., Egbetokun, A., & Memon, M. H. (2015). Human capital and economic growth: The role of governance. *The Pakistan Development Review*, 54(4), 529–548.

Naimur, R. (2010). MDGS. Inclusive Growth and Governance, One World Foundation India, New Delhi.

Pauw, J. B. D., Gericke, N., Olsson, D., & Berglund, T. (2015). The effectiveness of education for sustainable development. *Sustainability*, 7(11), 15693–15717. DOI:10.3390/su71115693

Radu, M. (2015). "Political stability-a condition for sustainable growth in Romania?." *Procedia Economics and Finance*, 30, 751–757. DOI:10.1016/S2212-5671(15)01324-6

Rød, E. G., Knutsen, C. H., & Hegre, H. (2020). The determinants of democracy: A sensitivity analysis. *Public Choice*, 185(1), 87–111.

Rontos, K., Syrmali, M. E., & Vavouras, I. (2015). Economic, political and social determinants of governance worldwide. *Journal of Social and Economic Development*, 17, 105–119. DOI:101007/s40847-015-0014-3

Safaei, J. (2006). Is democracy good for health?. *International Journal of Health Services*, 36(4): 767–786. DOI:10.2190/6V5W-0N36-AQNF-GPD1

Türke, R. E. (2012). Sustainable governance. *Systemic Management for Intelligent Organizations: Concepts, Models-Based Approaches and Applications* (pp. 237–247). DOI:10.1007/978-3-642-29244-6_14

UNDESA, & UNDP. (2012). *Governance and Development*.

UNDP (2020). United Nations Development Programme. New York. http://hdr.undp.org/en/data (accessed June 22, 2020)

WDI. (2020). *World Development Indicators*. The World Bank, Washington D.C. https://databank.worldbank.org/source/world-development-indicators (accessed on June 22, 2020).

WGI. (2020). *Worldwide Governance Indicators.* The World Bank, Washington D.C. https://databank.worldbank.org/source/worldwide-governance-indicators (accessed on June 22, 2020)

Wu, J. (2012). *Advances in K-means Clustering: A Data Mining Thinking.* Springer Science & Business Media, Heidelberg.

Xiaoqing, X. (2005). Investment in physical capital, investment in health and economic growth in China. *Investment Management and Financial Innovations*, 2(1), 23–29.

APPENDIX 1.1 List of Variables and Data Source

Code	Name	Description	Source
sust	Sustainability index	PCA of following sub-indices	
env	Environmental quality	PCA of following indicators	
		Forest area (% of land area)	WDI (2020)
		Renewable energy consumption (% of total final energy consumption)	WDI (2020)
		CO_2 emissions (metric tons per capita)	WDI (2020)
heal	Health quality	PCA of following indicators	
		Physicians (per 1000 people)	WDI (2020)
		Life expectancy at birth, total (years)	WDI (2020)
		Mortality rate, infant (per 1000 live births)	WDI (2020)
econ	Economic well-being	PCA of following indicators	
		GDP per capita (constant 2010 US$)	WDI (2020)
		Unemployment, total (% of total labor force)	WDI (2020)
		Inflation, consumer prices (annual %)	WDI (2020)
gov	Governance quality	PCA of following indicators	
		Control of corruption: estimate	WGI (2020)
		Government effectiveness: estimate	WGI (2020)
		Political stability and absence of violence/terrorism: estimate	WGI (2020)
		Regulatory quality: estimate	WGI (2020)
		Rule of law: estimate	WGI (2020)
		Voice and accountability: estimate	WGI (2020)
phycap	Physical capital	Gross capital formation (% of GDP)	WDI (2020)
humcap	Human capital	Education index	UNDP (2020)
infra	Infrastructure	PCA of following indicators	
		Individuals using the internet (% of population)	WDI (2020)
		Mobile cellular subscriptions (per 100 people)	WDI (2020)

APPENDIX 1.2 Descriptive Statistics

Variables	Obs	Mean	Std. Dev.	Min	Max
Panel A: High					
sust	640	0.632	0.628	−2.000	1.898
gov	640	2.703	1.048	0.569	4.585
phycap	640	23.442	4.646	12.371	41.449
humcap	640	0.805	0.083	0.546	0.940
infra	640	1.008	1.012	−1.696	2.921
Panel B: Middle					
sust	624	−0.090	0.771	−2.300	2.006
gov	624	−0.596	0.932	−3.318	2.264
phycap	624	24.132	6.291	7.542	47.943
humcap	624	0.620	0.120	0.213	0.834
infra	624	−0.166	1.180	−1.911	3.185
Panel C: Low					
sust	576	−0.604	0.729	−4.904	0.733
gov	576	−2.358	0.719	−4.513	−0.671
phycap	576	23.912	9.042	2.781	60.156
humcap	576	0.482	0.156	0.139	0.839
infra	576	−0.939	0.949	−1.919	2.200

APPENDIX 1.3 Cross-Section Dependency (CD) Test

Variables	CD-Test	p-Value
sust	60.904	0
gov	6.947	0
phycap	33.212	0
humcap	277.684	0
infra	301.797	0

Notes: Null hypothesis is the cross section independence. P-values close to zero indicate data are correlated across panel groups.

APPENDIX 1.4 Pesaran Panel Unit-Root Test Results

	Level		First Difference	
Variables	Constant	Constant & Trend	Constant	Constant & Trend
sust	−2.038*	−2.836***		
gov	−1.712	−2.472	−3.729***	−3.851***
phycap	−1.854	−2.408	−3.382***	−3.448***
humcap	−1.742	−2.177	−3.144***	−3.193***
infra	−1.811	−1.989	−2.521***	−3.153***

Notes: The numbers are the CIPS values. Null hypothesis is that the variable has unit-root. ***, ** and * denote significance levels at 1%, 5% and 10%, respectively.

APPENDIX 1.5 List of Countries in Clusters

Panel A: High

Australia	Austria	Bahamas, The	Barbados	Belgium
Botswana	Canada	Chile	Costa Rica	Cyprus
Czech Republic	Denmark	Estonia	Finland	France
Germany	Iceland	Ireland	Israel	Japan
Republic of Korea	Latvia	Lithuania	Luxembourg	Malta
Mauritius	Netherlands	New Zealand	Norway	Poland
Portugal	Singapore	Slovak Republic	Slovenia	Spain
Sweden	Switzerland	United Kingdom	United States	Uruguay

Panel B: Middle

Albania	Armenia	Bahrain	Benin	Brazil
Brunei Darussalam	Bulgaria	Colombia	Croatia	Dominican Rep.
El Salvador	Georgia	Ghana	Greece	Guyana
Hungary	India	Indonesia	Italy	Jamaica
Jordan	Kuwait	Malaysia	Mexico	Moldova
Morocco	North Macedonia	Panama	Peru	Philippines
Romania	Rwanda	Saudi Arabia	Senegal	South Africa
Sri Lanka	Thailand	Tunisia	Turkey	

Panel C: Low

Algeria	Azerbaijan	Bangladesh	Belarus	Bolivia
Burkina Faso	Burundi	Cambodia	Cameroon	Chad
China	Congo, Rep.	Cote d'Ivoire	Ecuador	Egypt, Arab Rep.
Eswatini	Gabon	Gambia, The	Guatemala	Haiti
Iran, Islamic Rep.	Kenya	Kyrgyz Republic	Madagascar	Malawi
Mali	Mauritania	Nepal	Pakistan	Paraguay
Russian Federation	Tanzania	Togo	Uganda	Ukraine
Vietnam				

2

GOVERNANCE AND ECONOMIC GROWTH

An Econometric Analysis with BRICS Countries

Dipankar Das and Debabrata Mukhopadhyay

Introduction

Globally each country continuously tries to emerge in world development platform. Development of the economy depends on economic growth, although economic growth depends on the roles of social, economic, and political institutions in the countries. Political institution means political parties that lead the governments in countries and play a crucial role in the development process. Regarding economic growth, policy makers' decisions are vital.

In the last three decades, BRICS (Brazil, Russian Federation, India, China, South Africa) countries have emerged as developing countries in the world. The BRICS, i.e., the groups of countries, have been increasing their share of global trade and investment and it is likely to become even more significant in the future. Regarding BRICS, all the countries have experienced rapid GDP growth (with GDP typically calculated in Purchasing Power Parity exchange rates rather than nominal exchange rates). Some other potential members of the developing countries particularly Indonesia and Mexico have experienced relatively large economies. It means the volume of GDP is larger compared to other countries. Like much of the rest of the developing world, they have also sought to add to their holding of foreign exchange reserves. India's trade share has increased in recent times and it is almost 2%. Among the other BRICS countries, Brazil even increased its global trade share.

Generally, the acronym 'BRIC' formed the combination of four countries, namely, Brazil, Russia, India, China, and it was coined by Jim O'Neill of Goldman Sachs in 2001. Initially, it was the acronym of 'BRIC' after in the year 2010 the country South Africa joined. Presently BRICS countries deserve as emerging countries in socio-economic view as well as rapid GDP growth

DOI: 10.4324/9781003530688-4

context. Overall, in the last few decades, BRICS countries are very significant in the global economic platform in the context of per capita GDP growth. Not only that these countries are fuelled by economic growth, they are with a large resource base, favourable demographic and lower labour costs and their social inclusion policies helped global economic development. However, BRICS was established earlier aiming to promote peace, development, security, and cooperation among the member countries. According to Goldman Sachs (an investment and banking company), they have a huge potential to form a powerful economic block in the world. The role of BRICS is most significant to the global economy in terms of population (40% of the world) and GDP (25% of world GDP). Moreover, BRICS countries have 30% of the land coverage of the global economy. Apart from potentiality or socio-economic development, especially financial development is very crucial in BRICS countries. Moreover, banking sector expansion plays a more important role in financial development and ultimately it influences the economic growth of the countries. In the research, it is demonstrated that financial development positively influences economic growth (Leitao, 2010).

Effective public governance ensures the adoption of laws and their accessibility to citizens. As a result, this helps to improve the economic growth of the nation (Burgess, 2012). The existence of the rule of law in a country provides stability, which will undoubtedly increase investments because investors will feel protected by the implementation of laws by the judiciary, which will ensure full justice. Although the rule of law was insignificant, the sign of this coefficient corresponds to our a priori expectation. The coefficient for political stability and absence of violence/terrorism turned out to be insignificant, but the sign is positive. Younis et al. (2008) make note that a stable political environment in a country not only increases the accumulation of human capital and physical capital but also stimulates the growth process.

The study under the backdrop has employed panel static models [ordinary least squares (OLS) and fixed effects (FEs) estimator] from 2002 to 2020 to investigate the effects of governance factors by the World Bank World Governance Indicators (WGI) on economic growth to the BRICS countries.

Governance Factors

The six dimensions of governance indicators developed by the World Bank are described as follows:

I. Voice and Accountability: It means that the peoples of the countries can decide to select freely their government and have freedom to vocal independence, freedom of speech, and freedom of associations and must be responsible for civil rights of the country. All such factors indicate the voice and accountability of the countries.

II. Political Stability and Absence of Terrorism/Violence: Political stability and absence of violence are necessary for every country and that are the responsibility of the peoples. The possibility of destabilization or unconstitutional overthrow of the government, including domestic violence and terrorism, is measured by several indicators in the country such as fake administration, bad law, etc.

III. Government Effectiveness: It means that any decisions of the government, such as government policies and implications, and the credibility of the authority's commitment to implement various policies on responses by the government. To explain the degree of responses by the government on the quality of public service, civil service, independence of political pressure, etc.

IV. Regulatory Quality: Encouraging foreign business and protecting the private sector by eliminating all unfriendly policies such as price control, banking supervision, and restriction of capital movement.

V. Rule of Law: Every citizen of the country has confidence in their social rules and in particular the quality of contract enforcement, property rights, the police, and the courts. The effectiveness of the judiciary systems of the country may give protection to foreign investors.

VI. Control of Corruption: Public power of bureaucratic regulation exercised for private gain creates corruption in the country and may hinder foreign investors. Massive corruption leads to inefficient plans for the foreign party due to uncertainty and ambiguity created in return.

For the research purpose, all the governance indicators are developed and measured by the World Bank. According to the World Bank, the estimated values of each governance indicator lie between –2.5 and +2.5 approximately. The minimum value of any indicator –2.5 explains the weak governance performances of each country. Besides, the maximum value +2.5 explains the strong governance performances of each country. Its expected sign is ambiguous. Good governance positively affects economic growth. In contrast, poor governance negatively affects per capita GDP growth in BRICS countries.

Literature Review

Economic growth of a country means GDP growth. The stable economic growth of the countries depends on many factors like capital inflows, governance factors, technological advancement, etc. However, in the long run economic growth results in enormous inequality in income and wealth in many countries for many reasons. The countries where inequality in income challenges create political pressure through taxation policy to the countries, which affects the economic growth as well as investment policy.

Bagchi and Svejnar (2015) and Jorgenson (2018) argued that most GDP in developing countries is concentrated among the most powerful, frequently politicians and their ancillary people. As a result, this politically powerful people may have adverse effect on economic growth in the countries. It was generally revealed that politically accumulated income or wealth inequality has an adverse effect on economic growth in the country. This is an instance in a research of Morck, Yeung, and Yu (2000) and Omar and Inaba (2020).

Furthermore, few research studies have used panel data analysis; for example, Lee and Kim (2009) found that there is bi-directional causation between institutions, governance, and economic growth, using a sample of 63 countries for the period 1965–2002. They also divided the sample countries into two groups, namely, the high-income countries group (high and upper middle income) and the low-income countries (low and lower middle income) group. Their findings indicated that institutions are statistically significant determinants of growth in both groups of countries, but the role of institutions diminishes in high-income countries, as more variables are added to the model specification. These results were consistent with another panel data analysis by Law et al. (2013), who found the causal effect between institutions and economic development using the panel Granger causality test. The findings also suggest that causality patterns between institutions and economic performance vary at different stages of income level. Better institutional quality leads to faster economic development in higher income countries, whereas economic development tends to enhance institutional quality in lower income countries group. Similar results were revealed in Valeriani and Peluso's (2011) studies and they examined the institutional framework through which economic growth occurs and growth differences among countries. The study concluded that the quality of economic institutions had a positive impact on the growth and development of a nation.

Moreover, corruption plays a role in advancing both inequality and growth in developing countries. It amasses wealth in the hands of a few ruling parties (World Bank, Khan & Naeem, 2020). Convicted cases in crimes involve the distribution of state resources and require the reimbursement of any misappropriated or stolen funds. Corruption in state finances is the reason for inequality in developing countries because funds meant for the poor are misappropriated (Khan & Naeem, 2020). These events are mostly found in the case of BRICS countries.

The impact of corruption on economic growth is an ongoing topic that has caused debates among researchers. Many studies indicate that corruption can have adverse effects on the growth of the economy (Baklouti & Boujelbene, 2019). Notably, Hodge, Shankar, Rao, and Duhs (2011) claim that corruption adversely affects investment, human capital, and political instability leading to negative economic growth. Gründler and Potrafke (2019) analysed data from 175 countries during the period 2012–2018 to find the relationship between corruption and economic growth. The authors conclude that one standard deviation increase in the reversed Transparency International's Perception of Corruption Index leads to an approximately 17% decrease in the real per capita GDP. They add that corruption negatively influences growth by reducing FDI and raising inflation.

Singh (2022) employed the panel cointegration technique to examine the relationship between growth and the six governance indicators. He concluded that development and governance are complementary. This means that growth is necessary for enhancing good governance, whereas governance promotes growth in the BRICS nations. In the same vein, using two-stage least squares (2SLS) and generalized method of moments (GMM) regression model.

Moreover, some researchers suggest that the direction of the governance–growth relationship varies according to countries' economic and social factors. Fawaz et al. (2021) categorized a sample of 11 developing nations from 1996 to 2008 according to income levels (high or low). Using FE methods, they showed that, as compared to high-income nations, voice and responsibility hampered economic progress in low-income countries. The cause might be the low credibility of the media in these nations, whether free or not. They also concluded that the rule of law and corruption control significantly impacted economic development.

Furthermore, the relationship between income per capita as a proxy of the stage of development and governance indicator was analysed in Quibria (2014). A simple regression line of a composite index of governance on the logarithm of real GDP per capita was estimated. The slope coefficient of the estimated regression line was found to be positive with a high R-squared value. In addition, relationships between various dimensions of the WGI and the income per capita were also estimated. The study found the slope coefficients ranging between 0.391 and 0.526. It was 0.391 for voice and accountability, 0.403 for political stability, 0.483 for regularity quality, 0.496 for corruption perception, 0.513 for rule of law, and 0.526 for governance effectiveness.

Although the relationship between governance and economic growth is well documented, the positive associations are insufficient for establishing the direction of causality between the two variables because the cross-section nature of the technique employed in the literature does not allow different countries to exhibit different patterns of causality (Law et al., 2013). Moreover, the results of cross-section analysis can quickly change with addition or reduction in the number of countries. Das et al. (2013) and Das and Das (2014) investigated the relationship between governance indicators and economic growth and economic confidence across some countries and regions and found some good impacts of governance upon growth.

A lot of empirical studies support that economic growth depends on governance (Kaufmann et al., 2000; Knack, 2002). These studies concluded that governance factors have a positive impact on economic growth. Kaufmann and Kraay (2002) explored the interrelationship between governance and growth through several domains grouped into six main indicators. They conclude that per capita income and the quality of governance are significantly, strongly, and positively correlated across countries. Thus, better governance leads to an increase in per capita income and the opposite phenomenon is observed when the level of governance is low, followed by economic stagnation because of negative growth rates.

Objectives of the Study

The major aim of this chapter is to examine growth and governance relationships in BRICS countries. The first objective of the study is to examine the idea of 'Good Governance', which states that improvement in governance capabilities leads to an increase in the rate of economic growth in the economy. On the contrary, the idea of 'good enough governance' is examined under the second objective which advocates that improvement in economic performance causes a subsequent improvement in the quality of governance.

Methodology and Analysis

In this chapter, the study will empirically evaluate the relationship between governance and economic growth in BRICS countries over the period 2002–2020. The econometric model is used for the balanced panel in this study and the study has used the OLS method and FE method at the country level. Before that the study has also the stationarity of the time-series data is checked with the augmented Dickey-Fuller (ADF) (1979, 1981, and 1984) test. The study also gets significant results stationary level at first differences by using a balanced panel data method.

Data

The study utilizes annual balanced panel data for BRICS countries, namely, Brazil, Russia, India, China, and South Africa, for the period from 2002 to 2020. The data for all the variables are collected from the World Bank database. According to Wong et al. (2005), GDP per capita is the most widely used economic growth measurement. Therefore, the per capita GDP (GDP) growth is taken as a proxy for economic growth, which has been taken from World Development Indicators of the World Bank. The governance indicators, namely, Voice and Accountability, Political Stability and Absence of Violence, Government Effectiveness, Regulatory Quality, Rule of Law, and

Control of Corruption, are taken from the World Bank Governance Indicators (WGI). Moreover, Gross Capital Formation (as % of GDP) is another crucial factor for economic growth in BRICS countries and is drawn from World Bank data source.

Econometric Methodology

Since most of these studies relied on a linear modelling framework, one explanation for the conflicting findings from the empirical literature relates to the failure to account for the level effect of corruption. This rationale has fuelled several threshold regression-based contributions aimed at identifying the cut-off level where corruption might have a positive, negative, or neutral economic impact (Trabelsi & Trabelsi, 2021).

The regression equation for each emerging economy is usually taken in the following form:

$$y_t = \alpha + \sum_{j=1}^{k} \beta_j X_{jt} + \varepsilon_t$$

The above regressions model y_t represents the per capita GDP growth in the BRICS economy and $X_j's$ [j = 1, 2 ..., $k(7)$] are the explanatory variables including all types of governance components with the time series dimension (t = 2002, 2001, ..., 2020). The disturbance or error term ε_t considers both the unobservable unit of observation-specific effects and the remainder of the disturbance and follows all the usual assumptions of the classical linear model. Again, α denotes the intercept term and β denotes a vector of coefficients.

Empirical Results

Table 2.1 shows that the ADF test statistics for the first differences of all the variables are statistically significant implying that the null hypothesis of the ADF test that there is a unit root for the first differences cannot be accepted and it is implying that the variables are stationary at the first difference level. The empirical analysis employs annual data on six governance indicators and gross capital formation in BRICS countries. In addition, the ADF test is performed with respect to the variables under consideration to test the stationarity. Table 2.1 reports the results of the ADF tests on the said variables. They show that the first differenced forms of the concerned variables are revealed to be stationary at 1% significance. Therefore, it is assumed that all concerned variables are integrated of order one in all the countries. Only except in the case of the Rule of law as cgovernance indicator in Brazil, of Voice and accountability in India, and in case of Control of corruption in Russian Federation are the second difference at a 1% level of significance.

TABLE 2.1 Augmented Dickey-Fuller (Denoted by ADF) Test Statistics for the Period 2002–2020

Countries	Brazil				Russian Federation			
Variables	Stationary at Level	ADF Test Statistics (p-Value)	Coefficient of the 1st lag (p-Value)	D-W Statistics	Stationary at Level	ADF Test Statistics (p-Value)	Coefficient of the 1st Lag (p-Value)	D-W Statistics
GDP growth	1st Diff.	−4.8 (0.00)*	−1.88 (0.00)*	1.929	1st Diff.	−5.16 (0.00)*	−1.29 (0.00)*	2.12769
Voice and accountability	1st Diff.	−3.78 (0.01)	−0.96 (0.00)*	2.010	1st Diff.	−3.52 (0.02)	−0.92 (0.00)*	1.88611
Political stability	1st Diff.	−5.28 (0.00)*	−1.31 (0.00)*	2.036	1st Diff.	−5.01 (0.00)*	−1.74 (0.00)*	2.37185
Government effectiveness	1st Diff.	−5.9 (0.00)	−1.45 (0.00)*	1.879	1st Diff.	−3.71 (0.01)*	−0.98 (0.00)	1.82605
Regulatory quality	1st Diff.	−3.91 (0.00)*	−1.00 (0.00)*	1.811	1st Diff.	−6.39 (0.00)*	−1.43 (0.00)*	2.22352
Rule of law	2nd Diff.	−5.12 (0.00)*	−1.32 (0.00)*	2.042	1st Diff	−4.81 (0.00)	−1.16 (0.00)*	1.93582
Control of corruption	1st Diff.	−3.80 (0.01)	−0.97 (0.00)*	1.927	2nd Diff.	−7.76 (0.00)*	−1.56 (0.00)*	2.10144
Gross capital formation (% of GDP)	1st Diff.	−3.76 (0.01)	−0.97 (0.00)*	1.756	1st Diff	−4.50 (0.00)*	−2.81 (0.00)*	2.19904

Countries	India				China				South Africa			
Variables	Stationary at Level	ADF Test Statistics (p-Value)	Coefficient of the 1st Lag (p-Value)	D-W Statistics	Stationary at Level	ADF Test Statistics (p-Value)	Coefficient of the 1st Lag (p-Value)	D-W Statistics	Stationary at Level	ADF Test Statistics (p-Value)	Coefficient of the 1st Lag (p-Value)	D-W Statistics
GDP growth	2nd Diff.	-4.24 (0.0059)*	-2.21 (0.0011)	1.69	1st Diff.	-3.1 (0.0455)	-1.36 (0.00)*	1.6881	1st Diff.	-3.15 (0.04)**	-1.04 (0.00)*	1.57
Voice and accountability	2nd Diff.	-6.87 (0.00)*	-1.48 (0.00)*	1.6653	1st Diff.	-4.39 (0.00)*	-1.09 (0.00)*	2.0842	1st Diff.	-2.55 (0.12)	-0.63 (0.02)**	1.5482
Political stability	1st Diff.	-6.13 (0.00)*	-1.31 (0.00)*	1.9036	1st Diff.	-6.73 (0.00)*	-1.37 (0.00)*	1.7970	1st Diff.	-3.27 (0.03)**	-1.20 (0.00)*	1.9282
Government effectiveness	1st Diff.	-6.01 (0.00)*	-1.48 (0.00)*	1.9257	1st Diff.	-3.69 (0.01)**	-1.30 (0.00)*	1.9393	1st Diff.	-5.30 (0.00)*	-1.30 (0.00)*	2.131
Regulatory quality	1st Diff.	-3.78 (0.01)**	-0.97 (0.00)*	2.015142	2nd Diff.	-3.12 (0.04)**	-1.20 (0.00)*	1.87	1st Diff.	-8.3 (0.00)*	-1.58 (0.00)*	2.097
Rule of law	1st Diff.	-6.09 (0.00)*	-1.25 (0.00)*	1.694832	1st Diff.	-3.38 (0.02)**	-0.96 (0.00)*	1.833406	1st Diff.	-5.14 (0.00)*	-1.28 (0.00)*	1.998028
Control of corruption	1st Diff.	-6.92 (0.00)*	-1.51 (0.00)*	2.251828	1st Diff.	-5.07 (0.00)*	-1.39 (0.00)*	1.351604	1st Diff.	-3.34 (0.02)**	-0.85 (0.00)*	1.695863
Gross capital formation (% of GDP)	1st Diff.	-3.05 (0.05)**	-0.79 (0.00)*	1.859036	1st Diff.	-3.01 (0.05)**	-0.59 (0.00)*	1.746704	1st Diff.	-4.10 (0.00)*	-1.05 (0.0009)	1.986819

Source: Authors' computations.

*Indicates significance at 1% level of significance, **indicates significance at 5% level of significance, ***indicates significance at 10% level of significance.

Furthermore, this section discusses the empirical results obtained by following the econometric methodology stated in the previous section. This study selected BRICS countries and each country is most crucial in this group in the context of economic development. Figures 1–5 refer to the trend of GDP growth in five countries during 2002–2020. In that figure, it is shown that the trend of GDP growth in BRICS countries gradually at decline over the periods except Brazil, China, and rest of the countries it reached at negative value during the year 2020. But GDP growth was a rising trend in the first phase of the stipulated period.

Therefore, the study has presented the results of a simple time-series linear equation analysis in Table 2.1. Thus, the results showed that the governance indicators are highly significant in explaining the variation in economic growth across the BRICS countries. Table 2.1 has two parts: the first part considers only the significant governance indicators with respective BRICS countries and the second part of Table 2.1 explains the empirical results by using static panel data with FE methodology. Firstly, there are two governance sub-components and gross capital formation is statistically significant at 1% level and 5% level in Brazil. Such components are political stability, government effectiveness. This is also indicated by the high value of R^2 in all the BRICS countries except South Africa. It describes these results in detail; the governance indicators such as political stability and government effectiveness are negatively significant at 1% levels in Brazil. This result is mismatched with a usual relation, and generally stable political system and government effectiveness boost up the economic growth. On the other gross capital formation is also positively impact on economic growth and statistically significant at the 5% level in Brazil.

In the case of China and Russian Federation, only one governance sub-component is statistically significant, i.e., control of corruption. The value of the coefficient is considered positive and statistically significant at a 5% level in Russian Federation and it is negatively related to the growth at a 5% level in the case of China (Nguyen & Luong, 2020). On the other gross capital formation is also positively impact on economic growth and statistically significant at a 1% level in Russian Federation. In India, governance indicators like Voice and accountability are statistically significant at a 5% level. The coefficients for the governance indicator are positively significant indicating that if voice and accountability are properly established, then the BRICS countries will be able to perform effective economic growth (Figure 2.1).

The second part of Table 2.2 depicts static panel data results. The only two governance indicators, i.e., government effectiveness and control of corruption, are negatively significant at 5% level and positively significant at a 1% level, respectively, in BRICS countries. This result is mismatched with a usual relation; generally stable political system and government effectiveness boost up the economic growth.

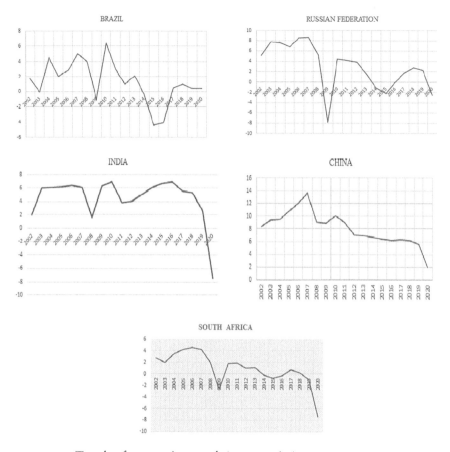

FIGURE 2.1 Trends of economic growth (county wise).

Source: Compiled by authors based on the data collected from World Development Indicators of World Bank.

Summary and Conclusion

The purpose of this study is to assess whether and to what extent the six governance indicators influence the economic growth in BRICS countries over the period 2002–2020 by using a series linear regression approach as well as a panel data model with a FE approach. This study aims to assess the impact of governance indicators on economic growth in BRICS countries. The results of the empirical tests show that improving the effectiveness of governance and political stability positively and significantly promotes economic growth in the countries covered by this study. Similarly, the results reveal that the control of corruption has a positive influence on economic growth, and its estimated coefficient is significant.

TABLE 2.2 Empirical Results during the Period 2002–2020

Countries	Brazil		Russian Federation		India		China		South Africa	
Variables	Coefficient	Prob	Coefficient	Prob	Coefficient	Prob	Coefficient	Prob	Coefficient	Prob
1st part										
C	-0.701494	0.35	-0.838043	0.25	0.445316	0.55	-0.112862	0.69	-0.422129	0.48
Voice and accountability	1.619941	0.90	1.284939	0.91	44.79634	0.02	6.572696	0.34	-22.74987	0.40
Political stability	-8.155733	0.00	6.186785	0.19	-3.242026	0.49	-4.547703	0.12	5.529347	0.27
Government effectiveness	-11.81987	0.05	-7.291940	0.31	-7.362297	0.22	6.568819	0.23	3.380301	0.61
Regulatory quality	12.96959	0.13	-10.02163	0.16	8.690126	0.57	0.942639	0.78	-1.899845	0.80
Rule of law	7.343369	0.39	9.565043	0.36	3.033408	0.72	-12.89381	0.16	1.155561	0.88
Control of corruption	-11.20327	0.12	33.09952	0.02	-1.046058	0.69	-6.982925	0.09	-0.035815	0.99
Gross capital formation (% of GDP)	1.209939	0.03	1.799545	0.00	0.525748	0.11	-0.050213	0.68	-1.116678	0.07
R^2	0.65		0.80		0.58		0.57		0.42	
Adj R^2	0.40		0.66		0.28		0.27		0.01	

Variables	Coefficient	Std. Error	t-Statistic	Prob
2nd part				
C	4.976266	0.445751	11.16378	0.0000
Government effectiveness	-3.191628	1.547737	-2.062125	0.0429
Control of corruption	3.994002	1.356022	2.945380	0.0044
R^2	78			
Adj R^2	70			

Source: Authors' computations.

Moreover, in China and Russian Federation, there is only one governance sub-component that is statistically significant, which is the control of corruption. Moreover, control of corruption is statistically significant at a 5% level and has positive impact in Russian Federation and it is negatively related with the growth at a 5% level in the case of China. On the other gross capital formation is also positively impact on economic growth and statistically significant at 1% level in Russian Federation. In India, governance indicators like Voice and accountability are statistically significant at a 5% level. The coefficients for the governance indicator are positively significant indicating that if voice and accountability are properly established, then the BRICS countries will be able to perform effective economic growth.

The main implication of this study is that strong efforts are needed within BRICS countries to improve the quality and effectiveness of regulatory mechanisms; to bring down corruption levels; to strengthen the rule of law; to achieve political stability and reduce internal violence; and to make governments more accountable to their own citizens. Furthermore, an exogenous increase in income – through multilateral aid, for instance – will feed in better governance. A future extension of this study will work on testing the effect of multipurpose aid in improving governance in BRICS countries.

References

Bagchi, S., & Svejnar, J. (2015). Does wealth inequality matter for growth? The effect of billionaire wealth, income distribution, and poverty. *Journal of Comparative Economics*, 43(3), 505–530. https://doi.org/10.1016/j.jce.2015.04.002

Baklouti, N., & Boujelbene, Y. (2019). Shadow economy, corruption, and economic growth: An empirical analysis. *The Review of Black Political Economy*, 47(3), 276–294. https://doi.org/10.1177/0034644619885349

Burgess, M. (2012). Dangers of environmental extremism, analysis of debate over India's social forestry programme. *Economic and Political Weekly*, 27(40), 2196–2199.

Das, R. C., & Das, U. (2014). Interrelationships among growth, confidence and governance in the globalized world-An experiment of some selected countries. *International Journal of Finance and Banking Studies*, 3(4), 68–83.

Das, R. C., Das, U., & Ray, K. (2013). Linkages among confidence, governance and growth in the era of globalization-A study of some Asian countries. *Vidyasagar University Journal of Economics*, XVII, 35–46.

Fawaz, F., Mnif, A., & Popiashvili, A. (2021). Impact of governance on economic growth in developing countries: A case of HIDC vs LIDC. *Journal of Social and Economic Development*, 23(1), 44–58.

Gründler, K., & Potrafke, N. (2019). Corruption and economic growth: New empirical evidence. *European of Journal Political Economy*, 60, 101810. https://doi.org/10.1016/j.ejpoleco.2019.08.001

Hodge, A., Shankar, S., Rao, D. P., & Duhs, A. (2011). Exploring the links between corruption and growth. *Review of Development Economics*, 15(3), 474–490. https://doi.org/10.1111/j.1467-9361.2011.00621.x

Jorgenson, D. W. (2018). Production and welfare: Progress in economic measurement. *Journal of Economic Literature, 56*(3), 867–919. https://doi.org/10.1257/jel.20171358

Kaufmann, D., & Kraay, A. (2002). Growth without governance. *Policy Research Working Paper No.* 2928: The World Bank.

Kaufmann, D., Kraay, A., & Zoido-Lobatón, P. (2000). Governance matters. *Finance Development*, 37(2), 10.

Khan, R. E. A., & Naeem, H. M. (2020). Corruption, income inequality and human resource development in developing economies. *Asian Journal of Economic Modelling*, 8(4), 248–259. https://doi.org/10.18488/journal.8.2020.84.248.259

Knack, S. (2002). *Governance and Growth: Measurement and Evidence*. Munich, Germany: University Library of Munich.

Law, S. H., Lim, T. C., & Ismail, N.W. (2013). Institutions and economic development: A granger causality analysis of panel data evidence. *Economic Systems*, 37, 610–624. https://doi.org/10.1016/j.ecosys.2013.05.005

Lee, K., & Kim, B.Y. (2009). Both institutions and policies matter but differently for different income groups of countries: Determinants of long-run economic growth revisited. *World Development*, 37, 533–549. https://doi.org/10.1016/j.worlddev.2008.07.004

Leitao, N. C. (2010). Financial development and economic growth: A panel data approach. *Theoretical and Applied Economics*, 10(551), 15–24.

Morck, R., Yeung, B., & Yu, W. (2000). The information content of stock markets: Why do emerging markets have synchronous stock price movements? *Journal of Financial Economics*, 58(1–2), 215–260. https://doi.org/10.1016/S0304-405X(00)00071-4

Nguyen, T. A. N., & Luong, T. T. H. (2020). Corruption, shadow economy, and economic growth: Evidence from emerging and developing Asian economies. *Montenegrin Journal of Economics*, 16(4), 85–94. https://doi.org/10.14254/1800-5845/2020.16-4.7

Omar, M. A., & Inaba, K. (2020). Does financial inclusion reduce poverty and income inequality in developing countries? A panel data analysis. *Journal of Economic Structures*, 9, 37–49. https://doi.org/10.1186/s40008020-00214-4

Quibria, M. G. (2014). Governance and developing Asia: Concepts, measurements, determinants, and paradoxes. ADB Economics Working Paper, Series No. 388. Asian Development Bank.

Singh, B. P. (2022). Does governance matter? Evidence from BRICS. *Global Business Review*, 23(2), 408–425.

Trabelsi, M. A., & Trabelsi, H. (2021). At what level of corruption does economic growth decrease? *Journal of Financial Crime*, 28(4), 1317–1324.

Valeriani, E., & Peluso, S. (2011). The impact of institutional quality on economic growth and development: An empirical study. *Econ Papers*. https://econpapers.repec.org/article/sppjkmeit/1203.htm

Wong, P., Ho, P., & Autio, E. (2005). Entrepreneurship, innovation, and economic growth: Evidence from GEM data. *Small Business Economics*, 24, 335–350.

Younis, M., Lin, X. X., Sharahili, Y., & Selvarathi, S. (2008). Political stability and economic growth in Asia. *American Journal of Applied Sciences*, 5(3), 203–208. https://doi.org/10.3844/ajassp.2008

3

EFFECT OF COST OF GOVERNANCE ON REAL GROWTH

Does Corruption and Violent Conflict Play a Role in the ECOWAS Region?

Okunlola Olalekan Charles, Imran Usman Sani, and Olumide A. Ayetigbo

Introduction

Mainly, the government performs two functions: protection (security) and provisions of certain public goods. The protection function consists of creating the rule of law and enforcing property rights, which helps minimize risks of criminality and protect life and property and the nation from external aggression. Under the provisions of public goods are defense, roads, education, health, and power, among others (Ogundipe & Oluwatobi, 2013). Good governance by the government can create an enabling environment for economic growth by providing stability, transparency, and predictability in the business and investment climate, as well as by improving public services and reducing corruption. On the other hand, an over-bloated public service can lead to a considerable cost of running a government. Cost of governance refers to the resources (such as financial and human capital) that are required to run a government and provide public goods and services (Revenue Mobilisation Allocation and Fiscal Commission (henceforth RMAFC), 2023).

The cost of governance can impact economic growth in various ways. High corruption and inefficiency in government can increase the cost of governance (measured by government spending) and reduce economic growth, as resources are not being allocated effectively. The cost of governance and its impact on economic growth is a complex and dynamic relationship, influenced by various factors such as the efficiency and effectiveness of government institutions, corruption levels, and the economy's overall state. According to RMAFC (2023), the cost of governance is subdivided into recurrent and capital expenditure. An increased cost of governance (measured by government spending) leads to an increased growth rate (Barro,

DOI: 10.4324/9781003530688-5

1990; Barro & Sala-i-Martin, 1992; Roux, 1994; Harrod, 1960; Domar, 1946). Barro (1991) and OECD (2021) have argued that this is not often true for some countries, especially developing ones.

The effect of the cost of governance on economic growth has neither been resolved theoretically nor empirically, not even in the ECOWAS region. There have been growing concerns about how much the cost of governance (measured by government spending) has impacted the economic growth in ECOWAS countries. The rising cost of governance remained a challenge for ECOWAS countries; the size of public spending has expanded, generating interest among scholars. Following statistics from the African Development Bank (ADB), government expenditure experiences a yearly increase. This increase in government expenditure can be attributed to increased population, inflation, foreign aid, continual development, etc. Similarly, macroeconomic performance in ECOWAS has generally been dissatisfying despite many political commitments to achieve stability in the various economies and convergence at the sub-regional level.

The macroeconomic performance of ECOWAS members varies across countries; some have excellent and high macroeconomic performance, while for some, it is low or stagnant when compared. For instance, the average inflation for Senegal between 2000 and 2020 was 2% compared to that of Nigeria, which was 15.5% within the same period. In 2021, the Human Development Index for Nigeria, Ghana, and Senegal stood at 0.53, 0.63, and 0.51, respectively (HDI report, 2021). The report ranked Nigeria 163rd, Ghana 138th, and Senegal 170th in the world in terms of development. This ranking puts Nigeria and Senegal among the low human development countries, while Ghana is among the medium human development countries. Life expectancy for Nigeria (52.07) was also less than that of Ghana (64.3) and Senegal (68.01) in 2021 (World Bank, 2021). Also, in comparing the adult literacy rate between Nigeria, Ghana, and Senegal at 59.5%, 76.57%, and 56.30%, respectively (World Bank, 2021), Senegal still falls behind these countries. The number of people in multidimensional poverty and living below the income poverty line stood at 12.1% and 28.6% for Ghana, 17.5% and 30.9% for Nigeria, and 51.7% and 37.8% for Senegal, respectively (HDI report, 2021). According to World Bank statistics (2021), the GDP per capita for these countries of comparison stood at Ghana (2,363.30 USD), Nigeria (2,065.75 USD), and Senegal (1,636.89 USD).

It is, however, evident that as government spending increases in the ECOWAS region, there is no commensurate increase in the region's economic growth and development. This and the absence of a consensus in the literature on the link between the cost of governance (measured by government spending) and real growth have made it instructive to investigate the association between the cost of governance and real growth in ECOWAS countries.

There has been intense debate by economists on the issue of whether the government should intervene to correct short-run fluctuations in economic activity. There have been contributions from economists such as Solow, Barro, Keynes, and Wagner and various schools of thought such as the classical, neoclassical, Keynesian, etc. Classical economists oppose government intervention, while the Keynesian school of thought stands for government intervention. The classicalists believe that market forces bring the economy to long-run equilibrium through adjustment in the labour market. The classical and neoclassical economists deem fiscal policies ineffective due to the well-known crowding-out effect. The crowding-out effect implies that as the cost of governance increases, public goods are substituted for private goods, lowering private spending on education, health, transportation, and other goods and services. Based on the classical evaluation, when governments borrow to finance spending, pressures in the credit market result in higher interest rates, which hinder private investment.

The debate that fiscal policies enhance economic growth has gained additional anchor by introducing new growth theories. Unlike the neoclassical growth model formulated by Solow (1956), which did not propose the channels through which government spending may influence long-run economic growth, the new growth theories suggest that there are both temporary effects from the government intervention during the transition to equilibrium and a possible long-term impact from government spending on economic growth.

From the classical, neoclassical, and keynesian points of view, they all had different views regarding government expenditure and economic growth. For example, the neoclassical who based their research on Solow's (1956) growth model or its version of optimal growth formalized by Cass (1965) and Koopmans (1965) following previous proof in Ramsey (1928) were of the view that government expenditure is detrimental to economic growth in the long run. To them, government expenditure engenders the crowding-out effect. In times of budget deficit, taxes are raised, which increases production costs and leads to increased prices and low demand, or the government results in borrowing. In addition, government spending discourages private investments. On the other hand, Keynesians say that government expenditure does not obstruct economic growth; instead, it accelerates it through full employment, increased aggregate demand, etc. Thus, government expenditure is an exogenous force that changes the aggregate output.

However, evidence from past studies has revealed a growing concern and controversies on the role of the cost of governance (measured by government spending) on real growth. Some studies (Solow, 1956; Huang, 2006 for China and Taiwan; Magazzino, 2010 for EU countries; Dogan & Tang, 2006 for Indonesia, Malaysia, Singapore, and Thailand; Abu-Bader & Abu-Qarn, 2003 for Egypt; Chimobi, 2009 for Nigeria) found a negative relationship between the cost of governance (measured by government spending) on real growth. Similarly, some studies (Gwartney et al., 1998; Schalteger & Torgler, 2006; Mitchell, 2005; M'amanja & Morrissey, 2005) found a negative link between government expenditure and economic growth, while others (Barro, 1990; Barro & Sala-i-Martin, 1992; Roux, 1994; Harrod, 1960; Domar, 1946; Keynes, 1936; Olugbenga & Owoye, 2007; Gisore et al., 2014; Bleaney, Gemmel, & Kneller, 2001; Sevitenyi, 2012; Omoke, 2009; Abu-Bader & Abu-Qarn, 2003, for Israel and Syria; Govindaraju et al., 2010, for Malaysia; Wahab & Rihanat, 2011, for Nigeria; Kalam & Aziz, 2009, for Bangladesh; Kumar, 2009, for China, Hong Kong, Japan, Taiwan, and South Korea; Keho, 2015, for Gabon, Senegal, and Burkina Faso; Ebaidalla, 2013, for Sudan; and Gisore et al., 2014, for East Africa) saw, instead, that government expenditure plays a positive role in influencing economic growth. Das and Mukherjee (2019) arrived at the conclusion that the government's R&D expenditure and per capita GDP growth rates have long-run associations for high-income and upper middle-income groups with Japan, Germany, South Korea, France, the UK, India, and Brazil.

From the above empirical issues, one can notice the diversity in most of the results, which can be attributed to using different econometric techniques. Accordingly, and as such, this study will be making use of the panel data regression technique by the inclusion of other essential control variables such as foreign exchange rate (FER), conflict, control of corruption, and the interactive terms to ascertain the relationship between government expenditure and economic growth in ECOWAS within the time frame of 1999 to 2021.

Materials and Methods

This study adopts the panel data analysis to examine the impact of the cost of governance (measured by government spending) on the real growth of ECOWAS. Following Sadorsky (2012) and Adeyemi (2012), we estimate the relationship between the cost of governance and real growth using the production function. The model in Adeyemi (2012) includes general government final consumption expenditure as a proxy for recurrent spending, labour force, stock of capital, and gross domestic product in the production function to investigate the links between government expenditure and economic growth. In the present study, we follow the exact model specification with Sadorsky (2012) and Adeyemi (2012) with modifications to investigate the relationship between the cost of governance (measured by government spending) and real growth from ECOWAS.

The production modelling framework given below shows that output (Y) is written as a function of the cost of governance (TGE), capital (K), and labour (L):

$$Y_{it} = f\left(\mathrm{TGE}_{it}, K_{it}, L_{it}\right) \tag{3.1}$$

where Y is GDP/output, TGE is total government expenditure, K stands for capital, and L stands for labour.

We then adapt Equation (3.1) to become a linear model stated in the log form as follows:

$$RGDP_{it} = f\left(TGE_{it}, COR_{it}, FER_{it}, CONF_{it}, INTR_{it}\right) \qquad (3.2)$$

where RGDP is a real gross domestic product, COR is corruption, FER is the foreign exchange rate, CONF is violent conflict, and $INTR_{it}$ stands for inter-active terms.

The natural log of Equation (3.2) gives the following equation:

$$RGDP_{it} = a_i + \delta_{it} + \beta_{1i}TGE_{it} + \beta_{2i}FER_{it} + \beta_{3i}CON_{it} + \beta_{4i}COR_{it} \qquad (3.3)$$
$$+ \beta_{5i}INTR_{it} + \varepsilon_{it}$$

where $I = 1$, N, for each country in the panel, $t = 1$, T denotes the period, and ε represents the stochastic error term. In addition, the parameters a_i and δ_i allow for country-specific fixed effect and deterministic trend, respectively.

Equation (3.3) relies on the specification of the Keynesian model, which explains how the cost of governance (TGE) stimulates aggregate demand and output in the short run. The main idea of the Keynesian model is that the total government expenditure (TGE) or demand in the economy determines the level of output, employment, and inflation (Wray, 2007). Similarly, the Mundell-Fleming model explains how the FER can influence an open economy's trade balance and growth rate. It showcased how the balance between the demand and supply of goods, money, and foreign assets can influence output. The model also suggests that government can stimulate or restrain the aggregate demand and achieve economic stability and growth by manipulating government spending and taxes (Sarantis, 1986). This supports using foreign exchange (FER) in Equation (3.3).

Furthermore, the Collier-Hoeffler theory of greed and grievance argues that the occurrence and continuation of civil wars hinder economic growth. Violent conflict (CON) can distort economic growth by destroying physical and human capital, diverting resources from productive to unproductive activities, discouraging investment and trade, and undermining social and political stability (Thies & Baum, 2020). To promote economic growth, the inclusive and extractive institution theory posits that the institutions should be inclusive (i.e., institutions must promote the participation, representation, competition, and rights of the majority of the population and also protect and enforce the interest of the public) (Saha & Sen, 2021). This is why corruption (COR) is included in Equation (3.3).

Furthermore, corruption can play different roles in the public sector, depending on the quality of governance and the size of the government (Afonso & de Sá Fortes Leitão Rodrigues, 2022). Similarly, government spending can have varying effects on the demand and supply sides of the economy, depending on the level and nature of conflict and instability (Dalyop, 2019; Bar-Nahum et al., 2020). The impact of government spending on economic growth can be positive or negative, depending on whether it enhances or impedes the efficiency and productivity of the economy. These arguments, along with the claim of the Schumpeterian theory of creative destruction (Saha & Sen, 2021) and the Collier-Hoeffler theory of greed and grievance (Spagnol, 2019), provide explanations for the interaction variables between corruption and the cost of governance (COR*TGE), violent conflict and the cost of governance (CONF*TGE), and corruption and violent conflict (COR*CONF).

We use panel cointegration techniques to examine the relationship between government spending and real growth for a sample of 15 ECOWAS countries. These techniques are interesting because estimations from cross-sections of time series have more freedom degrees and are more efficient than estimations from individual time series. Moreover, panel cointegration techniques are instrumental when each cross-section's time series dimension is short. Our empirical analysis follows four steps: (i) we proceed with panel unit root tests for stationary, (ii) we look for long-term cointegration between variables, (iii) we estimate the long-run relationships between variables, and (iv) we study the marginal effect of the moderating roles of corruption and conflict using the approach in Okunlola and Ayetigbo (2022), Akinlo and Okunlola (2022), and Okunlola (2022).

To estimate the long-run relationships in Equation (3.3), the study adopts the Dynamic Ordinary Least Squares (DOLS) and Fully Modified Ordinary Least Squares (FMOLS) techniques. Both methods correct for the problems of serial correlation and endogeneity that arise when using the panel ordinary least squares (POLS) method on non-stationary variables. The DOLS estimates the cointegrating equation by adding leads and lags of the changes in the explanatory variables to the OLS regression. This is done to eliminate the serial correlation and endogeneity problems. The FMOLS estimates the cointegrating equation by modifying the OLS regression with a correction term that accounts for the serial correlation and endogeneity problems (see Bhardwaj et al., 2022; Khan et al., 2019).

Data Source and Measurement

The data used in this study were secondary from 1999 to 2021. First, data on TGE, real gross domestic product (RGDP), and FER were sourced from the World Development Indicators (WDI) of the World Bank. Data on corruption (COR) was sourced from the World Governance Indicator (WGI) of the

World Bank. Lastly, from the Center for Systemic Peace database, we sourced data on the conflict (CONF) from the Major Episodes of Political Violence (MEPV), 1946–2015 (see Okunlola & Okafor, 2022).

Data Analysis and Empirical Results

Stationarity Test

In this study, we computed three types of unit root tests to examine the order of integration of variables at the level and first difference: Im et al. (2003), tests of Fisher using augmented Dickey and Fuller (ADF) (1979), and Phillips and Perron (1988). These tests are included in the second group and assumed individual unit root processes across the cross-section. For all these tests, the null hypothesis is that there is a unit root, and the alternative hypothesis is that there is no unit root. Furthermore, the study assumes that the test regressions contain an intercept and no deterministic trend. Finally, the number of lags selected is selected automatically using Schwarz Information Criterion (SIC). The results of unit root tests are reported in Table 3.1.

Table 3.1 indicates that, at the level, there is a unit root for Conflict (CONT) and its interactive terms CONF*TGE and COR*CONF panel data series. In contrast, other variables are stationary after the first differencing, implying that they are integrated of order one, I(1).

Cointegration Tests

In this study, we employ Pedroni's (1999, 2004) cointegration tests to check for long-run association in a heterogeneous panel. Pedroni (2004) proposes seven statistics distributed on two cointegration test sets. The first set comprises four-panel statistics: v-statistic, rho-statistic, PP-statistic, and ADF-statistic. These statistics are classified on the within-dimension and consider typical autoregressive coefficients across countries. The second set comprises three group statistics: rho-statistic, PP-statistic, and ADF-statistic. These tests are classified on the between-dimension and are based on the individual autoregressive coefficients for each country in the panel. The null hypothesis is that there is no cointegration ($H_0 : \sigma_i = 1$), whereas the alternative hypothesis is that there is cointegration between variables. Panel cointegration tests of Pedroni (2004) are based on the residual of Equation (3.3. The estimated residuals are defined as follows:

$$\varepsilon_{it} = \sigma_i \varepsilon_{it} + \omega_{it} \qquad (3.4)$$

The study assumes that the tests run with individual intercepts and deterministic trends. Four models were estimated; the first is the baseline model, then

TABLE 3.1 Unit Root Test Results

		ADF	PP	IPS	RMKs
LNGDP	I(0)	39.159 (0.122)	24.697 (0.740)	−1.053 (0.146)	I(1)
	I(1)	124.9*** (0.000)	302.6*** (0.000)	−8.24*** (0.000)	
COR	I(0)	27.121 (0.617)	30.878 (0.421)	−0.123 (0.451)	I(1)
	I(1)	115.7*** (0.000)	212.6*** (0.000)	−7.68*** (0.000)	
TGE	I(0)	38.191* (0.095)	47.76** (0.011)	−1.161 (0.123)	I(1)
	I(1)	102.1*** (0.000)		−7.05*** (0.000)	
FER	I(0)	43.655* (0.051)	24.637 (0.743)	−0.801 (0.211)	I(1)
	I(1)	122.6*** (0.000)	140.9*** (0.000)	−8.25*** (0.000)	
CONF	I(0)	34.8585 0.001	13.978 0.174	−3.119 0.001	I(0)
	I(1)		87.1*** (0.000)		
COR*TGE	I(0)	24.416 (0.659)	29.351 (0.395)	−0.156 (0.438)	I(1)
	I(1)	100.0*** (0.000)	196.2*** (0.000)	−6.87*** (0.000)	
CONF*TGE	I(0)	27.27*** (0.001)	40.5*** (0.000)	−2.97*** (0.002)	I(0)
COR*CONF	I(0)	39.88*** (0.000)	31.0*** (0.002)	−3.75*** (0.000)	I(0)

Source: Authors' calculations (2023).

Note: * Selected based on Schwarz Bayesian Criterion. ***, **, * indicate the level of significance at 1%, 5%, and 10%, respectively.

the interaction of corruption and government expenditure (COR*TGE), the interaction of conflict and government expenditure (CONF*TGE), and the last is the interaction of conflict and corruption (CONF*COR). The results from the tests for the data set for the models are reported in Table 3.2.

Table 3.2 indicates four cointegrating variables exist for the baseline model at 5% significance levels. Table 3.2 also reported that model II has six cointegrating variables, model III has five, and model IV has four cointegrating variables at a 5% significance level. Therefore, these results confirm the existence of long-term cointegration between the variables in the models.

TABLE 3.2 Cointegration Test Results

	Baseline		COR*TGE		CONF*TGE		CONF*COR	
Alternative Hypothesis: Common AR Coefs. (Within-Dimension)								
Panel v-statistic	17.917***	(0.000)	-2.416	(0.992)	8.682***	(0.000)	-2.225	(0.987)
Panel rho-statistic	1.631	(0.949)	1.234	(0.891)	1.524	(0.936)	-0.035	(0.486)
Panel PP-statistic	-1.202	(0.115)	-2.156**	(0.016)	-0.451***	(0.006)	-2.723***	(0.003)
Panel ADF-statistic	-0.168	(0.433)	-3.126***	(0.001)	-0.423**	(0.036)	-0.330	(0.371)
Weighted								
Panel v-statistic	19.494***	(0.000)	-2.457	(0.993)	9.449***	(0.000)	-2.248	(0.988)
Panel rho-statistic	1.614	(0.947)	1.296	(0.903)	1.411	(0.921)	0.165	(0.566)
Panel PP-statistic	-1.466**	(0.041)	-1.718**	(0.043)	-0.669	(0.252)	-2.148**	(0.016)
Panel ADF-statistic	-0.187	(0.426)	-2.852***	(0.002)	-0.583	(0.279)	-0.383	(0.351)
Alternative Hypothesis: Individual AR Coefs. (Between-Dimension)								
Group rho-statistic	3.015	(0.999)	1.593	(0.944)	2.201	(0.986)	0.608	(0.728)
Group PP-statistic	-1.859**	(0.032)	-4.293***	(0.000)	-0.094	(0.463)	-2.816***	(0.002)
Group ADF-statistic	-0.619	(0.268)	-3.715***	(0.000)	-0.024**	(0.041)	-1.755**	(0.039)

Source: Authors' calculations (2023).

Long-Run Estimations

We estimated the long-run of equation (3.3), where the dependent variable is real GDP. The independent variables are TGE, FER, corruption, conflict, and interaction variables. In the context of a panel estimate, the ordinary least squares (OLS) estimator is asymptotically biased, and its distribution depends on nuisance parameters. To correct this bias, we estimated the long-run structural coefficients of equation (3.3) by using the fully modified OLS (FMOLS) and the dynamic OLS (DOLS) panel approaches proposed by Pedroni (2001, 2004). To correct the problems of endogeneity and serial correlation, FMOLS uses a non-parametric approach, whereas DOLS uses a parametric approach. As our variables are measured in natural logarithms, the coefficients estimated from the long-run cointegration relationship can be considered long-run elasticities. The results of long-run estimates for the model are reported in Table 3.3.

Discussions

Table 3.3 shows that TGE has a positive and statistically significant effect on real GDP. For instance, in the baseline model, the result of the DOLS shows that the coefficient of government expenditure is 0.513, implying a positive effect on economic growth. From the baseline result, a 1% increase in government expenditure increases real GDP by 51.3%. In all the models, the coefficients of government expenditure are all positive. This implies the increase in government expenditure improves economic growth in ECOWAS countries. As stated earlier in the study, government expenditure has shown varying impacts (positive, negative, and neutral) on economic growth. On the positive side, the cost of governance (measured by government spending) can stimulate economic growth in several ways. For example, the cost of governance (measured by government spending) on infrastructure, such as roads, bridges, ports, and airports, can boost economic growth by providing the necessary physical and institutional framework for businesses to operate and expand (Ansar et al., 2016; Zhang & Ji, 2018; Du et al., 2022; Ziolo, 2022).

Similarly, Government investment in education and training can increase the workforce's productivity, leading to higher economic growth and better job opportunities (Kousar et al., 2023; Li, 2022; Kampelmann et al., 2018). In addition, government funding for research and development can stimulate innovation, leading to new products and technologies that drive economic growth (Raghupathi & Raghupathi, 2019; Bellucci et al., 2019). Also, the cost of governance (measured by government spending) on social welfare programmes, such as healthcare and social security, can help reduce poverty and inequality, leading to a more stable and productive workforce (Corlet Walker et al., 2021; Cammeraat 2020; Marshall, 1994).

TABLE 3.3 Panel OLS–FMOLS–DOLS Long-Run Estimates

VRBs	COR	TGE	CONF	FER	COR*TGE	CONF*TGE	COR*CONF
Baseline Model							
DOLS	7.717*	0.513***	2.152**	1.163			
	(0.078)	(0.007)	(0.010)	(0.112)			
FMOLS	1.353	0.788***	2.768***	1.395**			
	(0.630)	(0.001)	(0.001)	(0.020)			
POLS	3.670***	1.148***	2.436***	0.755***			
	(0.000)	(0.000)	(0.000)	(0.000)			
Interaction of Cost of Governance and Corruption (Model II)							
DOLS	12.909***	1.307***	1.644***	0.997**	-1.230***		
	(0.000)	(0.000)	(0.001)	(0.011)	(0.000)		
FMOLS	3.826***	0.238***	0.164***	0.312***	-0.298***		
	(0.005)	(0.008)	(0.000)	(0.004)	(0.006)		
POLS	21.038***	1.518***	0.320	-0.147	-1.280***		
	(0.000)	(0.000)	(0.275)	(0.331)	(0.000)		
Interaction of Cost of Governance and Conflict (Model III)							
DOLS	11.082***	0.518***	1.558	0.793		-0.023	
	(0.002)	(0.002)	(0.194)	(0.150)		(0.840)	
FMOLS	3.397***	0.932***	5.650***	0.729***		-0.344***	
	(0.000)	(0.000)	(0.000)	(0.000)		(0.001)	
POLS	3.275***	1.202***	5.561***	0.716***		-0.444***	
	(0.000)	(0.000)	(0.000)	(0.000)		(0.000)	
Interaction of Conflict and Corruption (Model IV)							
DOLS	12.540***	0.436***	1.525	0.753*			0.337
	(0.000)	(0.005)	(0.357)	(0.064)			(0.828)
FMOLS	3.262***	0.927***	-3.824***	0.799***			-5.554***
	(0.000)	(0.000)	(0.000)	(0.000)			(0.000)
POLS	3.207***	1.167***	-3.802**	0.788***			-5.588***
	(0.000)	(0.000)	(0.028)	(0.000)			(0.000)

Source: Authors' calculations (2023).

Note: Selected based on Schwarz Bayesian Criterion. ***, **, * indicate the significance level at 1%, 5%, and 10%, respectively.

However, the cost of governance (measured by government spending) can also adversely affect economic growth, mainly if it is not managed effectively. Firstly, if the government borrows too much to finance its spending, it can crowd out private investment, leading to higher interest rates and reduced economic growth (Thia, 2020; Chien et al., 2022; Traum & Yang, 2015). On the other hand, if the cost of governance (measured by government spending) is wasteful or misdirected, it can have little impact on economic growth and may even lead to a decline in productivity (Wuyts, 2020; Abbott & Jones, 2021; Shaddady, 2022). Also, to finance the cost of governance (measured by government spending), the government may need to raise taxes, which can reduce incentives for work and investment, leading to lower economic growth. With the result of this study, we can conclude that the cost of governance (measured by government expenditure) boosts real GDP in ECOWAS. In this study, corruption and conflict significantly affect real growth in ECOWAS countries.

Is the Cost of Governance–Real Growth Nexus Contingent on Corruption or Conflict?

Furthermore, Table 3.3 shows that all the interactive variables significantly affect real GDP. For instance, in model II, the coefficient of the interactive variable of corruption and the proxy for the cost of governance is negative. This is called buffering interaction (see Okunlola & Ayetigbo, 2022; Akinlo & Okunlola, 2022). The effect of the cost of governance on economic growth can be further moderated by corruption. When corruption is present, it can increase the cost of governance, as corrupt officials siphon off resources for personal gain. This can lead to a reduction in economic growth as resources are diverted away from productive sectors of the economy.

Furthermore, corruption can create an environment of uncertainty, deterring foreign investment and reducing economic growth. This is because foreign investors are less likely to invest in countries where corruption is rampant, as they perceive the risks to be higher. This can lead to reduced economic growth, as the government cannot attract the foreign investment needed to drive economic development.

The result of model III in Table 3.3 also shows that the interactive variable of conflict and cost of governance is negative and statistically significant for both FMOLS and POLS estimations. By implication, when conflict is present, the cost of governance can increase due to the need for security and defense spending, increased government borrowing to fund reconstruction efforts, and a decrease in foreign investment. These factors can negatively impact economic growth. Also, the impact of the cost of governance on economic growth can be moderated by the type and severity of the conflict. For example, in a post-conflict society, the cost of governance may initially be high due to the need for reconstruction and reconciliation efforts. Still, over time, the cost of governance may decrease as stability is restored and foreign investment increases. Additionally, the role of conflict in moderating the relationship between the cost of governance and economic growth can depend on the institutional capacity of the government to manage the conflict. If the government can effectively manage the conflict and minimize its negative impact on economic growth, then the cost of governance may have a smaller effect on economic growth.

The result in model IV in Table 3.3 also shows that conflict and corruption are harmful and can be referred to as buffering interaction. The interaction of corruption and conflict can significantly negatively affect economic growth. Corruption refers to the misuse of public office for private gain. At the same time, conflict can be defined as a situation where two or more parties have conflicting interests, goals, or values and perceive a threat to those interests.

In a conflict-ridden society, corruption can be exacerbated due to the lack of transparency and accountability in government operations and the need for government officials to use their power to maintain their position and control resources. As a result, corruption can further undermine the stability of society and fuel conflict. When combined with conflict, corruption can also lead to a decline in foreign investment, reduced government revenue, and increased public spending on defense and security, further weakening the economy. Moreover, the interaction between corruption and conflict can create a vicious cycle, as the lack of economic growth can fuel further corruption and conflict. In addition, the absence of opportunities and the perception of injustice can increase the likelihood of social unrest and violence. At the same time, corrupt practices can erode the government's legitimacy and reduce its capacity to address the underlying causes of conflict.

Conclusion

The effect of the cost of governance (measured by government spending) on economic growth can be positive and negative, depending on how the funds are used. In this study, we support the second view of a positive effect of the cost of governance on real growth in ECOWAS countries. However, the cost of governance can also be an important factor in economic growth. For example, a well-functioning government can provide essential public goods and services, such as infrastructure, education, and healthcare, necessary for economic growth. Also, the effectiveness of the cost of governance on real growth depends on how the funds are used. Moreover, the usage of funds can be influenced by corruption and conflict. This study found that the effect of the cost of governance is negatively moderated by corruption and conflict. This implies that corruption and violent conflict reduce the impact of the cost of governance on real economic growth in ECOWAS countries.

The finding suggests that a well-managed government can contribute positively to economic growth. Therefore, the governments of ECOWAS countries should prioritize transparency and accountability in their operations. This can be achieved by ensuring government officials are accountable for their actions, promoting open government policies, and transparently reporting the cost of governance (measured by government spending). Furthermore, the government of ECOWAS countries should ensure that it is stable and predictable. This can be achieved by fostering political stability, ensuring the rule of law, and providing a business-friendly environment that attracts investment.

References

Abbott, A., & Jones, P. (2021). The cyclicality of government foreign-aid expenditure: Voter awareness in "good" times and in "bad". *Public Choice*, 186(1), 97–117.

Abu-Bader, S., and Abu-Qarn, A. S. (2003). Government expenditures, military spending, and economic growth: Causality evidence from Egypt, Israel, and Syria. *Journal of Policy Modeling*, 25(6–7), 567–583.

Adeyemi, O. O. (2012). Corruption and local government administration in Nigeria: A discourse of core issues. *European Journal of Sustainable Development*, 1(2), 183–183.

Afonso, A., & de Sá Fortes Leitão Rodrigues, E. (2022). Corruption and economic growth: Does the size of the government matter? *Economic Change and Restructuring*, 55(2), 543–576. https://doi.org/10.1007/s10644-021-09338-4

Akinlo, A. E., & Okunlola, C. O. (2022). The effect of economic freedom on quality of life: Exploring the role of political risk factors in Africa. *Journal of Interdisciplinary Economics*. https://doi.org/10.1177/02601079221121894

Ansar, A., Flyvbjerg, B., Budzier, A., & Lunn, D. (2016). Does infrastructure investment lead to economic growth or economic fragility? Evidence from China. *Oxford Review of Economic Policy*, 32(3), 360–390.

Bar-Nahum, Z., Finkelshtain, I., Ihle, R., & Rubin, O. D. (2020). Effects of violent political conflict on the supply, demand and fragmentation of fresh food markets. *Food Security*, 12(3), 503–515. https://doi.org/10.1007/s12571-020-01025-y

Barro, R. (1990). Government spending in a simple model of endogenous growth. *Journal of Political Economy*, 98(5), 103–125.

Barro, R., & Sala-i-Martin X, (1992). Public finance in models of economic growth. *Review of Economic Studies*, 59, 645–661.

Barro, R. J., (1991). Economic growth in a cross section of countries. *Quarterly Journal of Economics*, 106, 407–443.

Bellucci, A., Pennacchio, L., & Zazzaro, A. (2019). Public R&D subsidies: Collaborative versus individual place-based programs for SMEs. *Small Business Economics*, 52(1), 213–240.

Bhardwaj, M., Kumar, P., Kumar, S., Dagar, V., & Kumar, A. (2022). A district-level analysis for measuring the effects of climate change on production of agricultural crops, i.e., wheat and paddy: Evidence from India. *Environmental Science and Pollution Research*, 29(21), 31861–31885

Bleaney, M., Gemmell, N. and Kneller, R., (2001). Testing the endogenous growth model: Public expenditure, taxation and growth over the long run. *Canadian Journal of Economics/Revuecanadienne d'économique*, 34(1), pp. 36–57.

Cammeraat, E. (2020). The relationship between different social expenditure schemes and poverty, inequality and economic growth. *International Social Security Review*, 73(2), 101–123.

Cass, David. (1965). Optimum growth in an aggregative model of capital accumulation. *Review of Economic Studies*, 32, 233–240.

Chien, F., Chau, K. Y., Aldeehani, T. M., Huy, P. Q., Tan, L. P., & Mohsin, M. (2022). Does external debt as a new determinants of fiscal policy influence sustainable economic growth: Implications after COVID-19. *Economic Change and Restructuring*, 55(3), 1717–1737.

Chimobi, O. P. (2009). Government expenditure and national income. A causality test for Nigeria. *European Journal of Economic and political Studies*, 2, 1–11.

Corlet Walker, C., Druckman, A., & Jackson, T. (2021). Welfare systems without economic growth: A review of the challenges and next steps for the field. *Ecological Economics*, 186, 107066. https://doi.org/10.1016/j.ecolecon.2021.107066

Dalyop, G. T. (2019). Political instability and economic growth in Africa. *International Journal of Economic Policy Studies*, 13(1), 217–257.

Das, R. C., & Mukherjee, S. (2019). Do spending on R&D influence income? An enquiry on world's leading economies and groups. *Journal of the Knowledge Economy*, 11(4), 1295–1315.

Dickey, D. A., & Fuller, W. A. 1979. Distribution of the estimators for autoregressive time series with a unit root. *Journal of the American Statistical Association*, 74, 427–431.

Dogan, E. and Tang, T. C. (2006). Government expenditure and national income: Causality test for five south east Asian countries. *International Business & Economics Research Journal*, 5(10), 49–58.

Domar, E. D. (1946). Capital expansion, rate of growth, and employment. *Econometrica*, 14(2), 137–147. https://doi.org/10.2307/1905364

Du, X., Zhang, H., & Han, Y. (2022). How does new infrastructure investment affect economic growth quality? Empirical Evidence from China. *Sustainability*, 14. https://doi.org/10.3390/su14063511

Ebaidalla, E. M. (2013). Causality between government expenditure and national income: Evidence from Sudan. *Journal of Economic Cooperation and Development*, 34(4), 61–76.

Gisore, N., Kiprop, S., Kalio, A., Ochieng, J., & Kibet, L. (2014). Effect of government expenditure on economic growth in East Africa: A disaggregated model. *European Journal of Business and Social Sciences*, 3(8), 289–304.

Govindaraju, D. R., Houle, D., & Omholt, S. (2010). Phenomics: The next challenge. *Nature Reviews Genetics*, 11(12), 855.

Gwartney, J. D., Lawson, R. A. and Holcombe, R. G. (1998). The size and functions of government and economic growth. *Joint Economic Committee.*

Harrod, R. F. (1960). The theory of economic growth. *The Economic Journal*, 70(278), 277–293.

Huang, C. J. (2006). Government expenditure in China and Taiwan: Do they follow Wagners's law? *Journal of Economic Development*, 31(2), 139–148.

Im, K. S., Pesaran, M. H., & Shin, Y., 2003. Testing for unit roots in heterogeneous panels. *Journal of Econometrics*, 115, 53–74.

Kalam, M. A., & Aziz, N. (2009). Growth of government expenditure in Bangladesh: An empirical enquiry into the validity of Wagner's law. *Global Economy Journal*, 9(2), 1–18. https://doi.org/10.2202/1524-5861.1422

Kampelmann, S., Rycx, F., Saks, Y., & Tojerow, I. (2018). Does education raise productivity and wages equally? The moderating role of age and gender. *IZA Journal of Labor Economics*, 7(1), 1. https://doi.org/10.1186/s40172-017-0061-4

Keho, Y. (2015). Foreign direct investment, exports and economic growth: Some African evidence. *Journal of Applied Economics and Business Research*, 5(4), 209–219. https://www.academicpublishingplatforms.com/article.php?journal=JAEBR&doi=143

Keynes, J. M. (1936). *The General Theory of Employment, Interest and Money, published by Harcourt, Brace, and Company, and printed in the U.S.A. by the Polygraphic Company of America*, New York; First Published: Macmillan Cambridge University Press.

Khan, M. W. A., Panigrahi, S. K., Almuniri, K. S. N., Soomro, M. I., Mirjat, N. H., & Alqaydi, E. S. (2019). Investigating the dynamic impact of CO_2 emissions and economic growth on renewable energy production: Evidence from FMOLS and DOLS tests. *Processes*, 7(8), Article 8. https://doi.org/10.3390/pr7080496

Koopmans, T. C. (1965). On the concept of optimal economic growth. In P. Braunerhjelm (Ed.), *The econometric approach to development planning* (pp. 225–287). Amsterdam: North-Holland.

Kousar, S., Ahmed, F., Afzal, M., & Segovia, J. E. T. (2023). Is government spending on education and health necessary for human capital development? *Humanities and Social Sciences Communications*, 10(1), Article 1. https://doi.org/10.1057/s41599-023-01514-3

Kumar, S. (2009). An empirical evaluation of export demand in China. *Journal of Chinese Economic and Foreign Trade Studies*, 2(2), 100–109.

Li, L. (2022). Reskilling and upskilling the future-ready workforce for industry 4.0 and beyond. *Information Systems Frontiers*, 1–16. https://doi.org/10.1007/s10796-022-10308-y

M'Amanja M., & Morrissey O. (2005). Fiscal Policy and Economic Growth in Kenya. *CREDIT Research Paper No 05/06.*

Magazzino, C. (2010). Wagner's law in Italy: Empirical evidence from 1960 to 2008.*Global and Local Economic Review*, 14 (1), 91–116.

Marshall, P. (1994). Welfare: Inequality and poverty. In P. Curwen (Ed.), *Understanding the UK Economy* (pp. 353–390). Macmillan Education UK. https://doi.org/10.1007/978-1-349-13475-5_10

Mitchell, J. D. (2005). The impact of government spending on economic growth, backgrounder, 1831. www.heritage.org/research/budget/bg1831.cfm

OECD. (2021). *Government at a Glance 2021*. OECD Publishing. Available at https://doi.org/10.1787/1c258f55-en

Ogundipe, A. A., & Oluwatobi, S. (2013). Government spending and economic growth in Nigeria: Evidence from disaggregated analysis. *Journal of Business Management and Applied Economics*, 2(4), 1–10.

Okunlola, O. C. (2022). Contingencies in the relationship between trade and internal conflict in Nigeria: The role of the quality of the political institution. *International Journal of Social Economics*, 49(12), 1727–1738.

Okunlola, O. C., & Ayetigbo, O. A. (2022). Economic freedom and human development in ECOWAS: Does political-institutional strength play a role?. *Journal of the Knowledge Economy*, 13, 1751–1785.

Okunlola, O. C., & Okafor, I. G. (2022). Conflict–Poverty relationship in Africa: A disaggregated approach. *Journal of Interdisciplinary Economics*, 34(1), 104–129.

Olugbenga, A. O., & Owoye, O. (2007). Public expenditure and economic growth: New evidence from OECD countries. *Business and Economic Journal*, 4(17), 13–25.

Omoke, P. (2009). Government expenditure and national income: A causality test for Nigeria. *European Journal of Economics and Political Studies*, 2, 1011.

Pedroni, P., (1999). Critical values for cointegration tests in heterogeneous panels with multiple regressors. *Oxford Bulletin of Economics and Statistics*, 61, 653–670.

Pedroni, P., (2004). Panel cointegration: Asymptotic and finite sample properties of pooled time series tests with an application to the PPP hypothesis. *Econometric Theory*, 20, 597–625.

Phillips, P. C. B., & Perron, P., (1988). Testing for a unit root in time series regressions. *Biometrika*, 75, 335–346.

Raghupathi, V., & Raghupathi, W. (2019). Exploring science-and-technology-led innovation: A cross-country study. *Journal of Innovation and Entrepreneurship*, 8(1), 5. https://doi.org/10.1186/s13731-018-0097-0

Ramsey, Frank P. (1928). A mathematical theory of saving. *The Economic Journal*, 38, 543–559.

Revenue Mobilisation Allocation and Fiscal Commission. (2023). Reducing Cost of Governance. Available at https://rmafc.gov.ng/2019/11/reducing-cost-of-governance/

Roux, A. (1994). Defense, human capital and economic development in South Africa. African Defense review no. 19.

Sadorsky, P., 2012. Energy consumption, output and trade in South America. *Energy Economics*, 34, 476–488.

Saha, S., & Sen, K. (2021). The corruption–growth relationship: Does the political regime matter? *Journal of Institutional Economics*, 17(2), 243–266. https://doi.org/10.1017/S1744137420000375

Sarantis, N. (1986). The Mundell-Fleming model with perfect capital mobility and oligopolistic pricing. *Journal of Post Keynesian Economics*, 9(1), 138–148.

Schalteger, C. A., & Torgler, B. (2006). Growth effects of public expenditure on the state and local level: Evidence from a sample of rich government. *Applied Economics*, 38, 1181–1192.

Sevitenyi, I. N. (2012), Government expenditure and economic growth in Nigeria: An empirical investigation (1961–2009). *The Journal of Economic Analysis*, 3(1), 38–51.

Shaddady, A. (2022). Is government spending an important factor in economic growth? Nonlinear cubic quantile nexus from Eastern Europe and Central Asia (EECA). *Economies*, 10(11), Article 11. https://doi.org/10.3390/economies10110286

Solow, R. M. (1956). A contribution to the theory of economic growth. *Quarterly Journal of Economics*, 70(1), 65–94.

Spagnol, G. (2019). Correlation between corruption and conflict. https://ieri.be/en/print/1654

Thia, J. P. (2020). Deficits and crowding out through private loan spreads. *The Quarterly Review of Economics and Finance*, 77, 98–107. https://doi.org/10.1016/j.qref.2020.01.009

Thies, C. F., & Baum, C. F. (2020). The effect of war on economic growth. *Cato Journal*, 40(1), 199–212.

Traum, N., & Yang, S.-C. S. (2015). When does government debt crowd out investment? *Journal of Applied Econometrics*, 30(1), 24–45.

United Nations Development Programme. 2021. *Human Development Report 2021/22: Uncertain Times, Unsettled Lives: Shaping Our Future in a Transforming World*. United Nations Development Programme. https://hdr.undp.org/sites/default/files/hdr2021-22pdf

Wahab, A. L., & Rihanat, I. A. (2011). An analysis of government spending on educational sector and its contribution to GDP in Nigeria. *International Journal of Financial Economics and Econometrics*, 3(1), 163–170.

World Bank. (2021). Life expectancy at birth, total (years) – Nigeria, Ghana, Senegal. *World Development Indicators*. https://data.worldbank.org/indicator/SP.DYN.LE00.IN

Wray, L. R. (2007). A post keynesian view of central bank independence, policy targets, and the rules versus discretion debate. *Journal of Post Keynesian Economics*, 30(1), 119–141.

Wuyts, W. (2020). Market distortions encouraging wasteful consumption. In W. Leal Filho, A. M. Azul, L. Brandli, P. G. Özuyar, & T. Wall (Eds.), *Responsible Consumption and Production* (pp. 443–453). Springer International Publishing. https://doi.org/10.1007/978-3-319-95726-5_45

Zhang, Y. F., & Ji, S. (2018). Does infrastructure have a transitory or longer-term impact? Evidence from China. *Economic Modelling*, 73. https://doi.org/10.1016/j.econmod.2018.03.014

Ziolo, J. (2022). Infrastructure investment and European economic growth. In S. D. Giacomo & P. de Mauro (Eds.), *Infrastructure investment and economic growth* (pp. 225–241). Edward Elgar Publishing. https://doi.org/10.4337/9781789906358.00016

4

ASSESSING THE ROLE OF GOOD GOVERNANCE IN THE CONTEXT OF RUSSIA-UKRAINE WAR

Abhishek Mitra and Eyasin Khan

Introduction

Governance refers to some characteristics that are generally associated with a system of national administration. The New Webster's International Dictionary defines the term in much the same way as journalists from the New York Times or The Economist: 'act, manner, office, or power of governing; government', 'state of being governed' or 'method of government or regulation'. In this respect, Morten Boas has shown that 'before being studied at the global level, governance was employed generically in academic discourse' (Boas, 1998: 117–134). One of the eminent thinkers, Goran Hyden has argued that it refers mainly to running governments and other public agencies or private ones with social purposes (Bawley, 1999). Scholars of international relations in contrast now use the term almost exclusively to describe phenomena that go beyond a synonym for 'government' and the legal authority with which such policies are vested. For instance, the Commission on Global Governance defines 'governance' as 'the sum of the many ways individuals and institutions, public and private, manage their common affairs. James Rosenau closely associated with the term and for him, whether at the grassroots or global levels, it 'encompasses the activities of governments, but it also includes the many other channels through which "commands" flow in the form of goals framed, directives issued, and policies pursued' (Ghali, 1992) The emergence of governance can be traced at the country level to a disgruntlement with the state-dominated models of economic and social development so prevalent throughout the socialist bloc and much of the Third World in the 1950s, 1960s and 1970s. At the theoretical level, 'global governance' can be traced to a growing dissatisfaction among

DOI: 10.4324/9781003530688-6

students of international relations with the realist and liberal-institutionalist theories that dominated the study of international organization in the 1970s and 1980s. In particular, these failed to capture adequately the vast increase, in both numbers and influence, of non-state actors and the implications of technology in an age of globalization (World Bank, 1994: xiv). One of the key features of good governance is participation. Major forms of participation could be either direct or through legitimate intermediate institutions or representatives. It is important to point out that representative democracy does not necessarily mean that the concerns of the most vulnerable in society would be taken in decision-making. This means freedom of association and expression on the one hand and an organized civil society on the other hand. In modern days discussion, civil society takes a valuable place to approaching a democratic space.

Basically, good governance is a collection of words. Good governance also requires a strong legal framework that is enforced impartially. It also requires full protection of human rights, particularly those of minorities and other unprivileged sections of the society. Impartial enforcement of laws requires a strong independent judiciary and an impartial and incorruptible police force. Transparency means that decisions taken and their enforcement are done in a manner that follows rules and regulations. It also means that information is freely available and directly accessible to those who will be affected by such decisions and their enforcement. Access to information in a single window is one of the new features of the digitization age. It also requires that enough information is provided and that it is provided in easily understandable forms and media. Good governance requires that institutions and processes try to serve all stakeholders within a reasonable time frame. There are many vital actors and many viewpoints in a given society. Good governance requires mediation of the different interests in society to reach a broad consensus in society on what is in the best interest of the whole community and how this can be achieved. It also requires perspectives in broad and long-term which is needed for the sustainable human development and how to achieve the goals of such development. This can only result from an understanding of the historical, cultural and social contexts of a given society or community. A society's well-being depends on ensuring that all its members feel that they have a stake in it and do not feel excluded from the mainstream of society. This requires all groups, but particularly the most vulnerable, to have opportunities to improve or maintain their well-being. Good governance means that processes and institutions produce results that meet the needs of society while making the best use of resources at their disposal. The concept of efficiency in the context of good governance also covers the sustainable use of natural resources and the protection of the environment. Accountability is a key requirement of good governance. Not only governmental institutions but also the private sector and civil society organizations must be accountable to the public and to their institutional stakeholders. Many reports suggest that bureaucracy increased in the wake of Russia-Ukraine war, for that, citizens are facing many problems in terms of accessing information, which violate the ideal goal of e-governance.

The former Secretary-General Boutros-Ghali wrote, "The time of absolute and exclusive sovereignty, however, has passed" (UNDP, 1997: 2–3). The status of 'Sovereignty' and its relevance are contested increasingly within international organizations and forums. According to World Bank observation, Governance is defined as the manner in which power is exercised in the management of a country's economic and social resources. The World Bank has identified three distinct aspects of governance: (i) the form of political regime; (ii) the process by which authority is exercised in the management of a country's economic and social resources for development; and (iii) the capacity of governments to design, formulate, and implement policies and discharge functions (OECD, 1995: 14). UNDP describe Governance is the exercise of economic, political and administrative authority to manage a country's affairs at all levels. It comprises mechanisms, processes and institutions through which citizens and groups articulate their interests, exercise their legal rights, meet their obligations and mediate their differences (Fukuyama, 1995; Putnam et al., 1993). OECD viewed the idea of governance denotes the use of political authority and exercise of the political control in a society in relation to the management of its resources for social and economic development. This broad definition encompasses the role of public authorities in establishing environment in which economic operators function and in determining the distribution of benefits as well as the nature of the relationship between the ruler and the ruled (Adams, 1997). According to the International Institute of Administrative Sciences, 'Governance' refers to the process whereby elements in society wield power and authority, and influence and enact policies and decisions concerning public life, and economic and social development very rightly observed that, Governance is a broader notion than government. Governance involves interaction between these formal institutions and those of civil society. According to the Tokyo Institute of Technology, "the concept of governance refers to the complex set of values, norms, processes and institutions by which society manages its development and resolves conflict resolution, formally and sometimes informally. During the Cold War, governmental representatives of newly independent countries were successfully on the defensive within UN and related international forum; they remained largely untouched by the rich scholarly debate about the 'new political economy', 'social capital' and 'public goods" (UNDP, 1996: 3). By playing off East versus West, moreover, developing countries deflected many criticisms by donors and investors if they hinted at shortcomings in economic and political management. Suggestions about what was wrong with economic and social policies in developing and socialist bloc countries were viewed as siding with the 'enemy' in the East-West struggle. And the 'other' side could be persuaded to be less critical, and even financially supportive, as part of the worldwide competition. Not only the rise of Russia-Ukraine war but also various international crises have had an impact on governance. Ironically, OPEC's ability to increase oil prices in 1973–1974 and again in 1979 strengthened the collective bargaining strength of the Group of 77 and produced foreign exchange shortages and unsustainable indebtedness that, in turn, forced many non-oil-exporting developing countries to accept intrusive structural adjustment. Outside interference in economic policy was the quid pro quo of desperately needed international finance, especially from the International Monetary Fund (IMF) as the lender of last resort, or the seal of approval required by other funders. Global governance invokes shifting the location of authority in the context of the integration and fragmentation process. Rosenau describes that it is the process as 'a pervasive tendency for which major shifts in the location of authority and the site of control mechanisms are under way for every continent, shifts that are as pronounced in economic and social systems as they are in political systems' The essential challenge for international cooperation jumps out from the title of his edited volume, *Governance without Government* (1992). Mobilizing support from the bottom up involves increasing the skills and capacities of individuals and altering the horizons of identification in patterns of global life. Elsewhere, Rosenau characterizes global governance as 'systems of rule at all levels of human activity, from the family to the international organization, in which the pursuit of goals through the exercise of control has transnational repercussions' (Luck, 1999). Oran Young has argued that the value of the concept is that identifiable social practices can be envisaged and sometimes undertaken to improve economic, social and environmental performance even without the formal institutions capable of authoritatively taking action (Rosenau, 1999: 293). The phenomenal economic expansion and technological progress of the 1990s have not benefited the world's citizens equally. The unevenness of the economic playing field and the power of players on it are evident. Using the three essential components of the human development idea, equality of opportunity, sustainability and empowerment of people, a bleaker picture emerges from UNDP and other UN reports than from conventional wisdom. For instance, income per capita and average purchasing power in some 100 countries were lower in the middle of 1995 than in the 1980s; it was actually lower than in the 1970s and in 1935, it was lower than in the 1960s (Sen, 1999: 112). If information technologies are driving growth or are a prerequisite for it, the increasing concentration of income, resources and wealth among people, corporations and countries does not bode well. The richest 20 percent of the world's population living in the wealthiest countries account for over 93 percent of internet users while the bottom 20 percent account for only 0.2 percent (Weiss, 2000: 795–814).

Today, the discussion of good governance occupies an important place in the practice of social science studies around the world. The government's role is not only to maintain law and order and protect it from foreign attacks but also to establish good governance. The term good governance was coined in the World Bank report in 1992, in which good governance basically refers to four aspects – good management in the public sector, accountability, adequate infrastructure and transparency and preservation of information. In addition, the report also discussed the issue of weak governance. Governance is a common term today but it has a brief history. In 1989, the World Bank first used the term governance in relation to lending to African countries. The World Bank was of the opinion that many countries in the African continent received loans and foreign aid, but they could not establish proper governance and their initial assumption was that there was a crisis of governance in those countries. The success of the government is now not only the establishment of proper rule of order in the country but also the establishment of good governance.

Recently, in view of the Russia-Ukraine war, once again the question of good governance is revolving in the practice of social science research. The present study discusses the history and evolution of good governance in relation to governability and also focuses on the future possibilities and problems of good governance as a practice in the context of Russia-Ukraine war.

Government, Governance and Good Governance

As such, the logical link between the patterns of governance at the national and global levels lies in solving the collective action puzzle to provide public goods. Philip Cerny observed that 'In both modern domestic political systems and the modern international system, the state has been the key structural arena within which collective action has been situated and undertaken' and as a result of a multiplicity of interactions, 'the authority, legitimacy, policy making capacity, and policy-implementing effectiveness of the state will be eroded and undermined both within and without' (Weiss, Forsythe, & Coate, 2017). Globalization has profound consequences for the nature of collective action in both domestic and international politics. Philip Cerny also argues that, as market activity intensifies and economic organization becomes increasingly complex, the institutional scale of political structures is no longer capable of providing a suitable scale of public goods. In effect, economic globalization is undermining the effectiveness of state-based collective action, which was extremely weak in the first place. Although the state remains a cultural force, its effectiveness as a civil association has also declined. The result may be a crisis of legitimacy. State-based collective action has not reached its end, but it is significantly different from in the past. In the contemporary world, proponents and theorists of global governance face enormous difficulties in making hard-hitting policy prescriptions. In the face of anarchy and disorder, what mechanisms should be primarily responsible for global governance? It is a million dollar question. Is there a way to structure a reasonable measure of coordination and cooperation among governments, intergovernmental organizations, non-governmental organizations and the private sector that would constitute meaningful, or at least improved, patterns of global governance? If it is the product of purposeful decisions and goal-oriented behaviour, how can global governance exist in the absence of a clear consensus about goals? To what extent does global governance depend on shared values and norms?

One common reaction, especially among representatives of governments, is to fall back on familiar ways of thought by attempting to recapture the 'good old days' of state-centric authority. Russian and Chinese reactions in the Security Council join those of developing countries there and in the UN General Assembly in trying to emphasize the centrality of the state and forestall erosions of its prerogatives. There is one notable similarity to democratization at the national level because more inclusive and participatory, hence, truly democratic mechanisms for consultations and ultimately governance must be created at the global level as well. They should be malleable enough to respond to an ever-changing environment. There is a crucial similarity in the reasoning of both theorists like Rosenau and practitioners like the members of the Commission on Global Governance to distinguish 'governance' from 'government'. At the global level, there can be no single model or form, nor does even a single structure or set of structures. The need of present day is therefore effective where it is relevant, a bit like postmodern thinking.

For the moment, we are unable even to describe accurately the dimensions of international economic and social interactions – what James Rosenau has aptly described as causal chains that follow crazy-quilt patterns. The proverbial bottom line is: there is no clear-cut equivalent at the global level to the national prescriptions of democratization and economic liberalization as the constituent components of human governance. In light of its universality and scope, the UN will have a special role, albeit not a monopoly, in future leadership for global governance. One group of UN watchers was supportive of the world organization's involvement. They saw global governance in terms of both the playing field and the players lagging behind globalization, and there was broad consensus that the United Nations should have a significant, but as yet undefined, role in "bridging the gap", which is to be the case the UN system should do better than in the past in swimming against the powerful currents of orthodoxy. As Amartya Sen, the 1998 Nobel laureate in economics who has played a major intellectual role within the periphery of outside the United Nations, prods us to recall at the dawn of the twenty-first century: 'The need for critical scrutiny of standard preconceptions and political-economic attitudes has never been stronger'. In this context, intergovernmental organizations, both universal and regional and local, should be strengthened. This is the most constant refrain throughout over half a century of the UN's stewardship over economic and social ideas. There is of course more than a dollop of institutional self-interest behind this conviction. But more important is the dramatic reality that some countervailing power is required to offset the excesses of a decentralized system of states pursuing their national interests in combination with the private sector pursuing individual gains. The need for a more cohesive and effective multilateral system is logical and evident. At the same time that a longing for a monolithic and top-down view of governance is comprehensible, it seems misplaced in an increasingly decentralized world. At a historical juncture when both problems and solutions transcend national borders and there is no likelihood of a central sovereign, the decibel level of calls from internationalists to strengthen intergovernmental institutions is understandably loud but ultimately wistful. We should think creatively about ways to pool the collective strengths and avoid the collective weaknesses of governments, intergovernmental organizations, NGOs and global civil society. This irony is behind the UN's convening of the Millennium Assembly in September 2000 and the growing emphases on the private sector and NGOs by the last two secretaries-general paradoxically, this is the conceptual and operational challenge for proponents of global governance and of the UN in the light of a changing world political economy.

Good Governance in the Context of Russia-Ukraine War

In the context of Russia-Ukraine war, the world economy, especially the European economy, has been affected very much. Not only economic insecurity in Europe but political control is also a subject of question. The war has caused a huge security crisis in many parts of Europe. Russia's invasion has also strengthened NATO's deterrence posture and increased its forward presence in many parts of Eastern Europe. Historic change has also been observed in this area. For example, Finland and Sweden, two countries which have until now shunned NATO's membership to avoid antagonizing Russia, are also set to join the alliance in a historic shift. Since the end of the Cold War and the advent of US-Russia arms control, nuclear weapons have become less important. However, the past year has seen regular nuclear weapon threats from Russia, some veiled, some from escalation and some directly aimed at NATO. Warnings have also emerged from the West, with the US President declaring the risk of a nuclear Armageddon to be at its highest level for last 60 years, bringing the nuclear issue firmly back to the forefront of large discussion. As the major supplier of energy, food and fertilizer commodities, Russia's conflict with Ukraine has caused disruption in supply chain for both developing and developed countries. The most major change observed by many thinkers is that Europe's shipping away from reliance on Russian gas. European states are trying to purchase gas from elsewhere and accelerating the move to renewable energy. It has been observed by major studies for the last few months.

Russia and Ukraine are the major exporters of agriculture fertilizers; the disruption to global food chains drove up prices to all time highs, fuelling a cost of living crisis in both developed and developing countries. Many sources suggest that an estimated 14 million people were displaced due to the war. Nowadays the term governance has got a lot of significance. In 1989, the World Bank used the term governance for the first time in relation to lending to African countries. The World Bank was of the opinion that many countries on the African continent have failed to properly implement loans and foreign aid. The World Bank was of the opinion that there is a crisis of governance in those countries. The success of the government is not only governing but also implementing good governance. According to a World Bank report, the term good governance has four characteristics – good management in the public sector, accountability, adequate infrastructure and transparency and preservation of information. Good governance also refers to the exercise of power for the proper utilization of economic and social resources for the purpose of development. This 1992 report included not only good governance but also bad governance or poor governance. It means inappropriate use of resources, lack of distribution of resources, lack of transparency, corruption, inadequate information, which cover the issues involved in poor governance. However, good governance also involves some non-economic aspects, such as transparency, accountability, transparent elections, protection of human rights, participation, etc. The standard of good governance depended in many cases on the proper implementation of these good governance factors.

In this scenario, good and bad governance discussions are taking place once again. In wartime conditions, good governance was replaced by bad governance in many areas where the major focus of the state is security. A group of thinkers believe that the lack of good governance has been seen in many parts of the world in the wake of the Russia-Ukraine war. The war is believed to have exacerbated the financial depression several times over. This impact of war recession has controlled many things. The war has created a security crisis in parts of Europe and Asia. Bureaucratic control is believed to have increased greatly within states due to the security crisis. Increased bureaucratic control is not considered very conducive to a democratic system. The war sparked an arms race across Europe, creating a crisis of insecurity among the common people. As a result of the war, many people have been displaced, and as a result, the migration problem has become acute. Alleged abuse of women and children has created a human rights crisis. Protection of human rights is a major aspect of good governance. The Europe-wide human rights crisis is believed to have stalled the momentum of good governance. Many people in Ukraine have been left homeless as a result of the war. For those people, immigration problems have arisen in various parts of Europe. In addition to this crisis, the food and oil crises have made the serious problems. Prices of goods in several places have gone up excessively. In view of these problems, government regulation and control has increased in many areas. As a result, a strange crisis has arisen in the administration.

The impact of Russia-Ukraine war has also resulted in (i) significant loss of human capital; (ii) destruction of agricultural trading infrastructure; (iii) huge damage to production capacity; (iv) the loss of electricity; and (v) a reduction in private consumption of more than one-third relative to the pre-war levels. EU also observes the problems very minutely and opines the following views:

- Russia's unprovoked war aggression against Ukraine has disastrous consequences for people in Ukraine and also globally. Security issues are a major concern rather than other issues.
- Russia's war of aggression has dramatically changed and aggravated the food security crisis in several parts of Europe.
- EU sanctions against Russia are specifically designed *not to* target food and agricultural products.

However, it did not save the entire EU from the devastating effects of the war. For the above cases, good governance is believed to have been hampered largely. The Council called on member states to work together to tackle global food insecurity via the following four strands of action:

(a) Solidarity through emergency relief and support for affordability
(b) Boosting sustainable production, resilience and food system transformation
(c) Facilitating trade by helping Ukraine to export agricultural products via different routes and supporting global trade
(d) Effective multilateralism and strong support for the central role of the UN Global Crisis Response Group to coordinate the global efforts. EU leaders also discussed on food security and affordability at the Special meeting of the European Council, which took place on 30–31 May 2022. They strongly condemned the destruction and illegal appropriation by Russia of agricultural production in Ukraine and called on Russia to:

- end its attacks on transport infrastructure in Ukraine;
- lift the blockade of Ukrainian Black Sea ports; and
- allow food exports.

The European Council invited member states to accelerate work on the solidarity lanes put forward by the European Commission to facilitate food exports from Ukraine and called for a comprehensive global response to food security challenges. A special meeting of the European Council on mobility of people and goods on 30–31 May 2022 decided the following facts: the invasion of Ukraine has had a significant impact on the mobility of people and goods in the EU across all modes of transport. Among the main issues are fuel supplies and fuel prices, as well as logistical challenges linked to border crossings and overall airspace restrictions. In addition, imports of goods and the large influx of Ukrainian refugees towards EU countries have led to operational challenges for the sector. In terms of solidarity with Ukrainian refugees, member states have decided on a number of measures like establishing transport and information hubs at the main border crossings and facilitating humanitarian aid transport.

Concluding Observations

From the beginning of 2023, the intensity of war has been decreasing. As a result, the economic conditions of Europe have slowly improved, but it's not the right time to say what will be the larger impact of the war in the future. Although it is true to say that the war has a serious impact on the governance issue, we will have to wait a little longer for a policy analysis of the role of major powers during the war. The crisis of the Russia-Ukraine war has forced the thinker to think a little differently. While governance was once seen as a good outcome of pure states' internal matter, after the war crisis, it became clear that good governance could also be affected by international events or crises. Even when the government of a country is well run, a crisis like war can change the administrative strategy of that state. It has been seen earlier in history that a democratic government has changed its mode of administration in the context of war. The Russia-Ukraine crisis has proven this. War is one such thing that forces the state to revert to its old traditional way of thinking.

References

Adams, N. (1997). *Worlds Apart: The North-South Divide and the International System*, London: Zed Books.
Bawley, D. (1999). *Corporate Governance and Accountability; What role for the Regulator, Director and Auditor?*, Westport, CT: Quorum, 1999.
Boas, M. (1998). Governance and multilateral bank policy; the cases of African development bank and the Asian development bank. *European Journal of Development Research*, 10(2).
Fukuyama, F. (1995). *Trust, The Social Virtues and the Creation of Prosperity*, New York: Free press
Ghali, B. (1992). *An Agenda for Peace*, New York: United Nations.
Luck, E. C. (1999). *Mixed Messages: American Politics and International Organization, 1919–1999*, Washington, DC: DC Brooking Institution Press.

OECD. (1995). *Participatory Development and Good Governance*, Paris: OECD.

Putnam, R., Leonardi, R., & Nanetti, R. (1993). *Making Democracy Work: Civic Traditions in Modern Italy*, Princeton University Press, Princeton, New Jersey

Rosenau, J. N. (1999). Toward an ontology for global governance. In M. Hewson and T. Sinclair (eds.) *Approaches to Global Governance Theory*, Oxford: Oxford University Press.

Sen, A. (1999). *Development as Freedom*, Oxford: Oxford University Press.

UNDP (1996). Human Development Report: Economic Growth and Human Development, January, 01. https://hdr.undp.org/content/human-development-report-1996

UNDP. (1997). *Governance for Sustainable Human Development*. New York: United Nations.

Weiss, T. G. (2000). Governance, good governance and global governance: Conceptual and actual challenges. *Third World Quarterly*, 21(5), 795–814.

Weiss, T. G., Forsythe, D. P., & Coate, R. A. (2017). *The United Nations and Changing World Politics*, Boulder, CO: Westview.

World Bank. (1994). *Governance - the World Bank's experience (English). Development in practice Washington, D.C.: World Bank Group*. http://documents.worldbank.org/curated/en/711471468765285964/Governance-the-World-Banks-experience

5

AN EMPIRICAL STUDY ON ASSESSMENT OF EFFECTIVE GOVERNANCE ON ECONOMIC GROWTH IN BRICS COUNTRIES

Sagnik Maity and Amit Majumder

Introduction

Governance is the activity or action of directing and controlling a group, nation, or other entity. In simple terms, "Governance" means a different approach to management an altered state of orderly rule, or a new way of regulating society. It helps in considering various perspectives and enforcing a group's informal agreement to reach a common objective (Keping, 2018). In a larger context, "Global governance" refers to the collaborative effort of institutions, methods, and interventions that help governments and the governed work together to achieve firmness in the face of disasters, crises, and calamities (Governance, 2014). In this background, the effective governance of the nation is essential for economic expansion. A vast number of compelling elements affecting long-term economic growth were revealed across a range of publications like employment growth (Seyfried, 2011), financial independence (Salim et al., 2017), and governance performance (Liu et al., 2018) as significant factors behind economic growth. Progress in economic growth is desirable since it would help the government serve the country's needs more effectively (Hussain et al., 2021). Various studies suggest that economic growth and governance have some relation. Several studies have shown that economic independence is beneficial to economic growth over the long run (Umer, 2014) (Malanski & Póvoa, 2021). Although around the world the pattern of economic growth of all the nations was not uniformly accelerated, the UNCTAD's 2016 study indicated that the economies of emerging markets have grown rapidly over the past decade (UNCTAD, 2016). One of the significant factors is that the growth condition and labour force of a country are both affected by the governance of that country.

DOI: 10.4324/9781003530688-7

Against this backdrop, the present research emphasizes the relevance of governance in the relationship between the labour force and the economic growth of the nation in the context of the most emerging nations of the World Economy, that is, BRICS nations.

Literature Review

There has been a wide range of studies that employed DEA to measure the economic growth of the country.

Studies Based on Economic Growth Using Economic Variables

A study done on the DEA's utility in the macroeconomic analysis by Färe et al. (1994) used the MPI to examine the expansion of productivity in 17 OECD countries between 1979 and 1988. The researchers also use the GDP as output and capital stock and employment as input. As a result, the TFP increase in nations was entirely driven by innovation and technological advancement. Later, the same method was followed by Rao and Coelli (1998) and Kaüger et al. (2000); 60 countries worldwide were measured between 1965 and 1990, while another 87 were analysed between 1960 and 1990.

Another study done on the macroeconomic performance of 19 OECD nations from 1970 to 1990 was conducted by Lovell et al. (1995). This case study defines macroeconomic performance as a country's ability to deliver four essential services to its residents: a high level of real GDP per capita, low inflation, low unemployment, and a favourable trade balance. And they also added carbon and nitrogen emissions (Škare & Rabar 2016). Data studies revealed a shift in performance rankings and a fall in Europe's relative performance (Lovell et al., 1995).

In a study, Lovell and Pastor (1995) assessed the economic performance of 16 Ibero-American countries from 1980 to 1991. They found that Venezuela and Mexico were the most efficient and productive, while Nicaragua, Bolivia, and Peru had the lowest performance. According to the findings, Colombia, Mexico, Argentina, Brazil, and Uruguay had the best-managed economies, while Peru, Bolivia, and Nicaragua had the worst. In addition to having two of the three strongest economies, Colombia and Uruguay also had effective macroeconomic management (Lovell & Pastor, 1995; Škare & Rabar, 2016).

Escaith (2006) analysed the economic growth patterns in Latin America. The geographical scenario was applied to several methods for extrapolating growth tendencies, including DEA. The economies of Mercosur and Chile, Mesoamerica, and the Andean Community are broken down into 1991–1997, 1998–2002, and 2003–2005, respectively and analysed. The findings indicate that structural reforms have had little effect on total factor productivity (TFP) and that years of underinvestment have weakened productive capacity (Escaith, 2006).

Twenty-eight European nations, most of which are EU members, had their economic development models analyzed by Škuflić et al. (2013) in three separate years (2000, 2004, and 2008) to find the major growth determinants. Inputs used in this study to analyse economic growth include productivity and the proportion of GDP attributable to exports; outputs include the percentages of GDP attributable to gross earnings, personal consumption, and the GDP per capita. As a result, Croatia ranks lowest in efficiency because the other transition nations in another sample have joined the EU while Croatia has not. The authors found that EU membership boosts efficiency (Škuflić et al., 2013).

A study on happiness as a new research subject and key new development in economics is predicated on the question of how to increase social welfare beyond the GDP of 130 nations over a decade from 2000 to 2009 (Debnath & Shankar, 2014; Škare & Rabar, 2016). Researchers looked at a wide range of countries. The DEA was used to compare the levels of contentment in each of the three groups of countries that had been grouped together economically. Given that they wanted to maximize happiness as an outcome, they employed a BCC output-oriented approach. Due to the importance of subjective criteria in measuring happiness, the authors argue that excellent governance alone cannot maximize happiness. Consistently, the findings revealed how the government might boost citizen satisfaction by studying their habits and anticipations. Consequently, the current notion of effective governance needs to evolve (Debnath & Shankar, 2014).

Some Economic Growth Studies Using Non-Economic Variables

A study done by some researchers measures the green economic growth in Chinese cities and found that, according to the data, China has had positive green economic growth, with the greatest progress happening in cities located in the country's northeast and along its eastern coast (Zhao et al., 2022).

A group of researchers used the window DEA model to assess the effect of economic expansion on environmental efficiency in a study. They found a consistent N-shaped relationship between environmental performance and regional GDP growth for global and total pollutants, while for local pollutants, results show an inverted N-shape (Halkos & Polemis, 2018).

A study uses the DEA to measure welfare beyond GDP based on economic growth. These techniques are used to measure the economic success of companies and nations (Lábaj et al., 2014).

Namazi and Mohammadi show DEA based on TOPSIS analysis of economic growth and the natural resources of the country and draw the conclusion that countries with significant economic dependence on natural resource exports or low political stability could fall into this difficulty zone if they do not innovate. This is especially true for countries that rely heavily on oil exports (Namazi & Mohammadi, 2018).

Research Gap

Previous research demonstrates that DEA applications have been widely employed to quantify efficiency by taking into account a wide range of input and output variables. According to the previous study, there is a relationship between economic growth, employment rate, and the governance of the country especially for emerging economies like BRICS nations. Literature reviews have not turned up a large body of empirical research that compares one country's efficiency to another based on the amount of aid and investment received from abroad. The existence of this knowledge gap drives researchers to pursue the goals.

Objective

The study evaluates the effectiveness of the country's governance based on its utilization of foreign aid and investment to accelerate economic growth.

Data and Methodology

Data

In this study, the BRICS countries were used as a benchmark against which to compare the impact of effective governance on economic growth. All five nations are represented in the sample: Brazil, Russia, India, China, and South Africa. All information was obtained from the World Bank database. The data has been collected over a ten-year span, from 2011 to 2021, in order to determine the level of efficiency achieved by the countries.

Variables Used in the Study

The present study used DEA to analyse two input and three output variables. After a thorough analysis of prior literature, this study takes IBRD loan and IDA credit and FDI as inputs and GDP, employed labour force, and export as outputs that measure economic growth. Below is a breakdown of these factors.

Input Variables

IBRD Loan and IDA Credit

IBRD and IDA originate from the World Bank Group. The credit facility is provided by IDA to the world's poorest countries in order to improve their economic prospects and living conditions. In contrast, the IBRD aids middle-income and credit-worthy developing nations, whereas the World Bank assists all developing nations. A study showcases that IBRD loans and IDA credit evaluate and enhance the country's economic growth (Butkiewicz & Yanikkaya, 2005; Frey & Schneider, 1986). In this study, researchers found that every BRICS nation availed itself of a foreign loan and took it as input.

FDI

Numerous studies demonstrate that FDI has a significant effect on economic growth (Campos & Kinoshita, 2002; Ram & Zhang, 2002). In addition, several studies have shown that FDI can help a country develop so long as certain conditions are met, such as the availability of human capital (Borensztein et al., 1998; Xu, 2000). However, some research suggests that certain countries with advanced financial systems may benefit from the growth-boosting effects of FDI (Alfaro et al., 2004; Durham, 2004). Therefore, it is evident that FDI affects economic growth; however, it also depends on how the government uses it. In this study, it is utilized as an input.

Output Variables

GDP

The gross domestic product (GDP) is a monetary measure of all final products and services produced in a country within a certain time period (Callen, n.d.). Researchers agree that GDP is a reliable indicator of economic expansion. According to a study, excellent governance also impacts GDP consumption (Bercu et al., 2019). So, the GDP is one of the most important factors in the country's economic expansion (Fayissa & Nsiah, 2013). Researchers took it as an output factor.

Export

Export has an effect on economic growth. Many studies show that foreign exchange is boosted by an increase in exports, which in turn allows for more imports of services and capital goods, all of which contribute to higher productivity and faster economic growth (Abou-Stait, 2005; Al-Yousif, 1997; Fayissa & Nsiah, 2013; Feder, 1983; Lucas Jr, 1988; Vohra, 2001). The discovered connection motivated the factor to be used as an output.

Employment

In a country, transparency, lawfulness, good policy, involvement, accountability, responsiveness, and corruption-free are all characteristics of good governance. Despite the fact that there are a variety of metrics that may be used to comprehend the nature of good governance, the researchers here opted for the employment element as an output (Aguilera, 2007; Capron & Guillén, 2009; Copeland & ter Haar, 2013). In order to determine the employment rate, the study used data from the World Bank data based on the International Labour Organization's (ILO) unemployment model.

Statistical and Econometric Tests Used

Different academics have devised several parametric and non-parametric methods to measure the efficacy of decision-making units (DMUs). DEA was developed by Charnes et al. in 1978 to find the efficiencies of the DMUs (Charnes et al., 1978). Different studies have used it as a tool to gauge the effectiveness of DEA in different nations (Kocher et al., 2006; Kočišová, 2015). There are two broadly used models: one based on a constant return to scale named CCR (developed by Charnes et al., 1978), and another is BCC (developed by Banker et al., 1984) based on the variable return to scale. Whereas the CCR model illustrates the overall technical efficiency (OTE), the BCC model concentrates on pure technical efficiency (PTE).

Using this method, the most efficient DMUs are given a score of 1, while the least efficient ones receive a score close to 0. Consider a system with n DMUs, each with p number of inputs and q number of outputs. A test DMU0 ("o" indicates a focused DMU) has been given a relative efficiency score according to the following model:

$$Max \frac{\sum_{r=1}^{q} v_r y_{r0}}{\sum_{i=1}^{p} u_i x_{i0}}$$

Subject to

$$\frac{\sum_{r=1}^{q} v_r y_{rj}}{\sum_{i=1}^{p} u_i x_{ij}} \leq 1; \left(j = 1,2,3,...,n\right); \left(i = 1,2,3,...,p\right); \left(r = 1,2,3,...,q\right);$$

$$\left(u_i, v_r \geq 0\right). \tag{5.1}$$

In the equation (5.1),

y_{rj} = *Output "r" produced by DMU "j"*
v_r = *Weight of the output "r"*
x_{ij} = *Input "i" employed by DMU "j"*
u_i = *Weight of the input "i"*

It is turned into a linear programming problem to evaluate each DMU's relative efficiency score.

$$Max \sum_{r=1}^{q} v_r y_{ro}$$

Subject to

$$\sum_{r=1}^{q} v_r y_{ro} - \sum_{i=1}^{p} u_i x_{ij} \leq 0; (j = 1,2,3,\ldots,n) \tag{5.2}$$

$$\sum_{i=1}^{p} u_i x_{ij} = 1;$$

$$u_i, v_r \geq 0$$

There are two oriented models to find the efficiency of the DMU. One is input-oriented, and the other is output-oriented. In this study, researchers follow an output-oriented model. In it, DEA maximizes output for a given amount of input; that is, it reveals how much a DMU can raise output for a certain level of input. In CRS and VRS modes, the performance scores will be distinct (Huguenin, 2013). The purpose of the study is to determine the government's effectiveness in bringing economic growth to the country through the use of foreign investment and foreign loans. Here, the efficiencies represent the nation's governance.

Before doing the efficiency test, descriptive statistics of the variables were calculated in order to comprehend the characteristics of the data. Researchers have also run the "isotonicity" test to understand whether the inputs positively affect the output (Golany & Roll, 1989). OTE and PTE scores are calculated for the BRICS nations from 2011 to 2021. Efficiency and consistency scores have been used to rank countries.

Analysis and Findings

The descriptive data and isotonicity test outcomes are shown in Tables 5.1 and 5.2. The researchers check the isotonicity assumption to ensure the results are reliable. Descriptive statistics have been done on the five nations over a decade based on 55 observations. The standard deviation of the data, the average, the maximum and minimum values, and the skewness are all shown in the table. Researchers also conduct the isotonicity test, which claims that an increase in inputs should not lead to a decrease in outputs and that a decrease in outputs should not lead to a rise in inputs. A correlation has been computed (Table 5.2), which shows a positive relationship between the variables that fulfil the assumption of the test.

TABLE 5.1 Descriptive Statistics

	N	Range	Minimum	Maximum	Mean	Std. Deviation	Skewness
IBRD loan (000)	55	39,563,625.00	177,959.00	39,741,584.00	14,489,678.53	13,564,605.76	0.675
FDI (000)	55	332,457,889.19	1,521,139.95	333,979,029.13	79,334,584.85	89,099,793.17	1.477
GDP (0000	55	17,410,477,135.7	323,585,509.6	17,734,062,645.3	3,700,737,037.6	4,417,126,763.06	1.762
Export (000)	55	3,462,400,220.05	91,109,021.41	3,553,509,241.46	773,602,120.76	904,661,737.51	1.598
Employed labour force (000)	55	745,739.16	14,737.68	760,476.84	274,556.55	286,029.85	0.748

Source: Authors' calculation.

TABLE 5.2 "Isotonicity" Test

	IBRD loan (000)	FDI (000)	GDP (0000)	Export (000)	Employed Labour Force (000)
IBRD loan (000)	1				
FDI (000)	0.196805	1			
GDP (0000	0.195682	0.913196	1		
Export (000)	0.175871	0.930638	0.984161	1	
Employed labour force (000)	0.597163	0.809614	0.852988	0.871143	1

Source: Authors' calculations.

After the test, the study further proceeds to evaluate the efficiency scores under the CCR (Table 5.3) and BCC (Table 5.4) methods. Table 5.3 represents the overall technical efficiency scores of the five nations from 2011 to 2021. The last row consists of the mean of the DMUs. The mean efficiency scores of the DMUs are as follows: Brazil (0.934997979), Russia (0.62025066), India (0.978297422), China (0.929454801), and South Africa (0.67968133). In the last column of the same table, yearly DMU means are displayed, with 2015 having the highest score. Figure 5.1 displays the combined year-wise efficiency of the five countries studied.

Table 5.4 shows the pure technical efficiency scores of the five nations under the BCC method, and the last row consists of the mean of the DMUs, Brazil (0.993974782), Russia (0.998200435), India (0.987396544), China (0.99281295), South Africa (0.985601088). As per the yearly DMU mean, 2021 has the highest score, 1, and the lowest score can be seen in 2020. All the year-wise efficiency under BCC is shown in Figure 5.2.

The further analysis proceeds with the calculation of the final rank of the DMUs in Table 5.5. Final ranks are derived from rank using AM and rank using consistency coefficient (CC = AM/SD). Table 5.5 shows the rank based on AM, which is derived using the mean of DMUs under CCR and BCC. In the rank based on AM shows, India came out at the top position, and Russia came last. The same result can be seen in the rank based on CC. In the final efficiency result, India came out at the top, followed by Brazil, China, South Africa, and Russia.

Details of the nation's year-wise efficiency can be seen in Table 5.6. Also, the year-wise efficient and inefficient data with maximum score, minimum score, and standard deviation are shown in Table 5.6. As a result, the highest number of effective DMUs was observed in 2021, with four effective DMUs, and the highest number of ineffective DMUs was shown in 2014, with five ineffective DMUs.

TABLE 5.3 Overall Technical Efficiency (OTE) Scores of the DMUs

Year	Brazil_Eff	Russia_Eff	India_Eff	China_Eff	South Africa_Eff	Mean of the Years
2011	1	0.213662255	0.945773774	0.765210878	1	0.784929381
2012	0.961797667	0.262486309	1	0.803486882	0.775193311	0.760592834
2013	1	0.286066933	0.992018296	0.836994845	0.505497766	0.724115568
2014	0.881784999	0.528684781	0.988961885	0.890800324	0.547664844	0.767579366
2015	0.934770051	1	0.976701268	0.939086271	1	0.970111518
2016	0.852334625	0.366782487	0.986941907	1	0.736387423	0.788489288
2017	0.889866568	0.436635496	1	1	0.812964544	0.827893322
2018	0.854505386	1	1	1	0.545067118	0.879914501
2019	0.909918469	0.728439003	1	1	0.567890139	0.841249522
2020	1	1	0.87087451	0.988423617	0.661665883	0.904192802
2021	1	1	1	1	0.324163601	0.86483272
Mean of DMUs	0.934997979	0.62025066	0.978297422	0.929454801	0.67968133	

Source: Authors' calculations.

TABLE 5.4 Pure Technical Efficiency Score of the DMUs

Year	Brazil_Eff	Russia_Eff	India_Eff	China_Eff	South Africa_Eff	Mean of Years
2011	1	0.990666021	0.969203178	0.979795046	1	0.987932849
2012	0.994574416	1	1	0.983158184	0.985409969	0.992628514
2013	1	1	0.998528886	0.985913589	0.988851529	0.994658801
2014	1	1	0.990350695	0.989846214	0.970286689	0.99009672
2015	1	1	0.977835706	0.993625428	1	0.994292227
2016	0.960044462	0.99381274	1	1	0.99078813	0.988929066
2017	0.983314716	0.995726023	1	1	1	0.995808148
2018	0.995789011	1	1	1	1	0.999157802
2019	1	1	1	1	0.993252029	0.998650406
2020	1	1	0.925443524	0.988603989	0.913023625	0.965414228
2021	1	1	1	1	1	1
Mean of DMUs	0.993974782	0.998200435	0.987396544	0.99281295	0.985601088	

Source: Authors' calculations.

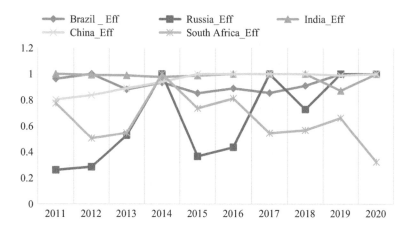

FIGURE 5.1 Year-wise efficiency of the five countries under OTE.

Source: Authors' calculations.

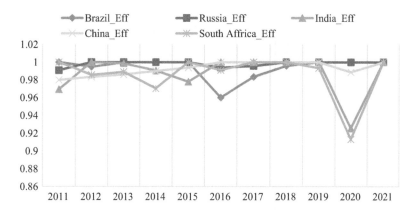

FIGURE 5.2 Year-wise efficiency of the five countries under PTE.

Source: Authors' calculations.

Focus on the output of DMUs in accordance with the output-oriented model. Those that ~~who~~ are inefficient display their deficit in Table 5.7. This table will help to understand the amount of output needed in that set of inputs to achieve the efficient mark. Those DMUs have no shortfall and are considered efficient DMUs (Marschall & Flessa, 2011). From the table, in most cases, China and India made the efficient mark, with the lowest efficacy showing South Africa.

Results and Discussion

This research shows that BRICS countries benefit significantly from international loans and investments. They are examining the effects of foreign aid

TABLE 5.5 Measures of Rank Based on Efficiency Scores and Consistency Coefficient

DMU	SD	AM (BCC & CCR)	CC	Rank Based on AM	Rank Based on CC	Sum of Rank	Final Rank
Brazil	0.052136	0.96448638	18.49931	2	2	4	2
Russia	0.299654	0.809225548	2.700537	5	5	10	5
India	0.031723	0.982846983	30.98207	1	1	2	1
China	0.070378	0.961133876	13.65674	3	3	6	3
South Africa	0.214007	0.832641209	3.890723	4	4	8	4

Source: Authors' calculation.

AM, *arithmetic mean; SD, standard deviation; CC, consistency coefficient.*

TABLE 5.6 Summary of Year-wise Efficient Nations (Under OTE)

Year	Mean of the Years	Numbers of DMUs		Descriptive Statistics		
		Efficient	Inefficient	Max	Min	SD
2011	0.784929381	2	3	1	0.213662	0.333585
2012	0.760592834	1	4	1	0.262486	0.294942
2013	0.724115568	1	4	1	0.286067	0.316349
2014	0.767579366	0	5	0.988962	0.528685	0.213699
2015	0.970111518	2	3	1	0.93477	0.031787
2016	0.788489288	1	4	1	0.366782	0.259204
2017	0.827893322	2	3	1	0.436635	0.232587
2018	0.879914501	3	2	1	0.545067	0.197503
2019	0.841249522	2	3	1	0.56789	0.188792
2020	0.904192802	2	3	1	0.661666	0.146101
2021	0.86483272	4	1	1	0.324164	0.302243

Source: Authors' calculations.

TABLE 5.7 Shortfall of Output Factor

Year	Shortfall GDP (Brazil) (0,000,000)	Shortfall Export (Brazil) (0,000,000)	Shortfall Employed Labour Force (Brazil) (0,000,000)	Shortfall GDP (Russia) (0,000,000)	Shortfall Export (Russia) (0,000,000)	Shortfall Employed Labour Force (Russia) (0,000,000)	Shortfall GDP (India) (0,000,000)	Shortfall Export (India) (0,000,000)	Shortfall Employed Labour Force (India) (0,000,000)	Shortfall GDP (China) (0,000,000)	Shortfall Export (China) (0,000,000)	Shortfall Employed Labour Force (China) (0,000,000)	Shortfall GDP (South Africa) (0,000,000)	Shortfall Export (South Africa) (0,000,000)	Shortfall Employed Labour Force (South Africa) (0,000,000)
2011	0	0	0	7,52,959	2,11,245	26	10,453	2,565	2	2,31,702	61,559	23	0	0	0
2012	9,792	1,163	0	6,20,470	1,66,952	20	0	0	0	2,08,677	53,197	18	12,598	3,419	0
2013	0	0	0	5,72,129	1,47,869	18	1,494	380	0	1,86,384	45,849	15	39,217	11,129	2
2014	32,926	3,626	1	1,83,579	49,770	6	2,276	523	0	1,28,417	30,191	9	31,485	9,131	1
2015	12,576	1,622	1	0	0	0	5,018	994	1	71,751	15,322	5	0	0	0
2016	31,110	3,878	2	2,20,426	56,990	12	3,036	582	1	0	0	0	11,584	3,262	1
2017	25,539	3,197	1	2,03,109	52,993	9	0	0	0	0	0	0	8,776	2,399	0
2018	32,639	4,777	2	0	0	0	0	0	0	0	0	0	33,733	9,298	1
2019	18,545	2,619	1	63,119	17,947	3	39,554	7,400	0	0	0	0	29,564	8,070	1
2020	0	0	0	0	0	0	0	0	6	17,202	3,197	1	17,264	4,765	1
2021	0	0	0	0	0	0	0	0	0	0	0	0	87,359	27,251	3

Source: Authors' calculations.

Shortfall = (*Predicted* − *Actual*)/10,000,000.

and investment on a country's exports, workforce, and GDP. Researchers agree that effective governance is crucial for any foreign assistance or investment to yield results; i.e., deficits in a country's growth may result from poor governance.

Country-wise Results and Discussion

China: From 2011 to 2015, China faced several challenges, including global economic uncertainty, a decline in export demand, and efforts by the Chinese government to transition to a more sustainable and consumption-driven economic model. All this can be seen in Tables 5.3 and 5.4, where China is behind the efficiency mark. After that, the Chinese government maintained its efficiency till 2020 due to the policy implementation of the 12th Five-Year Plan. In 2020, most BRICS nations' healthcare systems and economics were adversely impacted by the COVID-19 pandemic. While numerous nations had challenges in managing the transmission of COVID-19, China encountered the initial impact, leading authorities to enforce stringent measures of confinement, which are projected to result in a minimum 6% decline in economic growth by 2020 (The Conversation, 2021). It is evident from Table 5.7, which presents shortfall for GDP and exports that lag behind the efficiency level. China's GDP contracted 6.8% in Q1 2020 due to the state-wide lockdown imposed during the apex of the COVID-19 pandemic (The BBC, 2021). In 2021, the new COVID-19 variant and the collapse of the Chinese property market were devastating to the Chinese economy (The Economic Times, 2021). However, targeted fiscal policies and strong global export demand helped China recover its operational capacity (Wang et al., 2023). It can be seen from Table 5.3.

South Africa: South Africa exhibited a shortfall in its GDP, exports, and employment rate for most of the year. This occurrence can be attributed to various factors, including a global economic slowdown, domestic structural challenges, and policy uncertainty. Furthermore, due to COVID-19, the World Bank predicts South Africa's labour force will be down to approximately 1.5 million people by the end of 2020; although two-thirds of jobs increased, the earnings of those still employed will decline by 10–15% (The World Bank, 2021). The International Labour Organization calculated that a decline of 10.5% from pre-crisis levels (Q4 2019) was anticipated, equating to a loss of 305 million full-time employees (assuming a 48-hour working week). The prior prediction was for a decline of 6.7%, which would imply a loss of 195 million full-time jobs. It happened because lockdown procedures had been expanded and made permanent (ILO, 2020). The pandemic has made the bad financial situation in South Africa even worse. With the government having to borrow funds to mitigate the effects of COVID-19, the country's ties to the BRICS are crucial to its recovery, particularly in boosting commerce and investment (BRICS info, 2020). Despite all the attempts, economic inefficiency was high in 2021 (Table 5.3) due to poor governance.

Russia: The aftermath of the 2008 financial crisis, geopolitical tensions, and economic sanctions imposed on Russia all contributed to a less favourable global economic climate. It had an impact on Russia's export-oriented sectors. Also, the oil and gas dependency affected Russia's economy from 2011 to 2015. Table 5.3 shows Russia's shortfall against the member countries in this study. According to a report titled "Key socio-economic consequences of COVID-19 pandemic in Russia 2021", published by the Statista Research Department (SRD), 60% of Russians surveyed in 2021 cited an increase in unemployment as the most pressing social and economic issue resulting from the COVID-19 pandemic in their country (SRD, 2021). Although the unemployment rate declined before the COVID-19 crisis, real wages decreased. Large disparities persist between urban and rural sectors of society (The Standard Bank South Africa, 2022). From Table 5.5, Russia came out in the last rank, which indicates poor governance in terms of the allocation of foreign funds.

Brazil: The OTE score of Brazil in Table 5.3, from 2014 to 2019, is near the efficiency mark but never touches it. It happened due to political instability, commodity price volatility, and economic recession. Despite the adverse health, social, and economic consequences of the COVID-19 pandemic, Brazil has demonstrated effective governance in efficiently distributing foreign aid. It is seen from the 4.1% decline in GDP experienced in 2020, followed by a recovery in 2021. In 2021, GDP growth was forecasted to rise to 5.3% thanks to a slight upward trend in commodity prices and a rebound in domestic and foreign demand (World Bank, 2021).

India: India shows an efficient governance framework using foreign aid and investment. It demonstrates efficient operational capabilities in five out of ten years, while in the remaining four out of five years, the country is close to the efficient threshold. Notably, 2020 stands out with an operational efficiency of 80% (Table 5.3) because India is one of the major countries affected by the COVID-19 pandemic. GDP, unemployment rate, interest rate, inflation rate, and industrial output are the five indicators liable for this type of economy's reaction (Barbate et al., 2021). GDP fell 6.6% in fiscal 2021 due to the pandemic (CRISIL Global Research and Risk Solutions, 2022). The unemployment rate reached a record high during the lockdown (average of rural and urban rates). It increased from 7.2% in January 2020 to 23.5% in April 2020 (Unemployment, 2022). Not only was unemployment at an all-time high but also inflation. In April, retail inflation reached its highest level in eight years, 7.79% (Trading Economics and MoSPI, 2020). RBI reduces the interest rate to encourage banks to extend credit. The reverse repo rate was decreased to 4%, the repo rate was decreased to 4.40%, the marginal standing facility rate was decreased to

4.65%, and the CRR was decreased by 1% (Barbate et al., 2021). The extended lockdown interrupted industry output in March, April, and May 2020. According to the Ministry of Statistics and Programme Implementation, the index of industrial production (IIP) declined by 10.4% to 118.1% in July (Indian express, 2020). However, India managed to recover its economy in 2021. It was driven by many factors, including robust vaccination campaigns, easing COVID-19 restrictions, strong agricultural performance, increased government spending on infrastructure, and global economic revival (UNCTAD, 2021). These measures, coupled with reforms aimed at enhancing ease of doing business, contributed to a rebound in manufacturing and services sectors, fostering economic growth and restoring investor confidence.

Other Global Economic Events

The contained study investigates the objectives' unfolding. The primary goal of the research was to learn about the development aid and lending practices of the BRICS countries. Data shows (Table 5.6) that most countries are having trouble maintaining efficiency in 2014; demand is subdued as a result of inflationary pressures and the global economy's weakness. The price of crude oil peaked in July 2014, and since then, it has been steadily falling, which has brought about a decrease in the cost of gasoline. Even though there are many potential causes, it is speculated that low global demand is to blame for the 2014 economic slowdown. China, Brazil, and Russia (essentially the well-known BRICS grouping) have all sustained the emerging global slowdown that began a year ago (Radulescu et al., 2014).

In 2021, BRICS countries controlled 26% of the global economy and were home to 3.2 billion people, or more than 40% of the global total (Chen Yurong, 2022). Added uncertainties in 2021, such as the conflict between Russia and Ukraine, disruptions to global supply chains, and soaring inflation in major economies, have slowed the recovery of the COVID-19 global economy. But for the first time, in 2021, commerce between China and India reached over $100 billion, totalling $125.66 billion. In the meantime, business ties between China and South Africa increased by 50.7% in the same time frame (Chen Yurong, 2022).

This efficiency analysis reveals that four out of five DMUs will function efficiently in 2021 (Table 5.6). As per the IMF, global growth will grow to 6.0% in 2021 and 4.9% in 2022. These adjustments are in response to new information and shifts in government policy regarding the pandemic. With the expected passage of more budgetary aid in the second half of 2021 and better health measures across the board, the outlook for advanced economies, and the United States in particular, has been revised upward by 0.5 percentage points for the year 2022 (Gita Gopinath, 2021).

Conclusion

This chapter aims to examine the governance and economic growth of BRICS nations from 2011 to 2021 based on foreign investment and aid. Researchers selected IBRD loans, IDA credits, and FDI as inputs and GDP, exports, and employment as outputs for this study. Researchers utilize data envelopment analysis to evaluate the efficacy of five nations. Before conducting the DEA, researchers conducted the isotonicity test to determine the input–output variable relationship.

According to the findings, India is the most efficient country to govern foreign loans and aid to achieve economic growth and employed workforce. In managing foreign aid and investments, efficiency is a product of effective governance. There is so much evidence that India has a very efficient governing system that utilizes investments to bring economic growth to the country. One study shows the effective use of investment in PPP mode has a favourable effect on GDP in the long run (Chotia & Rao, 2018). Also, some researchers use other models like ARDL and FMOLS to find out that FDI inflows and foreign aid are beneficial to economic growth in India (Kumar et al., 2022).

Correspondingly, the outcome indicates that South Africa placed last. The inefficiency demonstrates that the government fails to allocate funds effectively, and the rise in inflation has a detrimental impact on economic growth (Nuru & Gereziher, 2022).

The study implies that based on year-wise data, throughout the decade, BRICS countries may have successfully increased their economic growth, but a downfall can be seen in the employment rate. To sustain stability, the role performed by the BRICS countries is vital not just in the G20 but also in global economic policy (Mminele, 2016). The BRICS are developing economies, but they still need to establish domestic strategies to address issues such as a shortage of fiscal and monetary policies, inadequate government support for national priorities, mismanagement, and economic malfeasance. In this setting, BRICS nations cannot blindly implement the policies designed for developed nations because there is a wide range of cultural values, ideological positions, and social demography (poverty, unemployment) among the BRICS nations, all of which have an outsized impact on economic decisions made between them. BRICS needs to improve international cooperation towards common goals, an open exchange of information about the obstacles confronted by each country, and the adoption of consensus-based solutions reached via open and honest communication. With this agreement in place, BRICS nations may be able to improve their markets without any foreign financial aid and investment. This will result in financial independence, which will benefit their domestic market and the global economy and will serve as an example of effective governance.

References

Abou-Stait, F. (2005). *Working Paper 76-Are Exports the Engine of Economic Growth? An Application of Cointegration and Causality Analysis for Egypt, 1977–2003.*

Aguilera, R. V. (2007). *Corporate Governance and Employment Relations: Spain in the Context of Western Europe.* SSRN.

Alfaro, L., Chanda, A., Kalemli-Ozcan, S., & Sayek, S. (2004). FDI and economic growth: The role of local financial markets. *Journal of International Economics*, 64(1), 89–112.

Al-Yousif, Y. K. (1997). Exports and economic growth: Some empirical evidence from the Arab Gulf countries. *Applied Economics*, 29(6), 693–697.

Banker, R. D., Charnes, A., & Cooper, W. W. (1984). Some models for estimating technical and scale inefficiencies in data envelopment analysis. *Management Science*, 30(9), 1078–1092.

Barbate, V., Gade, R. N., & Raibagkar, S. S. (2021). COVID-19 and Its Impact on the Indian Economy. *Vision*, 25(1), 23–35. https://doi.org/10.1177/0972262921989126

Bercu, A.-M., Paraschiv, G., & Lupu, D. (2019). Investigating the energy–economic growth–governance nexus: Evidence from central and eastern european countries. *Sustainability*, 11(12), 3355.

Borensztein, E., de Gregorio, J., & Lee, J.-W. (1998). How does foreign direct investment affect economic growth? *Journal of International Economics*, 45(1), 115–135.

BRICS info. (2020, November 24). BRICS Partnership to Help S. Africa Recover from COVID-19 – Expert. http://infobrics.org/post/32311

Butkiewicz, J. L., & Yanikkaya, H. (2005). The effects of IMF and World Bank lending on long-run economic growth: An empirical analysis. *World Development*, 33(3), 371–391.

Callen, T. (n.d.). *Gross Domestic Product: An Economy's All.* IMF. Retrieved February 14, 2023, from https://www.imf.org/en/Publications/fandd/issues/Series/Back-to-Basics/gross-domestic-product-GDP

Campos, N. F., & Kinoshita, Y. (2002). Foreign direct investment as technology transferred: Some panel evidence from the transition economies. *The Manchester School*, 70(3), 398–419.

Capron, L., & Guillén, M. (2009). National corporate governance institutions and post-acquisition target reorganization. *Strategic Management Journal*, 30(8), 803–833.

Charnes, A., Cooper, W. W., & Rhodes, E. (1978). Measuring the efficiency of decision making units, *European Journal of Operational Research*, 2(6), 429–444.

Chen Yurong, Z. H. (2022). Analysis: How BRICS promotes global economic recovery post-COVID – CGTN. https://news.cgtn.com/news/2022-06-21/Analysis-How-BRICS-promotes-global-economic-recovery-post-COVID-1b2ycQz8SA0/index.html

Chotia, V., & Rao, N. V. M. (2018). Infrastructure financing and economic growth in India: An empirical investigation. *Journal of Financial Management of Property and Construction*, 23(3), 258–273.

Copeland, P., & ter Haar, B. (2013). A toothless bite? The effectiveness of the European Employment Strategy as a governance tool. *Journal of European Social Policy*, 23(1), 21–36.

CRISIL Global Research and Risk Solutions. (2022, July 29). *Indian Economy: States of aftermath*. CRISIL Report. https://www.crisil.com/en/home/our-analysis/reports/2022/07/crisil-insights-indian-economy-states-of-aftermath.html

Debnath, R. M., & Shankar, R. (2014). Does good governance enhance happiness: A cross nation study. *Social Indicators Research*, 116, 235–253.

Durham, J. B. (2004). Absorptive capacity and the effects of foreign direct investment and equity foreign portfolio investment on economic growth. *European Economic Review*, 48(2), 285–306.

Escaith, H. (2006). *Can Latin America Fly? Revising Its Engines of Growth*.

Färe, R., Grosskopf, S., Norris, M., & Zhang, Z. (1994). Productivity growth, technical progress, and efficiency change in industrialized countries. *The American Economic Review*, 84, 66–83.

Fayissa, B., & Nsiah, C. (2013). The impact of governance on economic growth in Africa. *The Journal of Developing Areas*, 47, 91–108.

Feder, G. (1983). On exports and economic growth. *Journal of Development Economics*, 12(1–2), 59–73.

Frey, B. S., & Schneider, F. (1986). Competing models of international lending activity. *Journal of Development Economics*, 20(2), 225–245. https://doi.org/10.1016/0304-3878(86)90022-2

Golany, B., & Roll, Y. (1989). An application procedure for DEA. *Omega*, 17(3), 237–250.

Gopinath, Gita. (2021). World economic outlook update, July 2021: Fault lines widen in the global recovery. https://www.imf.org/en/Publications/WEO/Issues/2021/07/27/world-economic-outlook-update-july-2021

Governance, G. (2014). *Global Rules for Development in the Post-2015 Era*. United Nations.

Halkos, G. E., & Polemis, M. L. (2018). The impact of economic growth on environmental efficiency of the electricity sector: A hybrid window DEA methodology for the USA. *Journal of Environmental Management*, 211, 334–346. https://doi.org/10.1016/J.JENVMAN.2018.01.067

Huguenin, J.-M. (2013). Data Envelopment Analysis (DEA). *Un Guide Pédagogique à l'intention Des Décideurs Dans Le Secteur Public. IDHEAP–Cahier*, 278(2013), 7–81.

Hussain, H. I., Haseeb, M., Kamarudin, F., Dacko-Pikiewicz, Z., & Szczepańska-Woszczyna, K. (2021). The role of globalization, economic growth and natural resources on the ecological footprint in Thailand: Evidence from nonlinear causal estimations. *Processes*, 9(7), 1103.

ILO. (2020). ILO: As job losses escalate, nearly half of global workforce at risk of losing livelihoods. http://www.ilo.org/global/about-the-ilo/newsroom/news/WCMS_743036/lang--en/index.htm

Indian express. (2020, September 11). IIP India growth rate data July 2020: India's industrial output falls 10.4% in July, shows govt data. https://indianexpress.com/article/business/economy/india-iip-index-of-industrial-production-data-july-2020-6592098/

Kaüger, J. J., Cantner, U., & Hanusch, H. (2000). Total factor productivity, the East Asian miracle, and the world production frontier. *Weltwirtschaftliches Archiv*, 136(1), 111–136.

Keping, Y. (2018). Governance and good governance: A new framework for political analysis. *Fudan Journal of the Humanities and Social Sciences*, 11, 1–8.

Kocher, M. G., Luptacik, M., & Sutter, M. (2006). Measuring productivity of research in economics: A cross-country study using DEA. *Socio-Economic Planning Sciences*, *40*(4), 314–332.

Kočišová, K. (2015). Application of the DEA on the measurement of efficiency in the EU countries. *Agricultural Economics*, *61*(2), 51–62.

Kumar, P., Kumari, N., & Sahu, N. C. (2022). Floods and economic growth in India: Role of FDI inflows and foreign aid. *Management of Environmental Quality: An International Journal*, *33*(5), 1114–1131.

Lábaj, M., Luptáčik, M., & Nežinský, E. (2014). Data envelopment analysis for measuring economic growth in terms of welfare beyond GDP. *Empirica*, *41*(3), 407–424. https://doi.org/10.1007/S10663-014-9262-2/METRICS

Liu, J., Tang, J., Zhou, B., & Liang, Z. (2018). The effect of governance quality on economic growth: Based on China's provincial panel data. *Economies*, *6*(4), 56.

Lovell, C. A. K., & Pastor, J. T. (1995). *Macroeconomic Performance of Sixteen Ibero-American Countries over the Period 1980–1991*. Instituto Valenciano de Investigaciones Económicas.

Lovell, C. A. K., Pastor, J. T., & Turner, J. A. (1995). Measuring macroeconomic performance in the OECD: A comparison of European and non-European countries. *European Journal of Operational Research*, *87*(3), 507–518.

Lucas Jr, R. E. (1988). On the mechanics of economic development. *Journal of Monetary Economics*, *22*(1), 3–42.

Malanski, L. K., & Póvoa, A. C. S. (2021). Economic growth and corruption in emerging markets: Does economic freedom matter? *International Economics*, *166*, 58–70.

Marschall, P., & Flessa, S. (2011). Efficiency of primary care in rural Burkina Faso. A two-stage DEA analysis. *Health Economics Review*, *1*(1), 1–15.

Mminele, D. (2016). Daniel Mminele: The role of BRICS in the global economy. https://www.bis.org/review/r160720c.htm

Namazi, M., & Mohammadi, E. (2018). Natural resource dependence and economic growth: A TOPSIS/DEA analysis of innovation efficiency. *Resources Policy*, *59*, 544–552. https://doi.org/10.1016/J.RESOURPOL.2018.09.015

Nuru, N. Y., & Gereziher, H. Y. (2022). The effect of fiscal policy on economic growth in South Africa: A nonlinear ARDL model analysis. *Journal of Economic and Administrative Sciences*, *38*(2), 229–245.

Radulescu, I. G., Panait, M., & Voica, C. (2014). BRICS countries challenge to the world economy new trends. *Procedia Economics and Finance*, *8*, 605–613. https://doi.org/10.1016/S2212-5671(14)00135-X

Ram, R., & Zhang, K. H. (2002). Foreign direct investment and economic growth: Evidence from cross-country data for the 1990s. *Economic Development and Cultural Change*, *51*(1), 205–215.

Rao, D. S. P., & Coelli, T. J. (1998). A cross-country analysis of GDP growth catch-up and convergence in productivity and inequality. *Centre for Efficiency and Productivity Analysis (CEPA) Working Paper No. 5*, 98.

Salim, R. A., Rafiq, S., & Shafiei, S. (2017). Urbanization, energy consumption, and pollutant emission in Asian developing economies: An empirical analysis. *ADBI Working Paper*.

Seyfried, W. (2011). Examining the relationship between employment and economic growth in the ten largest states. *Southwestern Economic Review*, *32*, 13–24.

Škare, M., & Rabar, D. (2016). Measuring economic growth using data envelopment analysis. *Amfiteatru Economic Journal*, *18*(42), 386–406.

Škuflić, L., Rabar, D., & Škrinjarić, B. (2013). Assessment of the efficiency of Croatia compared to other European countries using data envelopment analysis with application of window analysis. *International Journal of Sustainable Economy*, 5(1), 104–123.

SRD. (2021). COVID-19 socio-economic consequences Russia 2021 | Statista. https://www.statista.com/statistics/1230034/covid-19-pandemic-socio-economic-consequences-russia/

The BBC. (2021). China's economy grows 18.3% in post-Covid comeback – BBC News. https://www.bbc.com/news/business-56768663

The Conversation. (2021). How the pandemic has changed China's economy – Perhaps for good. https://theconversation.com/how-the-pandemic-has-changed-chinas-economy-perhaps-for-good-167597

The Economic Times. (2021). Why China's economy is threatened by a property giant's debt problems – The Economic Times. https://economictimes.indiatimes.com/news/international/business/why-chinas-economy-is-threatened-by-a-property-giants-debt-problems/articleshow/86097524.cms?from=mdr

The Standard Bank South Africa. (2022). The economic context of Russia – Standard Bank TradeClub. https://www.tradeclub.standardbank.com/portal/en/market-potential/russia/economical-context?clear_s=y#

The World Bank. (2021). South Africa economic update: South Africa's labor market can benefit from young entrepreneurs, self-employment. https://www.worldbank.org/en/country/southafrica/publication/south-africa-economic-update-south-africa-s-labor-market-can-benefit-from-young-entrepreneurs-self-employment

Trading Economics MoSPI. (2020). India inflation rate MoM – September 2022 Data – 2011–2021 historical. https://tradingeconomics.com/india/inflation-rate-mom

Umer, F. (2014). Impact of trade openness on economic growth of Pakistan: An ARDL approach. *Journal of Business & Economic Policy*, 1(1). www.jbepnet.com

UNCTAD. (2016). *Trade and Development Report 2016*. UN Trade and Development.

UNCTAD. (2021). Trade and development report 2021: From recovery to resilience: The development dimension. https://shop.un.org/

Unemployment. (2022). Retrieved October 11, 2022, from https://unemploymentinindia.cmie.com/kommon/bin/sr.php?kall=wsttimeseries&index_code=050050000000&dtype=total

Vohra, R. (2001). Export and economic growth: Further time series evidence from less-developed countries. *International Advances in Economic Research*, 7(3), 345–350.

Wang, Y., Wang, X., Zhang, Z., & Cui, Z. (2023). Role of fiscal and monetary policies for economic recovery in China. *Economic Analysis and Policy*, 77, 51–63. https://doi.org/10.1016/J.EAP.2022.10.011

World Bank. (2021). Brazil overview: Development news, research, data | World Bank. https://www.worldbank.org/en/country/brazil/overview#1

Xu, B. (2000). Multinational enterprises, technology diffusion, and host country productivity growth. *Journal of Development Economics*, 62(2), 477–493.

Zhao, X., Ma, X., Shang, Y., Yang, Z., & Shahzad, U. (2022). Green economic growth and its inherent driving factors in Chinese cities: Based on the metafrontier-global-SBM super-efficiency DEA model. *Gondwana Research*, 106, 315–328.

6

THE EFFECT OF GOOD GOVERNANCE INDICATORS ON ECONOMIC GROWTH THROUGHOUT SELECTED ASIAN COUNTRIES

Promila Das and Manohar Giri

Introduction

Appropriate governance has been diagnosed as a critical factor in current economic progress. It is highly important to boost the country's competitiveness and keep the economy running smoothly. Governance is described as "the manner in which power is exercised in the management of a country's economic and social resources for development" (World Bank, 1991). Development organizations are growing ever more aware that effective governance is a means of influencing a variety of other goals, including economic development and growth, in addition to being a noble goal in and of itself (Gisselquist, 2012). In contrast, poor administration can prevent the economy from reaching its full potential. Corruption as a component of poor governance suggests that only a portion of resources are utilized in economic activity. As a result, the public cannot fully profit from the activities. Government spending on health, education, and infrastructure appears to not be used efficiently for reducing poverty and achieving broader development goals due to the negligible administrative capability inside the state and the inadequate citizen accountability from service providers (World Bank, 2004). "Good governance is the single most critical ingredient in reducing poverty and supporting development", as Kofi Annan, a former UN Secretary-General, declared (UNDP, 2002). Furthermore, excellent governance can foster long-term economic growth with high levels of productivity and innovation.

Governance factors like transparency, law and order, and preventing corruption can have a significant effect on economic growth. Good governance fosters a stable and predictable business environment, attracts foreign investment, and fosters entrepreneurship, all of which help to drive economic growth. On the other side, weak governance can lead to a loss of investor

DOI: 10.4324/9781003530688-8

confidence, resource misallocation, and a drop in entrepreneurship, resulting in slower economic growth. Thus, governance indicators are critical in influencing the economic expansion and development of the nation.

Since 1996, the World Bank's "Worldwide Governance Indicators" (WGI) have been periodically analysed for 215 nations across six governance aspects. The WGI (World Bank, 2022) is made up of six sub-indicators. These sub-indicators are classified as "Voice and Accountability", "Political Stability", "Government Effectiveness", "Regulatory Quality", "Rule of Law", and "Control of Corruption". These governance indicators seek to produce a quantitative assessment of governance performance to aid in the establishment of policy reforms and monitoring procedures. It is usually believed that an economy will grow faster if the Worldwide Governance Indicators (WGI), namely, low political instability, systems for voice and accountability, continued control of corruption, and the rule of law, are all trending in the right direction. The present study intends to investigate the effect of WGI indicators on economic growth using World Bank estimates for selected Asian countries, namely, Afghanistan, Bangladesh, China, India, Pakistan, and Sri Lanka from the year 2002 to 2021. Additionally, the study seeks to determine which of the WGI indicators contributes the most to economic growth. There are various factors behind the choice of the six Asian nations. Firstly, these nations have a wide range of governance structures, from authoritarian to democratic, making it possible to examine the relationship between governance and economic growth in a variety of contexts. For example, the federal democratic system of India and the centralized governance of China are very different. Secondly, taken as a whole, these nations account for a sizable share of the world's population and make major economic contributions. Analysing how governance affects economic growth might provide insights that are relevant to a wider context. Thirdly, the socioeconomic conditions of any nation vary, spanning from acute poverty to swift industrialization and technical progress. It is imperative that policymakers and economists comprehend the ways in which governance impacts growth in such heterogeneous situations. Lastly, a few of these countries—such as China, India, and Pakistan—have strong economic linkages with one another and significant geopolitical sway, which may have an effect on each other's rates of economic growth. Understanding regional dynamics can be gained by examining the interaction between their governance and growth.

Review of Literature

The Good Governance

Governance describes the broad involvement of institutions other than the government in political and decision-making processes. It covers how public organizations and leaders obtain and use authority to govern public policy and offer services and goods that are public (de Ferranti et al., 2009). The concept of governance was embraced and refined by a number of international businesses in the late 1980s to combat excess and waste in the administration of public monies. The World Bank has the power to determine which nations have effective governance due to its role in supplying them with the socioeconomic resources necessary for development. To prevent future corruption efforts from happening, governance helps fix any gaps in the system (Meteb, 2015). In this empirical investigation, governance is an explanatory variable that is not readily observable. Several proxies for governance are used by academics and researchers. Some used different comprehensive indices of good governance, such as the International Country Risk Handbook (Olson et al., 2000), WGI (Adedokun, 2017), and others adopted the governance quality sub-index, like government effectiveness in WGI (Kurtz & Schrank, 2007) and six sub-indices in WGI (Setayesh & Daryaei, 2017).

The level of government performance has a strong effect on growth of the economy (Rothstein & Teorell, 2008). Often used as a gauge to assess the effectiveness of governance are the Worldwide Governance Indicators (Absadykov, 2020). The World Governance Index (WGI) was created by Kaufmann et al. (1999b), and it consists of six fundamental aspects of governance, including a stable political environment and a lack of terrorism and violence, voice and accountability, effective government, high-quality regulations, anti-corruption measures, and the rule of law (Kaufmann et al., 2010). Several studies have used these indicators as regressors, including Kurtz and Schrank (2007) and Neumayer (2002). The WGI and per capita income have been compared, and Kaufmann and Kraay (2002) discovered that there is a correlation between the two that is favourable in all nations. Chauvet and Collier (2004) discover that bad governance in developing nations inhibits economic progress. A number of important institutions, including property rights that are clearly defined, fair enforcement contracts, little misinformation among consumers and sellers, and macroeconomic stability environment conditions, are necessary to ensure economic growth (North, 1991; Rodrick & Subramanian, 2003). Considering the aforementioned arguments, the present study evaluates the WGI as a gauge of the effectiveness of governance and investigates how it relates to the economic growth of the selected Asian countries.

WGI Affecting Economic Growth

The association between economic growth and governance has been extensively discussed in the literature. Singh (2022) looked at the connection between growth and the six governance measures using the panel cointegration method. He came to the conclusion that governance and development go hand in hand. Governance serves as a critical soft infrastructure for all economies in order to accomplish long-term economic growth and development. Due to its relationship to economic growth, governance has become a vital subject in any study of development (Gaghman, 2019). If an economy successfully integrates its microeconomic and institutional systems in order, its macroeconomic progress will probably be more consistent and profound (Brouwer, 2003). Governance is a wide and comprehensive notion and concentrates on how the administration exercises its authority to regulate various aspects of the economy and society (World Bank, 1994). The significance of the association between economic growth and governance was first explored in the early 1990s (World Bank, 1994; Perkins et al., 2006), and since then, it has almost become obvious (Kadhim, 2013). According to research (Kaufmann et al.,1999b, 1999a; Campos & Nugent, 1999), greater governance has a favourable effect on economic growth. Good governance promotes economic growth, according to the United Nations, the World Bank (Kaufmann and Kraay, 2002), and the International Monetary Fund (IMF). Governance boosts a nation's economic success and promotes wise policymaking (Rodrik, 2008).

Many researchers have conducted a number of studies that support the assertion that WGI is strongly correlated with economic growth. Nzama et al. (2023) used generalized quantile panel regression to explore the influence of government performance on financial and trade openness in 35 specialized countries worldwide. They discovered that the chosen nations would increase their efforts towards global integration through financial and trade opportunities if they had above-average governmental effectiveness, that is, if they had a well-established government bureaucracy and a substantially strong state heritage. Alam et al. (2017) examined how well the government performed in 81 low-income, middle-class, and high-income economies. They found a significant correlation between government effectiveness and economic growth, in both high- and low-income economies. Similar to how rising trade and capital flow are frequently associated with higher economic growth. For the trade-growth nexus, this has been repeated in a number of studies, which include but are not limited to Asada (2022), Nguyen and Bui (2021), Alam and Sumon (2020), Çevik et al. (2019), or Kouadio and Gakpa (2021), Estrada et al. (2015), and Agenor et al. (2018) for the financial services linkage.

Beyene (2022) investigated the impact of every government-related attribute on economic growth in 22 African countries by putting them all together to create a composite governance index. The result reveals that the composite governance index had a beneficial influence on economic growth considering the drawbacks of both corruption and ineffective government as a whole. Orji et al. (2022) found that decreasing corruption boosts economic growth in Nigeria. They discovered through the use of multivariate regression methods that increasing the rate of corruption prevention causes an increase in growth rates of 0.54% while holding other economic variables constant.

Radulovi (2020) investigated the impact of institutional quality on South-East European economic progress and compared these effects between EU (European Union) and non-EU countries from 1996 to 2017, employing World Governance Indicators (WGI) to evaluate the institutional quality and economic growth rate through the panel autoregressive distributed lag (ARDL) approach, and found that institutional quality and economic growth have a long-term relationship for all relevant variables in EU countries, whereas in non-EU countries only government effectiveness, political stability and lack of conflict, institutional quality, and voice and responsibility are significant statistically. Furthermore, the author discovered that in EU countries, institutional quality and economic expansion have no short-term correlation, whereas in SEE's non-EU countries, the significance of institutional quality, authority, and responsibility is higher.

Samarasinghe (2018) evaluated the effect of governance and institutional quality on economic growth in 145 countries from 2002 to 2014 using fixed effects and random effects panel regression models. The author discovered a 10% significant positive relationship between economic growth and political stability and the lack of violence, as well as a 5% significant positive association between economic growth and the reduction of corruption.

Han et al. (2014) looked at the possibility that development success might be predicted by governance metrics. They discovered that variables other than voice and accountability and the rule of law that had a positive impact on a country's prosperity were government effectiveness, political stability, corruption control, and regulatory quality. The author suggested that low-income nations try to improve regulatory quality, the rule of law, and government performance while lowering corruption. On the other hand, middle-income and high-income nations will benefit if political stability, accountability, and voice are improved.

According to Iqbal and Daly, the absence of the rule of law, insufficient political and public policies, and a lack of dependable infrastructure comprise a poor institutional environment that is incapable of fostering the growth and development of a market economy. They contended that while democracy is connected with economic growth in transition economies, lower levels of corruption are related to rapid economic growth in democratic countries (Iqbal & Daly, 2014).

According to North (1990), strong, efficient institutions can boost economic growth by reducing uncertainty. Economic growth and voice and accountability were found to have a negative correlation by Gani (2011), who also examined the relationship between these variables. Also, he demonstrated a negative correlation between the reduction of corruption and economic expansion in developing nations. He believed that the primary obstacles to economic growth were regulatory quality, the rule of law, and the voice and accountability of developing nations. Furthermore, since high levels of corruption degrade the effectiveness of institutions, these nations can increase economic growth by reducing corruption.

Shapkova and Disoska (2017) used panel regression analysis to examine the effects of institutions and trade on economic growth in Central and Eastern European and Western Balkan transition economies between 2000 and 2016. The findings revealed a favourable association between economic growth and the rule of law, corruption control, voice and accountability, and regulatory quality. According to estimates made on a large sample of 106 countries by d'Agostino et al. (2016), there were significant negative effects on economic growth from the relationships between corruption and military spending and corruption and investment. They were also robust across various corruption metrics, economic development levels, and country groups. This implies that measures aimed at reducing corruption, in conjunction with those aimed at reducing military burdens, such as regional security accords, would have a significant impact on economic growth.

Oanh et al. (2021) revealed that institutional quality significantly influences growth in 48 Asian countries, particularly in lower-income countries, using the quantile regression methodology. This finding is consistent with the findings of Fikadu et al. (2019), Abdullahi et al. (2019), and Dickson et al. (2021) on the favourable influence of institutional quality on the economic development of Africa. According to Fraj et al. (2018), there must be an interaction between the country's governance and other efficient economic channels for there to be a link between governance and growth. They came to the conclusion that government regulation hinders economic progress based on a sample of 50 nations. Yet when they thought about how governance and exchange rate flexibility interacted, they discovered that when exchange rates are flexible, governance is in favour of development. In other words, the exchange rate is an effective means by which the government affects economic expansion. In the same context, good governance will enable FDI to advance the process of economic development, according to Yahyaoui and Bouchoucha (2019).

Research Gap and Objectives

While many research works have looked at the connection between economic growth and good governance indicators in different settings (Kurtz & Schrank, 2007; Rodrik, 2008; Shapkova and Disoska, 2017; Beyene, 2022), there is still a dearth of studies that particularly address the complex effects of good governance indicators on growth within a particular group of Asian nations, viz., Afghanistan, Bangladesh, China, India, Pakistan, and Sri Lanka. Previous studies frequently take a broad approach, examining these variables globally or in certain regional contexts, omitting a thorough examination of the various socio-political environments and economic frameworks found in different Asian countries. Therefore, given their varied political, social, and economic characteristics, there is a research gap in thoroughly examining and comparing the various effects of good governance indicators on economic growth within a subset of selected Asian nations. A targeted investigation of the distinct governance elements and their differing effects on economic growth in the framework of varied Asian countries is necessary to fill this research gap and advance knowledge of the connection between governance and the growth of the economy in this area.

The primary aim of the study is to analyse the effect of Worldwide Governance Indicators (WGI) on economic growth (GDP) for six Asian countries, viz., Afghanistan, Bangladesh, China, India, Pakistan, and Sri Lanka. The main objectives of the study are as follows:

1. To explore the status of selected Asian countries on WGI indicators, namely, Political Stability, Government Effectiveness, and Regulatory Quality
2. To analyse the impact of WGI indicators on the economic growth of the selected six Asian countries

The study's dataset comprises the GDP and Worldwide Governance Indicators (WGI) at the country level for a subset of six Asian countries between 2002 and 2021.

Methodology

Data

Data for this study is gathered from the official website of the World Bank (WB). The dataset included in the study consists of Worldwide Governance Indicators (WGI) and the economic indicator (GDP) from 2002 to 2021 for six Asian countries, viz., Afghanistan, Bangladesh, China, India, Pakistan, and Sri Lanka. The data points provide country-level statistics for the selected period 2002–2021.

Model

Panel regression is used for the present study to see the effect of Worldwide Governance Indicators on economic growth (GDP) for the selected six Asian countries. Panel data is made up of data collected for the same entities monitored throughout time. Panel models can be used to mitigate the effects of entity- and time-specific properties in order to prevent omitted variable bias when estimating the effect of independent variables on the dependent variable. It is described as follows:

$$Y_{it} = \alpha_{it} + \beta_{it}X_{kit} + \varepsilon_{it}$$

where Y_{it} denotes the dependent variable for the ith entity measured at time t; X_{kit} are the values of the kth independent variables for the ith entity at time t; ε_{it} is the error term.

Dependent Variables

Several proxies were considered for measuring the economic growth, such as wholesale price index (WPI), gross domestic product (GDP), consumer price index (CPI), and inflation. WPI, CPI, GDP, and inflation are all related to the economic growth of a country. In this study, GDP (at current US dollars) was chosen as the dependent variable since economic growth is the method of steadily bettering a nation's financial situation, particularly through an increase in the economy's physical output of goods and services (Andesta et al., 2022). Economic growth is measured using a variety of macroeconomic variables. The World Bank (2004) chooses to quantify yearly economic growth as a percentage increase in the GDP or gross national product (GNP). According to a number of studies, both the direct and indirect methods of government governance have an impact on economic growth. Economic growth is frequently measured using annual real GDP per capita. Lahouij (2017), for example, used GDP per capita calculated using constant US dollars from 2005 to determine economic growth. Many studies employ PPP-adjusted GDP per capita (Harttgen et al., 2012; Islam, 1998; Wong et al., 2005), while some researchers use GDP per capita (e.g., Fayissa & Nsiah, 2013; Al Mamun et al., 2017); others use GDP growth rate.

Independent Variables

The Worldwide Governance Indicators measure six different areas of governance, including voice and accountability, political stability, government effectiveness, regulatory quality, rule of law, and corruption control. Data was collected by the World Bank for over 200 countries between 1996 and 2021. The value of these indicators across each dimension ranges between –2.5 and +2.5.

In the present study, we used three WGI dimensions, namely, Political Stability, Government Effectiveness, and Regulatory Quality, as independent variables. Many studies used both Political Stability and Government Effectiveness as independent variables. Zhuo et al. (2021) used data collection from 31 nations from 2002 to 2018 and GMM and system GMM approaches. Using the ARDL model, according to Kesar and Jena (2022), the political stability of the BRICS countries between 2002 and 2018 had a positive impact on growth. Government efficacy has been studied extensively in academic literature for a long time, and it has been defined from a variety of angles (see Moynihan and Pandey, 2004; Acemoglu et al., 2010; Brewer et al., 2007; Lee & Whitford, 2009; Acemoglu & Robinson, 2012, Garcia-Sanchez et al., 2013; Garcia-Sanchez et al., 2016; Montes and Paschoal, 2016). The Predictors are explained below:

Political Stability (PS)[1]: The likelihood that the government would not be dethroned or destabilized through violent or illegal means like terrorism and acts of political terrorism.

Government Effectiveness (GE)[1]: The legitimacy of the government, the standard of public services, the performance and level of independence of the resilience of the civil service to political pressure, and the efficiency of creating and carrying out strategies.

Regulatory Quality (RQ)[1]: The effectiveness of the government in formulating and implementing regulations and policies that promote the growth of the private sector.

Results and Discussion

Descriptive statistics for selected worldwide growth indicators and GDP are provided in Table 6.1. The lowest value for Political stability was observed for Pakistan (–2.41) while China recorded the highest value (–0.23) for political stability during the study period. The mean value for this indicator varies between –0.464 (China) and –2.385 (Afghanistan). The mean value for Government's effectiveness ranges between –1.403 (Afghanistan) and –0.2095 (China) indicating the Afghanistan government was least effective while China Government was most effective during the study period. The mean value for regulatory quality was observed lowest for Afghanistan and highest for China indicating that China has the most effective regulatory control while Afghanistan has the least effective. The average value for GDP indicates that China has the highest GDP among the selected Asian countries followed by India, Sri Lanka, Bangladesh, Pakistan, and Afghanistan.

Panel Data Models for Economic Growth

We create several regression models, such as fixed effect, random effect, and pooled regression models. Several tests were conducted to see the appropriate model to be used for the study. The results of these tests are summarized in Table 6.2. The Hausman test can be used to differentiate between a fixed effects model and a random effects model in a panel study. Fixed effects (FE)

TABLE 6.1 Descriptive Statistics for GDP and WGI across Selected Asian Countries

Political Stability

Countries	Mean	Min	Max	Std.
Afghanistan	−2.385	−2.46	−2.04	0.22
Bangladesh	−1.2885	−1.86	−0.9	0.27
China	−0.464	−0.66	−0.23	0.12
India	−1.084	−1.51	−0.62	0.23
Pakistan	−2.236	−2.41	−1.55	0.41
Sri Lanka	−0.7075	−1.8	−0.09	0.56

Government's Effectiveness

Afghanistan	−1.403	−1.63	−0.91	0.17
Bangladesh	−0.771	−0.94	−0.63	0.07
China	0.2095	−0.16	0.84	0.29
India	0.016	−0.23	0.41	0.18
Pakistan	−0.631	−0.83	−0.38	0.14
Sri Lanka	−0.138	−0.44	0.07	0.12

Regulatory Quality

Afghanistan	−0.903	−1.43	−0.73	0.23
Bangladesh	−0.511	−0.64	−0.41	0.15
China	0.173	−0.27	0.63	0.34
India	0.094	−0.13	0.27	0.26
Pakistan	−0.47	−0.67	−0.36	0.21
Sri Lanka	−0.098	−0.246	0.098	0.31

GDP ($ Million)

Afghanistan	14,162.16	3,854.24	20,564.5	5,989.19
Bangladesh	1,75,598.8	54,724.08	4,16,265	1,14,849.3
China	80,39,467	14,70,550	1,77,34,062	49,20,009
India	17,50,021.06	5,14,937.95	31,76,295.07	7,90,214.44
Pakistan	60,278.86	16,536.54	94,493.85	28,225.95
Sri Lanka	2,18,359.7	79,904.99	3,56,128.22	88,029.07

Source: Authors' calculation.

are preferred under the null hypothesis because they are at minimum as reliable as random effects (RE), whereas RE are preferred under the alternative because they are more potent.

The Hausman test presented in Table 6.2 indicates that the fixed effect model is better than the random effects model for this sample study.

Results for the fixed effect panel regression model is presented in Table 6.3. Results indicate that political stability and government effectiveness and regulatory quality all have positive and statistically significant effects on GDP. The results suggest that political stability, government effectiveness, and

TABLE 6.2 Tests Conducted for Selection of Models

Test	Null vs. Alternate Hypothesis	Test Statistics from Our Data	Conclusion
F test for fixed effects versus OLS	Null: No fixed effect	$F = 31.994$	Reject null hypothesis
	Alternative: Fixed effect is better	$df1 = 5$, $df2 = 117$,	Fixed effect model better than OLS model
		P-value < 0.000	
Hausman test for fixed versus random effects model	Null: Random effect exists	Chi square 8.236, $df = 3$	Reject null hypothesis
	Alternate: Fixed effects models are better	P-value = 0.016	Fixed effect model better than random effect model

Source: Authors' calculation.

regulatory quality all are important determinants of economic growth among selected Asian countries. This implies that countries that are politically stable with effective governments and greater regulatory quality experience faster growth in their economy.

Government effectiveness is thought to be a most significant factor in determining a country's economic growth followed by regulatory quality and political stability, as evidenced by the fact that the estimated impact size for GE is bigger than the estimated effect size for RQ and PS. It differs slightly from the results found in the literature (Samarasinghe, 2018; Gani, 2011; Iqbal & Daly, 2014); this could be because only six countries are examined in the study. Adjusted R-squared and F-statistics suggest that the estimated model has a good fit.

The research findings make a substantial contribution to the knowledge of how governance parameters affect the economic growth paths of different countries in the study area. The important points are listed below.

Firstly, the study probably shows a significant positive correlation between economic growth and good governance measures in the Asian countries that were chosen. Stronger and more sustained economic growth is typically seen in nations with better degrees of political stability, rule of law, transparency, and other governance-related characteristics. The literature listed in the review section is supported by these findings (Oanh et al., 2021; Fikadu et al., 2019; Abdullahi et al., 2019; Dickson et al., 2021).

Secondly, although there is a generally positive association, it is likely that different Asian countries have differing effects of particular governance measures on economic growth. Different historical contexts, institutional frameworks, cultural influences, and government policies can all have an impact on

TABLE 6.3 Economic Growth and Worldwide Growth Indicators (Fixed Effect Models)

Predictors	Estimate	t-Value	Pr(>|t|)	Significance
PS (political stability)	0.47828	2.4936	0.014	**
GE (government effectiveness)	1.3929	4.271	0	***
Regulatory quality (RQ)	0.7432	3.635	0	***
Total sum of squares:	43.685			
Residual sum of squares:	37.048			
R-squared:	0.653			
Adj. R-squared:	0.603			
F-statistic:	10.032 on 3 and 111 DF			
p-value:	9.82E–05			

Source: Authors' calculations.

how much governance indices influence a nation's economic success. For example, in one country, political stability may have a significant influence, but in another corruption control may become a crucial component.

Conclusion

Effective governance is essential for every country's development since it can contribute favourably to economic growth. In the study, the relationship between three measures of good governance given by Worldwide Governance Indicators and economic growth has been explored. The results show that China was the most politically stable country, while Afghanistan had the most chaotic political situation. Of the selected Asian nations, China has the greatest GDP, followed by India, Sri Lanka, Bangladesh, Pakistan, and Afghanistan. Findings show that political stability, government effectiveness, and regulatory quality all have positive and statistically significant effects on GDP. The findings also imply that within a small group of Asian countries, political stability and governmental performance and regulatory quality play significant roles in determining economic growth. Furthermore, it is revealed that government effectiveness—rather than political stability and regulatory quality—is the significant predictor of a country's economic growth.

Governments should broaden their focus from merely considering economic factors to including political and economic factors that influence economic growth. They should do all possible efforts to improve economic growth and achieve good governance. A series of political actions may be necessary; the following are our recommendations:

Governments ought to implement a rigid anti-corruption strategy. Lack of corruption will boost investor and consumer confidence as well as institutional effectiveness in society. As a result, lawmakers must adopt proactive measures to combat corruption, such as raising wages. Governments should ensure political stability to improve the environment for investment. People may spend more because of the political unrest because they fear that their savings would lose all of their value, which would cause saving rates to fall. On the other hand, when political uncertainty grew, investors' appetite for fixed capital also decreased. Political instability consequently has a detrimental impact on investment and savings, two key factors that promote economic growth.

Lastly, it is crucial to stress the value of regional cooperation in advancing good governance. The economic growth of neighbouring nations will undoubtedly be aided by the reduction of political tensions in any area because doing so will promote investment and prosperity in those nations.

Note

1   https://info.worldbank.org/governance/wgi/Home/Documents

References

Abdullahi, S., Rusmawati, S., Normaz, W. & Nur, S. M. (2019). Public debt, institutional quality, and economic growth in sub-Saharan Africa. *Institutions and Economies*, 11(3), 39–64.

Absadykov, A. (2020). Does good governance matter? Kazakhstan's economic growth and worldwide governance indicators. *Otoritas: Jurnal Ilmu Pemerintahan*, 10(1), 1–13. doi:10.26618/ojip.v10i1.2776

Acemoglu, Daron, Egorov, Georgy, & Sonin, Konstantin. (2010). Political selection and persistence of bad governments. *The Quarterly Journal of Economics*, 125, 1511–1575.

Acemoglu, Daron, & James Robinson. (2012). *Why Nations Fail: The Origins of Power, Prosperity and Poverty*. New York: Crown Publishers.

Adedokun, A. J. (2017). Foreign aid, governance and economic growth in Sub-Saharan Africa: Does one cap fit all?. *African Development Review*, 29(2), 184–196. doi:10.1111/1467-8268.12249

Agenor, Pierre-A., Leanardo, G., Enisse, K., & da Luiz, S. (2018). The effects of prudential regulation, financial development, financial openness on economic growth. Bank for International Settlement Working Paper No. 752. Available online: https://ssrn.com/abstract=3302300

Al Mamun, M., Sohag, M. K., & Hassan, M. K. (2017). Governance, resources and growth. *Economic Modelling*, 63(C), 238–261. doi:10.1016/j.econmod.2017.02.015

Alam, Khandaker Jahangir, & Khairul Kabir Sumon. (2020). Causal relationship between trade openness and economic growth: A panel data analysis of Asian countries. *International Journal of Economics and Financial Issues*, 10, 118–126.

Alam, Md R., Erick K, and Bizuayehu Getachew B. (2017). Government effectiveness and economic growth. *Economic Bulletin*, 37, 222–227. Available online: www.accessecon.com/Pubs/EB/2017/Vomule37/EB-17-V37-I3-P21

Andesta, H. Y., Gunarto, T., & Aida, N. (2022). Influence of good governance on ASEAN economic growth. *International Journal of Economics, Business and Entrepreneurship*, 5(2), 16–23. doi:10.23960/ijebe.v5i2.196

Asada, H. (2022). Effects of foreign direct investment, trade openness, and human capital development on the economic growth of Thailand. *International Journal of Asian Business and Information Management*, 13, 89.

Beyene, A. B. (2022). Governance quality and economic growth in sub-Saharan Africa: The dynamic panel model. *Journal of Economic and Administrative Sciences*. doi:10.1108/JEAS-08-2021-0156

Brewer, Gene, Choi, Yujin, & Walker, Richard. (2007). Accountability, corruption and government effectiveness in Asia: An exploration of World Bank governance indicators. *International Public Management Review*, 8, 204–225.

Brouwer, G. (2003). Macroeconomics and governance. Commonwealth of Australia, Treasury Working Paper.

Çevik, E. İ., Atukeren, E., & Korkmaz, T. (2019). Trade openness and economic growth in Turkey: A rolling frequency domain analysis. *Economies*, 7(2), 41.

Campos, N. F., & Nugent, J. B. (1999). Development performance and the institutions of governance: Evidence from East Asia and Latin America. *World Development*, 27(3), 439–452. doi:10.1016/S0305-750X(98)00149-1

Chauvet, L., & Collier, P. (2004). *Development Effectiveness in Fragile States: Spillovers and Turnarounds*. Centre for the Study of African Economies, Department of Economics, Oxford University (Mimeo). Retrieved from https://inee.org/sites/default/files/resources/doc_1_Development_Effectiveness_in_FS.pdf

d'Agostino, G., Dunne, J. P., & Pieroni, L. (2016). Government spending, corruption and economic growth. *World Development*, 84, 190–205.

de Ferranti, D. M., Jacinto, J., Ody, A., & Ramshaw, G. (2009). *How to Improve Governance: A New Framework for Analysis and Action*. Brookings Institution Press. www.brookings.edu

Dickson, O. W., Masai, W. & Samuel, M. N. (2021). Institutional quality and economic growth: Evidence from sub-Saharan Africa countries. *African Journal of Economic Review*, 9(4), 106–125.

Estrada, G., Donghyun P., & Arief R. (2015). Financial development, financial openness, and economic growth. Asian Development Bank Economics Working Paper Series No. 442. SSRN 45p

Fayissa, B., & Nsiah, C. (2013). The impact of governance on economic growth in Africa. *The Journal of Developing Areas*, 47(1), 91–108.

Fikadu, A., Wondaferahu, M. & Tesfaye, M. (2019). Impact of institutional quality on economic performance of Eastern Africa: A panel data analysis. *Jurnal Perspektif Pembiayaan Dan Pembangunan Daerah*, 7(2), 169–182.

Fraj, S., Hamdaoui, M. & Maktouf, S. (2018). Governance and economic growth: The role of the exchange rate regime. *International Economics*, 156, 326–364.

Gaghman, A. (2019). The Importance of good governance on achieving sustainable development case study: Yemen. In *Economies of the Balkan and Eastern European Countries (EBEEC 2019)* (pp. 170–192).

Gani, A. (2011). Governance and growth in developing countries. *Journal of Economic Issues*, 45(1), 19–40.

Garcia-Sanchez, María I., Cuadrado-Ballesteros, B, & Frias-Aceituno, J-V. (2013). Determinants of government effectiveness. *International Journal of Public Administration*, 36, 567–577.

Garcia-Sanchez, María I., Cuadrado-Ballesteros, B. & Frias-Aceituno, J-V. (2016). Does media freedom improve government effectiveness? A comparative cross-country analysis. *European Journal of Law and Economics*, 42, 515–537.

Gisselquist, R. (2012). Good governance as a concept, and why this matters for development policy. UNU-WIDER Working Paper 2012/30.

Han, X., Khan, H. & Zhuang, J. (2014). Do governance indicators explain development performance? A cross-country analysis. ADB Economics Working Paper Series. Mandaluyong: Asian Development Bank.

Harttgen, K., Klasen, S., & Vollmer, S. (2012). Economic growth and child undernutrition in Africa. United Nation Development Program (Working Paper No. 2012-013), UNDP. Retrieved From. Oct- 30- 2012 http://web.undp.org/africa/knowledge/WP-2012-013-Harttgen-klassen-economicgrowth-undernutrition.pdf

Iqbal, N. & Daly, V. (2014). Rent-seeking opportunities and economic growth in transitional economies. *Economic Modelling*, 37, 16–22.

Islam, M. (1998). Export expansion and economic growth: Testing for cointegration and causality. *Applied Economics*, 30(3), 415–425. doi:10.1080/000368498325930

Kadhim, A. (Ed). (2013). *Governance in the Middle East and North Africa: A Handbook*, Routledge. Books.google.com

Kaufmann, D., & Kraay, A. (2002), Growth without governance. Policy Research Working Paper No. 2928, World Bank: Washington DC, USA.

Kaufmann, D., Kraay, A., & Mastruzzi, M. (2010). The Worldwide Governance Indicators: Methodology and Analytical Issues. Draft Policy Research Working Paper: The World Bank.

Kaufmann, D., Kraay, A., & Zoido-Lobatan, P. (1999b). Governance matters. Policy Research Working Paper No. 2196, World Bank: Washington, DC, USA.

Kaufmann, D., Kraay, A., & Zoido-Lobaton, P. (1999a). Aggregating governance indicators. Policy Research Working Paper No. 2195, World Bank: Washington, DC, USA.

Kesar, A., & Jena, P. K. (2022). Corruption and economic growth: Empirical evidence from BRICS nations. *Studies in International Economics and Finance* (pp. 183–202). Springer. doi:10.1007/978-981-16-7062-6_10

Kouadio, Hugues Kouassi, & Landry Lewis Gakpa. 2021. Financial openness and economic growth in Côte D'ivoire: The total factor productivity channel. *International Journal of Financial Research*, 12, 138–149.

Kurtz, M. J., & Schrank, A. (2007). Growth and governance: Models, measures and mechanisms. *The Journal of Politics*, 69(2), 538–554. doi:10.1111/j.1468-2508.2007.00549.x

Lahouij, H. (2017). Governance and economic growth in developing economies: A comparative study. Masters Theses. Eastern Illinois University. 2724. https://thekeep.eiu.edu/theses/2724

Lee, Soo-Young, & Whitford, Andrew B. (2009). Government effectiveness in comparative perspective. *Journal of Comparative Policy Analysis*, 11, 249–281. Available online: https://www.tandfonline.com/doi/abs/10.1080/13876980902888111

Meteb, A. M. (2015). The importance of corporate governance in Saudi Arabia economy. *Journal of WEI Business and Economics*, 4(1), 14–27. http://westeastinstitute.com/journals/wp-content/uploads/2015/05/2.Alotaibi-Mohamed-Meteb.pdf

Montes, Gabriel Caldas, & Paschoal, P. (2016). Corruption: What are the effects on government effectiveness? Empirical evidence considering developed and developing countries. *Applied Economics Letters*, 23, 146–150. Available online: https://www.tandfonline.com/doi/abs/10.1080/13504851.2015.1058900?journalCode=rael20

Moynihan, Donald P., & Pandey, Sanjay K. (2004). Testing how management matters in an era of government by performance management. *Journal of Public Administration Research and Theory*, 15, 421–439.

Neumayer, E. (2002). Do democracies exhibit stronger international environmental commitment? A cross-country analysis. *Journal of Peace Research*, 39(2), 139–164. doi:10.1177/0022343302039002001

Nguyen, M. L. T., & Bui, T. N. (2021). Trade openness and economic growth: A study on asean-6. *Economies*, 9(3), 1–15.

North, D. (1990). *Institutions, Institutional Change, and Economic Performance*. Cambridge: Cambridge University Press.

North, D. C. (1991). Institutions. *The Journal of Economic Perspectives*, 5(1), 97–112. doi:10.1257/jep.5.1.97

Nzama, L., Sithole, T., & Kahyaoglu, S. B. (2023). The impact of government effectiveness on trade and financial openness: The generalized quantile panel regression approach. *Journal of Risk and Financial Management*, 16(1), 14.

Oanh, K. T., Hac, D. L. and Anh, H. N. (2021). Role of institutional quality in economic development: A case study of Asian countries. *Problems and Perspectives in Management*, 19 (2), 357–369.

Olson, M., Sarna, J. N., & Swamy, A. V. (2000). Governance and growth: A simple hypothesis explaining cross-country differences in productivity growth. *Public Choice*, 102(3–4), 341–364. doi:10.1023/A:1005067115159

Orji, A., Ogbuabor, J. E., Dunu, O. U., Mba, P. N. and Anthony-Orji, O. I. (2022). Corruption and population increase in Nigeria: Analysis of their impact on selected macroeconomic variables. *Journal of Xi'an Shiyou University, Natural Science Edition*, 18(2), 313–332.

Perkins, Dwight Heald, Radelet, Steven C., Lindauer, David L., & Block, Steven A. (2006). *Economics of Development*. New York: WW Norton & Company.

Radulović, M. (2020). The impact of institutional quality on economic growth: A comparative analysis of the EU and non-EU countries of Southeast Europe. *Economic Annals*, 65(225), 163–181.

Rodrick, D., & Subramanian, A. (2003). The primacy of institutions (and what this does and does not mean). *Finance and Development*, 40(2), 31–34. https://www.imf.org/external/pubs/ft/fandd/2003/06/pdf/rodrik.pdf

Rodrik, D. (2008). Thinking about Governance. In D. North, D. Acemoglu, F. Fukuyama & D. Rodrik (Ed.), *Governance, Growth and Development Decision-Making* (pp. 17–24). World Bank. Retrieved from https://documents1.worldbank.org/curated/en/373891468314694298/pdf/441860WP0REPLA1rnanceandgrowth0test.pdf

Rothstein, B., & Teorell, J. (2008). What is quality of government: A theory of impartial government institutions. *Governance: An International Journal of Policy, Administration and Institutions*, 21(2), 165–190. doi:10.1111/j.1468-0491.2008.00391.x

Samarasinghe, T. (2018). Impact of governance on economic growth. MPRA Paper No. 89834. Munich: Munich Personal RePEc Archive.

Setayesh, M. H., & Daryaei, A. A. (2017). Good governance, innovation, economic growth and the stock market turnover rate. *The Journal of International Trade & Economic Development*, 26(7), 829–850. doi:10.1080/09638199.2017.1334809

Shapkova, K. K. & Disoska, E. M. (2017). Influence of trade and institutions on economic growth in transitional economies: Evidences from countries from Central and Eastern Europe and Western Balkans. *Economic Analysis*, 50(3–4), 32–42.

Singh, B. P. (2022). Does governance matter? Evidence from BRICS. *Global Business Review*. 23(2), 408–425.

UNDP (United Nations Development Programme) (2002). Human Development Report 2002: Deepening Democracy in a Fragmented World. New York.

Wong, P., Ho, P., & Autio, E. (2005). Entrepreneurship, innovation and economic growth: Evidence from GEM data. *Small Business Economics*, 24(3), 335–350. doi:10.1007/s11187-005-2000-1

World Bank. (1991). Managing development: The governance dimension. World Bank Discussion Paper No. 34899. Washington, DC.

World Bank. (1994). *Governance - the World Bank's experience (English). Development in practice Washington, D.C.: World Bank Group*. http://documents. worldbank.org/curated/en/711471468765285964/Governance-the-World-Banks-experience

World Bank. (2004). *Beyond Economic Growth* An Introduction to Sustainable Development Retrieved from https://documents1.worldbank.org/curated/pt/454041468780615049/pdf/2489402nd0edition0Beyond0economic0growth.pdf

World Bank. (2022). Global Financial Development Development Report 2019/2020: Bank Regulation and Supervision a Decade after the Global Financial Crisis.

Yahyaoui, I. and Bouchoucha, N. (2019). Foreign direct investment and economic growth: The role of the governance. *Economics Bulletin*, 39(4), 2711–2725.

Zhuo, Z. O. A., Muhammad, B. and Khan, S. (2021). Underlying the relationship between governance and economic growth in developed countries. *Journal of the Knowledge Economy*, 12, 1314–1330.

7

DOES GOVERNANCE EXPLAIN GROWTH? AN EMPIRICAL ANALYSIS ON AFRICAN COUNTRIES

Catia Cialani, Alemu Tulu Chala, and Reza Mortazavi

1 Introduction

The issue of whether good governance influences economic growth is still widely investigated by scholars. The literature is very vast in the field, and it shows that differences in economic growth across countries depend in the long run on different institutional measures, for example, corruption, rules of law, and policy effectiveness which are generally used as proxy indicators for governance. There is no unique definition of the concept of governance. However, one that is well accepted and commonly used is the World Bank's (2017) definition which defines governance as "the process through which state and nonstate actors interact to design and implement policies within a given set of formal and informal rules that shape and are shaped by power". Six different indicators, namely, political stability and absence of violence/ terrorism, voice and accountability, government effectiveness, regulatory quality, control of corruption, and the rule of law, are produced by the World Bank (*Worldwide Governance Indicators (WGI)*, 2023). All these governance indicators can influence the economic outcome of a country in different ways. Good governance creates the foundations to increase the productivity of human capital and attract investments. Additionally, good governance plays an important role in the implementation of successful economic policies as already confirmed by studies carried out by Acemoglu et al. (2005), Kaufmann and Kraay (2002), and Dixit (2009). Because governance can play a key role in the economic development of a country, many studies have investigated empirically this research question focusing largely on developing countries. Also, the vast empirical literature seems to be concentrated principally in the African continent because of the poor economic performance.

DOI: 10.4324/9781003530688-9

The findings of previous most relevant works by Ahlerup et al. (2016), Ganau (2017), Salawu et al. (2018), Erdogan and Acaravci (2022), Feyisa et al. (2022), and Hussen (2023) have confirmed the importance of good institutions to facilitate economic growth in different areas and more even distribution of income within African countries.

The present work explores the impact of governance quality on per capita GDP growth for 45 African countries using World Bank data and the definition of governance and different proxy indicators as explained above. In addition to WGI, our study also considers a range of other variables, including educational enrolment, trade openness, gross capital, foreign direct investment (FDI), and government expenditure for the period 2002–2021. Our data provide a good source of information to test the possible influence of governance and institutional quality on the economic development of African countries. We estimate a dynamic panel model using a system of Generalized Method of Moments (GMM).

The results of our study contribute to the current literature to explain the association between governance and economic growth in Africa. Our findings, using more recent data, contribute to suggest to policymakers in African countries reforms on governance factors that can have adverse effects on economic growth. Previous studies have focused more on sub-Saharan countries or specific geographical areas of Africa. Hopefully, our analysis can provide a more comprehensive picture of the African continent.

The remaining sections of this chapter are organized as follows: Section 2 discusses the literature review, Section 3 presents the data and methodology used, Section 4 presents and discusses the results, and Section 5 concludes the study.

2   A Review of Selected Literature

This section provides an overview of the literature on how quality of governance has influenced economic performance. Since the literature in this field is very extensive, we will focus mainly on selected studies that have investigated how governance has influenced economic growth in African countries in the most recent times. During our analysis, we noticed that most of the literature seems to be mainly focused on sub-Saharan African countries. One explanation is that sub-Saharan African countries have a history of political and government instability, lack of laws, and serious problems of corruption that can be defined as bad governance (Fayissa and Nsiah, 2013). In addition, the sub-Saharan African countries are classified as the economies in the world with the lowest per capita income and the lowest institutional quality (Kebede and Takyi, 2017). Moreover, sub-Saharan African countries are characterized by a huge variety of ethnic diversity. In fact, there are over 2000 ethnic groups in Africa with their own languages, religious beliefs, and their own traditions and culture (Fosu et al., 2006). For the above reasons, African countries continue to appear in the majority of empirical studies on this topic.

The importance of good government in Africa was investigated by Fayissa and Nsiah (2013) for the period 1995–2004, employing GMM procedure for a sample of 39 sub-Saharan African countries. Their analysis, based on the World Bank governance indicators, showed that good governance significantly improves economic growth. Das et al. (2013) and Das and Das (2014) examined the interrelationships between governance indicators and economic growth, and economic confidence across some countries and regions and found some favourable impacts of good governance practices upon economic growth. Akinlo (2016) investigated the association of institutions and economic growth using Pooled OLS and GMM methods of estimation over the period 1986–2013 from 32 sub-Saharan African countries. The results of this study suggest that institutions, physical capital, and interest have a negative impact on economic growth, while human capital and money supply have a positive impact on economic growth. Using annual panel data from 27 sub-Saharan African countries for the period spanning 1996–2014, Kebede and Takyi (2017) apply a system GMM technique. Their results suggest that there is a unidirectional causality from economic growth to institutional quality. Furthermore, their findings show that trade openness, financial development, and debt are positively related to economic growth.

A comparable research question was investigated by Abdullahi et al. (2019) who examined the effect of public debts and the quality of institutions on the economic growth in 46 African countries during 2000–2014. These authors also used the GMM method, and their findings show that the institutional quality has both a direct and indirect impact on economic growth. They also found that the role of policy effectiveness, control of corruption, and regulatory quality can alleviate the negative impact of public debt on economic growth in sub-Saharan Africa.

Afolabi (2019) also used a panel data approach to examine the impact of governance on economic development in West Africa from 2002 to 2016 for 15 countries. He found that voice and accountability, political stability, government effectiveness, and the rule of law all have a positive impact on economic development, whereas regulatory quality and corruption control indices have a negative impact on short-term growth and have a positive impact on development in the long run. Similarly, Dickson et al. (2021) employed a two-step GMM estimation procedure to explore the effect of governance on the economic growth of 35 sub-Saharan African countries from 2006 to 2018. The findings of their work show that an improvement in the quality of the governance, expressed by the following indicators: government effectiveness, political stability and absence of violence, rule of law, voice and accountability, control of corruption, and regulatory quality, can improve the economic performance of the sub-Saharan African countries.

Using fixed effects and System GMM methods, a study by Fikadu et al. (2019) tested the impact of institutional quality on the economic performance of 14 Eastern African countries using panel data between 2005 and 2016. Based on their findings, the improvement of control of corruption and quality of government effectiveness play the most relevant role in a good economic performance. In addition, trade openness has also a significant positive effect on economic growth. Further studies carried out on sub-Saharan African countries by Salawu et al. (2018) and Adzima and Baita (2019) also found that "governance effectiveness" influences economic growth.

A paper from Ganau (2017) employs spatial econometric tools to examine the relationship between institutional factors and economic growth in Africa, using data for 50 African countries covering the period 1981–2001. The author uses three indices: (1) a democracy index to proxy for the level of democracy in a country, (2) a measure of legislative effectiveness to proxy for political and institutional quality and political effectiveness, and (3) number of government crises to proxy for political and regime instability. His results suggest that institutions may play a role in explaining short-run growth processes and that short-run economic growth is positively affected both by the high quality of national institutional settings and by institutional factors of neighbouring countries. His analysis also reveals that the low level of democracy has a negative effect on the economic growth of a country. In addition, it also seemed that the economic growth of a country is positively influenced by the level of democracy of the neighbouring countries and negatively by their level of the political instability. Feyisa et al. (2022) studied the impact of governance on economic growth in sub-Saharan Africa from 2005 to 2019 for 34 countries using the principal component analysis (PCA) method and the fixed and random effects estimations. The authors have found that corruption, government effectiveness, regulatory quality, and rule of law are positively associated with per capita GDP growth.

The study of Ekpo (2021) uses several governance indicators to investigate the relationship between the impact of the governments on the economic growth for 47 sub-Saharan African countries from 1980 to 2018. The findings of the paper show that lack of democracy, unemployment, and corruption negatively influence economic growth while private investment has a positive relationship with growth. Moreover, the author also finds that "political stability and voice and accountability" have a positive relationship with economic growth, while the rule of law, regulatory quality, and government effectiveness are negatively associated with economic growth.

Beyene (2021) has analysed the role of governance quality in influencing the economic growth of 22 selected sub-Saharan African Countries from 2002 to 2020 using GMM. The outcome of Beyene (2021) has confirmed that the composite governance index, constructed by PCA, is positively related to the economic growth of the selected countries. The author also found that corruption control and government effectiveness instead have a negative significant relationship with economic performance while other governance indicators, such as the rule of law and regulatory quality, exhibited a positive significant effect. Erdogan and Acaravci (2022) use a holistic approach to investigate the institutional and economic determinants of the economic development in 17 Saharan African countries for the period from 1990 to 2016. Their results show that democracy, peace, market size, and population growth have a positive and statistically significant impact on economic development, whereas foreign direct investment (FDI) has a negative one.

A more recent work, published by Hussen (2023), has used PCA and GMM estimation techniques to explore the impact of different institutional quality indices on the economic growth of 31 sub-Saharan African countries from 1991 to 2015. The author's findings show that there is a nexus between governance and economic growth; however, it differs across clusters of countries.

Although there are many studies that support the positive relationship between good governance and economic growth, there are almost no studies which found opposite results. A paper published by Sachs et al. (2004) found that slow economic growth for African countries cannot be accounted only for bad governance. Using a sample of 33 countries for the period from 1980 to 2001, the authors investigate the relationship between a set of World Bank governance indicators proposed by Kaufmann et al. (2003) along with some dummy variables and GDP per capita. The findings of their regressions suggest that even if countries have improved their governance, this has not helped them to improve their economic growth. The authors argue that some African countries are too poor to improve the economic situation and the well-being of their population even after establishing a democracy for a long time. The policy reforms were not sufficient to overcome the poverty trap and the inflows of foreign direct investments were not effective because of poor human capital and insufficient infrastructure across African countries.

We are aware that we have not probably covered all existing literature dealing with this topic; however, we can draw the conclusion that there is a strong relationship between the quality of the governance and the economic performance in the African countries.

3   Empirical Methodology

Our empirical model is based on the economic growth models originally developed by Solow (1956) and Swan (1956) and completed by Cass (1965) and Koopmans (1965) which are formalized by the traditional neoclassical production function. Economic growth is explained by a variety of variables (for example, physical and human capital, trade, among others) that have been introduced according to the evolution of the economic growth model. We introduce in our empirical model the common explanatory variables adopted in literature and described in Section 3.1.

3.1 Data

To investigate the impact of governance on economic growth, we use panel data from 45 African countries for the period from 2002 to 2021. The choice of the countries included in the sample is determined by the availability of data, and the list of countries is given in Appendix 7.1. The data used in the study are retrieved from the World Bank database. The Worldwide Governance Indicators (WGI) provide data on the six governance indicators ((1) Voice and Accountability; (2) Control of Corruption; (3) Government Effectiveness; (4) Political Stability and Absence of Violence/Terrorism; (5) Regulatory Quality; (6) Rule of Law) while the World Development Indicators provide the rest of the data. Below, we provide all definitions of the variables used in this study.

3.1.1 Dependent Variable

Our primary objective is to investigate how good governance affects economic growth. To this aim, we use the change in the natural log of gross domestic product (GDP) per capita, measured at purchasing power parity (PPP), in the current international dollar to measure growth. In the empirical literature, percentage change in GDP per capita is commonly used as a measure of economic growth (see, for example, Forbes (2000)).

3.1.2 Explanatory Variables

We include several traditional sources of growth as explanatory variables to reduce omitted variable bias. The theoretical models of Grossman and Helpman (1991) predict that trade openness enhances growth, while the endogenous growth models of Redding (1999) and Young (1991) suggest that openness to trade may also hamper growth. We measure openness to international trade (*Trade openness*) using the natural logarithm of the sum of exports and imports of goods and services as a percentage of GDP. In the neoclassical growth theory, capital accumulation is considered an engine of economic growth (Solow, 1957). We measure physical capital accumulation (*Gross capital formation*) using the natural logarithm of gross capital formation as a percentage of GDP. In endogenous growth theory, human capital plays an important role in economic growth (Barro, 2001; Lucas, 2015). We measure human capital (*Primary school*) using the natural logarithm of primary school enrolment as the percentage of gross enrolment. Endogenous growth models also show that FDI contributes to economic growth (Borensztein et al., 1998). We account for this using the natural log of net FDI inflows as a percentage of GDP. Finally, according to the endogenous growth models, there is a nexus between government expenditure and economic growth, with growth initially increasing with productive government spending before subsequently decreasing (Barro, 1990).

3.1.3   Correlation Analysis

Table 7.1 reports the correlation coefficients of the governance measures. As the results reported in this table show, governance effectiveness is very strongly correlated with rule of law ($r = 0.92$, $p < 0.01$), regulatory quality ($r = 0.89$, $p < 0.01$), and control of corruption ($r = 0.85$, $p < 0.01$) while strongly correlated with the remaining governance measures.

Rule of law is very strongly correlated with regulatory quality ($r = 0.88$, $p < 0.01$) and control of corruption ($r = 0.87$, $p < 0.01$) and strongly correlated with political instability ($r = 0.75$, $p < 0.01$) and voice and accountability ($r = 0.77$, $p < 0.01$). The only moderate correlation is between regulatory quality and political instability ($r = 0.64$, $p < 0.01$) and between political instability and voice and accountability ($r = 0.62$, $p < 0.01$).

Since there is a high correlation between the six governance measurements, we investigate the impact of each governance indicator on economic growth separately rather than considering the effect of all of them together. We do this to avoid the problem of multicollinearity.

TABLE 7.1 Pairwise Pearson Correlations of the six different governance measurements

Variables	(1)	(2)	(3)	(4)	(5)	(6)
(1) Government effectiveness	1.000					
(2) Rule of law	0.916***	1.000				
(3) Regulatory quality	0.887***	0.881***	1.000			
(4) Political instability	0.654***	0.749***	0.635***	1.000		
(5) Voice and accountability	0.682***	0.766***	0.749***	0.617***	1.000	
(6) Control of corruption	0.852***	0.872***	0.772***	0.692***	0.715***	1.000

Source: Authors' own estimations.

*** $p < 0.01$, ** $p < 0.05$, * $p < 0.1$. *Asterisk symbols* ***, **, *and* * *represent significance level at 1%, 5%, and 10%, respectively.*

3.2　Econometric Model

To investigate how governance affects economic growth, we follow Forbes (2000) and model growth as follows:

$$Growth_{it} = \theta \ln y_{it-1} + \beta Governance_{it-1} + \ln X'_{it-1}\gamma + \eta_t + \varepsilon_{it} \qquad (7.1)$$

where $i = 1,...,45; t = 2002,...,2021$. $Growth_{it}$ is the growth rate of GDP per capita of the country i at time t and lny_{it-1} is the natural logarithm of lagged GDP per capita. $Governance_{it-1}$ stands for governance indicators: Government effectiveness, rule of law, regulatory quality, political instability, voice and accountability, and control of corruption. $\ln X_{it-1}$ is a vector of the natural logarithm of lagged explanatory variables. As stated above, we control for openness to international trade (*Trade openness*), level of education (*Primary school*), foreign direct investment (*FDI*), physical capital accumulation (*Gross capital formation*) and government spending (*Government expenditure*) while η_t is the year dummy to control for year-specific effects, $\varepsilon_{it} (= \alpha_i + \upsilon_{it})$ is the error term which has a constant component and a component that changes over time and finally α_i is the country's individual effect which captures time-invariant characteristics of each country not included in the model.

As noted by Forbes (2000), the standard methods of panel data estimation techniques such as fixed effects and random effects are not appropriate since equation (7.1) includes a lagged dependent variable. This becomes apparent if we rewrite per capita GDP growth using the first difference of the natural logarithm of per capita income level as: $Growth_{it} = lny_{it} - lny_{it-1}$. Substituting this into equation (7.1) yields:

$$\ln y_{it} = \phi \ln y_{it-1} + \beta Governance_{it-1} + \ln X'_{it-1}\gamma + \eta_t + \varepsilon_{it} \qquad (7.2)$$

where $\phi = \theta + 1$. Arellano and Bond (1991) suggest that one can eliminate the endogeneity bias introduced by the lagged dependent variable by using the GMM estimators in the first difference, which is specified as follows:

$$\Delta \ln y_{it} = \phi \Delta \ln y_{it-1} + \beta \Delta Governance_{it-1} + \Delta X'_{it-1}\gamma + \Delta \eta_t + \Delta \varepsilon_{it} \qquad (7.3)$$

where Δ is the first difference operator. In the difference GMM, the lagged level variables are used as instruments for the differenced explanatory variables. However, when the lagged level explanatory variables are highly persistent, they become weak instruments. In this case, Arellano and Bover (1995) and Blundell and Bond (1998) suggest that the system GMM is preferred to the difference GMM. The system GMM is more consistent and efficient than the difference GMM because it uses more instruments; i.e., it uses the moment conditions from both the level equation (7.2) and the first difference equation (7.3).

In this study, we use the two-step system GMM. For the instrument to be valid, two conditions are required by the system GMM. We test for serial correlation of the error term using the Arellano and Bond tests for second-order autoregressive in first differences. We also test for instrument validity using Hansen's test of overidentifying restrictions. However, Roodman (2009) argues that instrument proliferation considerably weakens Hansen's test for the validity of instrumental exogeneity. To reduce the instrument counts, we follow Roodman (2009) and use collapsed instruments. Furthermore, we use Windmeijer's (2005) finite sample correction to obtain robust standard errors.

4 Empirical Results

In Table 7.2 we present the empirical results of the two-step system GMM. The Arellano and Bond tests for AR (2) in differences of the error term (reported at the bottom of Table 7.2) show that the error terms are not serially correlated. Based on Hansen's J test of overidentifying restrictions (also reported at the bottom of Table 7.2), we do not reject the null hypothesis that the instruments are valid. One can note that, except for one regression, the p-values are less than 0.05. Also, based on the difference-in-Hansen tests, we can reject the null hypothesis of no correlation between lagged difference variables and the error term. Taken together, these tests indicate that our two-step system GMM model satisfies the conditions required for the estimators to be consistent and efficient.

From our empirical findings, we can notice that the majority of the governance indicators are statistically significant with the only exception of political stability and voice and accountability. This result confirmed what it was found by Beyene (2021). We will proceed to discuss the output displayed above in detail. In column (1) of Table 7.2, we estimate the impact of government effectiveness on growth. As can be seen, the estimated coefficient of *Government effectiveness* is significantly positive (at the 5% level). According to the estimation results, we can infer that one-unit improvement in *Government effectiveness* would lead to a 7% increase of GDP per capita. This suggests that increasing the competence of the bureaucracy and the quality of public service delivery enhances economic growth. Our results are in line with the recent work of Feyisa et al. (2022) but diverges from Ekpo (2021), Beyene (2021), and Dickson et al. (2021). In column (2), we investigate the relationship between the rule of law and economic growth. The estimation results reported in the column show that the *Rule of law* has a significant positive coefficient, suggesting that the quality of contract enforcement, the police, and the judiciary promotes economic growth. In particular

TABLE 7.2 Two-Step System GMM Estimation Results

	(1)	(2)	(3)	(4)	(5)	(6)
GDP per capita$_{t-1}$	0.9322***	0.9305***	0.9216***	0.9294***	0.9381***	0.9429***
	(0.03)	(0.03)	(0.03)	(0.04)	(0.03)	(0.03)
Government effectiveness	0.0700**					
	(0.03)					
Rule of law		0.0659**				
		(0.03)				
Regulatory quality			0.0562**			
			(0.03)			
Political instability				0.0150		
				(0.02)		
Voice and accountability					0.0122	
					(0.02)	
Control of corruption						0.0472*
						(0.03)
Trade openness	0.0652	0.0779	0.0896	0.0663	0.0668	0.0625
	(0.05)	(0.05)	(0.06)	(0.05)	(0.05)	(0.04)
Primary school	−0.0260	−0.0378	−0.0358	−0.0512	−0.0532	−0.0308
	(0.03)	(0.04)	(0.04)	(0.05)	(0.04)	(0.05)
FDI	−0.0061	−0.0055	−0.0112	−0.0056	−0.0061	−0.0034
	(0.01)	(0.01)	(0.01)	(0.01)	(0.01)	(0.01)
Gross capital formation	−0.0036	0.0027	0.0073	0.0136	0.0142	0.0060
	(0.03)	(0.03)	(0.03)	(0.03)	(0.02)	(0.03)
Government expenditures	−0.0634**	−0.0589**	−0.0557*	−0.0270	−0.0233	−0.0509
	(0.03)	(0.03)	(0.03)	(0.04)	(0.03)	(0.03)
Time dummies	Yes	Yes	Yes	Yes	Yes	Yes

(Continued)

TABLE 7.2 (Continued)

	(1)	(2)	(3)	(4)	(5)	(6)
Arellano-Bond test for AR(2) in differences (*p*-values)	0.114	0.100	0.149	0.117	0.114	0.118
Hansen test of overidentifying restrictions (*p*-value)	0.432	0.291	0.545	0.435	0.326	0.288
Difference-in-Hansen test (*p*-value)	0.588	0.505	0.951	0.742	0.532	0.684
Number of instruments[a]	44	44	44	44	44	44
Number of countries	45	45	45	45	45	45
Number of observations	571	571	571	571	571	571

Source: Authors' own estimations.

Note:

[a] Number of instruments includes exogenous variables including time dummies. The significance level is denoted as: *** $p < 0.01$, ** $p < 0.05$, * $p < 0.1$.

a unit *Rule of law* enhancement of 6.6% GDP per capita. This result is in line with Afolabi (2019), Beyene (2021), Dickson et al. (2021), and Feyisa et al. (2022). We obtain a similar result when we investigate the impact of regulatory quality in column (3). The positive and significant coefficient of *Regulatory quality* suggests that the ability of the government to formulate and implement sound policies and regulations that encourage the development of the private sector helps spur economic growth. According to our estimation, an increase in unit of regulatory quality improvement would lead to a rise in the GDP per capita of 5.6%. Our finding does not support the outcomes of Abdullahi et al. (2019), Afolabi (2019), and Ekpo (2021) but nevertheless it is similar to the results of Beyene (2021) and Dickson et al. (2021). In column (4), we look at how political instability influences growth. As can be seen, the estimated coefficient of *Political instability* is not statistically significant. This finding is unexpected given that many African nations have been caught up in political turmoil. It is also in contrast to the conventional argument that unstable political systems impede investments by introducing uncertainties that discourage investors from undertaking productive investment projects. In column (5), we examine the *impact of voice and accountability*, such as the degree to which individuals' participation in political life, expressing their opinion without repression, and the independence of media, and we found that it has no significant impact on economic growth. Finally, we investigate the effect of corruption in column (6), and the result suggests that *control of corruption* marginally increases growth. This result is supported by Feyisa et al. (2022) but contrasts with Afolabi (2019) and Ekpo (2021). Taken together, the finding presented in this study suggests that government effectiveness, rule of law, and regulatory quality are the most important governance factors that influence the rates of growth.

Regarding the remaining variables, we find that lagged GDP per capita has a statistically significant (at the 1% level) and negative effect on economic growth (notice that $\theta = \phi - 1$). This finding is consistent with the neoclassical growth model prediction that countries with low levels of income grow faster than countries with high levels of income (Solow, 1956), which is also known as the conditional convergency hypothesis (Barro and Sala-i-Martin, 1992; Mankiw et al., 1992; Sala-i-Martin, 1996; Barro, 2015). Our finding shows that *Trade openness* does not have a statistically significant impact on growth; our result is not consistent with some of previous work as Zahonogo (2017), Ganau (2017), Kebede and Taky (2017), Bakluti and Boujelbene (2020), Bunje et al. (2022), and Ibrahim and Abdulmalik (2013) but they are in line with the findings of Hussen (2023).

In contrast to the findings of Fayissa and Nsiah (2013), Akinlo (2016), Bakluti and Boujelbene (2020), and Hussen (2023) who investigated human capital measured by primary school enrolment on economic growth, we show that *Primary school*, which proxies for a country's human development, has no significant impact on economic growth. However, our results are instead supported by previous studies of Barro and Lee (2001), Minier (2007), and Delgado et al. (2014); they must be interpreted with caution because the primary school enrolment might not represent sufficiently the human capital, which can include various levels of education and other formal training. Thus, to fully understand the impact of human capital, more comprehensive measures should be considered.

Surprisingly, *FDI* result suggests that it is not significantly associated with economic growth as also it was found by Hussen (2023) but not in line with the findings of Fayissa and Nsiah (2013) and Feyisa et al. (2022). One possible explanation is that the effects of FDI are hindered by governance indicators as lack of rule of law and political instability.

Unlike the prediction of the neoclassical growth model (Solow, 1956), we find that gross capital formation is not enhancing rates of economic growth; however, it is in line with the findings of Hussen (2023). Finally, consistent with the prediction of Barro (1990), we find that economic growth declines with government expenditure.

5   Conclusions

The aim of this work was to estimate the relationship between governance and economic growth in 45 African countries during the period from 2001 and 2022. We apply a dynamic panel system GMM method to estimate our model. The main findings suggest that four out of six dimensions of governance, namely, government effectiveness, rule of law, regulatory quality, and control corruption, have positive influence on economic growth. Our results are in line with the previous literature and confirm the noticeable relationship between the quality of governance and economic growth. Based on our empirical results, some recommendations and policy implications can be suggested. It would be very crucial that policymakers in Africa adopt policies to implement and enforce policies related to good governance. For example, to improve the government's effectiveness, it is crucial to formulate policies that increase credibility of the government in African countries. Concerning the rule of law, it is necessary to make a big effort at all levels of the government so that the citizens have confidence in the rules of society. It could be strategically important, for example, to educate citizens about their rights and take responsibility and adopt transparency in the decision processes to also reduce corruption. This means that economic growth requires citizens' trust in public institutions and effective management of public resources. Our findings also suggest that government expenditure can have a role in stimulating economic growth while trade openness, primary school education, and foreign direct investment do not seem to be relevant to improving the economic performance of our sample of African countries. The lack of statistically significant impact of FDI on growth can suggest that African countries should put effort to attract more investments and identify the channels that generate and facilitate their direct impact to speed economic growth.

Our research could be expanded by using longer time series when available and investigating the research question in different geographical areas in Africa, as well as considering the different level of income to which the countries belong to. Also, we think that further research on measuring different aspects of governance is warranted so as to make policymaking more functional and effective.

References

Abdullahi, S., Rusmawati, S., Normaz, W. and Nur, S. M. (2019). Public debt, institutional quality, and economic growth in sub-Saharan Africa. *Institutions and Economies*, Vol. 11(3), pp. 39–64.

Acemoglu, D., Johnson, S., and Robinson, J. A. (2005). Institutions as a fundamental cause of long-run growth. *Handbook of Economic Growth*, Vol. 1(A), Philippe Aghion, Steven N. Durlauf, eds., pp. 385–472. Elsevier, Amsterdam, The Netherlands.

Adzima, K. and Baita, K. (2019). The impact of governance on economic growth: An empirical assessment in sub-Saharan Africa. http://dx.doi.org/10.2139/ssrn.3470607 (access 29 August 2023).

Afolabi, J. O. (2019). The impact of governance on economic development in West Africa: A system GMM dynamic panel approach. *Acta Universitatis Danubius Economica*, Vol. 15(3), pp. 217–231.

Ahlerup, P., Baskaran, T. and Bigsten A. (2016). Government Impartiality and Sustained Growth in sub-Saharan Africa, *World Development*, Vol. 83, pp. 54–69.

Akinlo, T. (2016). Institution and economic growth in sub-Saharan Africa (1986–2013). *Emerging Economy Studies*, Vol. 2(2), pp. 170–180.

Arellano, M. and Bond, S. (1991). Some Tests of Specification for Panel Data: Monte Carlo Evidence and an Application to Employment Equations, *The Review of Economic Studies*, Vol. 58(2), pp 277–297.

Arellano, M. and Bover, O. (1995). Another look at the instrumental variable estimation of error-components models, *Journal of Econometrics*, Vol. 68(1), pp 29–51.

Bakluti, N. and Boujelbene, Y. (2020). An econometric study of the role of the political stability on the relationship between democracy and economic growth. *Panoeconomicus*, Vol. 67(2), pp. 187–206.

Barro, R. (1990). Government spending in a simple model of endogenous growth. *Journal of Political Economy*, Vol. 98(5), pp. 103–125.

Barro, R. J. and Lee, J.-W. (2001). International data on educational attainment: Updates and implications. *Oxford Economic Papers*, Vol. 53(3), pp. 541–563.

Barro, Robert J. (2001). Human capital and growth. *American Economic Review: Papers and Proceedings*, Vol. 91(2), pp. 12–17.

Barro, Robert J. (2015). Convergence and Modernisation. *Economic Journal*, Vol. 125(585), pp. 911–942.

Barro, Robert J. and Sala-i-Martin, X. (1992) Convergence. *Journal of Political Economy*, Vol. 100(2), pp. 223–251.

Beyene, A. B. (2021). Governance quality and economic growth in sub-Saharan Africa: The dynamic panel model. *Journal of Economics and Administrative Sciences*. https://doi.org/10.1108/JEAS-08-2021-0156

Blundell, R. and Bond, S. (1998). Initial conditions and moment restrictions in dynamic panel data models. *Journal of Economics*, Vol. 87(1), pp. 115–143. https://doi.org/10.1016/s0304-4076(98)00009-8

Borensztein, E., De Gregorio, J. and Lee, J-W. (1998). How does foreign direct investment affect economic growth? *Journal of International Economics*, Vol. 45(1), pp. 115–135.

Bunje, M. Y., Abendin, S. and Wang, Y. (2022). The effects of trade openness on economic growth in Africa. *Open Journal of Business and Management*, Vol. 10(2), pp. 614–642.

Cass, D. (1965). Optimum growth in an aggregative model of capital accumulation. *Review of Economic Studies*, Vol. 32(3), pp. 233–240.

Das, R. C. and Das, U. (2014). Interrelationships among growth, confidence and governance in the globalized world - An experiment of some selected countries. *International Journal of Finance and Banking Studies*, Vol. 3(4), pp. 68–83.

Das, R. C., Das, U. and Ray, K. (2013). Linkages among confidence, governance and growth in the era of globalization - A study of some Asian countries. *Vidyasagar University Journal of Economics*, Vol. XVII, 2012-13 ISSN – 0975-8003

Delgado, M. S., Henderson, D. J. and Parmeter, C. F. (2014). Does education matter for economic growth? *Oxford Bulletin of Economics and Statistics*, Vol. 76(3), pp. 334–359.

Dickson, O. W., Masai, W. and Samuel, M. N. (2021). Institutional quality and economic growth: Evidence from sub-Saharan Africa countries. *African Journal of Economic Review*, Vol. 9(4), pp. 106–125.

Dixit, A. (2009). Governance institutions and economic activities. *American Economic Review*, Vol. 99(1), pp. 5–24.

Ekpo, A. K. (2021). Governance, growth and development in sub-Saharan Africa: A revisit of the evidence. *The Nigerian Journal of Economic and Social Studies*, Vol. 63(2), pp. 153–186.

Erdogan, S., Acaravci, A. (2022). On the Nexus between institutions and economic development: An empirical analysis for sub-Saharan African countries. *The European Journal of Development Research*, Vol. 34, pp. 1857–1892.

Fayissa, B. and Nsiah, C. (2013). The impact of governance on economic growth in Africa. *The Journal of Developing Areas*, Vol 47(1), pp. 91–108.

Feyisa, H. L., Ayen, D. D., Abdulahi, S. M. and Tefera, F. T. (2022). The three-dimensional impacts of governance on economic growth: Panel data evidence from the emerging market. *Corporate Governance and Organizational Behavior Review*, Vol. 6(1), pp. 42–55.

Fikadu, A., Wondaferahu, M. and Tesfaye, M. (2019). Impact of institutional quality on economic performance of Eastern Africa: A panel data analysis. *Jurnal Perspektif Pembiayaan Dan Pembangunan Daerah*, Vol. 7(2), pp. 169–182.

Forbes, Kristin J. (2000). A reassessment of the relationship between inequality and growth. *American Economic Review*, Vol. 90(4), pp. 869–887.

Fosu, A., Bates, R. and Hoeffler, A. (2006). Institutions, governance and economic development in Africa: An overview. *Journal of African Economies*, Vol. 15(1), pp. 1–9.

Ganau, R. (2017). Institutions and economic growth in Africa: A spatial econometric approach. *Economia Politica*, Vol. 34, 425–444.

Grossman, G. M., and Helpman, E., (1991). *Innovation and Growth in the Global Economy*. MIT Press, Cambridge, MA.

Hussen, M. S. (2023). Institutional quality and economic growth in sub-Saharan Africa: A panel data approach. *Journal of Economics and Development*, Vol. 25, pp. 332–348.

Ibrahim, A., and Abdulmalik, M. R. (2013). Do trade openness and governance matter for economic growth in Africa? A case of EAC and WAEMU countries. *International Economica and Economic Policy*, Vol. 20, pp. 389–412.

Kaufmann, D. and Kraay, A. (2002). Growth Without Governance. Available at: https://ssrn.com/abstract=316861 (Access August 2023).

Kaufmann, D., Kraay, A. and Mastruzzi, M. (2003). Governance matters III: Governance indicators for 1996–2002. Policy Research Working Paper 3106 (June). Available at www.worldbank.org/wbi/governance/pubs/govmatters3.html access August 2023.

Kebede, J. G. and Takyi, P. O. (2017). Causality between institutional quality and economic growth: Evidence from sub-Saharan Africa, *European Journal of Economic and Financial Research*, Vol. 2(1), pp. 114.

Koopmans, Tjalling C. (1965). On the concept of optimal economic growth, in *The Economic Approach to Development Planning*. North-Holland Publishing Co., Amsterdam, pp. 225–287.

Lucas, Robert E., Jr. (2015). Human capital and growth. *American Economic Review: Papers & Proceedings*, Vol. 105(5), pp. 85–88.

Mankiw, N. Gregory, Romer, David and Weil, David N. (1992). A contribution to the empirics of economic growth. *Quarterly Journal of Economics*, Vol. 107(2), pp. 407–437.

Minier, J. (2007), Nonlinearities and robustness in growth regressions. *American Economic Review*, Vol. 97(2), pp. 388–392.

Redding, S. 1999. Dynamic comparative advantage and the welfare effects of trade. *Oxford Economic Papers*, Vol. 51(1), pp. 15–39.

Roodman, David. (2009). How to do xtabond 2: An introduction to difference and system GMM in Stata. *The Stata Journal*, Vol. 9(1), pp. 86–136.

Sachs, J. D., McArthur, J. W. Schmidt-Traub, G. Kruk, M. Bahadur, C. Faye, M. and McCord G. (2004). Ending Africa's poverty trap. *Brookings Papers on Economic Activity*, Vol. 1, pp. 117–240.

Sala-i-Martin, Xavier X. (1996) The classical approach to convergence analysis. *Economic Journal*, Vol. 106 (437), pp. 1019–1036. https://doi.org/10.2307/2235375

Salawu, M. B., Yusuff, A. S., Salman, K. K., Ogunniyi, A. I. and Rufa, A. M. (2018). Does governance influence economic growth in sub-Saharan Africa. *Global Journal of Human-Social Science: Economics*, Vol. 18(1), pp. 57–66.

Solow, Robert M. (1956). A contribution to the theory of economic growth. *Quarterly Journal of Economics*, Vol. 70(1), pp. 65–94.

Solow, Robert M. (1957). Technical change and the aggregate production function. *The Review of Economics and Statistics*, Vol. 39(3), pp 312–320.

Swan, Trevor W. (1956). Economic growth and capital accumulation. *Economic Record*, Vol. 32, pp. 334–361.

Windmeijer, F. (2005). A finite sample correction for the variance of linear efficient two-step GMM estimators. *Journal of Econometrics*, Vol. 126(1), 25–51.

World Bank. (2017). World Development Report, Governance and Law. https://www.worldbank.org/en/publication/wdr2017

World Bank. (2023). *The Worldwide Governance Indicators (WGI)* http://info.worldbank.org/governance/wgi/ (access 2 February 2023).

Young, A. (1991). Learning by doing and the dynamic effects of international trade. *The Quarterly Journal of Economics*, Vol. 106(2), 369–405.

Zahonogo, P. (2017). Trade and economic growth in developing countries: Evidence from sub-Saharan Africa. *Journal of African Trade*, Vol. 3(1), pp. 41–56.

APPENDIX 7.1 List of the Countries

Country Name	
Algeria	Guinea-Bissau
Angola	Kenya
Benin	Libya
Botswana	Madagascar
Burkina Faso	Mali
Burundi	Mauritania
Cabo Verde	Mauritius
Cameroon	Morocco
Central African Republic	Mozambique
Chad	Namibia
Comoros	Niger
Congo, Dem. Rep.	Nigeria
Congo, Rep.	Rwanda
Cote d'Ivoire	Senegal
Djibouti	Sierra Leone
Egypt	South Africa
Equatorial Guinea	Sudan
Eritrea	Tanzania
Ethiopia	Togo
Gabon	Tunisia
Gambia	Uganda
Ghana	Zambia
Guinea	

PART II

Growth and Governance Linkages for the Selected Countries of the World

8

GOOD GOVERNANCE AND KNOWLEDGE-BASED ECONOMIC GROWTH

A Study of Japan

Debasish Nandy

Introduction

The correlation between economic expansion and knowledge-based economies is notably significant, particularly in the context of Japan. The adoption of a knowledge economy model in the 1990s has yielded remarkable growth for Japan, thereby establishing its knowledge-based economy as a paradigm for other nations. This alternative trajectory for economic development, rooted in innovation, has been instrumental in Japan's ascent. As Schaede (2020) asserts, Japan's current business practices have propelled it to become the third-largest global economy and a dominant force in the Asian region. Notably, major Japanese corporations are actively engaged in pioneering novel and transformative innovation methodologies to facilitate their reinvention.

After gathering horrific experiences from World War II, the government of Japan changed its defense policy. From a warrior state, it became one of the world's most peaceful and developed states. Japan has become the best example of a technologically advanced country. The glaring economic growth of Japan is a combination of rapid industrialization, the monopoly in vehicle manufacturing, advancement in IT (Information and Telecommunication), supremacy in electronics, advancement in various branches of science and technologies, etc. Japan is a corruption-free country where criminalization of administration is almost absent. Japan applied Michael Foucault's power–knowledge relationship. Due to having absolute good governance and positive economic policy, the knowledge-based economic growth of Japan has been fostered. This chapter has attempted to combine these two themes. Due to good governance, the knowledge economy of Japan moves well. This chapter initiates a study how good governance helps the growth of the knowledge economy.

DOI: 10.4324/9781003530688-11

Research Objectives, Research Questions, and Methodology

This chapter is based on two research objectives: (1) To investigate the reasons behind the introduction of knowledge economy in Japan and (2) to delineate the various sectors of the knowledge economy of Japan. There are two research questions in this chapter: (1) What are the basic objectives behind introducing a knowledge economy in Japan? And (2) What are the major sectors and aspects of the knowledge economy of Japan? Both primary and secondary sources are used to develop the chapter. The content analysis method has been applied in this chapter. Government reports, books, journals, and news sources have been used in this chapter.

Review of Literature

To prepare this chapter, some relevant literature has been reviewed. In the literature review, government reports, books, and journals have been followed. According to *Annual Report on the Japanese Economy and Public Finance 2022* has analyzed the status of the Japanese economy in 2022 and the contribution of the knowledge economy. Carl and Thomas (2000) elaborately discussed the impact of the knowledge economy in Korea. Castro (2015) discussed knowledge management and innovation in knowledge-based and high-tech industrial markets. Drucker (1993) analyzed future management and knowledge economy. Hadad (2017) has discussed on knowledge economy, its characteristics, and dimensions. Nonaka and Takeuchi (1995) discussed the knowledge-creating company and how Japanese companies create the dynamics of innovation. Naqshbandi and Jasimuddin (2018) analyzed knowledge-oriented leadership and open innovation. Miwa et al. (2022) argued how high-speed rail and the knowledge economy are interconnected. In her comprehensive analysis, Schaede (2020) has undertaken a critical examination of Japan's business reinvention, shedding light on the significance of comprehending the emerging landscape of Japan and its implications. Skulska et al. (2018) discussed the knowledge-based economy in Japan. They also highlighted the potential role of knowledge cluster initiatives. Zeb (2022) highlighted the role of the knowledge economy in Asian business. There is a research gap to deal with this topic. So much research has been done so far on good governance and the knowledge economy of Japan. The existing literature is either on good governance or knowledge economy.

A Conceptual Outline

The concept of good governance is not a recent development, but rather one that has been present since the dawn of human civilization. At its core, governance refers to the process of decision-making and the subsequent execution or non-execution of those decisions. The term governance can be applied to a variety of contexts, including corporate, international, national, and municipal settings. An examination of governance involves an exploration of both formal and informal individuals involved in decision-making, as well as the formal and informal structures that have been established to facilitate and enforce these decisions. Governance encompasses the entire process of decision-making and its subsequent execution.

Grindle (2008) has mentioned that the notion of a proficient government is deemed highly commendable. Often, commendable ideas are attributed with greater significance in the process of development than they truly deserve. They may be perceived as influential factors in development, establishing a sequential framework for nations to follow to progress, which may not be pragmatic or historically accurate. Consequently, these influences contribute to the formulation of extensive agendas and convoluted reasoning. Ultimately, proponents of good governance, erroneously equating it with development, advocate that growth is the development pathway. One of the key actors in governance is the government, and depending on the level of government, numerous other stakeholders may participate in the governance process. Formal governmental frameworks offer a means of formulating and executing decisions, guided by principles of accountability, transparency, responsiveness, efficacy, equity, inclusivity, and adherence to legal norms. An analysis of governance requires an understanding of the various actors involved, the structures that have been established, and the principles that guide decision-making and execution. The knowledge-based economy has been introduced by the government of Japan. The knowledge-based economy can succeed through the application of good governance, especially the efficiency of the government. In the case of Japan, good governance enormously helps to develop a knowledge-based economy. The advent of science technology and innovation made Japan the leading economy of the world (Takahashi, 2016).

Good governance promotes the knowledge economy (KE). Hadad (2017) posits that the contemporary economy has undergone a significant shift toward the knowledge economy, which has been brought about by globalization and technological advancements. This transformation has resulted in the emergence of a new system of organization and work in the corporate world, which demands rapid skill development, comprehensive knowledge, and heightened accountability. Consequently, modern society has evolved into a learning society that is adaptable to change. In this context, educational institutions must strive to cultivate individuals who can effectively contribute to the development of their skills and achieve complete integration into the sociocultural milieu in which they reside. The knowledge economy is characterized by economies that are primarily propelled by the generation, distribution, and utilization of knowledge and information. Individuals who possess, employ, and transmit knowledge play a pivotal role in the knowledge economy.

According to Michel Foucault, a prominent French Post-Modernist, power is wielded as a tool of coercion by certain actors, extending beyond the confines of their discrete structures. Foucault posits that power is ubiquitous, diffused throughout society, and embodied in various forms such as discourse, knowledge, and regimes of truth (Foucault, 1991). In this context, knowledge is viewed as a form of power that can be harnessed for both hard and soft power purposes, aligning with Foucault's conceptualization of power. The term "soft power" was first introduced by Joseph S. Nye Jr. in his 1990 publication, *Bound to Lead: The Changing Nature of American Power*. Nye posits that a state can reduce its reliance on costly traditional economic or military resources by establishing international institutions that encourage others to limit or channel their activities and by legitimizing its power in the eyes of others. Soft power, as defined by Nye, is a composite of a nation's pedagogical components, culture, economics, and ideals. This form of power is reliant on intangible factors such as culture, morals, ideology, and esoteric knowledge.

According to Joseph Nye's definition (Nye, 2004), soft power refers to the capacity to achieve desired outcomes through attraction rather than coercion or payment. In the context of globalization, a state must maintain a delicate equilibrium between the use of hard force and the deployment of soft power. According to Robert Keohane and Joseph Nye, globalization is characterized by the expansion of economic freedom. This phenomenon involves the unimpeded and consistent movement of resources, such as capital, goods, services, and labor. In light of the acceptance of globalization, the least-developed nations are now faced with two obligations to enhance their democratic practices (Bandyopadhyaya, 2002). These obligations include the implementation of privatization and liberalization, which are the fundamental components of globalization. Liberalization, in particular, pertains to the elimination of all trade restrictions and economic safeguards. The assurance of good governance cannot be solely reliant on transparency. While transparency can be beneficial for citizens, it is imperative to recognize that unrestricted dissemination of information about individuals and natural resources may inadvertently foster unethical market forces that seek to exploit these resources for personal gain (Prabakaran, 2011).

Reasons Behind the Introducing Knowledge Economy in Japan

Yamamura (1997) has argued that Japan succeeded in transforming an agricultural economy into an advanced industrial economy.

1. Since the 1990s, Japan has undergone a process of reinvention, marked by a notable transition in its political economy from a regulatory-controlled system to one characterized by a neoliberal orientation (Rosenbluth and

Thies, 2010). Despite the significance of this transformation, it has received scant attention domestically and even less recognition on the international stage.

2. Tsutomu (2006) posits that Japan is perceived within the context of the knowledge economy; a comprehensive framework that encompasses various sectoral concerns related to development. These concerns include the national innovation system, science and technology, infrastructure, and the macroeconomic framework.

3. The deceleration in the expansion of capital services inputs emerged as a significant determinant behind the comparatively sluggish growth of Japan's market economy from 2005 to 2015, in contrast to the preceding decade of 1995–2005. This deceleration was primarily attributable to a decline in capital investment within Japan between 2005 and 2015, which was instigated by a confluence of events including the global financial crisis triggered by the Lehman Brothers' bankruptcy in 2008, the subsequent appreciation of the yen, and the Tohoku disaster in 2011.

4. The decline in total factor productivity (TFP) growth emerged as a significant contributor to the economic downturn. It is noteworthy that TFP growth exhibited a downward trend during the period spanning from 2005 to 2010, which included the global financial crisis. Furthermore, it is pertinent to mention that TFP growth did not witness a substantial recovery post-2010. A detailed exposition of this phenomenon will be presented subsequently.

Good Governance in Japan Toward Knowledge Economy

According to Yasuo et al. (2023), Japan's economic management system stands out as unique among other nations. Despite minimal direct state involvement in economic activities, the government exerts significant control and influence over businesses, surpassing that of most market economies. This control is primarily exercised through regular consultations with businesses and indirect manipulation of the banking industry. Consultation is facilitated through the establishment of joint committees and groups, which closely monitor the performance of various branches and sectors of the economy and frequently set goals. In the context of their engagement with the private sector, Japanese bureaucrats employ extensive discretionary authority instead of relying on explicit directives to provide "administrative guidance" as a means to execute official policies. Nevertheless, since the early 1990s, endeavors have been undertaken to curtail the utilization of these informal instructions, which have been criticized for fostering a climate of collusion between governmental authorities and large corporations.

Several agencies and government departments concern themselves with such aspects of the economy as exports, imports, investment, and prices, as well as with overall economic growth. The most important of these agencies is the Economic Planning Agency, which is under the Ministry of Economy, Trade, and Industry. The practice of long-term planning has been a major force in the functioning of the Japanese economy. According to the economic objectives of the government, various policy measures have been used to shift the allocation of resources among industrial sectors and to influence the organization of specific industries.

The comprehensive regulation of commercial activities, particularly within the financial industry, has been instrumental in establishing control. Nevertheless, in the early 1990s, the primary focus of authorities shifted from promoting economic engagement to reducing it. This strategic shift was perceived as a means to unlock fresh business opportunities and as a prerequisite for liberalizing Japan's domestic markets to international trade, thereby revitalizing the nation's stagnant economy at that time. Consequently, several deregulation measures were suggested and implemented to eliminate and streamline regulations.

The Knowledge Economy of Japan: Various Aspects

Shibata et al. (2006) shed light on the concept of the knowledge economy in Japan, extensively examining various sectoral aspects of its development. Their comprehensive analysis encompassed the macroeconomic framework, education and skill enhancement, the national innovation system, science and technology, information and communication technology, and infrastructure.

The literature contains various definitions of knowledge, which are often considered to be a fundamental component of intellectual capital or even the sole economic resource. Knowledge is seen as a factor that reduces uncertainty and determines the ability to adapt quickly to market demands. It can be understood as a collection of knowledge held by an entity or as systematically shaped and developed skills necessary for seizing opportunities (Skulska et al., 2018). Enterprises, organizations, individuals, and societies all play a role in creating, absorbing, transferring, and effectively utilizing this essential element of the knowledge-based economy (Carl & Thomas, 2000). According to Neoclassical Economics, the Austrian School, Penrose's Theory of Business, Nelson and Winter's Evolutionary Model of Technological Change, and Nonaka and Takeuchi, knowledge is a key aspect of economic phenomena. Recent research in the field of socioeconomic studies has focused on the concept of knowledge. Nonaka and Takeuchi (1995) argued that the generation of knowledge within an organization is a dynamic process that involves active engagement in activities, personal growth, and learning from others. This process, known as organizational knowledge creation, encompasses a company's ability to generate novel information, disseminate it effectively, and apply it in the development of goods and processes. By harnessing knowledge and fostering its continuous development, businesses can gain a competitive advantage in the global marketplace. The application of knowledge is much more essential for the knowledge economy. Productivity-based knowledge and market-oriented knowledge can play a significant role in the era of globalization. The applicability of knowledge has been found in Japan since the early 1990s. The schools, colleges, and universities of Japan used to offer knowledge-based curriculums that kept Japan far ahead of other countries (Nandy, 2024).

According to Lloyd and Payne (2003), there is a significant appreciation among scholars for discourses related to the knowledge economy. These discourses are highly regarded due to their potential to create a workforce that is more educated and less hierarchical. The aim of the knowledge-based workplace, which emerged after the Fordist era, is to eradicate the existing disparities between academic and vocational education, as well as mental and manual employment. The authors argue that educators are attracted to the notion that all individuals, irrespective of their race, gender, or social class, can acquire and effectively utilize advanced communication, critical thinking, and creative skills. Furthermore, they emphasize the importance of engaging employees in broader learning contexts, where they can take genuine ownership of their education.

Good governance is a must for flourishing free exercises of intellectuality. Japan ensures good governance not only through constitutional and administrative measures but also through "national character." The people of Japan are disciplined and work-loving. The way the Japanese government promotes innovation and free thinking is very positive for the knowledge economy. The policy of the government can be successful if the people understand the national priority. The knowledge-based economic policy of Japan has succeeded due to the convergence of the thinking of the government and citizens. The corruption-free government of Japan ensures promptness of policy implementation and has been able to make linkages between the academia–industry linkages. The destruction of the intellectual economy characterized by the free exchange of ideas can be attributed to the close associations between universities and businesses. Within this context, knowledge workers assume the role of entrepreneurial subjects, characterized by problematic configurations, as they engage in competition for knowledge with the aim of financial gain, while simultaneously networking and participating in social networks. The knowledge economy, as highlighted by Kenway et al. (2006), has emerged as a potent force permeating national and international policy circles. However, it is worth noting that the fundamental principles and methodologies of the knowledge economy remain unfamiliar to a vast majority of individuals outside the realm of economics in Japan. The knowledge economy of Japan also depends on the other countries where Japanese innovation and intellect are mostly required.

The concept of "lifelong learning," also known as *shai gakush*, has emerged as a prominent focus in Japan's educational reform agenda, as highlighted by Ogawa (2009). This emphasis became evident in December 2006, when the term "lifelong learning" was incorporated into Japan's educational constitution, known as the Fundamental Law of Education. In Europe, where endeavors are underway to cultivate knowledge-based economies, lifelong learning is recognized as a crucial strategy for addressing various significant social and economic challenges. These insights can be applied to Japan's newly established lifetime learning program. The transition from childhood to young adulthood for children entering school in 2018 will present them with unforeseen challenges in the year 2030. These obstacles will likely involve navigating careers that have yet to be developed, adapting to emerging technologies that have not yet been established, and addressing issues that have not yet been predicted. In recognition of this uncertainty, Japan has implemented a systematic approach to regularly updating its educational curriculum, drawing on data from teaching practices. These revisions occur approximately every ten years. However, the current curriculum reform in Japan acknowledges the need to modernize teaching and learning methods to foster 21st-century competencies.

One pivotal factor elucidating the triumph of the education system in Japan resides in the proficient implementation of comprehensive education for children. Teachers exhibit exceptional expertise and demonstrate comprehensive care for students' overall well-being, while students actively engage in collaborative endeavors. Moreover, parents prioritize the pursuit of knowledge and allocate additional resources for extracurricular learning, while communities provide unwavering support for educational endeavors. This distinctive model thrives on the harmonious collaboration of all components within the system.

Japan's knowledge-based learning system is market-oriented. However, categorically the knowledge-based learning system of Japan can be divided into three different dimensions. Firstly, an evidence-based educational strategy that emphasizes the application of knowledge is advocated. Secondly, a technical model of knowledge-based education is proposed, wherein technical skills take precedence over theoretical comprehension. Thirdly, goals-based education is implemented, wherein information is utilized to effect changes in the nation's society and economy. In the 1990s, Japan introduced a novel style of governance referred to as the "designated administrator system." Specifically, within the framework of conventional outsourcing and management outsourcing systems, the delegation of management responsibilities is limited to businesses supported by regional governmental institutions. This approach transcends the mere utilization of private-sector techniques and the commercialization of services.

Japan's Investment and Gain through Knowledge Economy

Annual Report on the Japanese Economy and Public Finance 2022 (2022), Japan's R&D efficiency is low in the post-pandemic times. Japan should enhance its R&D capabilities through open innovations by supporting startup enterprises, increasing doctorate holders and cross-border exchanges among research human resources, and enhancing industry–academia–government cooperation further. Japan should enhance investment in human resources in consideration of the quantitative and qualitative shortages in human resources for information technology (IT) that have become a bottleneck to digitalization.

There are several sectors of the knowledge-based economy where the government of Japan is focusing. The most important sectors of the knowledge economy are as follows.

Technology

"Deep tech" startups encompass small businesses that integrate advanced technological innovation and scientific discoveries to develop ground-breaking products. However, the process of creating a successful product in this industry is time-consuming, which may deter private venture capital firms from providing financial support. This raises the question of Kyoto University's contribution to this field. While the university's 11 Nobel laureates are a notable achievement, it also facilitates the establishment of new startups by students and academics through its two venture capital funds. Enecoat Technologies, for instance, received a substantial grant of 500 million yen ($3.6 million) from these funds. In 2015, the Japanese government granted the university $300 million to foster entrepreneurship. According to Oi (2022), Kyoto University excels in highly challenging scientific domains such as cleantech energy, regenerative medicine, and stem cell research. However, the commercialization of these deep-tech enterprises requires both time and significant financial resources. Since the launch of its innovation department and investment fund seven years ago, the number of startups founded by Kyoto University students has more than doubled to 242. The government of Japan is encouraging universities and research institutions for more innovative work which will connect the economic development.

The Japanese government has formulated a plan to allocate a substantial amount of US$87 billion to the Innovation Fund Ramps Up Alternative Focus, to foster a knowledge-based economy (Takeo & Ito, 2022). In line with this, Japan has established a target of 120 trillion yen in research and development (R&D) investment, to be distributed between the public and private sectors over a period of five years commencing from fiscal year

2021. This objective is outlined in the 6th Science, Technology, and Innovation Basic Plan, which aims to realize Society 5.0—a visionary societal model proposed by the Japanese government. Society 5.0 envisions the attainment of both economic growth and the resolution of social issues through the comprehensive utilization of cutting-edge technologies. To achieve this ambitious goal, the Kishida administration released the Integrated Innovation Strategy 2022 in June, which delineates the necessary steps to be taken.

The deliberate promotion of cutting-edge and emerging technology constitutes the second pillar of this initiative. Research and development will be strategically advanced to expedite the practical implementation of various technologies that hold the potential to bring about transformative change, such as quantum technology and artificial intelligence. Given its anticipated applicability across a wide array of fields, deep learning is designated as a priority area within the realm of AI technology. Additionally, efforts will be made to develop digital twins and sustainability applications, enabling swift responses to potential disasters such as significant earthquakes and increasingly intense rainfall. Ambitious objectives have been established for quantum technology, including the aim of attaining 10 million users in Japan by 2030, generating goods worth 50 trillion yen, and fostering the emergence of quantum unicorn firms.

Japan has undergone a rigorous process of structural reform since 2001, and it is currently witnessing the final stage of the decline of the industrial society that was initially established under the guidance of bureaucrats. As Japan endures these challenges and difficulties, a new type of society, one that values knowledge, will emerge. The knowledge-based economy (KBE) is constructed upon several crucial factors, one of which is globalization (Zeb, 2022). In developing and emerging economies, there are greater opportunities for growth and development due to the globalization of new technologies (Naqshbandi & Jasimuddin, 2018). However, in certain economies, particularly those in Asia, the landscape is somewhat distinct. Technology, communication, and information have revolutionized the KBE. In high-tech sectors, businesses can establish enduring competitive advantages.

Castro (2015) elucidated one of the most intricate business phenomena, namely, a firm's technological advantage, by adopting a particular perspective. The author demonstrated that an organization cannot achieve superior levels of innovation solely through its internal capabilities. Instead, the establishment of external connections plays a pivotal role in fostering enhanced and expedited innovation. Miwa et al. (2022) mentioned that Japan has developed its high-speed railway system as part of the knowledge economy. The basic argument besides this is without a faster communication system, economic dynamism is not possible.

Knowledge-based Management

The term "knowledge management" encompasses managerial activities involving the generation or acquisition of knowledge, the regulation of knowledge flow within organizations, and the efficient and effective utilization of knowledge for long-term organizational benefits. Vidal (2013) define knowledge management as organizational practices centered around the utilization and exploitation of knowledge. It can be argued that knowledge management facilitates the optimal utilization of personnel. Walczak (2005) underscores the significance of knowledge culture, asserting that knowledge management necessitates the establishment of a suitable organizational culture that fosters the creation and dissemination of knowledge within the organization.

The literature extensively discusses various dimensions of knowledge management. This study focuses on four key dimensions of knowledge, namely, the generation of knowledge, knowledge acquisition, knowledge distribution, and knowledge application. It is important to note that organizational knowledge and the ability to create are closely intertwined, as knowledge plays a pivotal role in fostering creativity and facilitating the generation of innovation. Furthermore, the presence of facilitators of knowledge exchange within an organization is of utmost importance, as they can greatly enhance the process of organizational innovation.

Knowledge Economy through Smart Cities

There exist significant disparities in the nuances and emphases within the notion of smart cities, as they encompass various aspects of intricate technological arrangements. These disparities are contingent upon specific circumstances and contexts. The innovation systems framework is a primary analytical approach employed to examine processes of innovation. This framework is based on the premise that societal and institutional frameworks, as well as research and business activities, contribute to shaping the nature of technological progress. The concept of innovation systems was initially developed to investigate the functioning of national systems of innovation, with a particular focus on how the five major actors within the system could actively foster innovation through interactions and networking within the national context (Nelson, 1993).

The Japanese government has shown a keen interest in smart cities due to its long-standing commitment to renewable energy sources, an area in which Japan has been a pioneer. Various projects, such as clustered photovoltaic (PV) generating, mega-solar generation, wind power stabilizing and power quality control, and microgrids, have received government support. Although these initiatives were not explicitly labeled as smart city projects, they encompassed some of the key functionalities associated with smart cities. In 2010, the Ministry of Economy, Trade and Industry introduced four significant smart city demonstration projects in different regions of Japan, marking the initiation of the innovation process for smart cities. The situation in Japan about the process of knowledge creation and dissemination can be regarded as advantageous. Smart city initiatives are considered to be noteworthy collaborative platforms that facilitate the testing of state-of-the-art technological advancements. The knowledge generated by the closely interconnected organizations involved in smart city projects holds significant value; however, its widespread dissemination has been limited (Yarime, 2018).

Private Sectors in Knowledge Economy

In June 2019, Tokyo announced a new guideline for universities and research institutions to manage risks of unintentional technology drain. In October 2019, the Ministry of Economy, Trade and Industry provided concrete plans to protect sensitive technologies in universities and research institutions, in cases such as research collaboration and accepting international students. In November 2019, Tokyo revised the Foreign Exchange Law to tighten the screening of inbound foreign direct investments in security-related fields, such as nuclear energy, electronics, and telecommunications. Tokyo is discussing further measures and researching options, including looking into the US case of visa restrictions for international students. Moreover, Tokyo is planning to establish a new think tank to apply commercial technologies, such as quantum technology and AI, to the national security field in FY 2021 (Togashi, 2020).

The technological industry in Japan is predominantly governed by the private sector. This can be attributed to several factors, including the substantial allocation of funds toward commercial technologies in Japan's science and technology budget, the long-standing emphasis on the commercial sector in technology policy, and the notable market dominance of dual-use technologies. Consequently, it can be inferred that the private sector plays a pivotal role in ensuring the efficacy of Tokyo's economic security strategy.

Japan's Projection of Knowledge Economy in the Global Milieu

The implementation of a knowledge economy immensely depends on good governance and the policy of trade liberalization. Japan has successfully been able to connect the knowledge economy with the trade liberalization policy. Now, a knowledge-based economy has become a key part of Japan's global economic engagement. The cognitive effort of Japan has been appreciated by the global community. The reliability and branding of Japan is unquestionable. Right from the Prime Minister of Japan, Foreign Ministers, Japanese diplomats, academicians, engineers, and intellectuals are projecting Japan's orientation on the knowledge economy. Japan has started to invest in many countries in the cognitive sector. The Japanese diplomatic missions in various countries are focusing on organizing some events to project Japan's moves toward a knowledge economy.

To achieve sustainable growth on a global scale, it is imperative to promote trade liberalization and investment, not to mention the significance it holds for Japan's economy. To combat protectionism and enhance the legal stability and predictability of global commerce, it is crucial to maintain and reinforce the multilateral trading system of the World Trade Organization (WTO). Additionally, Japan actively engages in various bilateral and multinational initiatives to safeguard intellectual property rights. Japan is carefully outsourcing and inviting global intelligence to work in Japanese firms and research institutions. The culture of Japan is reflected in the innovation and knowledge creation. The knowledge of Japan should be used for application in the national economy.

Japan engages in various bilateral and multinational activities to protect its intellectual property rights. The Ministry of Foreign Affairs of Japan (MFAJ, 201) has identified economic diplomacy as a priority area and has implemented measures to accelerate its development. These measures are focused on three aspects: (1) promoting rule-making to support free and open global economic systems through the promotion of various economic agreements, (2) fostering public–private partnerships to aid the internationalization of Japanese businesses, and (3) promoting resource diplomacy and foreign travel to Japan (MFAJ, 2021).

According to Japanese Prime Minister Kishida, the G20, widely recognized as the primary platform for global economic cooperation, is in urgent need of enhanced collaboration in light of the numerous challenges currently confronting the international community. The G7 Hiroshima Summit, held during Japan's G7 Presidency, underscored the significance of fostering cooperation among a diverse range of stakeholders beyond the G7, to effectively address the multitude of global challenges. Prime Minister Kishida further emphasized that the G20 Summit, held under the overarching theme of "One Earth, One Family, One Future," served as a platform for extensive deliberations on critical issues such as food security, climate change, and energy security, development, health, and digitization (Krishnan, 2023).

The current trend in the nation's economy is toward smart cities, which are facilitating the process of digitization. Japan's long-awaited digital transformation is being facilitated by the establishment of a new digital agency and other measures. The Super City Law aims to promote collaboration between the public and private sectors to achieve the digital transformation of cities. Japan has been an early and enthusiastic supporter of the G20 Global Smart Cities Alliance, which aims to promote knowledge-sharing and convergence on important issues such as privacy, interoperability, and commercial models. Smart cities provide a range of contemporary knowledge systems that generate economic value through mental activities.

Conclusion

In the current knowledge-based economy, resources and abilities will probably play a critical role in the survival of organizations amidst the dynamic and competitive environment. According to Drucker (1993), information has the potential to replace traditional factors of production such as equipment, capital, materials, and labor and may emerge as the most crucial component in the production process. Drucker further projected that knowledge resources, also referred to as knowledge workers, will be the key determinants of competitive advantage in the future. In the aftermath of World War II, the Japanese government prioritized the creation of a contemporary industrial society. This was achieved through the promotion of companies based on mass production standards and the establishment of an educational system aimed at producing a diligent and compliant workforce.

By the late 1980s, Japan had emerged as an exemplary industrial society. A select few highly prosperous corporate alliances possessed the capability to generate substantial labor output and offer their workforce lifelong job security. Innovation-driven businesses play a pivotal role in devising solutions for global markets. Japan, recognizing the significance of such enterprises, extends its support to them in their endeavors to create state-of-the-art technology and integrate it into society for the betterment of all. The focal point of Japan's competitive advantage lies in its emphasis on innovation and technology. Knowledge-intensive enterprises tend to favor insourcing rather than outsourcing when seeking resources from foreign countries, indicating a tendency for businesses to internalize their technological expertise (Banri, 2011). In light of the recent release of the preliminary results for the April–June 2023 GDP, we have revised our economic forecast. Based on our primary scenario, we now anticipate a growth rate of +2.1% for Japan's real GDP in the fiscal year 2023, followed by a growth rate of +0.8% in the fiscal year 2024 (Daiwa Institute of Research, 2023). In the policy frame of Japan, knowledge should be used for the national interests and economic development. It has been possible in Japan due to good governance and the effectiveness of the governmental agencies. The private sectors of Japan are the key sources to foster the knowledge economy. The connectivity between knowledge and economy is significantly established in Japan.

References

Annual Report on the Japanese Economy and Public Finance 2022. (2022). Report by Minister of State for Economic and Fiscal Policy, Cabinet Office, Government of Japan, Tokyo, pp. 1–19.

Bandyopadhyaya, J. (2002). *World Government for International Democracy and Justice*, Manuscript. Howrah, p. 41.

Banri, I. (2011). Technological knowledge and offshore outsourcing: Evidence from Japanese firm-level data. *RIETI Discussion Paper Series 11-E-052*, Tokyo, https://www.rieti.go.jp/jp/publications/dp/11e052.pdf, accessed on 14 October 2023.

Carl, D., and Thomas, A. (eds.) (2000). *Korea and the Knowledge-Based Economy. Information Society.* OECD, World Bank Institute, London, vol. 2000, pp. 11–12.

Castro, M. D. G. (2015) Knowledge management and innovation in knowledge-based and high-tech industrial markets: The role of openness and absorptive capacity. *Industrial Marketing Management*, 47, pp. 43–146.

Daiwa Institute of Research. (2023). *Japan's Economy: Monthly Outlook* (Aug 2023). https://www.dir.co.jp/english/research/report/jmonthly/20230905_023979.html, accessed on 12 October 2023.

Drucker, P. F. (1993). *Managing for the Future: The 1990s and Beyond.* Tuman Talley Books/Dutton, New York, pp. 1–360.

Foucault, M. (1991). *Discipline and Punish: The Birth of a Prison.* Penguin, London.

Grindle, M. (2008). Good governance: The inflation of an idea. Faculty Research Working Paper Series, Harvard Kennedy School, pp. 1–2.

Hadad, S. (2017). Knowledge economy: Characteristics and dimensions. *Management Dynamics in the Knowledge Economy*, 5(2), pp. 203–225. https://doi.org/10.25019/MDKE/5.2.03

Kenway, J. et al. (2006). *Haunting the Knowledge Economy.* Routledge, London, pp. 1–160.

Krishnan, A. (10 September 2023). G-20 Summit 2023 | Japan keen to deepen military ties with India amid 'harsh' security environment. *The Hindu.* https://www.thehindu.com/news/international/g-20-summit-2023-japan-keen-to-deepen-military-ties-with-india-amid-harsh-security-environment/article67292751.ece, accessed on 16 October 2023.

Lloyd, C. and Payne, J. (2003). The political economy of skill and the limits of educational policy. *Journal of Education Policy*, 18(1), pp. 85–107.

Ministry of Foreign Affairs of Japan (MFAJ). (8 April 2021). *Economic Diplomacy.* https://www.mofa.go.jp/policy/economy/index.html, accessed on 16 October 2023.

Miwa, N. et al. (2022). High-speed rail and the knowledge economy: Evidence from Japan. *Transportation Research Part A: Policy and Practice*, 159, pp. 398–416. https://doi.org/10.1016/j.tra.2022.01.019, accessed on 16 October 2023.

Nandy, D. (2024). Japan's free and open Indo-pacific (FOIP) policy and India. *Journal of Historical Archaeology and Anthropological Sciences*, 9(2), pp. 75–79.

Naqshbandi MM, Jasimuddin SM. (2018). Knowledge-oriented leadership and open innovation: Role of knowledge management capability in France-based multinationals. *International Business Review*, 27(3), pp. 701–713.

Nelson, R. (ed.) (1993). *National Innovation Systems: A Comparative Analysis.* Oxford University Press, New York.

Nonaka, I and Takeuchi, H. (1995). *The Knowledge-Creating Company: How Japanese Companies Create the Dynamics of Innovation.* Oxford University Press, Oxford, p. 53.

Nye, J. S. (2004), *The Means to Success in World Politics.* Public Affairs, New York.

Ogawa, A. (2009). Japan's new lifelong learning policy: Exploring lessons from the European knowledge economy. *International Journal of Lifelong Education*, 28(5), pp. 601–614. https://doi.org/10.1080/02601370903190011

Oi, M. (26 September 2022). Japan's push into 'deep tech' innovation. *BBC.* https://www.bbc.com/news/business-62719774, accessed on 15 October 2023.

Prabakaran, M. (2011). What is good governance? *SSRN*, 22 February 2011, http://dx.doi.org/10.2139/ssrn.1766267

Rosenbluth, F. and Thies, F. M. (2010). *Japan Transformed: Political Change and Economic Restructuring*. Princeton University Press, New Jersey, pp. 1–264.

Schaede, U. (2020). *The Business Reinvention of Japan: How to Make Sense of the New Japan and Why It Matters*. Stanford Business Books.

Shibata, T. (ed.) (2006) *Japan, Moving Toward a More Advanced Knowledge Economy (Vol. 2): Advanced Knowledge-Creating Companies (English)*. WBI Development Studies. World Bank Group, Washington, D.C. http://documents.worldbank.org/curated/en/884211468260931314/Advancedknowledge-creating-companies

Skulska, D. B. et al. (2018). An advancement of knowledge-based economy in Japan: The potential role of knowledge cluster initiative. *Stosunki Międzynarodowe International Relations*, 2(54), pp. 203–227.

Takahashi, M. (2016). Lifelong learning in Japan: Policy, concepts, and the present situation. *Advances in Social Science, Education and Humanities Research*, 88, pp. 151–156.

Takeo, Y. and Ito, K. (27 January 2022). Japan's $87 billion innovation fund ramps up alternative focus. *Bloomberg*. https://www.bloomberg.com/news/articles/2022-01-26/japan-s-87-billion-innovation-fund-ramps-up-alternative-focus#xj4y7vzkg, accessed on 15 October 2023.

Togashi, M. (2020). *Japan's Economic Security and the Role of the Private Sector*. Centre for Strategic and International Studies, https://www.csis.org/blogs/new-perspectives-asia/japans-economic-security-and-role-private-sector, accessed on 16 October 2023.

Tsutomu, S. (2006). *Japan: Moving Toward a More Advanced Knowledge Economy. Volume 1. Assessment and Lessons*. WBI Development Studies. World Bank, Washington, DC. http://hdl.handle.net/10986/7081, pp. 1–7

Vidal, A. J. (2013). Knowledge management and innovation performance in a high-tech SME industry. *International Small Business Journal*, 31(4), pp. 454–470.

Walczak, S. (2005). Organizational knowledge management structure. *The Learning Organization*, 12(4), pp. 330–339. https://doi.org/10.1108/09696470510599118

Yamamura, K. (1997). *Economic Emergence of Modern Japan*. Cambridge University Press, Cambridge.

Yarime, M. (2018). Smart cities as a Nexus of the energy and information and communication industries: An analysis of the innovation systems of smart cities in Japan and the United States. The International Conference on Innovation Studies (ICIS2018) & Innovation Academy for Yong Scholars (IAYS2018), Tsinghua University, 20-24 June 2018. https://repository.hkust.edu.hk/ir/Record/1783.1-93907, accessed on 18 September 2023.

Yasuo, M. et al. (17 August 2023). Economy of Japan. *Encyclopedia Britannica*, 17 Aug. 2023, https://www.britannica.com/money/topic/economy-of-Japan, accessed on 16 October 2023.

Zeb, S. (2022). The role of the knowledge economy in Asian business. *Future Business Journal*, 8(1), pp. 1–13, https://doi.org/10.1186/s43093-021-00112-6

9

GOOD GOVERNANCE AND ECONOMIC GROWTH

A Case Study on the Local Government of Bangladesh

Md. Saifullah Akon, Md. Juel Mia, and S. M. Rabby Raj

Introduction

In the realm of development discourse, the relationship between "good governance" and "economic growth" is almost symbiotic and has been a subject of sustained scholarly inquiry. Without ensuring good governance, sustainable economic growth is very difficult to achieve. Similarly, when a country starts to experience economic growth, it assists the country to improve the quality of governance. The concept of good governance basically came from the World Bank which considers good governance equivalent to flawless management of development. According to the World Bank (1992), governance is the process of exercising power to manage economic and social resources of a particular country for its development, and good governance is something that turns this development to be a strong and equitable one by creating and maintaining an optimal setting. Das et al. (2013) and Das and Das (2014) investigated the relationship between governance indicators and economic growth and economic confidence across some countries and regions in the world and Asia and found some good impacts of governance upon growth.

Bangladesh, a nation at the crossroads of economic progress and governance challenges, provides a compelling backdrop for exploring this intricate connection. The consistent and healthy growth in GDP (gross domestic product) and per capita income and the rapid reduction of poverty in recent years indicate that Bangladesh has secured a considerable socio-economic success. The government of this country is very keen on accelerating the development process through implementing various development projects, some of which are large enough to be termed "mega-projects". The economic growth

DOI: 10.4324/9781003530688-12

trajectory of Bangladesh, particularly since the late 20th century, has been noteworthy. Despite facing challenges, such as high population density, natural disasters, and socio-political complexities, the country has made significant strides in various economic sectors. The ready-made garment industry, remittances, and the agricultural sector have been notable contributors to the nation's economic growth. However, the question of whether this growth is underpinned by effective governance practices, especially at the local level, remains a critical inquiry.

Comprising a multi-tiered structure with union councils, upazila councils, and city corporations, the local government plays a pivotal role in implementing policies at the grassroots level. But Bangladesh's performance has been consistently poor in terms of governance indicators developed by the World Bank such as control of corruption, rule of law, government effectiveness, accountability, etc. (CEIC, 2023). So, it is a matter of debate to what extent the development approach of Bangladesh is sustainable. The sustainability of Bangladesh's economic growth is also questionable. The context of Bangladesh strongly suggests that only good governance can ensure sustainable economic growth in this country. The role of the local governmental bodies is very significant in this regard. The local government of Bangladesh can be broadly perceived as the legacy of the administrative system that originated in the British colonial era. So, doubts were raised many times in the past regarding how pro-people the local government is. However, despite all the limitations, deadlocks, and criticisms, the local government contributed significantly to diminishing the poverty rate and improving the living standards of the people of the grassroots level over the years. If good governance is ensured and maintained properly, the local government will play a more effective role in producing truly sustainable economic growth in the future.

The theoretical underpinnings of the study draw from a rich tapestry of literature that underscores the significance of good governance as a catalyst for economic advancement through mitigating risks, reducing corruption, and enhancing public trust. Good governance, characterized by transparency, accountability, rule of law, and effective public administration, becomes instrumental in ensuring the equitable distribution of opportunities and resources. Against this backdrop, this chapter tries to explore the relationship between good governance and economic growth and the role of the local government of Bangladesh in this regard. Apart from the introductory section, this chapter has been divided into five sections. The first section reviews the local government system of Bangladesh. The second section provides the major barriers to strong local government in Bangladesh. The third section analyzes the dichotomy of governance and growth in the local government of this country. The following section critically evaluates governance and its impact on the economic growth of the local areas. The final section provides concluding remarks from the authors.

Research Gap and Objective

There is a significant gap in understanding how good governance affects economic growth, especially when it comes to looking at the local government system in Bangladesh. While the connection between good governance and economic growth is widely acknowledged in global discussions, the practical application of these principles at the grassroots level in Bangladesh remains insufficiently studied. This chapter aims to fill this gap by examining the real-world dynamics and challenges between good governance and economic development within the local government structures of Bangladesh. In the context of Bangladesh's evolving economic landscape, where significant progress has been achieved, the specific role of good governance in sustaining growth needs closer examination. While the theoretical foundations propose that elements like transparency, accountability, rule of law foster an environment conducive to investment, their translation into practical outcomes at the local government level is not well-explored. Understanding these theoretical ideals of good governance manifest in everyday practices at the grassroots level is crucial for shaping effective policies, ensuring equitable development, and sustaining the momentum of Bangladesh's economic growth. Therefore, this chapter seeks to contribute empirical insights into the governance mechanisms at the local level and their impact on economic dynamics. However, considering these facts, the chapter intends to explore the following objectives:

  i) To assess the current state of local governance structures in Bangladesh by analyzing how principles of good governance are integrated into policies and practiced on the ground
 ii) To investigate challenges hindering the effective implementation of good governance principles at the local government level
iii) To explore the direct and indirect impact of good governance practices on local economic growth. This involves understanding how transparent decision-making and efficient resource allocation contribute to overall economic growth at the grassroots level.

Local Government System in Bangladesh

The structure of the local government in Bangladesh depends on the locality types. At the rural level, there is the three-tier structure of the government, namely—Zila (district) Parishad, Upazila (sub-district) Parishad, and Union Parishad (UP), and on the other side, currently the urban level local government consists of 11 largest cities with city corporation status and *Pourashavas* (municipalities). Except for the hill district councils of the country, for the development of the local area with civil and community welfare, the Ministry of Local Government, Rural Development and Cooperatives is primarily responsible. The local government in Bangladesh is a democratic institution established with an elected governance system where people have rights to participate even in the decision-making process and development practices; however, in different regimes the governance system falls into challenges due to interests of power politics. Changes in the local government acts and ordinances sometimes provided opportunities to the public for effective participation, sometimes reduced and neglected the opinions of the grassroots people. According to Article 11 of the constitution, the republic shall be democratic. At every level of the local government administration, effective participation of the people is required through their elected representatives to comprehend the fundamental principles of the constitution, for the same amendment is required in the Zila Parishad Act (Talukdar, 2014).

This chapter particularly focuses on the rural level local government. The Union Parishad works as the lowest level government institution in the country; it pays attention to providing services at the doorstep of the citizens in the rural areas of the country. The Union Parishad will be governed by one chairman and 12 members (nine general members from nine wards and another three reserved seats for female members), and they should be directly elected by the voters of that Union. Local Government (Union Parishad) Act 2009 has created a provision of standing committees to ensure transparency in the process and participation of the people in the decision-making and implementation of development works. According to the Act, the committee will consist of representatives from the Union Parishads, members of civil society, respected individuals in the community, and so on. However, it is observed that most committees at the local level are not active public representatives and other members of the committees are not aware of and interested in the functions and jurisdictions (Islam, 2017). The Upazila Parishad comprises a chairman, two vice-chairpersons (one of whom is a woman), the chairmen of all Union Parishads within the Upazila, the mayors of any municipalities (if any), and women members from reserved seats. Upazila Parishad Act 2009 and Upazila Parishad Act (Amendment) 2011 empowered the parishad to control and ensure transparency of the variegated departments of the ministries at the Upazila level; however, the reality is that the departments are not accountable to the Upazila Parishad (Liton, 2014). Researchers argued that the scope of participation of the people in the decision-making and implementation of the development projects is limited at the Upazila level compared to the Union level (Islam & Ahsan, 2021). On the other hand of the spectrum, the Zila Parishad Act 2000 provisioned an election by the Electoral college which has prevented the general people to elect their representatives in the parishad. According to the Act, the Zila Parishad will be formed with a chairman, 15 general members, and 5 female members from reserved seats following the electoral system where concerned Chairmen of sub-districts (Upazila level), Municipal Mayors and Councilors, and Union Parishad Chairmen and Members can cast their vote (Talukdar, 2014).

Barriers to Strong Local Government in Bangladesh

Though Bangladesh has long experiences of local government system, the structure is not yet appropriate for governing by the system itself, and historically the functionality of the local government is always controlled by the central government administration, specially by the central politicians and bureaucrats (Rahman, 2013). In the local government system for the rural areas of the country, the district-level Zila Parishad is formed without direct votes of the general peoples where the ruling political party always have an invisible influence on the electoral system. Such an electoral system at the district level goes against the democratic spirit of the country (Talukdar, 2014) and is a hindrance to introducing and imposing good governance in the rural level government institutions. From the role execution, policy implementation, and power sharing perspectives, the local government is facing a conflict triangulation among the Members of Parliament (MPs), chairmen of the Upazila Parishad, and bureaucrats. In the changing world, the decentralized local government is getting enormous significance and priority in the context of effective public administration and good governance; however, the local government institution in Bangladesh is less powerful and independent because of central dominance, largely dependent on a centrally controlled budget. Rahman (2013) illustrated that as the local citizens are not very conscious of the local government and its functionality, the central politician and the bureaucrats can establish their control over the local government institutions. The central government initiated provisions of incorporating citizen charter, ward meetings, and open budget at the Union Parishad level in 2009; however, still it has failed to ensure the participation of the people in the decision-making and implementation process, equal distribution of services, transparency in development projects, and accountability of public representatives (Panday & Rabbani, 2011). From central to local, currently questions are being raised on the proper practices of democracy in the country and people's spontaneous participation is incrementally decreasing at the local level. Shahedul Anam Khan, an associate editor of The Daily Star, explained in a roundtable discussion held in 2019 that

> at the Upazila-level elections, for example, the participation was 70 percent in 2009 which fell to 32 percent in 2019. This seems to be erosion in the confidence of the people in the election system. However, people are losing interest in election, not in democracy
>
> *(The Daily Star, 2019).*

As the local government is controlled by the central government, the practices of politics at the central level affect the local political environment. Corruption, nepotism, and mismanagement in the development works implemented by the local government institutions are almost common phenomena in the country; these create huge barriers to providing government services and ensuring equity and justice at the grassroots level. Research presented that the local leaders "do not have visionary leadership that is required for guiding the people to take part in the governance of the local government institutions" and they are "reluctant to involve themselves in the development of social condition of the community in the form of raising awareness, improvement of social coherence and community mobilization" (Panday & Rabbani, 2011). The present condition of governance systems at the local level is unsatisfactory for establishing a deeper democratic culture, good governance, and accountability of leaders and administrators. It is important to have good political will of the central government and true practices of democracy in the country for strengthening the local government system.

Governance and Growth: A Dichotomy in Local Government

There is a significant relationship between the terms "governance" and "growth". If a country manages to ensure good governance, it will generally have a positive impact on economic growth. Here, "good governance" can be defined as efficient management of administrative activities by the government of a country which positively influences the lives of the people from all walks of life. The World Bank evaluates "good governance" as the ability of the government of a particular country to implement various governance principles creating a framework for ensuring viable economic development (Mira, 2017). The absence of good governance may hinder infrastructural development, lower educational standards, and increase socio-economic inequality. As a result, economic growth slows down to a great extent (Roy, 2006). There was a significant contribution of good governance to the economic success achieved by the developed nations. Governance indicators such as controlling corruption, maintaining a strict rule of law, and ensuring accountability played a vital role in this regard (Zhuo et al., 2020). Similarly, improving the quality of governance is essential for a sustainable economic growth among the developing countries (Gani, 2011).

Bangladesh is a developing country having a population of over 165 million (BBS, 2022). In spite of some ups and downs, Bangladesh managed to retain consistent and vigorous economic growth in the previous decade. The current development vision of the government of Bangladesh is characterized by the Perspective Plan (2021–2041) (Mamun et al., 2023). This Perspective Plan will include Five Year Plan(s) (FYP) and the successful implementation of these FYPs is likely to realize Bangladesh's dream of transforming into a developed nation by 2041 under her much-hyped "Vision 2041". The role of Bangladesh's local government will be very significant in terms of implementing such a development plan. However, the local government of Bangladesh is plagued by intense corruption, incompetence, and mismanagement. There is also a lack of proper decentralization. So, to what extent this inefficient local government will be able to perform its due role in this regard is uncertain considering the fact that many objectives of the previous FYPs remained unachieved.

In fiscal year 2021–22, the GDP growth rate of Bangladesh stood at 7.10% (Ministry of Finance of Bangladesh, 2023). This growth rate crossed the milestone of 7% in FY 2015–16 and apart from the years in which the COVID-19 pandemic was at its peak, the GDP growth has been consistent in recent years. It apparently shows that Bangladesh's economy has been performing well for nearly a decade. However, there is a general perception that inequality among the Bangladeshi people is increasing rapidly, and those who live in the rural areas or the remote areas are hardly able to avail the benefits of the economic growth. The poverty rate in Bangladesh was 31.5% in 2010, which declined to 18.7% in 2022 (Ministry of Finance of Bangladesh, 2023). However, the Gini coefficient in terms of both income and consumption increased to a considerable extent. In Bangladesh, the Gini coefficient related to income increased from 0.458 in 2010 to 0.499 in 2022 (Rahman, 2023). As the Gini index measures inequality among the people and the higher the Gini coefficient is, the greater the inequality prevails, a considerable increase in the Gini coefficient proves that the perception of increasing inequality in this country is correct.

Despite the economic growth, the quality of services provided by the local government institutions has been poor over the years. Since the trust of the citizens in the local government institutions depends on the service delivery performance, the trust of the Bangladeshis in their local government institutions tends to be low (Islam & Ahsan, 2021). Bangladesh is a disaster-prone country, and the lack of good governance works as a barrier in terms of effective disaster management. As a result, the death toll rises after every disaster, be it natural or human induced. Zahid and Jahan (2022) found that the absence of good governance is directly responsible for the occurrence of landslides in the Chattogram area. On the other hand, the government of Bangladesh is led by a woman but Bangladeshi women's participation in the roles of political decision-making remains regrettably marginal. It is particularly true in terms of local government levels where only a handful of female personalities hold impactful leadership positions. Das et al. (2020) found that gender sensitivity and transparency had decreased among Union Parishads due to the centralized power of UP Chairs, politicization, and manipulation. Here, a Union Parishad is a significant unit of Bangladesh's rural local government.

Considering the sustainable development goals (SDG), the local government was supposed to play an essential role in terms of the localization of the SDGs. However, due to various politico-administrative, financial, planning, and behavioral challenges, Bangladesh's local government institutions at the rural level have not been able to make a significant contribution in this regard (Zahid, 2022). So, despite all the apparent economic success, a dichotomy between governance and growth prevails in Bangladesh which can be particularly visible in her local government institutions.

Governance and Its Impact on Economic Growth

There is a significant impact of governance on local economic growth anywhere in the world. It is valid for not only the developed countries but also the developing countries like Bangladesh. The existence and relevance of the local governmental institutions are generally embedded in their role and activities of socio-economic development within their respective local areas. The local governmental institutions play a crucial role in terms of local economic development through their process of local governance and local service delivery. In developing countries like Bangladesh, the socio-economic development initiatives of local governments mostly focus on poverty reduction and micro infrastructure improvement. Although Bangladesh is a signatory to the document related to the "Cardiff Consensus" which promoted local economic development to a great extent, the terms such as "local economy" or "local economic development" did not get any formal consideration in the documents of governmental plans (Ahmed, 2015).

In Bangladesh, most of the local areas are rural areas and the rural economy has traditionally been based on agriculture. So, the contribution of the agriculture sector to the GDP of this country used to be large. In 1981, the share of agriculture in the GDP was nearly a third which gradually declined over the years and stood at around 17% in 2014 (Toufique, 2017). Meanwhile, the share of the industrial sector in the GDP grew from 17% to 30%. So, a conspicuous structural transformation took place within the economy of this country. It is actually the result of the policies, approaches, and initiatives adopted by the government of Bangladesh in terms of rural development and urbanization. Toufique and Turton (2002) found that impactful external economic forces such as globalization and physical infrastructure development (i.e., constructing more roads and bridges, extending rural electrification, etc.) have been generating a rural landscape which is, to a considerable extent, "urban" in nature. In addition, the livelihood opportunities for the Bangladeshi rural population are increasingly diversifying, and more and more non-agricultural livelihoods are gradually emerging. So, Toufique and Turton (2002) suggested that the government should not confine the development of rural areas to a sectoral box. Rather, the government should embrace a holistic view of the local economy and the shifting dynamics of local livelihood opportunities.

Following the general elections of 2008, the Bangladesh Awami League-led coalition formed a government and introduced the term "Digital Bangladesh" which referred to a vision of initiating digitalization on a large scale throughout the country. The government began to work diligently to realize this vision, and in continuation of this, the Union Digital Centers emerged. Such digital centers also emerged in the Ward Councilors' offices of different *Pourashavas* and City Corporations. Because of these digital centers, not only e-services such as birth registration, passport application, application for government and private jobs, admission form fill-up for different educational institutions, online banking, online bill payments, etc. are becoming available for the people of local areas of this country but also employment opportunities like getting appointed as the operators of those digital centers are becoming feasible for the skilled persons of those localities (Bhuiyan & Abrar, 2022). The digital centers have brought different public services under one roof. Thus, they are saving a lot of time and money for the local population considering the fact that people had to either rush from one governmental office to another or visit the same office several times in order to avail of a particular service in the past. Despite having many limitations, these digital centers are playing a vital role in terms of improving the living standards of the people of local areas of Bangladesh.

In recent years, people's participation has become an essential element for ensuring good governance. So, the government of Bangladesh has tried to create sufficient opportunities for the local inhabitants through local government acts so that they can actively participate in the decision-making process. Ahsan and Jahan (2021) carried out an intensive study on these acts and found that these acts really provide such opportunities to a considerable extent, and the lower the level of a local governmental unit, the bigger the scope of getting involved in the decision-making procedure. So, the Bangladeshi people can more actively participate in the governing process in the tier of Union Parishad than the tier of Upazila or Zila Parishad, similarly more at the *Pourashava* level compared to the City Corporation level. However, to what extent the participation of the local people is effective in this regard is a matter of debate considering the fact that there exists intense corruption and a lack of efficiency in all tiers of local government bodies.

As poverty reduction is a major responsibility of the local governments in Bangladesh, statistical data suggests that their performance was quite well. Compared to urban areas, the poverty rate declined by a greater margin in the rural areas between 2010 and 2022. In 2010, the rate of income poverty in the rural areas was 35.2%, which came down to 20.5% in 2022, whereas this rate decreased from 21.3% to 14.7% in the urban areas during the same period (Ministry of Finance of Bangladesh, 2023). So, it would not be incorrect to assume that people's participation in the governing process played a catalytic role in the success of poverty reduction in rural areas. For ensuring practices of democracy and participatory development at the grassroots level, it is necessary to establish a strong, effective, and decentralized local government system. However, local government institutions in Bangladesh have faced and are facing huge ups and downs in its history. The current local government system allows Union Parishad to identify possible development projects at the local levels and prepare the proposals; however, the budgeting and implementation of the projects are approved and controlled by the upazila parishad/administration, zila parishad/administration, and national political leaders. The thing is that at the grassroot-level local government, the powers and responsibilities "are defined in general and vague terms while the powers of the central government functionaries are enshrined in specific and precise terms" (Sarker, 2006). Thus, it has created opportunities for national political leaders to gain control over the development projects of local government institutions. This often leads to the politicization of these projects, resulting in exploitation and political nepotism. Consequently, the projects tend to focus less on actual local development and more on serving political interests. The rural economy of Bangladesh is largely dependent on agriculture and fishing; for the marketing and trade of local products, it is necessary to build transportation facilities and other infrastructures at the grassroots levels. Maintaining relations with the local administration, the rural local government institutions of the country take initiative, make initial plans and proposals, and come forward to develop, conserve, and maintain the infrastructures that are needed for the rural economic growth and development. Existing news stories and research articles illustrated that despite the gradual economic progress of Bangladesh, corruption is still a big problem in the country, and in rural development projects corruption is almost common and a major impediment to local and national development (Dhaka Tribune, 2022; Nawar, 2023; Sarker, 2006). It is also evident that corruption, weak governance, political biases, and administrative complexities are often disrupting the coverages of social safety net programs, e.g., employment generation program for the poorest (EGPP), Vulnerable Group Feeding (VGF), Gratuitous Relief (GR), Food for Works (FFW), and Test Relief (TR) programs which are primarily aims at reducing chronic poverty and vulnerabilities of the people (Basher, 2020; Masud-All-Kamal & Saha, 2014).

The policies, practices, and initiatives adopted by a particular local government body ultimately influence the lives of all individuals and families of that locality. So, in order to retain the success of poverty reduction and sustain economic growth in the local areas of this country, good governance is a must. A greater extent of cooperation and coordination between the national government and the local governmental bodies in Bangladesh is required in this regard.

Conclusion

Undoubtedly, the local government institutions in Bangladesh are making a pivotal contribution to the social and economic development of the rural areas of the country. However, the lack of good governance in the local government institutions is obvious and almost common in all districts, Upazilas, and Unions. Compared to the investment for the rural areas, the development is not observed in a similar manner due to corruption, poor governance, lack of good political will, and interference of central government, ruling political party, and local bureaucracy. Development initiatives implemented by the local government should not be just for political interests and economic growth; development projects should consider local environmental sustainability and ensure sustainability from the viewpoint of empowering social institutions. Furthermore, this chapter also suggests that to uphold the democratic spirit of the country, direct participation of the local people in electing their representatives should be counted at all levels of the local government, and the voice of the community should be ensured in project initiation and implementation.

References

Ahmed, T. (2015, March 11). Local government and economic development. *The Daily Star*. Retrieved October 5, 2023, from https://www.thedailystar.net/supplements/24th-anniversary-the-daily-star-part-3/local-government-and-economic-development-71121

Ahsan, A. H. M., & Jahan, D. N. (2021). Manifestation of people's participation in the existing local government acts in Bangladesh. *Social Science Review [The Dhaka University Studies, Part-D]*, 38(1), 1–16. https://doi.org/10.3329/ssr.v38i1.56521

Basher, S. A. (2020, October 21). *Good intentions, poor results: The problem with social safety net programmes*. The Daily Star. https://www.thedailystar.net/opinion/news/good-intentions-poor-results-the-problem-social-safety-net-programmes-1981461

BBS (Bangladesh Bureau of Statistics). (2022). *Population & Housing Census 2022*. Government of Bangladesh.

Bhuiyan, A. R., & Abrar, M. (2022). Role of one stop shop for e-service delivery: Case study on Union Digital Center in Bangladesh. *Social Science Review [The Dhaka University Studies, Part-D]*, 39(1), 91–102. https://doi.org/10.3329/ssr.v39i1.64876

CEIC. (2023, October 1). *Bangladesh country governance indicators*. CEICdata. Retrieved October 3, 2023, from https://www.ceicdata.com/en/bangladesh/country-governance-indicators

Das, M., Nahar, N., Ahmed, A., & Nandi, R. (2020). Women's participation in decision making structures and processes: A case study on the local government institution in Bangladesh. *Social Science Review [The Dhaka University Studies, Part-D]*, 37(2), 267–286. https://doi.org/10.3329/ssr.v37i2.56511

Das, R. C., & Das, U. (2014). Interrelationships among growth, confidence and governance in the globalized world – An experiment of some selected countries. *International Journal of Finance and Banking Studies*, 3(4), 68–83.

Das, R. C., Das, U., & Ray, K. (2013). Linkages among confidence, governance and growth in the era of globalization – A study of some Asian countries. *Vidyasagar University Journal of Economics*, XVII, 35–46.

Gani, A. (2011). Governance and Growth in Developing Countries. *Journal of Economic Issues*, *45*(1), 19–40. https://doi.org/10.2753/jei0021-3624450102

Islam, M. S., & Ahsan, A. H. M. (2021). Citizens' satisfaction with local government service delivery performance in Bangladesh: Does citizens' confidence matter? *Social Science Review [The Dhaka University Studies, Part-D]*, *38*(2), 117–133. https://doi.org/10.3329/ssr.v38i2.64464

Islam, M. T. (2017). *Understanding the Effectiveness of Union Parishad Standing Committee: A Perspective on Bangladesh*. https://blogs.lse.ac.uk/southasia/2017/11/07/understanding-the-effectiveness-of-union-parishad-standing-committee-a-perspective-on-bangladesh/

Liton, S. (2014). Upazila Parishad: Victim of power politics. *The Daily Star*. https://www.thedailystar.net/upazila-parishad-victim-of-power-politics-31111

Mamun, A. A., Akon, M. S., & Shamsunnahar. (2023). Rethinking development effectiveness and governance in Post-COVID-19 period: Bangladesh perspective. In R. C. Das (Ed.), *Inclusive Developments Through Socio-economic Indicators* (pp. 127–140). https://doi.org/10.1108/978-1-80455-554-520231010

Masud-All-Kamal, Md., & Saha, C. K. (2014). Targeting social policy and poverty reduction: The Case of social safety nets in Bangladesh. *Poverty & Public Policy*, *6*(2), 195–211. https://doi.org/10.1002/pop4.67

Ministry of Finance of Bangladesh. (2023). *Bangladesh Economic Review*. Government of Bangladesh.

Mira, R. (2017). *Relationship between Good Governance and Economic Growth: A Contribution to the Institutional Debate about State Failure in Developing Countries*. Centre d'économie de l'Université Paris Nord.

Nawar, N. (2023, March 2). How corruption is perpetuated across generations in Bangladesh. *The Daily Star*. https://www.thedailystar.net/shout/news/how-corruption-perpetuated-across-generations-bangladesh-3260626

Panday, P. K., & Rabbani, M. G. (2011). Good governance at the grass-roots: Evidence from Union Parishads in Bangladesh. *South Asian Survey*, *18*(2), 293–315. https://doi.org/10.1177/0971523113513376

Rahman, M. F. (2023, May 23). Income inequality in Bangladesh keeps deepening. *The Daily Star*. Retrieved October 2, 2023, from https://www.thedailystar.net/business/news/income-inequality-bangladesh-keeps-deepening-3295226

Rahman, M. S. (2013). Role of the members of parliament in the local government of Bangladesh: Views and perceptions of grassroots in the case of Upazila administration. *Public Organization Review*, *13*(1), 71–88. https://doi.org/10.1007/s11115-012-0194-7

Roy, D. K. (2006). Governance, competitiveness and growth: The challenges for Bangladesh. *ADB Institute Discussion Paper*, *53*.

Sarker, A. E. (2006). The political economy of decentralized governance: An assessment of rural local government reforms in Bangladesh. *International Journal of Public Administration*, *29*(13), 1285–1309. https://doi.org/10.1080/01900690600928128

Talukdar, M. R. I. (2014). Zila Parishad Act needs amendment. *The Daily Star*. Retrieved October 20, 2023, from https://www.thedailystar.net/zila-parishad-act-needs-amendment-23953

The Daily Star. (2019). People's participation, democracy and local governance: Features of democracy in Switzerland and Bangladesh. Retrieved October 23, 2023, from https://www.thedailystar.net/round-tables/news/peoples-participation-democracy-and-local-governance-features-democracy-switzerland-and-bangladesh-1776718

The World Bank. (1992). *Governance and Development*. The World Bank, Washington, D.C.

Toufique, K. A. (2017). Bangladesh experience in rural development: The success and failure of the various models used. *Bangladesh Development Studies*, 40(1–2), 97–117.

Toufique, K. A., & Turton, C. (2002). *Hands Not Land: How Livelihoods are Changing in Rural Bangladesh*. Bangladesh Institute of Development Studies (BIDS).

Dhaka Tribune. (2022, January 25). Bangladesh still languishes among world's most corrupt countries. *Dhaka Tribune*. https://www.dhakatribune.com/bangladesh/262604/bangladesh-still-languishes-among-world-s-most

Zahid, A. (2022). Exploring the challenges of SDGs localisation by rural local government institutions in Bangladesh: A policy implementation perspective. *Social Science Review [The Dhaka University Studies, Part-D]*, 39(3), 93–111. https://doi.org/10.3329/ssr.v39i3.67436

Zahid, D., & Jahan, D. N. (2022). Disaster management and good governance: A review on Chattogram landslides. *Social Science Review [The Dhaka University Studies, Part-D]*, 39(1), 35–55. https://doi.org/10.3329/ssr.v39i1.64873

Zhuo, Z. O. A., Muhammad, B., & Khan, S. (2020). Underlying the relationship between governance and economic growth in developed countries. *Springer: Journal of the Knowledge Economy*, 12(3), 1314–1330. https://doi.org/10.1007/s13132-020-00658-w

10

MGNREGA, GOVERNANCE PRACTICES AND RURAL ASSETS CREATION

Any Association So Far for India and Its States?

Maitree Dey, Poulami Maity, and Ramesh Chandra Das

Introduction

The 2030 Agenda for Sustainable Development places great importance on issues like elimination of poverty (Goal 1), erasing hunger (Goal 2), enforcing gender equality (Goal 5), reducing income inequality (Goal 10) and maintaining justice and strong institutional support (Goal 16). A similar agenda holds for India too. The existing literature shows that the presence of hunger, poverty and unemployment restrict the growth and development of emerging nations like India. These problems are more serious in rural places. Based on Census 2011 data and the methodology of the Suresh Tendulkar Committee, 269 million people, which is 21.9% of the entire population, were living below the poverty line; in rural areas, the figure was 25.7%. A total of 260 million people in the whole country did not have enough money at the start of the new millennium to access the consumption basket that determines the poverty level. Of them, 75% were in rural areas. Of the world's hungry individuals, 22% reside in India. The high rate of poverty is concerning because alleviating poverty has been an important objective of the development planning process.

Various rural development programmes are introduced and adopted at different points in time by the Government of India to reduce poverty and unemployment and to meet the basic needs of life. The Mahatma Gandhi National Rural Employment Guarantee Act (MGNREGA) is a big-fat social welfare programme adopted by the Government of India in the year 2005 to alleviate poverty in rural areas by providing unskilled employment to rural youths. The main goal of MGNREGA is to increase the livelihood stability of individuals living in rural areas by providing each adult member of a rural

DOI: 10.4324/9781003530688-13

family who volunteers to perform unskilled manual labour with at least 100 days of paid employment per fiscal year. In addition, this project has other objectives such as generating productive assets, protecting the environment, empowering rural women, reducing rural-urban migration and fostering social equality. By developing productive assets on irrigation, rural connectivity, sanitation and water conservation, the initiative also seeks to foster sustainable agriculture and rural development. As of 28 December 2023, 7.91 crore assets have been geo-tagged. This demand-driven and rights-based structural project is the biggest poverty alleviation programme in the world which started with an initial outlay of Rs. 11,300 crore in the year 2006–07. Currently, the MGNREGA scheme has been allotted Rs. 60,000 crores by the Union Budget for the fiscal year 2023–24. Millions of rural households have benefited from the programme's employment opportunities, which have improved millions of people's livelihoods. As of 28 December 2023, 5.39 crore households benefitted from this initiative and 231.34 crore person days are produced this year by 14.35 crore active workers.

MGNREGA is not an exception to the widespread belief that characteristics like complexity, uniqueness and big project sizes induce corruption. The way the public sector is governed affects both the creation of assets and the degree of corruption. Effective governance reduces corruption and facilitates the creation of assets. Good governance may result in low levels of corruption and high levels of assets creation. On the other hand, poor governance may result in increased corruption and increased assets creation or increased corruption and decreased assets creation. For example, let us consider that a rural household wishes to apply to the block authority in order to get benefits under the MGNREGA programme. The block authority will forward the request for job execution to the higher authority if the governance practice is good. It may result in an improvement in the state governments' PAI (Public Affairs Index) scores. If the authority insists on a commission or some sort of rent-seeking activity to supervise the works' executions, it is a sign that the state's governance is inadequate. Even after the project is approved, the local government may still demand a part of the money designated for personal assets creation. Hence, presence of corruption, poor regulatory quality and poor government effectiveness reduce the state's PAI score. However, there exists a market for corruption in which government officials are on the demand side, who seek bribes to allot the work, and households are on the supply side, who provide bribes to get the work done. The two phases of governance are as follows: processing the application for work sanctioned and supervising the work process once it is sanctioned for this project. Three scenarios might cause the states' PAI score to decrease: (1) the local government does not function well at either of the stages; (2) the authority functions successfully in the second stage but not in the first; (3) in the first stage the authority functions well, but in the second level it is less effective. In the third instance, the corruption market functions efficiently. That indicates that the local administration requests a bribe from the families to carry out the work after it gets approved. As a result, though states' PAI scores decrease, the number of assets creations increases.

Therefore, there ought to be a relationship between the number of assets created and governance practices. Our study under the backdrop aims to examine any correlation between assets creation and governance in the 18 selected states as well as for India as a whole between 2014 and 2022. In this study, we take control of corruption, government effectiveness and regulatory quality as governance indicators for all India study. In the case of Indian states, the data on these indicators are not available. So as a proxy for governance indicator, we take PAI for the study of selected states.

Literature Review

A list of relevant studies on MGNREGA are surveyed for the justification of the present study. According to Alam and Alam (2014), the most disadvantaged and socially exploited members of the village benefit greatly from MGNREGA because of more work opportunities and increased wages; the poor population in the village now enjoys a higher level of living. MGNREGA has a substantial positive impact on rural workers in the state of Tamil Nadu, increasing their pay rates and giving them more negotiating leverage over higher caste employers while decreasing their reliance on them (Carswell & Neve, 2014). MGNREGA improves the purchasing power of the beneficiaries, food and non-food consumption, education and health. It also aids in the development of rural infrastructure and improves the livelihood of rural residents (Sharma et al., 2022; Kharkwal & Kumar, 2015).

In the Chitradurga district of Karnataka, Tiwari et al. (2011) investigate the effects of MGNREAGA on environmental sustainability and agricultural productivity. It also shows that, with long-term implementation, MGNREGA may create a sustainable environment. In just three years of implementation, it has proven to be very effective in reducing agricultural vulnerability caused by unpredictable rainfall, infertile soil and inadequate irrigation systems. Reddy et al. (2014) discovered that the MGNREGA mostly affects agriculture through the labour market in some Andhra Pradesh communities in terms of high salary and negotiating power. In that case, the farmers who are not participants of MGNREGA suffer mostly due to an increase in wage rate along with other input cost.

Rekha and Mehta (2019) draw that MGNREGA significantly improves the social and economic circumstances of the extremely poor, rural residents and a sizable segment of the caste system and other backward classes. The majority of rural Indians, according to Patwardhan and Tasciotti (2023), are heavily burdened by personal debt, whether it be institutional or non-institutional. MGNREGA increases rural income and lowers poverty while assisting low-income families in lowering their debt load. On the other hand, in the Annupur and Dindori districts of Madhya Pradesh, most of the job card holders are engaged in the cultivation of paddy and cereal and they have an income from farming in both districts. So, these schemes help the farmer as a subsidiary (Singh et al., 2022). Overall, it makes rural livelihood better and it has much scope for the inclusive development of social groups (Nazeer, 2015).

Remarkably, MGNREGA raises the pay rate for women more than it does for men (Reddy et al., 2014). This project has significant impact on women employment, household income, and agricultural output (Fernandez, 2015; Hussain & Singh, 2022). Even in Tamil Nadu, women participate in the MGNREGA plan at a very high rate—roughly 80% of all beneficiaries help rural women become self-sufficient and independent; this project has a significant influence on the empowerment of rural women (Rajlaxmi, 2017). Additionally, the majority of women chose to work under this programme since it allowed them to take care of their children and do domestic duties in addition to working less hours. On the contrary, males from Tamil Nadu move to Kerala in search of better salaries. According to Kadiya et al. (2016), the MGNREGA work requirements vary by Indian state, with some having very high rates of female involvement and others experiencing implementation issues. Three of India's 18 states—Tamil Nadu, West Bengal and Rajasthan—are found to be requesting the most labour under this scheme, according to this survey. This project increases the productive labour demand in the rural economy, reduces migration and helps to alleviate poverty through assets creation (Nazeer, 2015). Neogi et al. (2016) find that the MGNREGA scheme has helped in increasing fish cultivation in Indian states in the way that an increase in Rs. 1 lakh of MGNREGA fund for rainwater harvesting leads to an increase in the fish production of 2.6 quintals.

Goyal and Datta (2020) find that employment generation, specially women employment, under MGNREGA is increasing in India, but assets creation is not satisfactory although it differs across states. Deb (2017) finds that although MGNREGA allocates huge funds for rural development in India, due to a lack of proper planning for the implementation and lack of transparency, rural people cannot get maximum utilisation from this scheme. Ranjan (2016) conclude that MGNREGA reaches its aims to increase income, wage rate and purchasing power of the rural people. However, it fails to achieve the goal of sustainable assets creation. Turangi (2018) finds the performance of MGNREGA at Kalaburagi district of Karnataka, a drought prone area where the socio-economic condition is very poor. Although the implementation of MGNREGA for 11 years (2006–17) attempts to generate employment, it fails to create sustainable assets creation due to proper implementation of the scheme. MGNREGA has a significant influence on the creation of both private and public assets in India (Keerthi et al., 2014). According to survey respondents, the three districts of Madhya Pradesh have exceptionally strong individual and community asset generation under the MGNERA system (Mishra, 2011). However, Sinha (2020) finds that, because of an unlawful connection and a corrupt administration, MGNREGA is unable to maintain rural development in the state of Bihar, despite its immense ability to do so.

The output of MGNREGA is not the same for all the states, districts, blocks and even villages; it differs in different locations. Naskar (2019) finds that in a district of West Bengal, the average work days for the people under MGNREGA is hardly 50 and the participation of social caste and social tribe has decreased. Breitkreuz et al. (2017) try to seek the effects of MGNREGA in three states of India, namely, Kerala, Tamil Nadu and Odisha, and find that in Tamil Nadu 72% surveyors work for an average of 68 days under the project, in Kerala 46% people work for 57 days and in Odisha 61% participants work only for 36 days. This scheme faces some challenges like inadequate funds, corruption and problems in the implementation process. Therefore, MGNREGA fails to create sustainable assets due to corruption and lack of proper implementation planning.

Relevance of the Present Study

The extant literature survey has shown some works on the effects of MGNREGA on employment, income generation, security and sustainability of rural livelihood. Some studies say that there is a lack of implementation planning in the process of assets creation. However, studies regarding the assets creation by the MGNREGA initiatives and its related governance performance are lacking. But there should be a connection between good governance and assets creation under the MGNREGA scheme for its viability so far as the mission of rural development is concerned. The present study has attempted to find out the association between governance and rural assets creation, and the corresponding impact analysis of the former upon the latter in the 18 selected states as well as for overall India for the period of 2014–22.

Objectives of the Study

The present study has the following specific objectives:

1. To find the scenario of assets creation in different heads of the MGNREGA scheme across the selected Indian states over the period of 2014–22.
2. To examine the ranks of the selected states and the related rank correlation over years in different heads of assets creation.

3. To examine the association between governance indicators and assets creation during 2016–22 across the states.
4. To quantify the impacts of different governance indicators upon assets creations for the pooled data across the states for 2016–18 and 2019–22 separately.
5. To find the association between governance and assets creations in all India level for the period 2014–22 and its associated impact assessment.

Data and Methodology

The analysis is conducted from two perspectives: one covers India as a whole, while the other focuses on its major states. In case of overall India, the study has four variables: Assets Created (AC) under the project of the MGNREGA scheme and the three governance indicators, namely, Control of Corruption (CC), Government Effectiveness (GE) and Regulatory Quality (RQ). The data on assets created under MGNREGA are taken from the official website of MGNREGA (www.nregastrep.nic.in). We take ten heads of assets creation under which are, namely, Anganwadi/other rural infrastructure (ARI), drought proofing (DP), flood control and protection (FCP), micro irrigation works (MIW), works on individual land (WIL), land development (LD), rural connectivity (RC), rural sanitation (RS), water conservation & water harvesting (WCWH) and renovation of traditional water bodies (RTWB). The data on CC, GE and RQ are taken from the Worldwide Governance Indicators (WGI) database of the World Bank (www.govindicators.org). In the case of the study for the major states of India, there are 18 states on the list. It has two variables: Assets Created under the project of the MGNREGA scheme across states and the PAI. PAI measures the quality of governance in the states of India. The data on PAI is available from 2016 to 2022. During 2016–18, the PAI was calculated based on ten themes, namely, essential infrastructure, social protection, crime, law & order, delivery to justice, transparency and accountability, fiscal management, etc. Beginning in 2019, PAI integrated 13 SDGs into the development trajectory of the Indian states, along with three primary pillars: growth, equity and sustainability. Therefore, from 2016 to 2022, a one-on-one comparison would not be meaningful. Considering this, we split the time frame into two smaller periods for the analysis of Indian states: 2016–18 and 2019–22. The data on PAI is taken from the database of the PAI published by the Public Affairs Centre (https://pacindia.org).

For the analysis of trends of assets created in the project of MGNREGA in overall India as well as in 18 major states, simple line graphs are fitted. After that some descriptive statistics, i.e., mean and standard deviation (SD), are computed to have some basic ideas about the assets generated. We have calculated ranks for assets creation under MGNREGA and PAI for 18 states.

Using pooled data, we try to calculate correlation coefficients and regression coefficients between heads of assets creation and PAI for the states over the years 2016–18 and 2019–22 separately because of the differences in the natures of the databases in the two sub-periods for the latter. We then try to find the rank correlation for the heads of assets creation across the states over the period of 2014–22 with the help of Spearman's Rank Correlation method to find whether the states maintain the same pattern in their positions over the years.

The formula for the Pearson's correlation coefficient (r) between any two indicators (x, y) is:

$$r = \frac{cov(x,y)}{\sigma_x \sigma_y}$$

where the value of correlation coefficient (r) lies between –1 and +1, $cov(x, y)$ is the covariance of x and y, σ_x is the standard deviation of x and σ_y is the standard deviation of y.

The Spearman's Rank Correlation (R) formula is of the form

$$R = 1 - \frac{6\sum d^2}{n(n^2 - 1)}$$

where the value of Spearman's Rank Correlation (R) lies between –1 and +1, d = difference between the two ranks of each observation, and n = number of observations.

The statistical significance of the correlation coefficient is tested by the formula of t-statistics

$$t = \frac{R\sqrt{(n - 2)}}{\sqrt{(1 - R^2)}}$$

The hypothesis for rank correlation is

H_0: $R = 0$ (no rank correlation between variables)
H_1: $R \neq 0$ (presence of rank correlation between variables)

In the case of overall India, we have calculated correlation coefficients in the pairs of heads of Assets Created – Control of Corruption, heads of Assets Created – Government Effectiveness and heads of Assets Created – Regulatory Quality.

Results and Discussion

The study analyses the objectives in the following part involving the associated data and methodologies. To analyse the first one, we plot the trends of all the ten heads of Assets Creation for the selected states and overall India in the line diagram (Figure 10.1). The figure shows that in the whole India, works on individual land have increased most and assets on rural sanitation have declined drastically over the study period. Assets creation on land development, water conservation & water harvesting, Anganwadi/other rural infrastructure and micro irrigation works gradually have increased. On the

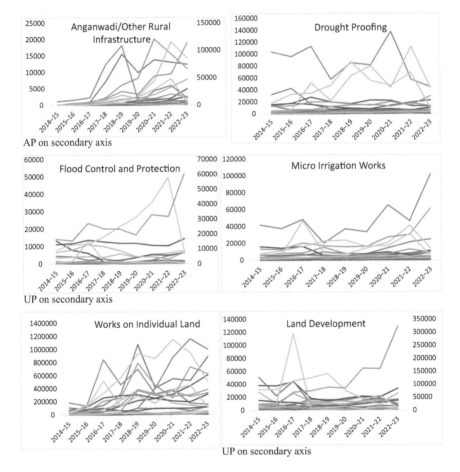

FIGURE 10.1   Trends of different heads of assets creation in 18 states and for overall India.

Note: In all India figure works on individual land is measured in the secondary axis.

Source: Drawn by the authors.

(*Continued*)

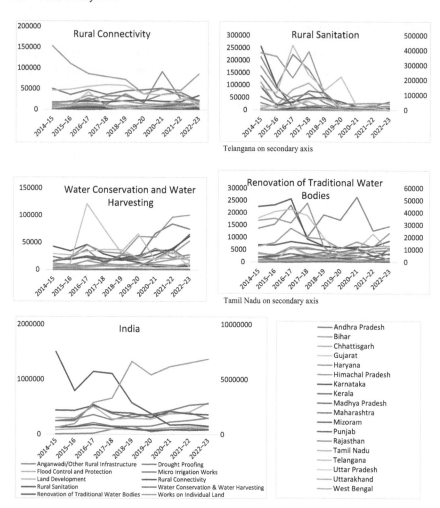

FIGURE 10.1   (Continued)

other hand, the number of assets creation on rural connectivity, renovation of traditional water bodies and rural connectivity have decreased.

In the case of the states, assets creation on ARI has increased for all the 18 states from 2014 to 2022. Andhra Pradesh has the highest number of assets creation on ARI from 2014–15 to 2018–19 and in 2018–19 it reaches its peak point and after that the downfall starts. Andhra Pradesh has the highest number of assets creation in DF from 2014–15 to 2020–21 except for the year 2018–19. In the head of FCP, Uttar Pradesh and West Bengal have significant increasing trends throughout the period. In 2021–22 and 2022–23, West Bengal and Uttar Pradesh reach the peak point of their trend lines, respectively. Andhra Pradesh, Uttar Pradesh, West Bengal, Telangana and

Bihar have increasing trends in the head of MIW. In most of the states, the trends on assets creation under WIL are rising. In the case of LD and WCWH, Telangana reaches its highest in 2016–17. The assets creation under RC decreases significantly for Uttar Pradesh. However, assets creation under RS has decreasing trends for most of the states. This may be because before 2014–15 more works under this head were done for most of the states. In the case of RTWB, while Kerala, West Bengal, Tamil Nadu and Uttar Pradesh face decreasing trends, Gujarat, Punjab, Madhya Pradesh and Telangana face rising trends.

As the trends on assets creation have ups and downs, we have calculated their average to find how many assets are created on an average and in which states. Table 10.1 presents the mean and SD values of all the selected states in the ten heads.

From the table, it is observed that in the heads of ARI, DP and MIW, Andhra Pradesh has the highest mean value. Andhra Pradesh creates on an average number of 2766786481 and 48051 assets under the heads of ARL, DP and MIW, respectively. However, Uttar Pradesh has the highest mean value in the head of FCP. In the case of WIL, West Bengal creates on an average the highest asset followed by Madhya Pradesh, Bihar, Uttar Pradesh and Andhra Pradesh.

Uttar Pradesh has the highest average assets creation in the heads of LD and RC. Telangana has the highest and Tamil Nadu has the second highest mean value of assets creation in the head of RS. Whereas in the case of WCWH, Tamil Nadu has the highest and Telangana has the second highest mean value of assets creation. Again, Tamil Nadu is able to create an average of 18451 assets, which is the highest number in the head of RTWB. In most of the heads, Haryana, Mizoram and Punjab are doing the lowest assets creation.

The trend lines and the mean values of assets creation cannot give us a clear picture of the ranks that the states held. So, we have calculated ranks for every state for all the 10 heads of assets creation from 2014 to 2022 and calculated Spearman's Rank Correlation to have a look at whether the states are able to maintain their positions or not. Only with the signs and values of the rank correlation, we cannot conclude whether the positive and negative relationships are significant or not. So, the Student's t-test is done. Table 10.2 presents the said results.

It is observed that all the rank correlation coefficients are positive and near 1 for all the states in all the heads. It indicates that the ranks of the states in a particular year are positively correlated with the previous year's rank of these states. All the calculated t-values are significant at a 5% level of significance. So, the null hypothesis (H_0) is rejected and the alternative hypothesis (H_1) is accepted. That means through the study period, states are maintaining their ranks and their ranks are not changing significantly.

TABLE 10.1 Mean (SD) Values of Assets Creation of 18 States

States	ARI	DP	FCP	MIW	WIL	LD	RC	RS	WCWH	RTWB
Andhra Pradesh	27667.4 (37499.9)	86480.6 (29801.8)	929.2 (336.3)	48051.1 (23598.4)	372735.9 (255114.3)	1998.6 (812.9)	28999.8 (25139.8)	86568.9 (92287.0)	24804.1 (9120.4)	16921.8 (5208.8)
Bihar	1425.9 (2285.2)	14441.6 (13855.3)	2082.0 (2051.4)	10878.2 (7937.1)	397856.3 (481922.0)	12923.6 (5468.7)	26952.1 (9366.2)	13122.6 (16595.6)	11415.0 (11753.7)	1579.3 (502.8)
Chhattisgarh	2638.7 (2634.2)	3182.2 (1053.4)	316.9 (169.6)	2415.2 (1002.7)	157333.6 (129381.9)	16460.7 (6115.9)	7802.2 (4722.6)	33951.2 (37294.7)	16352.2 (5788.7)	5295.2 (1329.3)
Gujarat	529.4 (546.1)	5813.6 (2227.1)	2213.9 (1328.5)	379.1 (336.0)	60645.7 (44707.0)	8332.1 (4011.7)	5355.2 (1019.7)	21783.8 (23983.9)	7757.2 (2414.5)	4352.2 (1242.5)
Haryana	124.0 (150.0)	324.6 (368.6)	200.8 (81.6)	2568.8 (932.8)	3802.3 (2942.7)	1670.8 (739.2)	2978.1 (1360.3)	1431.3 (1568.9)	871.6 (295.3)	491.1 (224.2)
Himachal Pradesh	428.4 (551.4)	726.1 (417.2)	4877.9 (1387.4)	2498.2 (678.5)	31074.2 (14483.9)	12036.4 (2751.7)	8706.0 (3264.8)	3589.9 (3533.7)	6350.1 (1361.4)	503.6 (136.1)
Karnataka	1294.3 (1564.7)	14893.1 (4886.4)	12076.7 (1385.0)	6575.2 (2084.1)	296265.4 (160411.0)	11302.7 (3435.6)	21498.7 (5058.6)	42622.4 (85838.0)	27524.8 (14575.7)	6999.9 (967.9)
Kerala	621.8 (924.0)	6864.3 (2452.0)	5673.7 (3541.2)	9920.3 (4456.3)	84765.3 (25612.6)	27426.2 (10975.7)	6867.3 (3598.3)	5664.0 (4398.1)	37371.9 (13050.5)	11655.9 (9400.7)
Madhya Pradesh	8161.8 (6243.4)	6224.9 (2981.2)	1089.0 (614.2)	376.2 (349.5)	455174.4 (347172.9)	19684.1 (17383.6)	41145.7 (10025.8)	49588.4 (40679.4)	39175.6 (27523.6)	2669.0 (1349.9)
Maharashtra	140.9 (296.5)	18950.6 (4876.7)	621.9 (251.6)	318.1 (157.8)	159108.7 (103874.2)	3900.8 (1743.3)	5588.9 (1439.6)	34423.9 (27390.2)	14100.7 (6302.7)	1980.9 (782.8)
Mizoram	314.7 (289.3)	495.7 (228.6)	244.8 (109.6)	227.7 (141.6)	7129.4 (5756.2)	2341.8 (740.0)	1870.4 (871.1)	656.4 (394.7)	884.4 (456.8)	166.0 (103.6)
Punjab	496.7 (548.2)	3236.8 (2071.6)	589.9 (234.2)	2535.1 (1370.8)	5054.1 (5694.1)	4628.8 (1849.7)	9325.3 (3548.5)	224.3 (236.9)	376.3 (246.4)	2914.7 (769.3)
Rajasthan	1471.4 (1205.4)	4253.1 (1215.7)	954.2 (350.1)	4828.2 (775.6)	219219.3 (142907.9)	3532.1 (1261.2)	18918.9 (6869.0)	16500.8 (36103.6)	13253.0 (5222.9)	4187.9 (1291.4)
Tamil Nadu	7212.9 (7208.2)	11285.1 (5344.7)	303.9 (317.5)	8954.3 (3158.4)	203747.0 (149823.9)	4678.2 (2728.6)	9470.6 (3927.2)	108529.2 (94776.2)	42342.7 (38161.6)	18451.1 (18698.7)

Telangana	5037.9	47841.4	2515.2	18486.1	243537.2	17316.9	13958.6	150958.2	42232.4	3957.9
	(7180.8)	(34977.1)	(4011.6)	(15226.9)	(172092.9)	(37902.7)	(13290.6)	(134823.4)	(38212.8)	(3412.3)
Uttar Pradesh	5365.8	17977.1	27884.0	23807.8	374854.9	111635.8	80329.0	43702.8	32429.8	8754.6
	(6152.4)	(5448.8)	(13578.8)	(15394.7)	(288940.5)	(93944.3)	(35858.4)	(54980.3)	(11515.3)	(2711.7)
Uttarakhand	298.2	1733.1	6743.6	3938.0	17777.1	10662.6	7935.9	8241.1	5928.6	858.4
	(235.0)	(1238.0)	(2765.2)	(2213.4)	(12783.9)	(6776.5)	(2906.5)	(11412.7)	(3493.1)	(348.6)
West Bengal	2046.9	44829.8	20720.3	16781.9	608197.0	32220.2	43138.0	18519.4	26912.2	10990.9
	(2736.5)	(24336.3)	(14326.7)	(8409.0)	(389715.3)	(16716.4)	(16201.3)	(14730.8)	(10160.4)	(8693.1)

Source: Calculated by the authors.

TABLE 10.2 Spearman's Rank Correlation Coefficients and Corresponding Estimated *t*-Values

Heads on Assets Creation	2015–16	2016–17	2017–18	2018–19	2019–20	2020–21	2021–22	2022–23
ARI	0.82 (5.83)	0.94 (10.83)	0.95 (12.66)	0.98 (18.03)	0.89 (8.01)	0.86 (6.67)	0.96 (14.70)	0.79 (5.14)
DP	0.98 (20.43)	0.92 (9.21)	0.94 (10.81)	0.99 (25.14)	0.98 (21.70)	0.98 (18.42)	0.94 (11.02)	0.90 (8.39)
FCP	0.91 (8.83)	0.95 (12.49)	0.87 (6.98)	0.98 (19.35)	0.96 (13.12)	0.96 (13.84)	0.98 (21.70)	0.92 (9.62)
MIW	0.98 (20.43)	0.97 (16.25)	0.90 (8.39)	0.97 (15.15)	0.95 (12.80)	0.96 (14.68)	0.98 (20.43)	0.89 (8.00)
WIL	0.90 (8.29)	0.96 (14.68)	0.88 (7.33)	0.92 (9.21)	0.91 (8.83)	0.86 (6.60)	0.91 (8.61)	0.91 (8.61)
LD	0.95 (12.21)	0.82 (5.77)	0.76 (4.74)	0.94 (11.02)	0.98 (19.35)	0.85 (6.37)	0.94 (11.23)	0.71 (3.99)
RC	0.95 (12.80)	0.92 (9.48)	0.87 (6.91)	0.91 (8.61)	0.81 (5.60)	0.90 (8.39)	0.91 (8.95)	0.79 (5.13)
RS	0.94 (11.46)	0.81 (5.47)	0.90 (8.29)	0.96 (13.84)	0.76 (4.74)	0.86 (6.72)	0.92 (9.34)	0.71 (4.03)
WCWH	0.95 (12.21)	0.90 (8.50)	0.94 (10.62)	0.87 (7.04)	0.90 (8.29)	0.78 (4.93)	0.90 (8.19)	0.83 (5.86)
RTWB	0.95 (12.21)	0.93 (10.26)	0.96 (13.12)	0.98 (20.43)	0.71 (4.01)	0.96 (13.46)	0.86 (6.84)	0.78 (4.96)

Source: Calculated by the authors.

Note: Estimated *t*-values are given within parentheses. All the rank correlation coefficients are significant at 5% level of significance.

Since governance indicator is an important factor to influence the assets creation under the MGNREGA scheme, it is required to correlate assets creation with governance indicators across the states. As mentioned earlier the PAI covers the role of governance at the state level, we use it as the proxy of good governance across the states. To link up PAI with assets creation statistically, Pearson's Correlation Coefficients between AC and PAI are calculated for each of the selected states using pooled data in two periods 2016–18 and 2019–22 separately, and the corresponding t-test is done for testing their statistical significance. Figure 10.2 gives an overview of the scenarios for PAI in the pooled data for the two phases and three governance indicators for all India level.

It is observed that all the PAI values in most of the states are with falling trends, meaning that the states have maintained lax governance at different stages. On the other hand, the governance indicators for CC, GE and RQ have improved over the years.

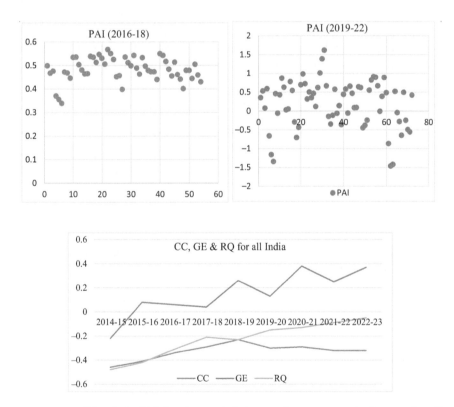

FIGURE 10.2 Trends in PAI for the pooled data and governance indicators for all India level.

Source: Drawn by the authors.

Table 10.3 presents the values of correlation coefficients and the corresponding estimated *t*-values. With respect to the correlation coefficient between AC and PAI, the values are positive for some heads and negative for some other heads. The negative value of the correlation coefficient means an increase in PAI is associated with a decrease in AC and vice versa, and the positive value of the correlation coefficient means the direct relationship between PAI and AC.

It is observed that for two heads, namely, WIL and RC, the correlation coefficients are negative and significant for both periods. In both periods, a decrease in PAI is correlated with an increase in assets creation on WIL and RC. This may be due to the lax governance in the states. This result supports the third case, which is stated in the introduction section. The possible reason is that the local government demands some bribe to execute the assets creation under these heads. As a result, more assets are created but the PAI score of that state has decreased. In the case of RTWB, the correlation coefficient is positive and significant. It implies that a decrease in PAI is associated with a decrease in AC on that head. This result supports the case 1, which is stated in the introduction section. However, for FCP and LD, the correlation coefficient is negative and insignificant in the first period, but in the second period, it is negative and significant. In the first period, decrease in PAI insignificantly

TABLE 10.3 Correlation Coefficients and Corresponding *t*-Values of AC & PAI (Pooled Data)

Heads on Assets Creation (States)	*Correlation Coefficients of AC & PAI (t-Values)*	
	2016–18	*2019–22*
Anganwadi/other rural infrastructure	−0.08(−0.56)	0.06(0.50)
Drought proofing	−0.05(−0.38)	0.04(0.35)
Flood control and protection	−0.13(−0.92)	−0.29(−2.67)*
Micro irrigation works	−0.09(−0.65)	−0.04(−0.31)
Works on individual land	−0.29(−2.28)*	−0.38(−3.68)*
Land development	−0.21(−1.57)	−0.23(−2.09)*
Rural connectivity	−0.48(−4.48)*	−0.31(−2.85)*
Rural sanitation	0.07(0.48)	−0.01(−0.08)
Water conservation & water harvesting	0.01(0.05)	0.14(1.21)
Renovation of traditional water bodies	0.29(2.31)*	0.10(0.85)

Source: Computed by the authors.

Note: (−) signs indicate that the variables are negatively correlated, and (+) signs indicate that the variables are positively correlated. (*) mark indicates significant correlation coefficient at the 5% level of significance.

increases the AC but in the second period, a decrease in PAI significantly increases AC under these heads. The probable cause might be the presence of high magnitudes of corruption which helped in more assets creation in the second period. Here, corruption might play the role of additional incentives to assets creation. The probable cause might be the presence of high magnitudes of corruption which helped in more assets creation in the second period. There may be good governance in the processing phase of getting the project sanctioned, but there is a high magnitude of lax governance in the execution phase leading to declining scores in the PAI, which means poor governance is associated with larger assets creations.

To get the impacts of PAI upon assets creation on different heads in the states, we have run regression of the latter being the dependent variable upon the former. This exercise is done across two sub-periods 2016–18 and 2019–22. The results are given in Table 10.4.

It is observed that the values of R-square for all heads in both periods are very low. This may be because we have run the regression with only one independent variable. However, we get some significant results in both periods. In the first period, the PAI affects RC significantly in a negative way. The result shows that if the PAI value decreases by one unit, it leads to increase in 205216 assets creation under the head of RC. In the case of WIL and RTWB, PAI affects the assets creation in a weakly significant negative way.

However, in the second period, FCP, WIL and RC have significant negative regression coefficients. The result shows that if the PAI value decreases by one unit, it leads to more 5238, 174869 and 8791 assets creations under the heads of FCP, WIL and RC, respectively. In the case of the LD, the result is negative and poorly significant. In the first period, ARI and DP have a negative and insignificant regression coefficient, but in the next period, they have insignificant positive values. Only for WCWH, we have insignificant positive values for both periods.

For overall India, we take CC, GE and RQ as governance indicators and calculate Pearson's Correlation Coefficient between AC & CC, AC & GE and AC & RQ separately. Only with the signs and values of the correlation coefficient, we cannot conclude whether the positive and negative relationships are significant or not. So, the Student's t-test is done. Table 10.5 represents the values of correlation coefficients and corresponding estimated t-values.

In the case of AC & CC, we get significant positive correlation values for ARI, DP and WIL. This means for these three heads corruption control leads to more assets creation, and assets creation and corruption control are increasing at all India level. However, for RC and RTWB, assets creation and corruption control have a negative weak association and for RS it is negative and poorly significant. For FCP, MIW and WCWH, the correlation coefficients are positive but insignificant.

TABLE 10.4 Regression Results of Different Heads on Assets Creation and PAI for State

Heads on Assets Creation (States)	2016–18			2019–22		
	t-Value	Regression Coefficient	R-Square	t-Value	Regression Coefficient	R-square
Anganwadi/other rural infrastructure	−0.563	−27683.3	0.0061	0.498	496.2	0.0035
Drought proofing	−0.377	−25511.1	0.0081	0.35	1752.6	0.0018
Flood control and protection	−0.915	−17497.4	0.0158	−2.536*	−5237.8*	0.0842
Micro irrigation works	−0.652	−19513.9	0.0081	−0.311	−1026.5	0.0014
Works on individual land	−2.181	−1509655.5	0.0838	−3.388*	−174869*	0.1409
Land development	−1.533	−101977.8	0.0433	−2.021	−17001.4	0.0552
Rural connectivity	−3.932*	−205216.2*	0.2291	−2.696*	−8791.2*	0.0941
Rural sanitation	0.483	106101.2	0.0045	−0.079	−406.8	0.0001
Water conservation & water harvesting	0.054	3097.5	0.0001	1.191	5372.5	0.0199
Renovation of traditional water bodies	−2.206	−18455.3	0.0855	0.84	700.4	0.0100

Source: Computed by the authors.

Note: (*) mark indicates significant correlation coefficient at 5% level of significance. At 5% level of significance with degrees of freedom 7, the *t*-statistic value is 2.365.

TABLE 10.5 Correlation Coefficient of AC & CC, AC & GE and AC & RQ for All India

Heads on Assets Creation (India)	Correlation Coefficient of AC & CC (t-Value)	Correlation Coefficient of AC & GE (t-Value)	Correlation Coefficient of AC & RQ (t-Value)
Anganwadi/other rural infrastructure	0.85(7.93)*	0.70(3.62)	0.72(3.97)*
Drought proofing	0.60(2.50)*	0.60(2.51)*	0.56(2.15)
Flood control and protection	0.21(0.59)	0.67(3.27)*	0.68(3.32)*
Micro irrigation works	0.22(0.61)	0.69(3.45)*	0.71(3.86)*
Works on individual land	0.81(6.39)*	0.87(9.84)*	0.92(15.95)*
Land development	0.03(0.09)	0.44(1.45)	0.42(1.37)
Rural connectivity	−0.39(−1.21)	−0.38(−1.15)	−0.59(−2.40)*
Rural sanitation	−0.56(−2.19)	−0.92(−15.63)*	−0.85(−7.93)*
Water conservation & water harvesting	0.36(1.10)	0.56(2.19)	0.71(3.82)*
Renovation of traditional water bodies	−0.42(−1.35)	−0.61(−2.54)*	−0.67(−3.25)*

Source: Computed by the authors.

Note: (−) signs indicate that the variables are negatively correlated, and (+) signs indicate that the variables are positively correlated. The (*) marks indicate significant correlation coefficient at 5% level of significance.

In the case of AC & GE, we get significant positive correlation coefficients for ARI, DP, FCP, MIW and WIL. For these heads, both assets creation and government effectiveness are increasing. For RS and RTWB, the correlation coefficients are negative and significant and for WCWH, the value is poorly significant. In the case of AC & RQ, we get positive and significant associations for ARI, FCP, MIW, WIL and WCWH. But this value is significantly negative for RC, RS and RTWB. For DP, the value is positive and poorly significant. The positive value of the correlation coefficient implies that an increase in governance indicators is associated with an increase in assets creation and vice versa, and the negative value of the correlation coefficient indicates that an increase in governance indicators is correlated with a decrease of assets creation. We can say that for assets creation under ARI, DP, FCP, MIW, WIL and WCWH, good governance plays a significant positive role. That means good governance leads to more assets creation under these heads. However, for assets creation under RC, RS and RTWB, good governance leads to a decrease in assets creation.

To get the impacts of governance indicators upon assets creation on different heads at all India level, we have run regression of the latter being the dependent variable upon the former. This exercise is done for the period of 2014–22. The results are given in Table 10.6.

When we consider the assets creation as the dependent variable, it is observed that control of corruption has a positive significant effect on the heads of ARI and WIL. This means assets creation increases with the increase in CC. An increase in CC indicates good governance and a reduction in corruption. The acceptable sign of the governance indicators should be positive in the sense that as the magnitude of good governance rises, the number of assets creation should increase. In the case of AC & GE, we get significant positive regression coefficients in the heads of ARI, FDP, MIW and WIL. This means the government effectiveness affects assets creation under these heads positively. Good governance factors become responsible for assets creation. Conversely, GE has a detrimental impact on the development of assets in the rural sanitation domain. For the RQ in this head, we obtain the same result. This can be because there is no longer a requirement to develop new assets in this category because a greater quantity of assets was created prior to the research period. It is observed that the regulatory quality affects assets creation positively in the heads of ARI, FDP, MIW, WIL and WCWH. But in the head of RTWB, it affects assets creation negatively. That means an increase in good governance leads to a decrease in assets creation under this head.

Conclusion

With the major objective of whether any relationship between good governance and assets creation under the MGNREGA project is there in Indian states in the pooled data format and all India level, the study finds that assets creations in the heads of Anganwadi/other rural infrastructure, micro irrigation works, works on individual land, land development and water conservation and water harvesting are rising across the states over the period 2014–22. However, states have maintained their ranks in the similar order over the years leading to the value of the rank correlation coefficient close to unitary. For the Indian states, the correlation coefficient and regression coefficient show striking negative signs in the case of PAI and assets creation which means poor governance quality of local authority is associated with an increase in assets creation in the states. There is good governance in the processing phase of getting the project sanctioned but there is a high magnitude of lax governance in the execution phase leading to declining scores in the PAI, which means poor governance is associated with larger assets creations. However, the correlation and regression coefficients of assets creation and governance indicators for the entire country are positive for most of the heads justifying good governance is associated with larger numbers of assets

TABLE 10.6 Regression Results of Different Heads on AC & CC, AC & GE and AC &RQ for all India Level

Heads of Assets Creation	AC & CC			AC & GE			AC & RQ		
	t-Value	Regression Coefficient	R-square	t-Value	Regression Coefficient	R-square	t-Value	Regression Coefficient	R-square
Anganwadi/other rural infrastructure	4.22*	615288 *	0.72	2.59*	184500*	0.49	2.75*	243869*	0.52
Drought proofing	2.00	487046	0.36	2.00	177038	0.36	1.78	210487	0.31
Flood control and protection	0.58	63610	0.05	2.41*	72824*	0.45	2.44*	93961*	0.46
Micro irrigation works	0.60	200400	0.05	2.50*	226370*	0.47	2.70*	301711*	0.51
Works on individual land	3.71*	29440319*	0.66	4.77*	11485283*	0.76	6.23*	15501755*	0.85
Land development	0.09	54992	0.00	1.30	254345	0.20	1.24	312435	0.18
Rural connectivity	-1.12	-339236	0.15	-1.07	-118772	0.14	-1.94	-240081	0.35
Rural sanitation	-1.81	-4086365	0.32	-6.16*	-2418365*	0.84	-4.22*	-2858317*	0.72
Water conservation & water harvesting	1.02	644783	0.13	1.81	365477	0.32	2.68*	592042*	0.51
Renovation of traditional water bodies	-1.23	-218315	0.18	-2.02	-114243	0.37	-2.40*	-162488*	0.45

Source: Computed by the authors.

Note: (*) mark indicates significant regression coefficient at 5% level of significance. At 5% level of significance with degrees of freedom 7, the t-statistic value is 2.365.

creations. But there are some assets like rural sanitation, renovation of traditional water bodies and rural connectivity where good regulatory quality and government effectiveness are probably responsible for a low number of assets creations.

With these good results, the study could have gone through several subpools of the data to examine the similar type of investigation objectives that the study preserves as the future agenda.

References

Alam, S. Md. & Alam, M. N. (2014). Good governance and employment generation through MGNREGA. *International Journal of Economics, Commerce and Management*, 2(9), 1–17. UK.

Breitkreuz, R., et al. (2017). The Mahatma Gandhi National Rural Employment Guarantee Scheme: A policy solution to rural poverty in India. *Development Policy Review (ODI)*, 35(3), 397–417.

Carswell, G. & Neve, G. D. (2014). MGNREGA in Tamil Nadu: A story of success and transformation? *Journal of Agrarian Change*, 14(4), 564–585.

Deb, D. (2017). Impact of MGNREGA on rural livelihood of Assam. *International Journal of Application or Innovation in Engineering and Management*, 6(8), 141–146.

Fernandez, D. (2015). Implementation of MGNREGA & its impact on rural Madhya Pradesh. *The Indian Journal of Industrial Relation*, 50(3), 505–516.

Goyal, S. & Datta, D. (2020). Performance of Mahatma Gandhi National Rural Employment Guarantee Act (MGNREGA): A review of women employment. *International Journal for Research Engineering & Management (IJREAM)*, 06(07), 2454–9150.

Hussain, A. & Singh, A. (2022). Analytical study of MNREGA's impact on rural livelihood of Indian states of Assam. *International Journal of Creative Research Thoughts (IJCRT)*, 10(10), 126–134. ISSN: 2320-2882.

Kadiya, S., Parashar, S. & Vatavwala, S. (2016). Work demand pattern analysis for MGNREGA: With special reference to 18 Indian states, *Scientific Paper Series Management, Economics Engineering in Agriculture and Rural Development*, 16(4), 2284–7995.

Keerthi, K., Bhattarai, M., Kamala, T. S. & Rao, P. P. (2014). MGNREGA impact on rural assets creation: A study in two villages of Prakasham district of Andhra Pradesh, India. http://oar.icrisat.org/id/eprint/8356

Kharkwal, S. & Kumar, A. (2015). Socio-economic impact of MGNREGA: Evidences from district of Udham Singh Nagar in Uttarakhand, India. *Indian Journal of Economics and Development*, 3(12), 1–10.

Mishra, S. K. (2011). Asset creation under MGNREGA: A study in three districts of Madhya Pradesh. 3(3), 19–30.

Naskar, K. (2019). MGNREGA and its impact on the village economy of West Bengal Economics with rural development. http://inet.vidyasagar.ac.in:8080/jspui/handle/123456789/5588

Nazeer, U. (2015) MGNREGA for inclusive development in India: An analysis, *Spanish Journal of Rural Development*, 6(1), 1–6.

Neogi C., Ray, K. & Das, R. C. (2016). Is MGNREG scheme complementary to fishing activities? A study on some selected states of India. *Journal of Research in Business & Social Science*, 5 (1), 47–53.

Patwardhan, S. & Tasciotti, L. (2023) The effect of the Mahatma Gandhi National Rural Employment Guarantee Act on the size of outstanding debts in rural India. *Journal of Development Effectiveness*, 15(4), 353–372.

Rajlaxmi, V. (2017). Impact of MGNREGA on women empowerment and their issues and challenges: A review of literature from 2005 to 2015. *Journal of Internet Banking and Commerce*, 22(S7), 1–13.

Ranjan, R. (2016). Mahatma Gandhi National Rural Employment Guarantee Act (MGNREGA): A critical appraisal of its performance since its inception. *Indore Management Journal*, 8(2), 55–73.

Reddy, D. Narasimha, Reddy, A. Amarender, Nagaraj, N. & Bantilan, Cynthia (2014). Impact of Mahatma Gandhi National Rural Employment Guarantee Act (MGNREGA) on rural labour markets. Working Paper Series No. 58. Patancheru-502324, Andhra Pradesh, India: International Crops Research Institute for the semi-Arid tropic. 40pp.

Rekha & Mehta, R. (2019). Impact of MGNREGA in improving socio-economic status of rural-poor: A study of Jodhpur district of Rajasthan. *International Journal of Humanities and Social Science Invention*, 8(03), 18–24.

Sharma, S. N., Chatterjee, S. & Dehalwar, K. (2022) Mahatma Gandhi National Rural Employment Guarantee Scheme: Challenges and opportunities. *Think India Journal*, 26(1), 0971–1260.

Singh, M. S., Modi, S. & Mourya, R. (2022). Livelihood security and sustainability of MGNREGA in tribal areas. *The International Journal of Social Science World*, 4(2), 63–76.

Sinha, P. (2020). MNREGA: An effective tool to reduce migration from Bihar. *Journal of Emerging Technologies and Innovative Research*, 7(2), 2049–5162.

Tiwari, R., Somashekhar, H. I., Ramakrishna, V. R., Murthy, I. K., Mohan Kumar, M. S., Parate, H., Kattumuri, M. & Ravindranath, N. H. (2011). MGNREGA for environmental service enhancement and vulnerability reduction: Rapid appraisal in Chitradurga district, Karnataka. *Economic and Political Weekly*, 46(20), 39–47.

Turangi, S. (2018). Assets creation and employment generation under Mahatma Gandhi National Rural Employment Guarantee Act: A study of Kalabugari district in Karnataka. *Economic Affairs*, 63(3), 695–702.

11

FISHERIES PRODUCTION, GROWTH AND GOOD GOVERNANCE

A Panel Data Analysis with Reference to India

Tonmoy Chatterjee and Kishan Agarwalla

Introduction

India, endowed with extensive inland and marine water resources, engages in the practice of capture and culture fisheries. The country's fisheries sector boasts a unique identity, thriving in a diverse range of ecosystems spanning from the pristine waters of the Himalayas to the expansive Indian Ocean. This natural diversity is widely considered to be a significant boon to India. The fisheries biodiversity within the nation encompasses a broad spectrum of physical and biological components, sustaining the livelihoods of millions. As the population continues to grow and the demand for fish protein rises, the imperative for sustainable development of aquatic resources becomes more pressing than ever before (Aigner & Chu, 1968; Alam et al., 2005; Anand, 2013). Meeting the increasing demands and ensuring a trajectory of growth that addresses current requirements while securing a more robust fishery for the future necessitates effective management of this sector (Anjani et al., 2005).

In the context of India, fisheries are not merely a source of food but are regarded as a vital contributor to nutrition, employment, and income. This sector provides livelihoods to approximately 16 million fishers and fish farmers at the primary level, with an additional twice that number along the fishery value chain (Anon. *Handbook of Fisheries*, 2013–14, 2014–15, 2015–16, 2017–18). Fish, being an affordable and rich source of animal protein, stands out as one of the healthiest options to alleviate hunger and malnutrition (Asamoah et al., 2012; Aziz et al., 2013; Balasubramanian et al., 2010). The fisheries sector holds immense potential to double the incomes of fishers and fish farmers, aligning with the government's vision. Evolving from a

DOI: 10.4324/9781003530688-14

traditional activity, fisheries have now transformed into a profitable enterprise (Banerjee, 2018; Barman, 2014; Bhattacharya, 2011).

Over the years, the total fish production in India has seen a remarkable increase, rising from 7.54 lakh tonnes in 1950–51 to 95.79 lakh tonnes in 2013–14. Inland fish production has climbed from 5.34 lakhs tonnes in 1950–51 to 34.43 lakhs tonnes in 2013–14, while marine fish production has surged from 2.43 lakh tonnes in 1955–56 to 61.36 lakhs tonnes in 2013–14. The share of inland fish production, however, has decreased from 71.04% in 1955–56 to 36.74% in 2012–13, contrasting with the rising share of marine fisheries from 28.99% in 1950–51 to 64.06% in 2013–14. The fisheries sector has emerged as a key contributor to foreign exchange earnings, solidifying India's position as one of the leading seafood exporting nations globally. Marine exports constitute about 5% of India's total exports and contribute 19.23% to agri-exports (2017–18). In the fiscal year 2018–19, marine product exports reached 13,92,559 metric tonnes, valued at Rs. 46,589 crore (USD 6.73 billion), with the substantial growth attributed to the boom in brackish water aquaculture (Anon. *Handbook of Fisheries*, 2013–14, 2014–15, 2015–16, 2017–18).

The pivotal role of fisheries production in India extends to significant contributions to the national economy, notably in the realms of food security, employment generation, and foreign exchange earnings. With its extensive coastline, elaborate river systems, and abundant water bodies, India provides an optimal setting for a diverse range of fisheries activities. The sector encompasses marine, inland, and brackish water fisheries, each presenting distinctive challenges and opportunities (Bose, 2014; Bunting, 2002). Recent years have witnessed a concerted effort to elevate fisheries production through the implementation of sustainable practices and enhanced governance. The governance of fisheries in India is characterized by an intricate interplay of regulations at both the central and state levels. The Ministry of Fisheries, Animal Husbandry, and Dairying formulates policies and provides guidelines at the central level, while state fisheries departments take on the responsibility of implementing and regulating activities within their respective jurisdictions (Jacon, 2003; Caruso, 2016; Chakraborty, 2016; Caoa et al., 2021). Effective coordination between these entities is imperative to ensure a cohesive and well-managed approach to resource utilization. Recognizing the significance of local communities and fisherfolk in decision-making processes, there is a growing acknowledgment of their essential role in fostering the sustainable development of the sector alongside governmental agencies (Clark, 1973; Coelli, et al., 1997; Ceyhan & Gene, 2014). In pursuit of comprehensive and sustainable development, efforts are being directed towards responsible fishing practices, including the promotion of aquaculture and the establishment of fish sanctuaries. Challenges such as overfishing, habitat degradation, and the impact of climate change persist, underscoring the need for a holistic approach to fisheries governance (Coelli et al., 2002; Coelli et al., 2005). Strengthening monitoring and enforcement mechanisms, fostering research and innovation, and encouraging international collaborations stand as pivotal elements in ensuring the enduring viability of India's fisheries sector.

India has experienced the implementation of diverse schemes and initiatives aimed at augmenting fisheries production and addressing the socio-economic needs of fishing communities. The Pradhan Mantri Matsya Sampada Yojana (PMMSY), designed to modernize the fisheries sector, places emphasis on infrastructure development, technology adoption, and capacity building. These measures are geared towards boosting fish production, mitigating post-harvest losses, and improving the income of fisherfolk (Cooper & Brand, 2007; Department of Animal Husbandry, Dairying and Fisheries, Ministry of Agriculture & Farmers Welfare, Government of India, 2018–19; Handbook of Fisheries Statistics, 2018). Despite these endeavours, challenges such as overfishing, habitat degradation, and the impacts of climate change persist, posing threats to the sustainability of fisheries. Initiatives are underway to encourage responsible fishing practices, encompassing the adoption of aquaculture and the establishment of fish sanctuaries. Sustainable fisheries governance requires a comprehensive approach that takes into account ecological, economic, and social considerations (Dessale, 2017; Devi, et al., 2014; Dilip, 2013; Ekramuddin, 2017; Hossain et al., 2015; Jayaram & Singh, 1977). The key to ensuring the enduring viability of fisheries in India lies in the reinforcement of monitoring and enforcement mechanisms, the promotion of research and innovation, and the facilitation of international collaborations. As the nation strives for inclusive and sustainable development, the establishment of a well-structured governance framework will play a pivotal role in unlocking the full potential of its fisheries sector (Esmaeili & Omrani, 2007; Grafton et al., 2006; Hallam & Machado, 1996; Igwe & Mgbaja 2014; Itam et al., 2014; Kaliba & Engle 2006).

Given that fisheries are a state subject, the governance of fisheries in India involves a pivotal role played by the states. The Central Government complements the states' efforts under the principles of cooperative federalism. While inland fisheries fall under the exclusive jurisdiction of state governments, marine fisheries are a shared responsibility between the central and coastal state/UT governments (Kirkley et al., 1999; Nobuyuki et al., 2008; Karthikeyan et al., 2019; Nayak & Kumar, 2019). Coastal states/UTs are responsible for the development, management, and regulation of fisheries within the 12 nautical miles territorial limit, while the government of India oversees fisheries in the Exclusive Economic Zone (EEZ) beyond 12 nautical miles up to 200 nautical miles (370 km). Effectively managing and regulating this common property resource is crucial for its sustainable and responsible utilization, emphasizing the need for close collaboration between the Center and the states. Neogi et al. (2016) observe that the MGNREGA (Mahatma Gandhi National Rural Employment Guarantee Act) scheme has helped in increasing fish cultivation in Indian states with the operation of governance factors.

Despite the transformation from traditional to commercial fishing activities in the region, the level of production and productivity remains insufficient, revealing a considerable gap between actual and potential output. The region has yet to harness the vast growth potential of fish production, particularly from pisciculture. The present study sets forth specific objectives: (a) to evaluate the fish production function in five selected states of India over a 15-year period, with unevenly spaced intervals, for an aggregated analysis of production function determinants; (b) to conduct a comparative analysis of selected factors determining the production function across different states over 15 years (unevenly spaced) to investigate whether the impact of each factor on the production function varies across states.

In alignment with the study's objectives, several statistical hypotheses have been formulated for testing: (a) a positive relationship between the 'number of Government schemes' and the production function; (b) a positive relationship between 'expenditure incurred' and the production function; (c) a positive relationship between 'net area under effective Pisciculture' and the production function; and (d) a positive relationship between the 'number of persons engaged in the professions' and the production function.

The remainder of this chapter is organized as follows. In section 2, we provide details about the sources of the dataset, sampling design, study periods, and the model selection process. Section 3 offers a comprehensive discussion of the various results obtained. Section 4 presents various comparative analyses among different states in India. Finally, in Section 5, we provide recommendations and draw conclusions based on the findings.

Theoretical Background

Fisheries production, growth, and effective governance are interconnected facets pivotal in shaping the sustainability and prosperity of the fisheries sector. Theoretical connections among these elements can be explored to comprehend their interdependent nature and their collective contribution to the holistic development of fisheries.

At the heart of this interrelation lies the concept of good governance. Fundamental to the sustainable expansion of fisheries production, effective governance practices establish the groundwork for responsible resource management when characterized by transparency, accountability, and participatory mechanisms (Crentsil & Ukpong, 2014). Good governance ensures that policies and regulations are clearly defined, rigorously enforced, and inclusive, fostering an environment conducive to sustainable fisheries practices.

Again, the association between good governance and the amplification of fisheries production is evident through an emphasis on regulatory frameworks and institutional capacities. Well-structured governance systems offer the necessary foundation to efficiently manage and allocate resources, preventing over-exploitation and the depletion of fish stocks (Banker et al., 1984; Barman, 2014). Furthermore, good governance promotes the adoption of contemporary technologies and practices that enhance productivity, leading to an upswing in fisheries production. Conversely, the expansion of fisheries production contributes to economic development and social well-being, establishing a positive feedback loop with good governance (Bennett et al., 2017; Charnes et al., 1978a; Charnes et al., 1978b). As fisheries production burgeons, it creates employment opportunities, augments income for fishing communities, and bolsters food security. This sustainable economic growth underscores the imperative of maintaining effective governance structures to safeguard the long-term health of fisheries resources.

In summary, the theoretical interconnections among fisheries production, growth, and good governance forge a dynamic relationship where each component reinforces and influences the others. A foundation of good governance facilitates sustainable growth in fisheries production, and the ensuing economic and social advantages underscore the ongoing necessity for effective governance to ensure the resilience and longevity of the fisheries sector (Kumar et al., 2008; Kaur et al., 2019; Musvver, 2019; Murugan, 2019). This interconnected framework underscores the significance of a holistic and well-coordinated approach to achieve a balanced and sustainable fisheries ecosystem. Mathematically, we can illustrate it in terms of the following expression:

$$Production = f(\text{Persons, Net Area, Expenditure incurred, Government Scheme}) \tag{11.1}$$

Table 11.1 describes the measurement of the variables mentioned in equation (11.1). In the next section, we try to express our theoretical understandings in terms of econometric modelling.

Data and Methodology

Source of Data

The study uses secondary data published by government sources such as the Assistant Director of Fisheries and Fish Farmer Development Agency (FFDA) of a few selected states of India were collected and the statistical software package 'STATA 14.0' is applied to interpret the result.

TABLE 11.1 Measurement of Variables

Variables	Measures
Production (Prod)	Approx. annual productions of fisheries (in Qtl.)
Government scheme (govtsch or loggovtsch)	Number of government Schemes operated
Expenditure incurred (exp or logexp)	Expenditure for inputs ('000')
Net area (netarea or lognetarea)	Net area under effective pisciculture (in hectare)
Persons (persons or logpersons)	Number of persons engaged in the professions

Sampling Design and Study Period

This study examines eight districts from each of five states in India, totaling 40 sample districts selected from an initial pool of 71. The selection was based on the highest production figures over six time periods spanning 15 years, from 1998–99 to 2013–14.

Panel Data Analysis

The research involved examining 40 sample districts across five states: Uttar Pradesh, Uttarakhand, Bihar, Jharkhand, and West Bengal. Eight districts were selected from each state, spanning six time periods over 15 years from 1998–99 to 2013–14. Consequently, a balanced panel dataset was created for analysis, comprising a total of 240 observations (eight districts × six time periods × five states). However, due to missing data and the need to address issues of Heteroscedasticity and Autocorrelation, only 217 observations were ultimately considered: Uttar Pradesh (28), Uttarakhand (55), Bihar (42), Jharkhand (42), and West Bengal (50).

Initially, the Durbin-Watson test confirmed the absence of autocorrelation in each district's observations. Subsequently, the Breusch-Pagan test revealed heteroscedasticity issues in Uttar Pradesh, Jharkhand, and West Bengal (Greene, 1980; Adkins, 2006; Adkins et al., 2011). To mitigate this, log values were applied to the variables, resolving the problem for some districts but persisting in Uttar Pradesh. To address this, outlier observations were systematically removed to eliminate heteroscedasticity problems. Apart from this, we consider natural log to eliminate the issue of heteroskedasticity from the data (Gujarati, 2004; Wooldridge, 2007; Gujarati, 2015; McManus, 2011). For the analysis of production function determinants, the study considered the production function as the dependent variable. The independent variables for each block included: (i) Government Scheme, (ii) Expenditure, (iii) Net Area, and (iv) Persons. Detailed measures for these variables are provided in Table 11.1.

Model Selection

In the Panel Data Regression Method, there are generally used three models, namely, the Pooled Regression Model, the Fixed-Effects Model, and the Random-Effect Model. For making a choice between the Fixed-Effects Model and the Random-Effect Model, we have applied the well-known Hausman Specification test. If the test statistic value of the Hausman Specification test is significant, the Fixed-Effects Model is preferred over the Random-Effect Model (Greene, 1980; Adkins, 2006; Acharya et al., 2019). In contrast, to select appropriate model between the Pooled Regression Model and the Random-Effect Model, we have performed the renowned Breusch and Pagan Lagrange Multiplier test (Zolfi et al., 2018; Gujarati, 2015; McManus, 2011). If the test statistic value of the Breusch and Pagan Lagrange Multiplier test is significant, then the Random-Effect Model is suitable for selection. Otherwise, one should select the Pooled Regression Model. If these two tests are producing contradiction regarding the selection of the model, then we have applied the Fixed-Effects Model as per convention. Industry-wise model specification for analysing the determinants of dividend policy is summarized and presented in Table 11.2.

TABLE 11.2 District-wide Selection of Model of Panel Regression on Determinants of Production Function

District	Observation	Hausman Specification Test	Breusch and Pagan Lagrange Multiplier Test	Selected Model
Uttar Pradesh	28	8.62 (0.0712)	0.00 (1.0000)	Fixed-Effect Model
Uttarakhand	55	9.77 (0.0444)	0.00 (1.0000)	Fixed-Effect Model
Bihar	42	Failed	0.00 (1.0000)	Pooled OLS Model
Jharkhand	42	6.44 (0.1686)	10.33 (0.0007)	Random-Effect Model
West Bengal	50	3.20 (0.5248)	0.00 (1.0000)	Fixed-Effect Model

Notes: We have considered 5% level of significance. Figure in the parentheses imply respective probability levels.

Analysis and Results

State-wise Empirical Analysis

Uttar Pradesh District

In examining the production function of Uttar Pradesh, we have employed the Fixed-Effect Model. The estimated regression equation of the model is illustrated as follows:

$$\text{Prod}_{it} = -2.0606 - 0.1109 \, \text{logpersons}_{it} + 1.5993 \, \text{lognetarea}_{it} + 1.4044 \, \text{logexp}_{it}$$
$$- 3.2758 \, \text{loggovtsch}_{it}$$

(2.1553) (0.1680)   (0.9009)   (0.2409)   (0.8050)
$R^2 = 0.6194 \, [11.89]$

[Notes: Significance at 5% level. Figures in the parentheses imply standard errors. Figure within the square bracket implies F value.]

The estimated regression analysis reveals that all the explanatory variables are statistically significant except logpersons and lognetarea. This finding is also consistent with the overall explanatory power of the model represented in terms of the F-statistic value (i.e. 11.89) drawn from R^2 value of 0.6194 with the probability value of 0.0001, signifying that it is statistically significant. Therefore, we see that the Fixed-Effect Model does provide an overall good fit. The production function of Uttar Pradesh is influenced highly by logexp and loggovtsch, respectively. In other words, logexp and loggovtsch have a positive influence on the production function of fisheries in Uttar Pradesh.

Uttarakhand District

To evaluate the production function determinant of Uttarakhand, we have selected the Fixed-Effect Model. The estimated regression equation of the Fixed-Effect Model is presented as follows:

$$\text{Prod}_{it} = 7829.537 + 2.5769 \, \text{Persons}_{it} + 34.8571 \, \text{Netarea}_{it} - 2.0091 \, \text{exp}_{it}$$
$$- 2616.476 \, \text{govtsch}_{it}$$

(3050.563) (1.3828)   (5.1622)   (0.7535)   (756.1715)
$R^2 = 0.5038 \, [15.07]$

[Notes: Same as those mentioned under equation (11.1))]

The estimated regression discloses that production function is positively and statistically significant dependent on Netarea. The other variables, i.e. Exp and Govtsch, are negative but statistically insignificant related to the production function. Furthermore, the overall significance of the model is represented by the F-statistic value (15.07) drawn from the R^2 value of 0.5038 with a probability value of 0.0000, which signifies that it is statistically significant at a 5% level; therefore, Fixed-Effect Model gives an overall good fit.

Bihar District

To find out the influencing factors of the production function of fisheries of Bihar district, we have selected the Pooled OLS regression model as follows:

$$\text{Prod}_{it} = -340.51 + 0.5043 \text{ Persons}_{it} + 18.903 \text{ Netarea}_{it} - 9.5177 \text{ Exp}_{it} + 1242.726 \text{ Govtsch}_{it}$$

(1708.713)   (0.07436)   (3.1100)   (2.6160)   (245.4823)

$R^2 = 0.7660$ [30.28]

[Notes: Same as those mentioned under equation (11.1).]

The results of the estimated equation display that all the independent variables are statistically significant and linked with the production function which is also evident from the F-statistic value (30.28) deduced from the R^2 value of 0.7760 with the probability value of 0.0000. This indicates that the production function of the fisheries of Bihar district depends highly on these chosen independent variables.

Jharkhand District

In explaining the factors having an impact on the production function of the Jharkhand district, we have applied the Random-Effect Model. The estimated regression outcomes of the model are shown as follows:

$$\text{Prod}_{it} = 0.8437 + 0.1074 \text{ logpersons}_{it} + 1.0647 \text{ lognetarea}_{it} - 0.0199 \text{ logexp}_{it} + 0.0328 \text{ loggovtsch}_{it}$$

(0.4724) (0.1518)   (0.0446)   (0.0124)   (0.0383)

$R^2 = 0.9517$ [Chi-value= 870.81]

[Notes: Same as those mentioned under equation (11.1).]

The outcomes of the estimated equation report that all the explanatory variables are found to be statistically insignificant except lognetarea. This result is also established by the Wald Chi-square value (i.e. 870.81) derived from an R^2 value of 0.9517 with a probability value of 0.0000. So, it concludes that the Random-Effect Model does not provide an overall good fit.

West Bengal District

For investigating the determinants of the production function of Fisheries of West Bengal District, we have selected the Fixed-Effect Model. The estimated equation of the Fixed-Effect Model is presented as follows:

$$\text{Prod}_{it} = 0.5211 + 0.2496 \text{ logpersons}_{it} + 1.0608 \text{ lognetarea}_{it} - 0.0722 \text{ logexp}_{it}$$
$$+ 0.0775 \text{ loggovtsch}_{it}$$

(0.5339) (0.0714)   (0.2453)   (0.9475)   (0.2701)

$R^2 = 0.6588$ [16.89]

[Notes: Same as those mentioned under equation (11.1).]

The estimated regression analysis unveils that logexp has a negative but statistically insignificant impact on the production function of the West Bengal district. However, the model's overall significance is underscored by an *F*-statistic of 16.87, derived from an R^2 value of 0.6588, with a probability value of 0.0000, indicating it is statistically significant at the 5% level. This implies that the Fixed-Effect Model gives us an overall good fit.

Comparative Analysis among the States

This section provides a comparative analysis across different states under study to explain the determination of the production function of different states in terms of their anticipated results.

The estimated regression results (Panel 3A of Table 11.3) shows that Persons (or logpersons) affects fisheries production positively in Uttar Pradesh, Uttarakhand, and Jharkhand, while it shows no significant impact on fisheries production in the case of Bihar and West Bengal.

The comparative analysis, presented in Panel 3B of Table 11.3, among the selected states indicates that Netarea (or lognetarea) serves as a positively significant factor in determining the production function of fisheries in all cases, with the exception of districts in Uttar Pradesh. Consequently, the Netarea (or lognetarea) variables are considered influential for the production function of fisheries in all states except for Uttar Pradesh.

Examining the comparative analysis of Exp (or logexp) in the determination of the production function for fisheries across different states yields mixed results. The results, as illustrated in Panel 3C of Table 11.3, indicate that Exp (or Logexp) is mostly an insignificant factor in explaining the production function of fisheries in the case of Jharkhand and West Bengal states. Uttarakhand and Bihar, on the other hand, exhibit negative and statistically significant influences of Exp (or Lognetarea) on the production function of fisheries. Additionally, a positive and significant influence on the production function is observed in the case of Uttar Pradesh.

TABLE 11.3 Relation between Persons (or Netarea or Exp or Govtsch) and Production
Function

States	Estimated Co-efficient	Standard Error	Null Hypothesis Accepted or Rejected
Panel 3A: Relation between Persons (or logpersons) and Production Function			
Uttar Pradesh	−0.1109	0.1680	Accepted
Uttarakhand	2.5769	1.3828	Accepted
Bihar	0.5043	0.0743	Rejected
Jharkhand	0.1074	0.1518	Accepted
West Bengal	0.2496	0.0714	Rejected
Panel 3B: Relation between Netarea (or lognetarea) and Production Function			
Uttar Pradesh	1.5993	0.9009	Accepted
Uttarakhand	34.8571	5.1622	Rejected
Bihar	18.903	3.1100	Rejected
Jharkhand	1.0647	0.0446	Rejected
West Bengal	1.0608	0.2453	Rejected
Panel 3C: Relation between Exp (or Logexp) and Production Function			
Uttar Pradesh	1.4044	0.2409	Rejected
Uttarakhand	−2.0091	5.1622	Rejected
Bihar	−9.5177	3.1100	Rejected
Jharkhand	−0.0199	0.0124	Accepted
West Bengal	−0.0722	0.9475	Accepted
Panel 3D: Relation between Govtsch (or Loggovtsch) and Production Function			
Uttar Pradesh	−3.2758	0.8050	Rejected
Uttarakhand	−2616.476	756.1715	Rejected
Bihar	1242.726	245.4823	Rejected
Jharkhand	0.0328	0.0383	Accepted
West Bengal	0.0775	0.2701	Accepted

Source: Authors' own calculation.

Note: Significance at 5% level.

The estimated regression results, presented in Panel 3D of Table 11.3,
suggest that Govtsch (or Loggovtssch) is an insignificant factor in determining the production function in Jharkhand and West Bengal states. In Bihar
districts, positive and statistically significant influences of Govtsch (or
Loggovtsch) on the production function are identified. Conversely, negative
and statistically significant relationships with the production function are
observed in Uttar Pradesh and Uttarakhand states.

Effectiveness from the Perspective of Governance

The given information explores the estimated regression outcomes concerning the impact of governance on the production function in various states

and districts. Here are key insights derived from the provided details: The influence of governance on the production function varies across different geographical areas. Specifically, in the states of Jharkhand and West Bengal, the findings indicate that governance does not significantly affect the production function. This implies that other factors may have a more pronounced role in shaping production dynamics within these states. In the districts of Bihar, the results reveal a positive and statistically significant correlation between governance and the production function. This suggests that effective governance practices in Bihar are linked to heightened productivity in the production process. The positive association implies that enhancements in governance could lead to improved economic outcomes in this region. Conversely, in the states of Uttar Pradesh and Uttarakhand, the analysis identifies a negative and statistically significant relationship between governance and the production function. This suggests that in these areas, suboptimal governance may be impeding or adversely affecting productivity in the production process. The findings propose that addressing governance challenges has the potential to enhance production outcomes in these particular regions.

Concluding Remarks

The comparative analysis of determinants of the production function of fisheries across different states interprets mixed results. The comparative analysis of determinants of production function across different states has derived significant evidence in support of explaining the production function except for Jharkhand. The estimated regression results interpret that all the explanatory variables are statistically significant in the case of Bihar. But in the case of Jharkhand, all the independent variables are statistically insignificant except Netarea (or Lognetarea). The outcome of the estimated regression results estimate that all the variables are statistically significant except persons (or Logpersons) in the case of Uttarakhand. Two out of the total number of explanatory variables are statistically significant in the case of Uttar Pradesh and West Bengal states. So, we derive significant evidence in support of explaining the production function of fisheries across different states. The results carry significant policy implications. In areas where governance is identified as either inconsequential or detrimental to the production function, there is a potential requirement for policy interventions targeting governance challenges. This may entail implementing reforms to enhance administrative efficiency, mitigate corruption, and strengthen regulatory frameworks, fostering a more favourable environment for economic activities. It is crucial to take into account the particular contextual factors that might contribute to these relationships. The observed effects of governance on the production function could stem from a variety of factors, including socio-economic, political, or historical elements. Further research and analysis are essential to comprehensively grasp the underlying mechanisms that drive these relationships.

Policy Caveats

Macroeconomic determinants of production function like human capital, physical capital, natural resources and technological knowledge available to workers, etc. can be considered for future research. These results can be used by the government for the implementation of effective government schemes in future in different states.

Limitations of the Study

First, data for the study has been gathered from Secondary data sources, i.e. Assistant Director of Fisheries and Fish Farmer Development Agency (FFDA). These sources sometimes suffer from reliability queries owing to methodology faults, printing errors, and hidden information. To lessen these drawbacks, the study has made efforts to eradicate the mistakes to a greater extent through constant editing to satisfy the objectives of the study, yet we cannot claim it as error free. Second, this study has made an analysis of production function on the basis of 40 sample districts which are taken by choosing 8 districts from each state. Hence, this chapter is analysed on the basis of different districts representing a few states under study. Thus, the production function of fisheries can be described in a better way if the sample size can be enlarged.

References

Acharya, S., Shukla, S., Sande, S., & Acharya, N. (2019). Educational panel discussion as a model of learning preference in the subject of medicine for undergraduates of a medical university. *Journal of Research in Medical Education & Ethics*, 9(2), 131–136.

Adkins, C. F. (2006). *An Introduction to Modern Econometrics Using Stata* (pp. 219–232). Stata Press.

Adkins, L., Griffiths, W. E., & Hill, R. C. (2011). *Using Stata for Principles of Econometrics* (pp. 442–466). John Wiley & Sons, Inc.

Aigner, D., & Chu, S. (1968). On estimating the industry production function. *American Economic Review*, 58, 826–839.

Alam, M. A., Rahman, & Quddu, S. (2005). Measurement of economic efficiency of production fish in bangladesh with translog stochastic cost Frontier. *Bangladesh Journal of Agricultural Economics*, XVIII(1&2).

Anand, M. D. (2013). A study on resource-use efficiency and sustainability of marine fishery (with reference to Tiruvallur District, Tamil Nadu). P.G & Research Departmnt of Economics, Presidency College, Chennai.

Anjani, K., & Katiha, et al. (2005). Technical efficiency in freshwater aquaculture in Uttar Pradesh. *The Indian Journal of Economics*, 86(341), 185–187.

Anon. (2013–14). *Handbook of Fisheries*. Government of India, Ministry of Agriculture, Department of Animal husbandry, Dairying and Fisheries, Krishi Bhavan, New Delhi.

Anon. (2014–15). *Handbook of Fisheries*. Government of India, Ministry of Agriculture, Department of Animal husbandry, Dairying and Fisheries, Krishi Bhavan, New Delhi.

Anon. (2015–16). *Handbook of Fisheries*. Government of India, Ministry of Agriculture, Department of Animal husbandry, Dairying and Fisheries, Krishi Bhavan, New Delhi.

Anon. (2017–18). *Handbook of Fisheries*. Government of India, Ministry of Agriculture, Department of Animal husbandry, Dairying and Fisheries, Krishi Bhavan, New Delhi.

Asamoah, E., Nunoo, F., & Asare, Y. (2012). A production function analysis of pond aquaculture in southern Ghana. *Aquaculture Economics & Management*, 16(3), 183–201.

Aziz, N., Janor, R., & Mahadi, R. (2013). Comparative departmental efficiency analysis within a university: A DEA approach. *Procedia- Social and Behavioral Sciences*, 90, 540–548. Elsevier.

Balasubramanian, G., Datta, K., Reddy, G., & Menon, M. (2010). Marketing system and efficiency of Indian major carps in India. *Agricultural Economics Research Review*, 23, 106–113.

Banerjee, S. (2018). The tragedy of fishing communities: A story from Vetka village, Odisha. *Economic and Political Weekly*, 42. https://www.epw.in/engage/article/tragedy-fishing-communities-story-vetka-village-odisha

Banker, R., Charnes, A., & Cooper, W. (1984). Some models for estimating technical and scale inefficiencies in data envelopment analysis. *Management Science*, 30(9), 1078–1092.

Barman, M. (2014). Problem and Prospects of Inland Fishery Development in the District of South 24 Parganas, West Bengal, India. http://hdl.handle.net/10603/122581

Bennett, N. J., et al. (2017). Conservation social science: Understanding and integrating human dimensions to improve conservation. *Biological Conservation*, 205, 93–108. Elsevier.

Bhattacharya, M. (2011). A study on the socio-economic of coastal fisheries with special reference to the Sundarbans of West Bengal, India. *International Journal of Current Research*, 3(12), 286–291.

Bose, T. (2014). Problems and prospects of inland fishery development in the district of South 24 Parganas, West Bengal. Thesis submitted to the University of Burdwan for the degree of Doctor of Philosophy in Arts.

Bunting, S. (2002). Overview of fish seed production and distribution in West Bengal, India. Working Paper.

Caoa, N., Eideb, A., Armstrongb, C., & Lea, L. (2021). Measuring capacity utilization in fisheries using physical or economic variables: A data envelope analysis of a Vietnamese purse seine fishery. *Fisheries Research*, Elsevier. https://doi.org/10.1016/j.fishres.2021.106087

Caruso, G. (2016). Fishery wastes and by-products: A resource to be valorised. *Journal of Fisheriessciences.com*, 10(1), 12–15.

Ceyhan, V., & Gene, H. (2014). Productive efficiency of commercial fishing: Evidence from the Sumsun Province of Black Sea, Turkey. *Turkish Journal of Fisheries and Aquatic Sciences*, 14, 309–320.

Chakraborty, M. (2016). Socio-economic conditions of fisherman of Bali Nolia Sahi, Puri, Orissa. *International Journal of Humanities & Social Science Studies*, II(VI), 283–290.

Charnes, A., Cooper, W. W., & Rhodes, E. (1978a). A data envelopment analysis approach to evaluation of the program follow through experiments in U.S. public school education. *Management Science Research Report No. 432*, Carnegie-Mellon University, School of Urban and Public Affairs, Pittsburgh, PA.

Charnes, W. W., Cooper, W., & Rhodes, E. (1978b). Measuring the efficiency of decision making units. *European Journal of Operational Research*, 2, 429–444.

Clark, C. (1973). *Report of the World Commission on Environment and Development*; Our Common Future.

Coelli, T., Rahman, S., & Thirtle, C. (2002). Technical, allocative, cost and scale efficiencies in bangladesh rice cultivation: A non-parametric approach. *Journal of Agricultural Economics*, 53, 607–626.

Coelli, T. J., Prasada Rao, D. S., O'Donnell, C. J., & Battese, G. E. (2005). *An Introduction to Efficiency and Productivity Analysis* (2nd ed.). Springer.

Coelli, T. J., et al. (1997). *An Introduction to Efficiency and Productivity Analysis* (vol. XVII, pp. 349). Spring.

Cooper, M., & Brand, D. (2007). Non-salmonids in a salmonid fishway: What do 50 years of data tell us about past and future fish passage? *Fisheries Management and Ecology*, 14(5), 319–332.

Crentsil, C., & Ukpong, I. G. (2014). Economics of fish production in Amansie-West district of Ghana: Implication for food security in West Africa. *Asian Journal of Agricultural Extension, Economics & Sociology*, 3(3), 179–188.

Das, R.C., Chatterjee, T., & Ivaldi, E. (2022). Nexus between housing price and magnitude of pollution: Evidence from the panel of some high- and low polluting cities of the world. *Sustainability*, *14*, 9283. https://doi.org/10.3390/su14159283

Department of Animal Husbandry, Dairying and Fisheries, Ministry of Agriculture & Farmers Welfare, Government of India. (2018–19). *Annual Report*.

Dessale, M. (2017). Technical efficiency in Teff production: The case of smallholder farmers in Jamma district, South Wollo Zone, Ethiopia. A Thesis Submitted to the School of Agricultural Economics and Agribusiness, Postgraduate Program Directorate Haramaya University.

Devi, P.B., et al. (2014). Health benefits of finger millet (Eleusine coracana L.) Polyphenols and dietary fiber: A Review. *Journal of Food Science and Technology*, 51(6), 1021–1040.

Dilip, A. (2013). A study on resource use efficiency and sustainability of marine fishery—With reference to Tiruvallur district, Tamil Nadu. Thesis submitted to the University of Madras in partial fulfillment for the award of the degree of Doctor of Philosophy in Economics.

Ekramuddin, Md. (2017). An overview of the impact of small scale fish farming on socio-economic growth in Birbhum district, West Bengal, India. *Journal of Entomology and Zoology Studies*, 5(4), 46–52.

Esmaeili, A., & Omrani, M. (2007). Efficiency analysis of fishery in Hamoon lake: Using DEA Approach. *Journal of Applied Sciences*, 7(19), 2856–2860.

Grafton, R., et al. (2006). Incentives-based approaches to sustainable fisheries. *Canadian Journal of Fisheries and Aquatic Science*, 63, 699–710.

Greene, R. (1980). Maximum likelihood estimation of econometrics frontier functions. *Journal of Econometrics*, 13, 27–56.

Gujarati, D. N. (2004). *Basic Econometrics* (4th ed., pp. 636–652). Tata McGraw-Hill Education.

Gujarati, D. N. (2015). *Econometrics by Example* (2nd ed., pp. 326–341). Palgrave Macmillan Education.

Hallam, D., & Machado, F. (1996). Efficiency analysis with panel data: A study of Portuguese dairy farms. *European Review of Agricultural Economics*, 23, 79–93.

Handbook of Fisheries Statistics. (2018). Government of India, Ministry of Fisheries Animal Husbandry and Dairying, Department of Fisheries.

Hossain, M., Alam, A., & Uddin, K. (2015). Application of stochastic frontier production function on small banana growers of Kushtia district in Bangladesh. *Journal of Statistics Applications & Probability*, 4(2), 337–342.

Igwe, K. C., & Mgbaja. (2014). Evaluation of pond fish production in Umuahia south local governments area of Abia state, Nigeria. *Global Journal of Science Frontier Research: D Agriculture and Veterinary*, 14, 39–48.

Itam, K., Etuk, E., & Ukpong, I. (2014). Analysis of resource use efficiency among small-scale fish farms in Cross River State, Nigeria. *International Journal of Fisheries and Aquaculture*, 6(7), 80–86.

Jacon, A. G. J. (2003). Fish farming. In *Encyclopedia of Food Sciences and Nutrition* (2nd ed., pp. 2479–2486). Science Direct.

Jayaram, K. C., & Singh, K. P. (1977). On a collection of fish from North Bengal. *Records of the Zoological Survey of India*, 72, 243–275.

Kaliba, A., & Engle, C. (2006). Productivity efficiency of catfish farms in Chitcot Country, Arkansas. *Aquaculture Economics & Management*, 10(3), 223–243.

Karthikeyan, M., et al. (2019). eMatsya-An innovative data acquisition system to collect fish catch data from reservoirs and other inland water bodies. *International Journal of Scientific & Technology Research*, 8(12), 47–52.

Kaur, R., Chattopadhyay, A. K., & Rakshit, D. (2019). Determinants of dividend policy with reference to select Indian companies: A panel data regression analysis. *An International Journal of Management Studies*, 9(3), 148–157.

Kirkley, J., Squires, D., & Walden, J. (1999). Assessing efficiency and capacity in fisheries. Prepared for the National Marine Fisheries Service workshop.

Kumar, M., Bhatt, G., & Duffy, C. J. (2008). An efficient domain decomposition framework for accurate representation of geodata in distributed hydrologic models. *International Journal of Geographical Information Science*, 23(12), 1569–1596.

McManus, P. A. (2011). *Introduction to Regression Models for Panel Data Analysis*. Indiana University: Workshop in Methods.

Murugan, K. (2019). Determinants of public expenditure in southern states of India: Panel data analysis. *Vision: Journal of Indian Taxation*, 6(1), 1–17.

Musvver, A. (2019). India's commodity trade with Saudi Arabia: A panel data approach. *Indian Journal of Economics and Development*, 15(3), 369–380.

Nayak, C., & Kumar, C. N. (2019). Crop diversification on Odisha: An analysis based on Panel data. *Agricultural Economics Research Review*, 32(1), 67–80.

Neogi, C., Ray, K., & Das, R. C. (2016). Is MGNREG scheme complementary to fishing activities? A study on some selected states of India. *International Journal of Research in Business & Social Science*, 5(1), 47–53.

Nobuyuki, Y., Yoshihito, S., & Masahiko, A. (2008). Panel data analyses to examine effects of subsidies to fishery productions in OECD countries. *Japanese Society of Fisheries Science*, 74, 1229–1234.

Wooldridge, J. (2007). *Textbook examples introductory econometrics: A modern approach*. South-Western Pub.

Zolfi, G., Jamalmanesh, A., & Torabipour, A. (2018). Analysis of hospital's financial liquidity using the linear regression model: A panel data study in Ahvaz teaching hospitals. *Indian Journal of Forensic Medicine & Toxicology*, 12(3), 270–275.

12

DOES GOOD GOVERNANCE AFFECT ECONOMIC GROWTH?

Evidence from Some Selected Developed Countries

Susobhan Maiti, Joshua Kodjo Asiedu, Surendranath Mandi, and Tanushree Gupta

Introduction

Economic growth is essential for countries to achieve economic development. Countries with higher economic growth, such as the United States and the United Kingdom, have been able to develop robust healthcare, education, transportation, and technological sectors as a result of their strong economic performance (Chakraborty & Jana, 2021). In contrast, many developing countries in sub-Saharan Africa have struggled to support their development due to poor economic performance. Widespread poverty in the region further complicates matters, making it challenging for these countries' governments to generate revenue for improving economic performance. Additionally, the standard of living in these developing regions is relatively low, with many people unable to afford healthcare and education. Developed countries consistently demonstrate strong economic performance, solidifying their dominance in the global economy. For instance, in 2021, the United States and China accounted for 23.93% and 18.45%, respectively, of the global economy (Molinillo et al., 2017) totaling 42.38% of the world's economic output. In terms of Gross Domestic Product (GDP) in nominal terms, the United States, China, Japan, Germany, and the United Kingdom contributed $23 trillion, $17.7 trillion, $4.9 trillion, $4.2 trillion, and $3.2 trillion, respectively. These nations exhibited varying growth rates: 5.7% for the United States, 8.1% for China, 1.6% for Japan, 2.9% for Germany, and 7.4% for the United Kingdom. Consequently, the standard of living in these countries has risen significantly due to their high GDP per capita. As a result of their increasing economic growth, these five nations wield substantial influence in international policies, as many other countries heavily rely on

DOI: 10.4324/9781003530688-15

them for financial aid. The drivers of economic growth in many developed countries are diverse. The service sector plays a pivotal role in the economic growth of the United States and the United Kingdom, while exports have a significant impact on the economies of China and Japan. China, in particular, has experienced remarkable economic growth attributed to several factors, including high levels of consumer demand, the development of the tertiary industry, financial advancements, and industrial expansion (Li et al., 2021). For several other Asian countries, particularly those in South Asia (Rahman et al., 2019), identify energy usage, gross capital formation, and remittances as the primary factors influencing economic growth in the region. In European countries, public expenditure on research and development (R&D) emerges as a key driver of economic growth (Groot et al., 2004), although it is not a common phenomenon in all types of countries in the world (Das & Mukherjee, 2019).

Governance is a critical factor that significantly influences economic growth. This influence is particularly evident in African countries, where some nations have witnessed economic improvements due to good governance, while others continue to grapple with poor economic performance resulting from inadequate governance. Feyisa et al. (2022) provide substantial evidence of the pivotal role that good governance plays in the economic growth of 39 sub-Saharan African countries, based on data spanning from 1995 to 2004. Their analysis also underscores that the impact of good governance is more pronounced in both high- and low-income African countries compared to middle-income countries. There is no universally accepted definition of good governance. However, the Office for the High Commissioner of Human Rights (OHCHR) defines governance as 'processes of governing, the institutions, processes, and practices through which issues of common concern are decided upon and regulated.' Moreover, good governance pertains to 'the political and institutional processes and outcomes that are necessary to achieve the goals of development.' The characteristics of good governance encompass transparency, responsibility, accountability, participation, and responsiveness.

To measure good governance, the World Bank constructed the World Governance Indicators (WGI). These six indicators are voice and accountability, political stability, absence of violence/terrorism, government effectiveness, regulatory quality, rule of law, and control of corruption (Kaufmann & Kraay, 2023). These indicators measure different aspects of governance. For example, while rule of law measures the views of the people of a country on how fair and efficient the judicial system in a country is, control of corruption examines how the people perceive the use of public power for private profits. Overall, these indicators provide an indication of state progress whereby the state or the government creates a progressive environment that leads to effective policy implementation.

Furthermore, the perceptions of economic agents in a country may either influence other foreign agents to participate in economic activity in that country or serve as a deterrent to them. For example, if a country is in conflict, many businesses will be discouraged from engaging in economic activity in the country. Also, if the judicial system is ineffective in delivering justice for the people, the people may resort to bribing judicial officers in order to win cases, thereby increasing the cost of the justice system which in turn increases the cost of business in the country. These are a few examples of how a poor governance system may discourage economic growth in a country. While the WGI is subjective, these perceptions provide an assessment on a scale of 0 to 100 or –2.5 to 2.5 of the performance of governance in a country. This allows countries to be compared to see whether government policies can be effective in the country or not. A taxation policy in a country with a low WGI score may not be as effective as a taxation policy in a country with a high WGI. This is because the conditions necessary for the effective implementation of government policies are not existent in those countries with low WGI.

Good governance can contribute to economic growth through two distinct approaches. The first of these approaches is the market-enhancing approach. It revolves around the establishment of an efficient market characterized by a significant reduction in corruption through the minimization of rent-seeking, the preservation of property rights, and the enforcement of the rule of law via a robust legal system. A strong legal system ensures the cost-effective resolution of conflicts and disputes. Moreover, governments must ensure the provision of public goods that cater to both the private sector and citizens' needs (Khan, 2007). The creation of efficient markets results in a notable decrease in transaction costs, which, in turn, fosters the growth and development of firms and businesses within these countries. Under favorable and efficient market conditions, both local and foreign private investors are incentivized to invest in businesses, thereby driving economic growth in the country. While the concept of efficient markets is integral to achieving economic growth, the reality is that markets often remain inefficient in many developing countries. Furthermore, numerous impoverished nations struggle to meet the criteria necessary for creating market-enhancing conditions due to the substantial public expenditure required for such an endeavor. Consequently, strong institutions become imperative for implementing growth policies in economically challenged countries. Weak institutions have hindered many sub-Saharan nations in their pursuit of growth objectives. In contrast, certain East Asian countries bolstered the capabilities of their governmental institutions to enhance their economic performance. This approach to good governance is growth-enhancing in nature. The growth-enhancing approach differs from the market-enhancing one in its emphasis on political stability, the government's proficiency in allocating and reallocating assets to productive sectors of the economy, and the government's ability to provide strong incentives (rents) essential for stimulating investment in their respective nations (Khan, 2007). It can be inferred that achieving good governance, whether through the market-enhancing or growth-enhancing approach, hinges on the presence of robust governmental institutions. The strength of these institutions is closely tied to the level of social and economic development within a country. Developed countries typically possess strong governments, whereas many developing nations face a deficiency in this regard. Consequently, countries like the United States and the United Kingdom are well-positioned to implement both market-enhancing and growth-enhancing strategies through their robust governmental institutions. While some East Asian countries, still facing challenges in economic growth, have addressed this by establishing strong institutions to drive growth efforts, other developing nations continue to grapple with the absence of capable governments and efficient markets needed to stimulate growth. Developed countries have established the essential conditions of good governance for fostering economic growth, whether through the market-enhancing or growth-enhancing approach. Considering this, this chapter aims to conduct a causal analysis of the relationship between good governance and economic growth. The following sections will delve into this objective.

Review of Literature

Many development economists believe that good governance, which means good management and direction of development strategies, has a positive effect on economic performance. The question is what aspects of governance are covered in the literature. It is said by the World Bank that a country's ability to put its governance ideas into practice, which allows markets to grow and the economy to expand, is a sign of good governance. The results of several statistical studies that looked at the link between 'market-enhancing governance' and good governance and economic growth were positive. However, good governance policies help developing countries achieve the same level of development as industrialized nations by requiring only the bare necessities: economic growth and political changes (Mira & Hammadache, 2018). One of the best ways to tell if an economy is healthy is to look at its growth. Sustainable growth rates that are higher help raise people's living standards and keep poverty at a minimum. A slowing of growth is thought to be caused by bad governance by some comparison researchers and development professionals. This is because they believe that growth and good governance usually go hand in hand (Aladlani, n.d.). According to the Worldwide Governance Indicators study, good governance entails having effective institutions and processes for exercising power, as well as for selecting, holding accountable, checking, and replacing governments. Furthermore, it is the ability of governments to manage resources efficiently and effectively, to make and stick to sensible policies and rules, and to inspire confidence in the institutions that rule them. The United Nations Development Programme defined good governance as 'the totality of authority exercised in the administration of a nation's matters, including the elaborate procedures, apparatuses, and institutions through which groups and populations express their interests, implement their legal rights, and arbitrate their differences' (United Nations Development Programme, 1997). Private enterprise, public administration, and civil society are all constituent parts of this authority, which spans the economic, political, social, judicial, and administrative spheres (Towah, n.d.). The importance of good governance in fostering economic expansion has grown in recent years. The United Nations will add 'Good Governance' as a Millennium Development Goal. High productivity and innovation levels are two key components of excellent governance that contribute to long-term economic prosperity. Many economists argue that improved economic output can be attributed to good governance, which they define as the quality control and direction of development policy (Fathia, 2021). Economic theories have failed to account for the importance of governance in production and economic development, even though its role in economic development has been recognized since the 18th century. The importance of good governance, however, has grown to the point that it is an essential part of every modern economic system. All aspects of behavior and social networks, including the political, economic, and legal ones, fall within the purview of governance, which is a subcomponent of an institution (North, 1990). Effective management of resources is directly linked to increased output from both individuals and businesses. When governance is weak, economic actors get more engaged in redistributing scarce resources, which stifles the free market and reduces the output of a country. Since good management reduces costs, it encourages the development of marketplaces in which participants can gain from one another. A stable and predictable macroeconomic environment with few unintended consequences is the result of effective governance. This allows for a more efficient allocation of resources, which boosts economic efficiency. Quality of governance is the availability of information that allows businesses and consumers to make educated decisions and encourages free-market competition. Economic expansion is aided by these elements (Legese Feyisa et al., 2022). Since the World Bank first utilized the notion of good governance in its 1989 report, it has been widely studied and applied to numerous disciplines of study. Several metrics of governance quality have been created by international organizations. One example is the Global Governance Indicators compiled by the World Bank. The WGI assess five aspects of government: citizen participation and transparency, political and physical safety, regulatory excellence, rule of law, and corruption suppression. Policymakers and researchers alike have increasingly relied on the WGIs (Huang & Ho, 2017). 'Is excellent governance useful to economic performance?' is one of the most frequently asked questions about governance. Numerous empirical studies have looked at how governance affects economic growth; most of them indicate that governance has a considerable impact (Huang & Ho, 2017). For instance, several studies (Dollar & Kraay, n.d.; Easterly & Levine, 2003; Groot et al., 2004; Huang & Ho, 2017) have suggested that governance has a positive impact on per capita income. The studies also find that in democratic nations, regulatory quality has a positive impact on both trade and economic growth; voice and accountability, effective governance, the rule of law, and corruption control have a favorable effect on economic growth (Azimi, 2022; Huang & Ho, 2017). The governance–growth nexus has been extensively documented in the literature to date (Mira & Hammadache, 2018; Rothstein & Teorell, 2008) Good governance, as defined by (Olson Jr. et al., 2000), is the engine that drives growth since it emphasizes high-quality policymaking in order to enhance services for citizens. However, the connection between the quality of governance and economic growth is not well understood (Azimi, 2022). According to Knack & Keefer (1995), good governance is a key factor in explaining investment because it improves the business climate and guarantees a stable capital market, both of which are necessary for the economy to expand. The quality of regulation ensures that effective and encouraging policies are formulated and implemented to support the development of the private sector and spur economic growth, while the rule of law empowers the market and provides equal opportunity for human capital engagement in economic activities and encourages foreign investments. Having a well-established administrative bureaucracy improves public sector performance and lessens corruption, which in turn boosts economic output (Azimi, 2022; Edgardo Campos et al., 1999). Almost all recent research has employed both time series and panel datasets to test the governance–growth nexus for the greatest economies, but in their own unique settings, providing a broader overview of the impact of governance on growth. Despite this, no research has been conducted on the asymmetrical effects of governance on growth for the world's leading economies, all of which are unique in terms of size and efficiency. This chapter is an original piece of writing that addresses an important topic and helps to bridge the gap between the previous research and the current state of knowledge. The present research work employs causality analysis and multiple regressions to examine data on the six variables from the world development indicators for the United States, China, Japan, Germany, and the United Kingdom from 2002 to 2022. Policymakers in all countries, but notably in developing countries, will benefit from understanding the meaning of the most important governance indicators and developing effective governance policies with the help of this research.

Objectives

The current investigation has a dual purpose. The first objective is to establish a causal relationship between countries' economic growth and indicators of good governance. The second goal of the chapter is to show how important the six indicators of good governance are in predicting economic growth in a limited group of developed countries using panel regression analysis.

Methodology and Data Source

Methodology

A common practice prior to handling time series data and for performing a co-integration test is to determine the stationarity of the series or its degree of integration, $I(d)$. For this augmented-Dickey-Fuller (ADF) Unit Root Test (Dickey & Fuller, 1979) has been used. It is essential to keep in mind that these tests presuppose the absence of any structural breaks (Gupta et al., 2022).

The present study uses the ADF unit root test to examine the stationarity of the data series. It consists of running a regression of the first difference of the series against the series lagged once, a constant and a time trend. This can be expressed as follows:

$$\Delta Y_t = \alpha_0 + \alpha_1 t + \alpha_2 Y_{t-1} + \sum_{j=1}^{p} \alpha_j \, \Delta Y_{t-j} + \varepsilon_t$$

The test for a unit root is performed on the coefficient of Y_{t-1} in the regression in this ADF process. If the coefficient deviates considerably from zero, the hypothesis that Y_t has a unit root is rejected. Stationarity is implied by rejecting the null hypothesis (Dickey & Fuller, 1979):

$H_0 : \alpha_2 = 0, \text{i.e.,} \, Y_t \text{ is a non} - \text{stationary series}$
$H_1 : \alpha_2 < 0, \text{i.e.,} \, Y_t \text{ is a stationary series}$

The null hypothesis, H_0, is accepted and the series is considered non-stationary or not integrated of order zero, I, if the estimated value of the ADF statistic is greater than McKinnon's critical values (Engle & Granger, 1991). If this fails, more differencing must be carried out until stationarity is obtained and the null hypothesis is rejected.

To determine whether or not one time period can be helpful in forecasting another, a statistical hypothesis test that can be called the Granger causality test is performed (Gupta et al., 2022). It is claimed that a time series X is a Granger cause of another time series Y if it can be shown that the values of the time series X convey statistically significant information about the values of Y in the future. The examination is carried out in the following way:

Let y and x be stationary time series. The null hypothesis is H_0: X does not Granger-cause Y.

The following regression should be used to determine the correct value to use for Y after it has been lagged. This is the limited model that must be purchased in order to receive SSRR. The next step is to strengthen the autoregression by including the lag values of x, as shown in the following equation:

$$y_t = a_0 + a_1 y_{t-1} + a_2 y_{t-2} + \ldots + a_m y_{t-m} + b_p x_{t-p} + \ldots + b_q x_{t-q} + residual_t$$

This is the model that does not have any restrictions for obtaining Sum square residual unrestricted (SSRUR).

The following serves as the test statistic in order to put the hypothesis to the test:

$$F = \left(\left(SSR_R - SSR_{UR} \right) / c \right) / SSR_{UR} / (n-1)$$

Where c represents the number of lagging terms that were taken, n represents the sample size, and l is the number of parameters that were estimated using the unconstrained equation.

If there are no lagged values of x that are kept in the regression, then one may accept the null hypothesis that x does not Granger-cause y. This is the only condition under which this hypothesis can be accepted (Maiti & Gupta, 2023).

In the next stage, a nonlinear panel regression has been carried out to find out the nexus between economic growth and different indicators of good governance. Panel data lets us take into account the information provided by time series, something we cannot do with a single cross section. A panel dataset also allows us to regulate for unobserved cross section heterogeneity. Test for a better model, i.e., whether the fixed effect or random effect model is the better one, has been checked using Hausman specification test. The fixed effect model turned out to be the better one as suggested by the Hausman specification test.

$$GDP_{it} = \beta_1 + \beta_2 PV_{it} + \beta_3 RQ_{it} + \beta_4 CC_{it} + \beta_5 GE_{it} + \beta_6 RL_{it} + \beta_7 VA_{it} + \beta_7 GE_{it}^2 + \varepsilon_{it}$$

The calculated equation is discovered to be nonlinear; it should be noted. Therefore, the sign of marginal effects will aid in determining whether a relationship is positive or negative for those factors that have a nonlinear relationship to the dependent variable. The Wald test has been used to determine the statistical significance of these variables (Maiti et al., 2023).

Data Source

In this chapter, seven variables, i.e., Political Stability and Absence of Violence/Terrorism (PV), Regulatory Quality (RQ), Control of Corruption (CC), Government Effectiveness (GE), Rule of Law (RL), Voice and Accountability (VA), and Real Gross Domestic Product (GDP), used as the proxy for economic growth have been used. The study is based on time series data from 2002 to 2022 for five countries, i.e., the United States, China, Japan, Germany, and the United Kingdom. All of them are having a mixture of good and weak governance as well as strong and weak economic growth rates, as has been collected from World Development Indicators (WDI) published by the World Bank.

Analysis of Data

This section presents the analysis of data. Table 12.1 shows the descriptive statistics of six indicators of good governance of the five developed countries during the study period. The table also shows the descriptive statistics of good governance.

It is found that during the study period, the mean value of the indicators of good governance is different from others. The mean value of the first indicator, i.e., political stability and absence of violence, is highest (1.020) for Japan and lowest for China (–0.461). Japan also has a low variation in this indicator which depicts the stable internal scenario within the country. In the case of regulatory quality, the United Kingdom shows the better picture among the countries. Control of corruption within a country is a significant indicator of good governance, and in this fact Germany is in a better position compared to the other countries. The United States is comparatively better in government effectiveness and rule of law than the other countries. Germany is in a better condition in voice and accountability.

For the ADF test, the optimum lag is selected based on the Schwartz Information Criterion (0–4 lags). It is found that the null hypotheses of unit roots cannot be rejected at conventional significance levels. Therefore, all the series are non-stationary in level but are stationary in the first difference (Maiti & Gupta, 2023). Therefore, all the series are integrated into the first difference.

Table 12.2 shows the two-way causality test between GDP and the various governance indicators for the five countries. With regard to Political Stability and the Absence of Violence/Terrorism (PV) and GDP, there is a bidirectional

TABLE 12.1 Descriptive Statistics of Six Indicators of Good Governance for the United States, China, Japan, Germany, and the United Kingdom

Country	Descriptive Statistics	PV	RQ	CC	GE	RL	VA
United States	Min.	−0.233	1.248	1.047	1.310	1.361	0.869
	Max.	0.678	1.641	1.874	1.740	1.639	1.345
	Mean	0.343	1.451	1.374	1.519	1.549	1.101
	CV	0.754	0.093	0.157	0.065	0.052	0.131
China	Min.	−0.657	−0.583	−0.618	−0.163	−0.700	−1.749
	Max.	−0.231	−0.164	0.054	0.841	0.035	−1.462
	Mean	−0.461	−0.289	−0.379	0.232	−0.402	−1.612
	CV	−0.253	−0.314	−0.504	1.325	−0.499	−0.052
Japan	Min.	0.879	0.495	0.937	1.017	1.149	0.931
	Max.	1.176	1.425	1.690	1.815	1.612	1.110
	Mean	1.020	1.185	1.431	1.511	1.396	1.017
	CV	0.069	0.171	0.138	0.137	0.104	0.049
Germany	Min.	0.574	1.470	1.727	1.331	1.550	1.298
	Max.	1.096	1.814	1.933	1.690	1.850	1.496
	Mean	0.787	1.611	1.821	1.542	1.662	1.394
	CV	0.204	0.067	0.031	0.069	0.045	0.036
United Kingdom	Min.	0.080	1.466	1.606	1.279	1.427	1.247
	Max.	0.673	1.868	2.003	1.868	1.875	1.597
	Mean	0.404	1.699	1.774	1.583	1.669	1.330
	CV	0.429	0.065	0.068	0.097	0.061	0.057

Source: Authors' own computations.

relationship between GDP and PV in the United States, the United Kingdom, and China. However, for Japan and Germany, there is a one-way causal relationship running from GDP to PV. In terms of Regulation Quality (RQ), there exists a bilateral causal relationship between RQ and GDP for Japan and the United States. On the other hand, there is a unilateral causal relationship running from RQ to GDP in China. Additionally, there is a one-way causal relationship running from GDP to RQ in Germany and the United Kingdom. With respect to Control of Corruption, a two-way causal relationship existed between CC and GDP for the United States and the United Kingdom. In contrast, there exists a one-way causal relationship running from CC to GDP. Furthermore, there also exists a one-way causal relationship running from GDP to CC in Japan and Germany. Regarding Government Effectiveness, from Table 12.2, there exists a bidirectional causal relationship between GE and GDP for only the United Kingdom. On the other hand, no causal relationship exists between GE and GDP for China. However, there

TABLE 12.2 Result of Granger Causality Test of Variables for the United States, China, Japan, Germany, and the United Kingdom

Null Hypothesis	Country									
	United States		China		Japan		Germany		United Kingdom	
	F-Statistic	Prob.	F-Statistic	Prob.	F-Statistic	Prob.	F-Statistic	Prob.	F-Statistic	Prob.
GDP does not Granger cause PV	0.433	0.66	3.971	0.05	1.138	0.35	0.128	0.88	0.139	0.87
PV does not Granger cause GDP	2.922	0.09	3.419	0.05	4.877	0.02	6.442	0.01	0.165	0.85
GDP does not Granger cause RQ	0.145	0.87	4.180	0.04	0.064	0.94	0.315	0.74	1.007	0.39
RQ does not Granger cause GDP	3.671	0.05	2.823	0.09	3.499	0.06	7.019	0.01	5.454	0.02
GDP does not Granger cause CC	0.321	0.73	4.080	0.04	3.516	0.06	0.662	0.53	1.196	0.33
CC does not Granger cause GDP	2.803	0.09	2.115	0.16	4.473	0.03	3.935	0.04	3.901	0.05
GDP does not Granger cause GE	0.434	0.66	5.712	0.02	2.606	0.11	2.526	0.12	0.793	0.47
GE does not Granger cause GDP	5.943	0.01	5.553	0.02	4.425	0.03	8.070	0	0.015	0.98
GDP does not Granger cause RL	0.008	0.99	1.127	0.35	1.693	0.22	0.575	0.58	2.635	0.11
RL does not Granger cause GDP	5.218	0.01	5.553	0.02	4.579	0.03	6.020	0.01	3.595	0.06
GDP does not Granger cause VA	1.710	0.22	1.127	0.35	6.110	0.01	0.169	0.85	0.015	0.98
VA does not Granger cause GDP	1.710	0.22	0.333	0.72	3.450	0.06	0.334	0.72	7.154	0.01

Source: Authors' calculations.

existed a one-way causal relationship running from GDP to GE for the United States, Japan, and Germany. In terms of Rule of Law (RL), there exists a bilateral causal relationship between RL and GDP for the United Kingdom only. For the other four countries, a unidirectional causal relationship was found running from GDP to RL. For Voice and Accountability (VA), there exists a two-way causal relationship between VA and GDP for China, the United States, and Germany. With respect to the United Kingdom, there exists a one-way relationship running from GDP to VA. For Japan, the unilateral relationship runs from VA to GDP.

Table 12.3 shows the result of panel regression of good governance on six indicators. It is found that political stability and absence of violence, regulatory quality, control of corruption, rule of law, voice and accountability, and square of government effectiveness have a positive impact on economic growth. From the table, it can be observed that regulatory quality and rule of law have a greater positive effect on economic growth than the other variables. A percentage increase in regulatory quality and rule of law leads to a 5.002 and 6.665 percentage increase in GDP, respectively. Regulatory quality and rule of law increase business confidence. Firms are more confident to conduct their economic activities in these countries as there are good laws and regulations that protect and promote their activities. These entire variables are statistically significant. The only indicator that has a nonlinear relationship with economic growth is government effectiveness and its effect on economic growth has been captured through the marginal effect. The result of the marginal effect shows a percentage increase in government

TABLE 12.3 Panel Regression Analysis – Economic Growth and Six Indicators of Good Governance

Explanatory Variable	Coefficient	t-Statistic	p-Value	Marginal Effect
C	7.431***	4.069	0.00	
PV	1.945**	2.425	0.02	
RQ	5.002**	2.193	0.03	
CC	1.082***	2.658	0.01	
GE	–3.992**	1.916	0.05	1.106 (7.025**)
RL	6.665***	2.529	0.01	
VA	1.297**	2.122	0.04	
GE^2	1.996**	–2.469	0.02	
Adjusted R-squared	0.751			
F-statistic	29.475			
Prob (F-statistic)	0			

Source: Authors' calculations; ***, ** and * significant at 1%, 5%, and 10% level, respectively (Maiti et al., 2023); Chi-square value is present in the first bracket ().

effectiveness leads to a 1.106 percentage increase in economic growth which may be due to government effectiveness and can increase the business operations and output of the different sectors. Governments in an effort to streamline processes in these countries may put in place many laws and regulations that increase the cost of doing business as well as slow down business operation discouraging firms from doing business. The F-statistics are highly significant confirming that the overall model is the best fitted one.

Conclusion and Recommendations

Good governance is important for economic growth and development. Some studies have highlighted the importance of good governance in the economic growth and development of countries (Fathia, 2021; Huang, 2017; Feyisa et al., 2022) Good governance creates the environment necessary for economic agents particularly businesses to be able to allocate resources efficiently and effectively. With good regulatory frameworks and laws, efficient markets are created leading to better distribution of scarce resources. In this chapter, good governance is examined in terms of six variables including political stability and absence of violence/terrorism, regulatory quality, control of corruption, government effectiveness, rule of law, and voice and accountability. Furthermore, the chapter has two primary objectives. First of all, the causal relationship between economic growth and good governance is determined for five countries, namely, the United States, China, Japan, Germany, and the United Kingdom. Secondly, the impact of these six government indicators on economic growth is examined. The analysis shows that the government's effectiveness, political stability and absence of violence/terrorism, regulatory quality, control of corruption, rule of law, and voice and accountability have a positive effect on economic growth. Also, there is a unidirectional or bidirectional causal relationship between economic growth and the six indicators of good governance in all the five countries. There are a few recommendations for governments and development agencies. First, countries must invest in their governance infrastructure. Governments need to pay attention to improving regulations, laws, and frameworks as well as encouraging the participation of the citizenry in the government process. This investment would encourage the entry of multinational firms into their country. Good governance would also promote the establishment of local businesses that would have confidence in doing business in the country leading to an increase in output. Secondly, development agencies need to support governments in their efforts to improve governance through research and funding. Research is important to enable governments to identify bottlenecks in their governance structures as well as the best practices needed to improve governance systems in their countries.

Limitations

A few limitations are there in the chapter. One of them is that the analysis is done for only five developed countries. Future research should also focus on the relationship between good governance and economic growth in developing and emerging economies. Also, future research can focus on the relationship between governance and economic growth in different regions such as Asia or sub-Saharan Africa.

References

Aladlani, A. H. (n.d.). *Governance and Economic Growth in the Arab World: Evidence from Panel Data Analysis.* Retrieved November 11, 2023, from https://scholarworks.wmich.edu/dissertations/3448

Azimi, M. N. (2022). Revisiting the governance-growth nexus: Evidence from the world's largest economies. *Http://Www.Editorialmanager.Com/Cogentecon, 10*(1). https://doi.org/10.1080/23322039.2022.2043589

Chakraborty, C., & Jana, A. (2021). Economic growth and trade-related variables: An empirical study using Indian data. In Das, R. C. (ed) *Global Tariff War: Economic, Political and Social Implications* (pp. 141–152). Emerald Publishing Limited. https://doi.org/10.1108/978-1-80071-314-720211011

Das, R. C., & Mukherjee, S. (2019). Do spending on R&D influence income? An enquiry on world's leading economies and groups. *Journal of the Knowledge Economy, 11*(4), 1295–1315. https://doi.org/10.1007/s13132-019-00609-0

Dickey, D. A., & Fuller, W. A. (1979). Distribution of the estimators for autoregressive time series with a unit root. *Journal of the American Statistical Association, 74*(366a), 427–431. https://doi.org/10.1080/01621459.1979.10482531

Dollar, D., & Kraay, A. (n.d.). *Growth Is Good for the Poor on JSTOR.* Retrieved September 17, 2023, from https://www.jstor.org/stable/40216063

Easterly, W., & Levine, R. (2003). Tropics, germs, and crops: How endowments influence economic development. *Journal of Monetary Economics, 50*(1), 3–39. https://doi.org/10.1016/S0304-3932(02)00200-3

Edgardo Campos, J., Lien, D., & Pradhan, S. (1999). The impact of corruption on investment: Predictability matters. *World Development, 27*(6), 1059–1067. https://doi.org/10.1016/S0305-750X(99)00040-6

Engle, R., & Granger, C. (1991). *Long-run Economic Relationships: Readings in Cointegration.* Oxford University Press. https://econpapers.repec.org/bookchap/oxpobooks/9780198283393.htm

Fathia, S. N. (2021). How good government governance affect the economic growth? An investigation on selected country around the world. *Asian Journal of Economics, Business and Accounting, 21*(1), 93–98. https://doi.org/10.9734/AJEBA/2021/V21I730405

Feyisa, L. H., Ayen, D. D., Abdulahi, M. S., Tefera, T. F.,. (2022). The three-dimensional impacts of governance on economic growth: Panel data evidence from the emerging market. *Corporate Governance and Organizational Behavior Review, 6*(1), 2022. https://doi.org/10.22495/cgobrv6i1p3

Groot, H. L. F., Linders, G. J., Rietveld, P., & Subramanian, U. (2004). The institutional determinants of bilateral trade patterns. *Kyklos, 57*(1), 103–123. https://doi.org/10.1111/J.0023-5962.2004.00245.X

Gupta, T., Sharma, D., & Maiti, S. (2022). *Global Trade and Economic Crisis*. In https://services.igi-global.com/resolvedoi/resolve.aspx?doi=10.4018/978-1-6684-5950-8.ch005 (pp. 86–111). IGI Global. https://doi.org/10.4018/978-1-6684-5950-8.ch005

Huang, C. C. (2017). The impacts of brand experiences on brand loyalty: Mediators of brand love and trust. *Management Decision*, 55(5), 915–934. https://doi.org/10.1108/MD-10-2015-0465/FULL/HTML

Huang, C. J., & Ho, Y. H. (2017). Governance and economic growth in Asia. *The North American Journal of Economics and Finance*, 39, 260–272. https://doi.org/10.1016/J.NAJEF.2016.10.010

Kaufmann, D., & Kraay, A. (2023). Worldwide Governance Indicators, 2023 Update (www.govindicators.org), Accessed on 11/10/2023.

Khan, M. H. (2007). Governance, economic growth and development since the 1960s. Working Papers. https://ideas.repec.org/p/une/wpaper/54.html

Knack, S., & Keefer, P. (1995). Institutions and economic performance: Cross-country tests using alternative institutional measures. *Economics & Politics*, 7(3), 207–227. https://doi.org/10.1111/J.1468-0343.1995.TB00111.X

Li, M., Sun, H., Agyeman, F. O., Heydari, M., Jameel, A., & Salah Ud Din Khan, H. (2021). Analysis of potential factors influencing China's regional sustainable economic growth. *Applied Sciences*, 11(22), 10832. https://doi.org/10.3390/APP112210832

Maiti, S., & Gupta, T. (2023). Impact of foreign trade and COVID-19 pandemic on Sri Lankan and Indian economy: A comparative study in Bhattacharyya et al (eds). *COVID-19 Pandemic and Global Inequality*, 139–152. https://doi.org/10.1007/978-981-99-4405-7_9

Maiti, S., Gupta, T., & Rajpal, G. S. (2023). Linkage between women empowerment and gender-based violence in India: Evidence from NFHS-5 data in Chakraborty & Pal (eds). *Gender Inequality and Its Implications on Education and Health: A Global Perspective*, 165–175. https://doi.org/10.1108/978-1-83753-180-620231015/FULL/XML

Mira, R., & Hammadache, A. (2018). Good governance and economic growth: A contribution to the institutional debate about state failure in Middle East and North Africa. *Asian Journal of Middle Eastern and Islamic Studies*, 11(3), 107–120. https://doi.org/10.1080/25765949.2017.12023313

Molinillo, S., Japutra, A., Nguyen, B., & Chen, C. H. S. (2017). Responsible brands vs active brands? An examination of brand personality on brand awareness, brand trust, and brand loyalty. *Marketing Intelligence and Planning*, 35(2), 166–179. https://doi.org/10.1108/MIP-04-2016-0064/FULL/HTML

North, D. C. (1990). *Institutions, Institutional Change and Economic Performance: Discovery Service for De Montfort University*. https://eds.p.ebscohost.com/eds/detail/detail?vid=11&sid=bd00d687-9a1f-4330-93a3-ce05f5b7762b%40redis&bdata=JkF1dGhUeXBlPWlwLHNzbyZzaXRlPWVkcy1saXZlJnNjb3BlPXNpdGU%3D#AN=510978&db=e000xww

Olson Jr., M., Sarna, N., & Swamy, A. V. (2000). Governance and growth: A simple hypothesis explaining cross-country differences in productivity growth. *Public Choice*, 102(3), 341–364. https://doi.org/10.1023/A:1005067115159

Rahman, M. M., Rana, R. H., & Barua, S. (2019). The drivers of economic growth in South Asia: Evidence from a dynamic system GMM approach. *Journal of Economic Studies*, 46(3), 564–577. https://doi.org/10.1108/JES-01-2018-0013/FULL/PDF

Rothstein, B., & Teorell, J. (2008). What is quality of government? A theory of impartial government institutions. *Governance*, *21*(2), 165–190. https://doi.org/10.1111/J.1468-0491.2008.00391.X

Towah, W. D. (n.d.). *ScholarWorks the Impact of Good Governance and Stability on Sustainable Development in Ghana*. Retrieved November 11, 2023, from https://scholarworks.waldenu.edu/dissertations

United Nations Development Programme. (1997). *Governance for Sustainable Human Development: A UNDP Policy Document*. 40. https://digitallibrary.un.org/record/492551

13

ROLES OF INDICATORS AND INHIBITORS OF GOOD GOVERNANCE IN SUSTAINABLE DEVELOPMENT AND ECONOMIC GROWTH

Begum Sertyesilisik

Introduction

Fostering sustainable development (SD) and sustainable and resilient economic growth is important for well-being, welfare, and sustainability of humanity facing to experience accelerated challenges of climate change increasing importance of and need for an effective fight against climate change. Kaushik (2023) described SD as a leading philosophy able to be applied to the foreseeable future to protect human beings and the earth. Omri and Mabrouk (2020)'s research on Middle East North Africa (MENA) economies revealed that economic growth and human development are interrelated and complement each other and that political and institutional governance supports SD. Governance covers how countries, companies, and entities are governed (IMF, n.d.). It includes not only institutions but also state and people relations, and mechanisms fostering collaboration across industries (United Nations Development Programme (UNDP), 2014). It covers decision-making and implementation processes (United Nations Economic and Social Commission for Asia and the Pacific (UNESCAP), n.d.). It dates back to human civilisation as it is among the main pillars upon which civilisations were built (Ramzy et al., 2019).

The SD and good governance (GG) interrelation is significant (Ramzy et al., 2019). GG is about the country's resources and affairs' administration in an accountable, citizen-centred, fair, and responsible way (Kaushik, 2023). GG is "... *responsible conduct of public affairs and management of public resources*" (Council of Europe (COE), n.d.). GG contributes to the governing process by adding the normative/evaluative perspective and it is about processes and outcomes vital for achieving development goals (OHCHR, n.d.).

DOI: 10.4324/9781003530688-16

It can be tested via the level of accomplishment/fulfilment of human rights promises (OHCHR, n.d.). As GG indicators can have the potential for supporting effectiveness in GG and in GG's potential contribution to SD and economic growth, support for achievement of GG's indicators and elimination of GG's inhibitors can comply with each other in supporting strategic effectiveness of GG and achieving SD and resilient and sustainable economic growth. Based on the literature review, this chapter aims to investigate roles of indicators and inhibitors of GG in SD and economic growth.

Relationship among GG, Its Indicators, and Sustainable Development

Humanity encounters and experiences challenges in achieving SD and UN SDGs. For example, according to the IMF (2023)'s report, "… *60% of low-income countries and 25% of emerging market economies in or at risk of debt distress… 350 million people in 79 countries face acute food insecurity*" (IMF, 2023). This situation puts emphasis on the importance of and need for effective GG to overcome challenges and difficulties that can make the GG and SD difficult to achieve. Effectiveness in GG can be supported by compliance with and performing well with respect to GG indicators.

Worldwide Governance Indicators (WGIs) and the COE's 12 Principles of Good Democratic Governance share common concerns and focus (e.g., rule of law). These indicators can support achievement of the UN's SDGs. GG can comply with the WGIs and the COE's 12 Principles of Good Democratic Governance. Both COE's 12 Principles of Good Democratic Governance and WGIs are in compliance with the UNDP's UN SDGs. Even if WGIs do not directly refer to sustainability and innovation, COE has principles directly on sustainability. The WGI has six aggregate governance indicators (Kaufmann & Kraay, 2023): voice and accountability (related with freedom of expression, citizens' ability to select government, etc.); political stability and absence of violence/terrorism (related with political instability, etc.); government effectiveness (related with quality of public services, government's commitment, etc.); regulatory quality (related with government's ability to establish and implement policies and regulations to support development of private sector); rule of law (related with agents' confidence in abide by the society's rules); control of corruption (related with the level of public power exercised for private gain) (Kaufmann & Kraay, 2023). Similarly, COE's 12 Principles of Good Democratic Governance are as follows (COE, n.d.): accountability; competence and capacity; efficiency and effectiveness; ethical conduct; human rights, cultural diversity, and social cohesion; innovation and openness to change; openness and transparency; participation, representation, fair conduct of elections; responsiveness; rule of law; sound financial management; sustainability and long-term orientation.

Performance in the GG indicators can provide input to the countries in enhancing their performance in their GG. For example, WGI's 2022 data (Kaufmann & Kraay, 2023) on countries' performance with respect to WGIs revealed that countries having 100 based on *"Upper bound of 90% confidence interval for governance, in percentile rank terms"* New Zealand appeared in 5 out of 6 WGIs, whereas Denmark and Finland were listed in 4 out of 6 WGIs, and American Samoa, Luxembourg, Norway, and Singapore appeared in 3 out of 6 WGIs as the WGIs and the countries having 100 in each WGI are, respectively, as follows (Kaufmann & Kraay, 2023): control of corruption (Denmark, Finland, and New Zealand); government effectiveness (Denmark, Finland, Luxembourg, Monaco, Norway, and Switzerland); political stability and absence of violence/terrorism (Andorra, Anguilla, American Samoa, Aruba, Brunei Darussalam, Cayman Islands, Cook Islands, Dominica, Greenland, Liechtenstein, Macao SAR China, Monaco, New Zealand, Niue, Singapore, San Marino, Jersey, and Channel Islands); regulatory quality (Australia, Denmark, Luxembourg, Macao SAR China, New Zealand, and Singapore); rule of law (Andorra, American Samoa, Austria, Switzerland, Denmark, Finland, Greenland, Guam, Iceland, Liechtenstein, Luxembourg, Monaco, Norway, New Zealand, Singapore, San Marino, Sweden, Jersey, and Channel Islands); and voice and accountability (American Samoa, Cook Islands, Finland, Guam, New Zealand, Niue, Norway, and Switzerland) (Kaufmann & Kraay, 2023). Accordingly, countries wishing to enhance and improve their performance on WGIs and GG can benefit from GG indicator-based benchmarks from other countries performing relatively better in particular indicator(s) and analyse the factors contributing to their high performance in particular indicator(s). Furthermore, they can consider these findings as potential input to their GG and SD policies covering ways for and establishing strategies for improving their GG with respect to indicators.

GG is important for SD and UN SDGs' targets (Ramzy et al., 2019). Biermann et al. (2014) emphasised the necessity of governance to be part of SDGs covering three aspects of governance (i.e., good, effective, and equitable governance). Camdessus, IMF Managing Director, addressed the United Nations Economic and Social Council in 1997 indicating GG's importance for all countries regardless of their development level (IMF, n.d.). GG's main characteristics are in compliance with WGIs and COE's principles. GG's main characteristics are: participatoriness, consensus orientedness, accountability, transparency, responsiveness, effectiveness and efficiency, equitability and inclusiveness, and compliance with the rule of law (UNESCAP, n.d.). It ensures inclusivity in decision-making, responsiveness to today's and future society's needs, and minimisation of corruption (UNESCAP, n.d.). Similarly, the Human Rights Council highlighted transparency, responsibility, accountability, participation, and responsiveness to people's needs as GG's main attributes (OHCHR, n.d.). For example, the accountability principle of GG can support the SDG2 Zero hunger (Ramzy et al., 2019). Similarly, UNDP (2014) highlighted accountability as a key theme affecting many aspects of GG. Regarding the participatory attribute of GG, Ramzy et al. (2019) emphasised that GG must support participatory relation among three main players (i.e., the government, private sector, and civil society) of GG. "...*Participation is both a right, and a means to more SD...*" (UNDP, 2014). Furthermore, GG and SDGs have the common concern of ending poverty (Ramzy et al., 2019). Additionally, the rule of law principle of governance is critical for SD (UNDP, 2014). Achievement of SDGs depends on effective governance mainly due to the requirement for strong political institutions and processes and governments' alignment of their policies with SDGs (GGI Development). Allen et al. (2019)'s research on GG's three institutional principles' effects on poverty reduction and inequality reduction revealed the enabling effects of SDG 16 on SDGs 1 and 10 (i.e., power reduction and reduced inequalities) at the national and subnational levels. Berliani and Violita (2021)'s research on how governance influences government public trust essential to achieve SDG revealed that the two WGIs (i.e., political stability and absence of violence/terrorism and control of corruption) affect public trust in government positively.

SD and GG are intertwined (Stojanovic et al., 2016; Kaushik, 2023), linked ideas (Kaushik, 2023), and like the same coin's two sides (Ramzy et al., 2019). Governance can contribute to SD both in developed and developing countries (Güney, 2017). The SD and GG interrelation is significant and they need each other so that they can be achieved (Ramzy et al., 2019). Similarly, Kaushik (2023) highlighted GG's essentiality for SD. GG is at the core of sustainability (Sharma, 2001, as cited in Stojanovic et al., 2016) and imperative to SD (Towah, 2019). GG is a prerequisite for sustainability (Bosselmann et al., 2008 as cited in Stojanovic et al., 2016). According to Kaushik (2023), even if GG does not ensure SD, GG's absence can obstacle growth. Ramzy et al. (2019)'s research supported the GG and SD relationship.

GG's contribution to and relation with sustainability and SD can be observed in all pillars of sustainability. "... *governance has been referred to as the fourth pillar of SD-together with social, environmental and economic factors*" (GGI Development). GG covers economic, social, and political dimensions of the SD (Ramzy et al., 2019). GG's relation to the sustainability's three pillars can be highlighted as follows:

- Economic aspect: GG is vital for reducing poverty (Towah, 2019), developing wealthy nations prioritising citizens' well-being (Kaushik, 2023), supporting countries' economic growth, and enhancing their human capital and social cohesion (Kaufmann & Kraay, 2023). For example, focusing on 39 countries in Sub-Saharan Africa, Assoum and Alinsato (2023)'s research revealed that the public debt's impact on per capita income depends on the governance quality level. According to Assoum and Alinsato (2023: 6)'s research, public debt's effect on per capita income is significant and positive in case the governance level is more than 21.78 points out of 100. Assoum and Alinsato (2023: 6)'s research findings highlighted GG's contribution to mitigate public debt's adverse impacts with the help of responsible management. Similarly, Stojanovic et al. (2016)'s research revealed a correlation between GG and GDP as well as between GG and inequality of income distribution. Countries' governance level increase can contribute to the welfare of the people and prevent scarcity of resources (Güney, 2017). Furthermore, Ramzy et al. (2019) highlighted GG's contribution to efficiency stating "GG is the best outcome of the minimum input". Effective and strategic GG can influence resource efficiency and effectiveness. For example, in Bhutan, GG has contributed to the effective use of resources and the expansion of health, education, and other services (Ura and Kinga, 2004).

- Environmental aspect: Effective and strategic GG can contribute to environmental sustainability. Gao, Murshed, Ghardallou, Siddik, Ali, and Khudoykulov (2023)'s research revealed that GG can support environmental quality, environmental conditions, and environmental innovations. Similarly, Ofori, Onifade, Ali, Alola, and Zhang (2023)'s study revealed that the financial development index, economic governance, institutional governance, voice of accountability, and control of corruption contribute to environmental quality and reduction in pollution. For example, according to Ofori et al. (2023: 5)'s research, a percentage increase in regulatory quality can result in enhanced environmental quality and a 2–3.08% reduction in CO_2 emission at a 1% significance level, whereas a percentage increase in governance effectiveness can cause 1.05–1.56% increase in environmental pollution. Furthermore, according to Ofori et al. (2023: 5)'s research, a percentage increase in renewable energy and economic growth can result in a reduction in environmental pollution by 0.14–0.22% and 0.51–0.60%, respectively. Focusing on the MENA economies, Omri and Mabrouk (2020)'s research revealed that improvement in political and institutional governance can enable MENA countries to reduce carbon emissions' adverse impacts on human development and economic growth. Recent studies (e.g., Alsaleh, Abdul-Rahim, and Abdulwakil, 2021; Saba and Biyase, 2022) highlighted the relationship among renewable energy, GG, and WGIs. Alsaleh, Abdul-Rahim, and Abdulwakil (2021)'s research emphasised that WGIs' enhanced practice and quality can contribute to European countries' bioenergy industry's growth. Saba and Biyase (2022)'s research emphasised the contribution of control of corruption, the rule of law, voice and accountability, and institutional quality to renewable electricity development.

- Social aspect: GG is vital for human rights protection (OHCHR, n.d.). Stojanovic et al. (2016)'s research highlighted GG's contribution to equality. Normative frameworks such as human rights standards and principles support governance's mechanisms and processes (UNDP, 2014). GG and human rights relationship can be supported via (OHCHR, n.d.): democratic institutions (e.g., supporting public participation in policymaking, and social groups' inclusion in decision-making processes); public service delivery (e.g., enhancing capacity of the state to provide public goods vital for human rights protection; enhancing accessibility and acceptability of services); rule of law (e.g., supporting public awareness of legal frameworks); and anti-corruption (supporting anti-corruption precautions through anti-corruption commissions, and monitoring how the public funds are used) (OHCHR, n.d.). GG can result in peaceful, stable, and resilient societies (UNDP, 2014). Effective governance allows society's participation in decision-making processes and the efficient application of resources for equitable and SD (Kaushik, 2023).

Recommendations for Fostering GG's Strategic Effectiveness and Resilience

As GG's performance regarding indicators of GG can reveal an indication about its success and effectiveness level, GG's scopes and its objectives' compliance with and their strategic effectiveness in the GG's indicators are important. GG's strategic and effective resilience against inhibitors of GG can further affect GG's success and effectiveness level. Both supporting high performance of GG with respect to indicators of GG while enhancing GG's resilience against its inhibitors, and eliminating inhibitors and their root causes in a synergic, holistic, and coherent way at all levels (i.e., at the company, industry, and country levels) can contribute to the success and effectiveness level of GG (Figure 13.1). This situation can further support establishment and flourishment of effective, strategic, and sustainable GG and SD, as well as their synergic, strategic, effective, holistic, coherent, and sustainable interaction at all levels (i.e., at the company, industry, and country levels), contributing to increase people's level at the Maslow (1943)'s Hierarchy of Needs and their motivation for contributing to and supporting both GG and SD (Figure 13.1). Furthermore, effective, strategic, and sustainable GG and SD, as well as their synergic, strategic, effective, holistic, coherent, and sustainable interaction at all levels, can further contribute to support GG's strategic success and effectiveness with respect to GG's indicators and to enhance GG's resilience against its inhibitors and to eliminate its inhibitors and their root causes (Figure 13.1).

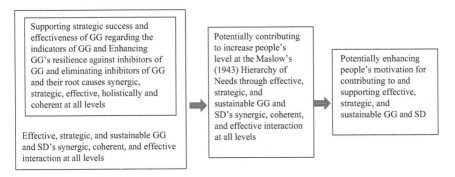

FIGURE 13.1   The main aspects of fostering GG's effectiveness and resilience.

Source: Sketched by the author.

Specific and unique aspects of all levels (i.e., company, industry, and country) need to be covered in supporting GG's indicators and the fight against GG's inhibitors. UNDP (2014) emphasised that "... *a single model of governance cannot and should not be imposed*". Stojanovic et al. (2016)'s research emphasised that different countries have different development needs and that even if GG affects SD indicators focused on their study, cross-sectional research from the countries' different categories perspective revealed GG dimensions' different effects on these indicators. Similarly, industry-level compliance with the GG indicators and fight against GG inhibitors need to be effectively and strategically achieved to influence and support industries' growth and economic growth considering industry-specific and country-specific aspects. For example, focusing on European countries' bioenergy industry, Alsaleh et al. (2021) highlighted the importance of authorities' emphasis on WGIs' effectiveness and transparency for achieving bioenergy security. Furthermore, Gao et al. (2023)'s research on the BRICS highlighted the importance of governments adopting policies to support clean foreign direct investment, environmental innovations, good democratic governance, and greener urbanisation policies. GG can be considered vital for being incorporated into development strategies (Kaushik, 2023). As different countries can have different development needs (Stojanovic et al., 2016), industries making significant contributions to their economy and growth can be different. For this reason, countries can consider in their GG and SD to prioritise industries playing effective roles in and making strategic contributions to their SD and economic growth. From this point of view, for example, as construction industry can be one of the main industries vital for many countries' SD and economic growth due to many factors (e.g., its contribution to infrastructures needed), prioritising construction industry related incentives and development policies in compliance with GG indicators and SD can be effective in various countries potentially depending mainly on their development level and on their construction industry's contribution to their SD and economic growth. Furthermore, the construction industry's development level in that country and its impacts on employment, economic growth, and GDP in that country can have the potential to influence this industry's significance level in that country's SD and GG. Effective compliance to GG and its indicators at the construction company level can contribute to the company's competitiveness which can further contribute to the construction industry's competitiveness which can contribute to SD and sustainable and resilient economic growth of the country. Furthermore, identification of that country's construction industry related GG's inhibitors, their main and sub-causes, and taking necessary effective precautions against these inhibitors and their causes can further support GG and SD. Additionally, the construction industry related SD and GG of that country can be updated based on the changing requirements and needs of their construction industry.

GG's compliance with UN SDGs can contribute to GG's strategic effectiveness at all levels. Complying with the definition of the SD in the Brundtland report, as SD is about the fulfilment of the needs of today's generation while ensuring/protecting the next generations' ability to meet their own needs, SD is based on inclusivity of the future generations to SD revealing and highlighting importance of GG's inclusivity. Furthermore, GG can support collective action through accountable actors' involvement and through coping with trade-offs among the SDGs (GGI Development). Additionally, Kaushik (2023) highlighted that public administration which is accessible, efficient, and responsible, as well as norms and institutions, and legal foundation for development need to be covered by governance's system.

Focusing on GG's indicators and focusing on GG's inhibitors are equally important for supporting GG and SD at all levels in an effective and strategic way. It is important to fight against inhibitors of GG and take necessary strategic and effective precautions against inhibitors of SD and GG and to enhance GG's resilience to the inhibitors. These precautions against inhibitors of GG need to be effective at all levels in a coherent and systematic manner in a way to support SD and economic growth. There are many inhibitors of GG (e.g., corruption, unfair human resources policies, failure in transparency, failure in compliance with ethics). For example, corruption is an inhibitor of SD and GG and it can emerge as a result of failure in SD and GG. Corruption can obstacle SD and GG and it can appear due to failure in SD and GG. Corruption is related to abusing public authority/trust for private benefit and it can be nurtured by poor governance as GG can support the fight against corruption (IMF, n.d.). Corruption can challenge governance and adversely affect economic performance, investments and economic growth, tax revenue, income inequality, macroeconomic management, and resources allocated to education and health (IMF, n.d.). Kaushik (2023) highlighted the importance of GG for anti-corruption initiatives and indicated that society can be equitable in case there is no favouritism, prejudice, and bribery. Furthermore, Sarhan and Gerged (2023)'s research supported companies' anti-bribery and corruption commitments and environmental management performance's positive link. Additionally, policies on anti-corruption, transparency, and accountability can contribute to development (e.g., education) (UNDP, 2014). Corruption control measures include enhanced transparency which can be supported by many aspects such as independent media and enhanced access to information (Allen et al., 2019). Furthermore, regarding measures at the company level, Sarhan and Gerged (2023) recommended managers to integrate anti-corruption related practices into their companies' strategic agenda to keep long-run sustainability through ethical initiatives. Additionally, at the country level, Sarhan and Gerged (2023) recommended regulators and policymakers to support the fight against bribery and corruption activities among companies and to support relevant mechanisms.

Countries can consider enhancing their performance with respect to the GG indicators as an integral part of their GG and SD policies and strategies at all levels, especially at the industry and country levels covering industry-specific and country-specific aspects, and addressing specific challenges and weaknesses. They can consider enhancing this process through indicator-based benchmarking from countries having high performance in specific GG indicator(s). They can integrate these findings into their GG and SD policies at the industry and country levels in enhancing their industry-specific and country-specific strategies for enhancing their SD and indicator-based GG performance covering their unique aspects. Furthermore, countries can consider changes in their GG indicator based annual performance to take necessary effective steps for enhancing their performance through identification of areas which need improvement and progress. For this reason, enhancing GG performance with respect to GG indicators is a dynamic process requiring active monitoring of the GG and SD performance so that necessary effective precautions can be taken on time to foresee potential performance deviations and/or to identify actual performance deviations and their main and sub-causes. Equally important is active monitoring of the performance regarding the GG inhibitors due to the need for eliminating their main and sub-causes and/or reducing their adverse impacts which can endanger and harm GG and SD of the countries and their industries. Both of these active monitoring processes (i.e., performance monitoring of GG indicators and GG inhibitors) need to be performed at the same time so that necessary effective pro-active and reactive precautions at the industry and country level can be taken in a coherent and strategic way to support GG and SD. These processes need to address GG and SD related unique aspects of the countries and their economies as well mainly due to Stojanovic et al. (2016)'s statement indicating that different countries can have different development needs. With the help of these active monitoring processes, achievement of effective and successful GG and SD can be supported. This situation can further support capacity fulfilment of countries and their industries in accomplishing their GG performance and SD which can further support their people's welfare and well-being and increase their level at the Maslow (1943)'s Hierarchy of Needs pyramid encouraging them to achieve their capacity too.

Establishment of and achieving effective, efficient, strategic, sustainable, and resilient GG and SD in a way to support sustainable economic development and sustainable economic growth can support and can be supported by effective, efficient, strategic, sustainable, smart, and resilient use of countries' and its industries' resources, capacity, and capabilities for supporting and enhancing country's and its industries' environmental-friendly and next-generation friendly SD and value-oriented sustainable economic development and growth. In this way, the country's and its industries' long-term relevant strategic capacity and capabilities can be supported by complying with and further supporting transition to the Society 5.0 and Industry 5.0. Furthermore, countries' and their industries' success in enhancing their GG's and SD's effectiveness, efficiency, sustainability, and resilience strategically can contribute to achievement of the goals and requirements of society 5.0. Society 5.0's goal is to achieve a human-centric super-smart society to enable the society to have a high-quality life (Huang, Wang, Li, Zheng, Mourtzis and Wang, 2022). Changes in industries [e.g., carbon capturing smart construction industry (Sertyesilisik, 2023); post-carbon transition and environmental justice to reduce environment footprint of the construction industry (Sertyesilisik, 2022); smart, circular, and competitive manufacturing industry (Sertyesilisik & Sertyesilisik, 2021)] can be further supported through effective, efficient, strategic, sustainable, and resilient GG and SD. Furthermore, countries achieving effective, efficient, strategic, sustainable, and resilient GG and SD can have the potential to contribute to global SD as their success can set an example for and act as a motivator for other countries and encourage them to further enhance their GG and SD. Failure in each country's GG and SD can harm the effectiveness, efficiency, sustainability, and resilience levels of other countries' GG and SD at the global level due to the opportunity cost and global interdependence of countries' GG and SD. Additionally, effective, efficient, strategic, sustainable, and resilient GG and SD can influence and be influenced by sustainable development plans to support industries and their outputs and services to reduce their environmental embodied footprint potentially affecting their investment, and trade decisions, trade-offs, opportunity cost, and priorities in these fields. Effective and successful widespread of effective, efficient, strategic, sustainable, and resilient GG and SD at the country and global levels can contribute to global sustainability and SD. As global sustainability and sustainability leadership are important for peace in the world (Sertyesilisik, 2018), effective, efficient, strategic, sustainable, and resilient GG and SD at the country and global levels can have the potential for contributing to global peace.

Conclusion

The chapter investigated and emphasised the roles of indicators and inhibitors of GG in SD and economic growth. Enhancing synergy for SD and economic growth through GG's, its indicators', and SD's strategic and coherent interaction at all levels can contribute to levelling up people in Maslow (1943)'s Hierarchy of Needs pyramid. As GG's performance regarding GG's indicators can reveal an indication about GG's effectiveness level, GG's scope and its objectives' strategic and coherent compliance with GG's indicators is important. Fostering synergy between GG and SD considering effective indicators complement with taking effective precautions against GG's inhibitors. Effective, strategic, and successful GG can contribute to SD and economic growth through supporting creation and enhancement of conditions, further supporting GG and SD transparency, fairness, synergy, and productivity. Effective indicators of GG can provide important input to SD whereas inhibitors of GG can hinder SD. Supporting achievement of GG's indicators and elimination of GG's inhibitors (e.g., corruption, unfair human resources policies, failure in transparency, failure in compliance with ethics) can comply with and complement each other in enhancing effectiveness of GG and achieving SD and economic growth. As GG's strategic and effective resilience against GG's inhibitors can influence GG's success and effectiveness, support for GG's high performance with respect to GG's indicators while supporting GG's resilience against GG's inhibitors and eliminating its inhibitors and their root causes in an effective, strategic, synergic, holistic, and coherent way at all levels (i.e., at the company, industry, and country levels) can contribute to the GG's effectiveness. Furthermore, achievement of SD respectful to GG and its indicators can support conditions enabling effective and strategic GG. Furthermore, compliance with GG's indicators in the SD of countries and their industries can have the potential to support effectiveness of policies, SD, and GG at all levels. Effective indicators integrated SD and GG can contribute to effectiveness and efficiency in resource allocation and usage contributing to the welfare and well-being of people and levelling them up in Maslow (1943)'s Hierarchy of Needs pyramid.

This chapter emphasised importance of the relationship among GG, GG's indicators and inhibitors, SD, and economic growth as well as the relationship between UN SDGs and GG highlighting importance of compliance with GG principles and elimination of inhibitors of GG at the company, industry, and country levels in a coherent, synergic, and effective way. Effective, coherent, and strategic compliance at the company level can support the company's competitiveness which can contribute to its industry's competitiveness which can further support SD and economic growth, and GG of the country. As GG's incorporation into development strategies is vital (Kaushik, 2023), this coherent, effective, and strategic compliance with GG principles and inhibitors in the SD at all levels (i.e., the company, industry, and country levels) can contribute to the creation of synergy in achieving SD and all three pillars of sustainability. Furthermore, as different countries can have different development needs (Stojanovic et al., 2016), and as industries' contribution to countries' economy and growth can differ from industry to industry and from country to country, countries can consider in their GG and SD which industries to prioritise (with respect to incentives, investments, etc.) considering industries' effective and strategic role in their SD, GG, and economic growth. For example, as construction industry can be among the main industries important for many countries' GG, SD, and economic growth with the help of its contribution to many aspects (e.g., the infrastructure needed), prioritising construction industry related incentives and development policies in compliance with GG indicators and SD, as well as increasing their construction industry's resilience to GG's inhibitors, can be effective in various countries' GG, SD, and economic growth depending on many factors including their construction industry's development level and contribution level to their SD and economic growth. This chapter can be useful to all stakeholders (e.g., researchers, politics, policymakers, humanity, companies, industries) of the SD and GG.

References

Allen, C., Metternicht, G., & Wiedmann, T. (2019). Prioritising SDG targets: Assessing baselines, gaps and interlinkages. *Sustainability Science*, 14(2), 421–438. https://doi.org/10.1007/s11625-018-0596-8

Alsaleh, M., Abdul-Rahim, A. S. & Abdulwakil, M. M. (2021). The importance of worldwide governance indicators for transitions toward sustainable bioenergy industry. *Journal of Environmental Management*, 294, 112960.

Assoum, F. & Alinsato, A. S. (2023). Only under good governance does public debt improve national income: Evidence from dynamic panel threshold model for Sub-Saharan African countries. *Journal of Government and Economics*, 10, 100078.

Berliani, A. D. & Violita, E. S. (2021). The role of governance in SDG through public trust in government: Study in selected OIC member states. *2021 IOP Conference Series: Earth and Environmental Science*, 716, 012100.

Biermann, F., Stevens, C., Bernstein, S., Gupta, A., Kabiri, N., Kanie, N., Levy, M., Nilsson, M., Pintér, L., Scobie, M. & Young, O.R. (2014). *Integrating Governance into the Sustainable Development Goals*. POST2015/UNU-IAS Policy Brief #3. Tokyo: United Nations University Institute for the Advanced Study of Sustainability.

Bosselmann, K., Engel, R. & Taylor, P. (2008). *Governance for Sustainability: Issues, Challenges, Successes*. Gland, International Union for Conservation of Nature.

Council of Europe. (n.d.). *12 Principles of Good Governance – Good Governance (coe.int)* https://www.coe.int/en/web/good-governance/12-principles

Gao, J., Murshed, M., Ghardallou, W., Siddik, A. B., Ali, H. & Khudoykulov, K. (2023). Juxtaposing the environmental consequences of different environment related technological innovations: The significance of establishing good democratic governance. *Gondwana Research*, 121, 486–498.

Güney, T. (2017) Governance and sustainable development: How effective is governance? *The Journal of International Trade & Economic Development*, 26(3), 316–335. https://doi.org/10.1080/09638199.2016.1249391

Huang, S., Wang, B., Li, X., Zheng, P., Mourtzis, D. & Wang, L. (2022). Industry 5.0 and Society 5.0—Comparison, complementation and co-evolution. *Journal of Manufacturing Systems*, 64, 424–428, https://doi.org/10.1016/j.jmsy.2022.07.010

IMF. (2023). Annual Report 2023 Committed to Collaboration. https://www.imf.org/external/pubs/ft/ar/2023/

IMF. (n.d.). *The IMF's Approach to Promoting Good Governance and Combating Corruption – A Guide* https://www.imf.org/external/np/gov/guide/eng/index.htm#P17_850

Kaufmann, D. & Kraay, A. (2023). *Worldwide Governance Indicators, 2023* Update www.govindicators.org, Accessed on 03.11.2023.

Kaushik, A. (2023). The role of good governance in achieving sustainable development: A study of India. *International Journal of Political Science and Governance*, 5(1) 101–106.

Maslow, A. H. (1943). A theory of human motivation. *Psychological Review*, 50(4), 370–396. https://doi.org/10.1037/h0054346

Ofori, E. K., Onifade, S. T., Ali, E. B., Alola, A. A. & Zhang, J. (2023). Achieving carbon neutrality in post COP26 in BRICS, MINT, and G7 economies: The role of financial development and governance indicators. *Journal of Cleaner Production*, 387, 135853.

OHCHR. (n.d.). About good governance. https://www.ohchr.org/en/good-governance/about-good-governance

Omri, A. & Mabrouk, N. B. (2020). Good governance for sustainable development goals: Getting ahead of the pack or falling behind? *Environmental Impact Assessment Review*, 83, 106388.

Ramzy, O., El Bedawy, R., Anwar, M., & Eldahan, O. H. (2019). Sustainable development & good governance. *European Journal of Sustainable Development*, 8, 2, 125–138.

Saba, C. S. & Biyase, M. (2022). Determinants of renewable electricity development in Europe: Do Governance indicators and institutional quality matter? *Energy Reports*, 8, 13914–13938.

Sarhan, A. A. & Gerged, A. M. (2023). Do corporate anti-bribery and corruption commitments enhance environmental management performance? The moderating role of corporate social responsibility accountability and executive compensation governance. *Journal of Environmental Management*, 341, 118063.

Sertyesilisik, B. (2018). Global sustainability leadership: A key for the peace in the world. In: Campbell, A. H. (Editor) *Global Leadership Initiatives for Conflict Resolution and Peacebuilding* (pp. 48–66), Oklahoma: IGI Global.

Sertyesilisik, B. (2022). Achieving post-carbon transition and environmental justice to reduce environment footprint of the construction industry and support sustainable development. In: Das, R. (Editor) *Globalization, Income Distribution and Sustainable Development* (pp. 223–234), Bingley: Emerald Ink Publishing.

Sertyesilisik, B. (2023). Carbon capturing smart construction industry model to foster green and sustainable total factor productivity growth of industries. In: Pal, M. (Editor) *The Impact of Environmental Emissions and Aggregate Economic Activity on Industry* (pp. 11–23), Bingley: Emerald Publishing Limited.

Sertyesilisik, E. & Sertyesilisik, B. (2021). Smart, circular, and competitive manufacturing industry as a key for enhancing resilience of the global economy. In: Pal, M. (Editor) *Productivity Growth in the Manufacturing Sector* (pp. 71–82), Bingley: Emerald Publishing Limited.

Sharma, S. K. (2001). Governance for realising a sustainable society. *Social Change*, 31(1/2), 165–173.

Stojanović, I., Ateljević, J. & Stević, R. S. (2016). Good governance as a tool of sustainable development. *European Journal of Sustainable Development*, 5, 4, 558–573.

Towah, W.D. (2019). The Impact of Good Governance and Stability on Sustainable Development in Ghana. Walden University. Doctoral Dissertation. Walden Dissertations and Doctoral Studies.

UNDP. (2014). Discussion Paper Governance for Sustainable Development Integrating Governance in the Post-2015 Development Framework, https://www.undp.org/sites/g/files/zskgke326/files/publications/Discussion-Paper--Governance-for-Sustainable-Development.pdf

UNESCAP. (n.d.) What is good governance? https://www.unescap.org/sites/default/files/good-governance.pdf

Ura, K., & Kinga, S. (2004). Bhutan—Sustainable Development Through Good Governance. The International Bank for Reconstruction and Development, the World Bank.

14

ROLE OF GOVERNMENT ASSISTANCE TO ENDORSE THE GROWTH OF UNORGANIZED RETAIL TRADING ENTERPRISES IN INDIA

Soumita Dasgupta, Akash Dandapat, Debashruti Jana, and Pinaki Das

Introduction

The Indian retail market is heavily slanted towards small unorganized retail trading enterprises. It has the highest retail density in the world, and a majority of them are smaller than 500 sqft (Kalhan, 2007; Sinha et al., 2015). According to the estimation of AC Nielsen and KSA Technopak, in 2001, India had 11 retail outlets for every 1,000 people (Guruswamy et al., 2005). Substantially, India's domestic logistics process is spatially separated. Products reach consumers from the producers through certain stages of assembly and wholesale to the retail outlet. Wholesaling activity is concerned with the sale of merchandised items to retailers or commercial users for intermediary use and not to the ultimate consumers. They create linkages between manufacturers and retail outlets and help in the distribution process of the economy with efficient utilization of time and cost constraints (Riemers, 1998). On the other hand, retailers create a link between the producers and final consumers of the distribution process and do not sell merchandise for further processing (Kotler, 1980; Nath, 2013).

Most consumers in developing countries preferred unorganized retail stores due to their variety and assortment of products. Lenartowicz and Balasubramanian (2009) tried to give a micro as well as macro perspective of those small retail formats that dominated in many developing countries. In underdeveloped markets, zoning requirements are often very loosely enforced. Therefore, the small retailing system represents a very easy and natural way adopted by the supply side to reach consumers through an intensive spatial dissemination of retail presence. Their findings suggest that the ability and willingness of small stores are influenced by the sales force. Differences in the

DOI: 10.4324/9781003530688-17

operational capabilities of small stores were much more effective than the uniform interaction style of multinational corporations. The introduction of consolidated retail formats can't force out the small retail stores due to the specific characteristics of emerging markets in developing economies, such as different shopping patterns among consumers, higher income variance, low-level disposable income, and some supply-side constraints like a lack of scope for information formation, storage management, and weak transportation facilities (D'Andrea et al., 2006; Lenartowicz and Balasubramanian, 2009; Mahajan et al., 2006).

Unorganized retail trade is a dominating feature of developing economies where the labour market is characterized by chronic underemployment (Dannhaeuser, 1980). Mehrotra et al. (2013) stated that though during the Tenth (2002–07) and Eleventh (2007–12) Five-Years Plan the growth rate of the Indian economy was unprecedentedly high, the nature of growth was characterized by joblessness and in formalization of jobs in organized sectors during 2004–05 to 2009–10. According to their findings, conventional sources like trade and repair were the most essential contributors to informal non-farm employment at that time, and retail trade accounted for most of the increase in employment for the sector. Out of 116 million in services, retail trade alone employed 35.7 million workers in 2009–10. Moreover, studies observed that unorganized retail units accounted for 98.6 percent of employment among total retail employees in urban India, while only 3.2 percent were from organized units (Mehrotra et al., 2013).

The unorganized sector comprises the units that engage in the production and sale of goods and services, operate outside of the state regulatory framework, and are not bound to abide by the labour laws and workers' employment conditions (Roever, 2016; Mukherjee &Goyal, 2012; Dandapat et al., 2020; Dandapat et al., 2021). According to the National Commission for Enterprise in the Unorganized Sector (NCEUS) of our country, "the unorganized sector consists of all unincorporated private enterprises owned by individuals or households engaged in the sale or production of goods and services operated on a proprietary or partnership basis with less than ten total workers". Gandhi and Chinnadorai(2017)stated that unorganized retail refers to traditional small retail operating inside a tiny geographical area, producing and selling goods or merchandise on a lower scale with slight or no standardization. Local grocery shops, small convenience stores, small pavement-side vendors, owner-manned general stores, chemists, footwear shops, pan and hand-cart shops, hawkers, etc. are examples of these low-cost traditional retail enterprises.

Government assistance plays a crucial role in enhancing the performance of unorganized enterprises (Peter et al., 2018). Some studies noted that these enterprises generally suffer from inadequate finance due to their opacity and informal nature of operation (Beck et al., 2005, 2008; Berger and Udell, 2006; Guiso and Minetti, 2010; Dietrich, 2012; Dandapat and Das, 2022). Government assistance assists small-scale enterprises in two different ways. First, direct and indirect credit assistance from the government, including grants and subsidies, eases the financial constraints for small informal enterprises and helps them improve performance by overcoming their imperfect ability to acquire finance through the creation of additional cash sources. Second, government intervention removed the problem of asymmetric information either by equalizing the accessibility of information or by developing the capabilities of collateral obligations (Kon & Storey, 2003; Liu et al., 2011; Xiang &Worthington, 2017). Vetrivel (2017) studied the kind of financial problems that unorganized traders faced in India. Problems of bad debt and difficulties in getting government subsidies or concessions have a pessimistic impact on unorganized workers, while the majority of them were facing the problem of limited financial resources. According to the study, the government should provide the facilities of short- and medium-term loans for those retailers who are financially weak.

However, India is one of those few countries where the role of government assistance in supporting the growth and development of unorganized retail trading enterprises (UREs) has not been adequately explored. This chapter aims to fill this gap by examining the effect of government assistance on the status of the growth of UREs in India and also investigating the regional variations and the types of government assistance received by UREs. This study is unique and important as it uses the unit-level data of the UREs of India to investigate the role of government assistance. The remaining part of the chapter is organized into four segments. The Database and Methodology part explicate the database and methodology applied for the empirical analysis of the study. The next part explore the regional disparities and the types of government assistance received by the UREs in India. Further, we discuss the impact of government assistance on the performance status of the UREs In the last part we conclude our observations.

Database and Methodology

Database

This study is based on unit-level data from the National Sample Survey Organisation (NSSO) 67th (2010–11) and 73rd (2015–16) rounds titled "Unincorporated Non-Agricultural Enterprises (Excluding Construction)". These surveys were designed to assess the various operational and economic characteristics of unincorporated non-agricultural enterprises, mostly those belonging to manufacturing, trade, and other services (excluding construction), at a more disaggregate activity category level. Here, for econometric analysis, we have considered only three types of firm status of growth classified by NSSO: expanding, stagnating, and contracting. For data integrity, we excluded firms operating for less than three years or with unspecified growth statuses.

Multinomial Logit Analysis of Status of Growth of UREs

Our analytical approach is guided by a robust theoretical framework, facilitating the examination of Unorganized Retail Enterprises' (UREs) growth status in India and the influence of government assistance. In our exploration, we harness the Multinomial Logit (MNL) model, a powerful tool tailored for situations where dependent variables exhibit multiple categorical outcomes. The MNL model is expressed as:

$$P_{it,j} = \frac{\exp\left(X'_{it,j}\beta_i\right)}{\sum_{i=1}^{m} \exp\left(X'_{it}\beta_i\right)}$$

where X_{it} is case-specific repressors, which include an intercept and other characteristics. Clearly, this model ensures that $0 < P_{it,j} < 1$ and $\sum_{j=1}^{m} P_{it,j} = 1$.
For model identification, one category serves as the base category, and coefficients are interpreted in relation to this base category. In the present study, we designate the expanding status of growth (the first category) as the base category. Thus, in the MNL model, we can express:

$$\Pr\left(Y_{it} = j \setminus Y_{it} = 1\right) = \frac{\Pr\left(Y_{it} = j\right)}{\Pr\left(Y_{it} = j\right) + \Pr\left(Y_{it} = 1\right)} = \frac{\exp\left(X'_{it}\beta_i\right)}{1 + \exp\left(X'_{it}\beta_i\right)}$$

Using $\beta_j = 0$ and cancellation of $\sum_{i=1}^{m} \exp\left(X'_{it}\beta_i\right)$ in the numerator and denominator.

This interpretation enables us to assess the impact of regressors on the likelihood of selecting alternative j over alternative 1.

In line with our theoretical framework, we formulate hypotheses regarding the influence of government assistance on URE growth. Specifically, we posit two hypotheses: H1, suggesting that government assistance positively affects URE growth, and H2, proposing that the impact of government assistance on URE growth varies based on certain control variables. To test these hypotheses, we employ a pooled regression analysis (where i stands for firm, and t stands for time), which we utilize to analyse a comprehensive dataset comprising 31,251,168 firm-level observations. The econometric model, specified as follows, allows us to empirically assess the relationships between government assistance, URE growth, and relevant control variables:

$$STGR_{it} = \beta_0 + \beta_1 GOVA_{it} + \sum \beta_k X_{it,k} + \gamma TD + \mu_{it} \qquad (14.1)$$

where

- $STGR_{it}$ denotes the status of growth of UREs for the i-th enterprise at time t.
- $GOVA_{it}$ represents the government assistance received by the i-th enterprise at time t.
- $X_{it,k}$ is a matrix of control variables encompassing key characteristics of UREs for the i-th enterprise at time t.
- β_k signifies the coefficients of the explanatory variables.
- k indicates the number of control variables (k =1, 2,..., 9).
- TD is the time dummy.

Results

Government Assistance Received by UREs in India

UREs constitute a significant part of the Indian economy, accounting for about 85 percent of the retail industry. It has also accounted for the largest share of employment and gross value addition among the entire unorganized distributive trade sector of our country and played a crucial role in achieving inclusive and sustainable economic growth by promoting entrepreneurship. Despite fostering these fundamental potentials, this sector is constantly left behind because of its informal structure and cannot get adequate support from the government. Only a small fraction of UREs in India have benefited from government assistance, indicating a lack of awareness, accessibility, and accountability among UREs and government agencies. It is observed that the number of retail enterprises getting assistance from the government was only 2 lakhs for the entire country in 2010–11, which again decreased in 2015–16 to 1.5 lakhs. Again, there is considerable variation across the regions of the country in terms of the extent and nature of government assistance to UREs.

Table 14.1 depicts the percentage share of UREs benefiting from government assistance that has increased from 2010–11 to 2015–16 for all the regions of the country except the western region. The western region of the country is experiencing a huge fall in the share of UREs receiving assistance from the government. UREs are operated either outside of the state regulatory framework or registered under local bodies like municipalities or panchayats rather than different acts like VAT, sales tax, the Shop and Establishment Act, etc., which may also be a major constraint to take

TABLE 14.1 Share of UREs Getting Government Assistance across Different Zones of India

Zone	No. of UREs			Govt. Assistance		
	2010–11	2015–16	% Point Change	2010–11	2015–16	% Point Change
North	26.44	26.42	–0.02	22.48	23.34	0.86
North East	4.39	4.33	–0.06	0.82	1.52	0.7
Central	6.22	6.42	0.20	7.74	11.57	3.83
East	22.92	22.42	–0.50	11.51	14.45	2.94
West	18.57	17.58	–0.99	19.88	7.52	–12.36
South	21.45	22.83	1.37	37.57	41.6	4.03
Total	100	100	—	100	100	—

Source: Authors' calculations based on NSSO unit-level data.

Note: North Zone: Chandigarh, Delhi, Haryana, Himachal Pradesh, Jammu & Kashmir, Punjab, Uttarakhand, and Uttar Pradesh.North East Zone: Arunachal Pradesh, Assam, Manipur, Meghalaya, Mizoram, Nagaland, Sikkim, and Tripura.Central Zone: Chhattisgarh and Madhya Pradesh. East Zone: Bihar, Jharkhand, Orissa, and West Bengal. West Zone: D & N Haveli, Daman & Diu, Goa, Gujarat, Maharashtra, and Rajasthan. South Zone: Andaman & Nicobar Island, Andhra Pradesh, Karnataka, Kerala, Lakshadweep, Pondicherry, Tamil Nadu, and Telangana.

advantage of the prevailing government assistance programmes. Among the major states of India, Himachal Pradesh emerges as the best performer in terms of increasing the share of UREs receiving government assistance; it has increased from 6 percent in 2010–11 to around 11 percent in 2015–16.

Figure 14.1 visually portrays the disparities in the distribution of UREs and the government assistance they receive across different regions of India. Notably, the northern part of India exhibits the highest concentration of UREs, closely followed by the eastern and southern regions. However, when it comes to the allocation of government assistance, the eastern region falls behind the other two regions. The southern region emerges as the frontrunner, receiving the highest percentage share of government assistance, while the northeastern region lags behind. Furthermore, the southern part of the country demonstrates the most substantial increase in the share of UREs benefiting from government assistance, which could be attributed to the abundance of registered UREs in this region.

The primary form of government assistance extended to UREs in India predominantly comprises financial loans, followed by subsidies (Figure 14.2). Types of assistance other than loans and subsidies have grasped a very marginal share. The government of India has initiated some flagship schemes to bring small unorganized enterprises under the formal credit system and provide them with affordable credit, such as the Credit Guarantee Fund Scheme for Micro and Small Enterprises (CGTMSE, 2000), the Pradhan Mantri

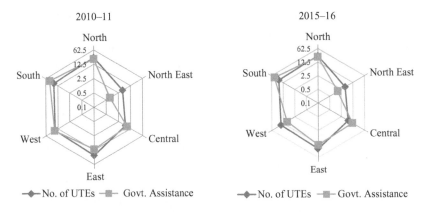

FIGURE 14.1   Distribution of UREs in terms of number and receiving government assistance in 2010–10 and 2015–16.

Source: Authors' calculations based on NSSO unit-level data.

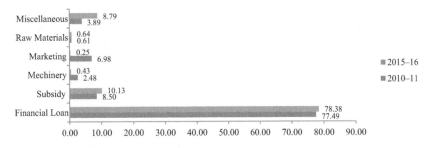

FIGURE 14.2   Types of government assistance received by UREs.

Source: Authors' calculations based on NSSO unit-level data.

Mudra Yojana (PMMY, 2015), etc. These schemes ease the borrowing process for non-farm income-generating activities and enable the provision of credit from any public sector bank (PSB), private sector banks, microfinance institutions, and nonbank financial institutions in the country.

Impact of Government Assistance on Growth Status

The role of government assistance in supporting the growth and development of UREs has not been adequately explored. Therefore, examining the effect of government assistance on the status of the growth of UREs in India is an essential and yet unexplored area of research. In this study, we have considered that UREs have perceived mostly three types of growth status: expanding, stagnating, and contracting. This classification has been made on the basis of the available information on the status of UREs that has been collected from the owners of the enterprises based on their "own perspective" by the NSSO. If enterprises experienced growth over the last three years of their operation, then the UREs have an expanding status of growth. Again, the stagnating status of growth implies that no growth has taken place in UREs or that the condition of UREs has been more or less the same over the last three years of operation. Lastly, if the status of UREs has deteriorated over the last three years of operation, then the status of growth of those UREs will be called contracting in nature.

In this study to measure the impact of government assistance on the status of growth of UREs, it is hypothesized that the status of growth is significantly affected by other firm-level characteristics like type of enterprise, nature of the operation, account maintenance, registration, agreement, sector, problem faced by the enterprise, size of fixed assets, and profitability, which act as the control variables in our empirical analysis. An enterprise may receive assistance from the government (GOVA) in the form of financial loans, subsidies, machinery and equipment, training, marketing, and raw materials. The Department for Promotion of Industry and Internal Trade (DPIIT) under the Ministry of Commerce and Industry of the central government is the nodal agency responsible for the different types of policy formulation to promote the growth of the domestic retail trade sector in the country. The government has various departments, such as the Director General of Foreign Trade, the State Financial Corporation, the District Supply and Marketing Society, etc., through which the government implements policies for the development of UREs. It was found that the mean value of GOVA increased and the standard deviation decreased from 2010–11 to 2015–16. It is hypothesized that government assistance will have a significant impact on the status of growth. It is a dummy variable that takes 1 if an enterprise receives government assistance and 0 otherwise.

Again, all the key characteristics of UREs like the type of enterprise (ESTTEs), nature of the operation (OPMNT), account maintenance (ACOUNT), registration (REGIST), prior agreement for work (AGRMNT), sector (SECTOR), and problem faced (PROB) by the enterprises are dummy variables, and they have taken either value one or zero. The size of the establishment (ESTTE) type of UREs is larger than the one-account (OATEs) type of UREs, which will hire labour from outside, have better market access, and have higher profitability. Similarly, UREs could be perennial, casual, or seasonal depending on the nature of their operation (OPNMNT). Perennial UREs (OPNMNT) are operating throughout the year, which means if an enterprise is perennial, then it has better work opportunities than the others. In the same way, the systematic bookkeeping practices (ACOUNT) of UREs indicate that regular maintenance of accounts helps to assess the performance of UREs and enhances the loan accessibility of that enterprise. Similarly, the registration (REGIST) attribute of UREs also helps to take advantage of various government policies that affect their status of growth. UREs can go for the prior agreement (AGRMNT) with any other units to sell their product partly or fully instead of the provision of supplying raw materials, technologies, designs, specifications, and plant and machinery by that particular unit, which helps in the functioning of the UREs. Again, it is hypothesized that urban sector (SECTOR) UREs will have a better status of growth than rural sector UREs. Moreover, we hypothesized that the net profit (PROF) and the size of the firm (SZFRM) would have a significant impact on the status of the growth of UREs. In this study, the size of a firm (ln SZFRM) is measured by taking the natural log of the volume of total fixed assets, and the net profit per employee (PROFTEMP) of UREs is measured by dividing the net surplus of the UREs by the number of estimated workers after deducting emoluments, rent, and interest from total factor income (Table 14.2).

TABLE 14.2 Notation, Specification, and Summary Statistics of Variables Used in the Regression Model

Notation	Specification	Mean	SD
Dependent Variable			
STGR	Status of growth is categorized as 0 if expanding, 1 if stagnating, 2 if contracting	1.65	0.64
Independent Variables			
GOVA	Government assistance: Whether the enterprise receives government assistance or not (Yes = 1, No = 0)	0.01	0.10
ESTTE	Nature of enterprises: Whether the enterprise is establishment or not (Yes = 1, No = 0)	0.35	0.48
OPMNT	Number of operating months of UREs	11.84	0.94
ACOUNT	Account maintain: Whether the enterprise maintain accountant or not (Yes = 1, No = 0)	0.20	0.40
REGIST	Registration: Whether the enterprise registered under act or not (Yes = 1, No = 0)	0.45	0.50
AGRMNT	Contracting: Whether the enterprise making contract with other parent entity or not (Yes = 1, No = 0)	0.00	0.05
SECTOR	Sector of enterprises: Whether the enterprise is urban located or not (Yes = 1, No = 0)	0.52	0.50
PROB	Faced problem: Whether the enterprise faced problem or not (Yes = 1, No = 0)	0.36	0.48
ln SZFRM	Size of the firm is measured by the volume of fixed asset (in Rs.crore)	11.92	1.89
PROFTEMP	Profit (in Rs. lakh) per employee of an enterprise is measured by dividing net surplus by the number of estimated workers after deducting emoluments, rent & interest from total factor income.	6630.2	12197.4
Time	Time dummy: 2010–11 = 0 and 2015–16 = 1	0.44	0.50

Source: Same as Table 14.1.

TABLE 14.3 Results of Multinomial Logit Regression

Number of Observations = 164,482
Wald chi2(22) = 11342.18; Prob> chi2 = 0.0000
Log Pseudo Likelihood = –146504; Pseudo R2 = 0.0425

STGR	Coef.	Std. Err.	z	P Value
Expanding (=0)(Base Outcome)				
Stagnating				
GOVA	–0.25576	0.054	–4.74	0.00
ESTTE	–0.43753	0.013	–33.07	0.00
OPMNT	–0.04498	0.006	–7.49	0.00
ACOUNT	–0.14854	0.015	–9.66	0.00
REGIST	–0.11264	0.012	–9.05	0.00
AGRMNT	–0.17051	0.103	–1.65	0.098
SECTOR	0.13915	0.011	12.37	0.00
PROB	0.378236	0.011	33.46	0.00
lnSZFRM	–0.03657	0.003	–10.13	0.00
PROFTEMP	–0.000014	0.00	–9.62	0.00
Time	0.224821	0.011	19.71	0.00
Constant	1.081898	0.077	13.98	0.00
Contracting				
GOVA	0.068385	0.084	0.81	0.42
ESTTE	–0.63576	0.024	–26.3	0.00
NOPN	–0.10976	0.009	–12.56	0.00
ACOUNT	–0.03603	0.027	–1.33	0.183
REGIST	–0.07807	0.022	–3.54	0.00
AGRMNT	0.325648	0.150	2.17	0.03
SECTOR	0.39727	0.020	19.29	0.00
PROB	1.632114	0.020	82.78	0.00
lnSZFRM	0.025588	0.007	3.44	0.001
PROFTEMP	–0.000033	0.000	–8.97	0.00
Time	0.421864	0.020	20.53	0.00
Constant	–1.32027	0.125	–10.55	0.00

Source: Same as Table 14.1.

Table 14.3 presents the results of the multinomial logit regression analysis spanning the years from 2010–11 to 2015–16. The findings reveal important insights into the growth dynamics of UREs in relation to government assistance and key firm-level characteristics.

Firstly, the analysis demonstrates that UREs receiving government assistance exhibit a distinct pattern of growth. Specifically, they are 0.255 units more likely to experience an expanding nature of growth compared to UREs that do not receive such assistance, indicating a positive association between government support and business expansion.

Additionally, several firm-level characteristics significantly influence URE growth status. These include the type of establishment, continuity of operation throughout the year, systematic bookkeeping practices, URE registration, prior work agreements with other businesses, and the challenges faced by UREs. UREs with certain characteristics are more inclined toward an expanding growth status as opposed to stagnation or contraction. For instance, establishment types other than "own account" UREs are more likely to experience growth. UREs operating consistently throughout the year and maintaining systematic bookkeeping practices tend to expand. Similarly, registered UREs are predisposed to growth, especially in rural areas compared to urban locales.

Moreover, the size of UREs plays a role in growth dynamics. Larger UREs are less likely to stagnate, suggesting that size positively impacts growth prospects. Notably, UREs encountering minimal problems and achieving higher profits per employee are more likely to experience expansion, underlining the importance of operational efficiency and profitability.

The inclusion of time dummies in the analysis reveals a concerning trend. UREs in 2015–16, relative to those in 2010–11 show a decreased likelihood of experiencing expansion. This indicates a worrisome deterioration in the growth prospects of UREs over time, highlighting the need for interventions and policies to support their sustainability and development.

Discussions

The findings of this study open up a rich landscape for discussing the status of UREs in India, the impact of government assistance, and the broader challenges that these enterprises face.

One striking observation is the limited extent of government support reaching UREs in India. The data indicates that a relatively small number of UREs benefit from government assistance, with discernible regional disparities in the distribution of this support. These regional variations may stem from differences in the prevalence of registered UREs across India's diverse geographical areas. Notably, financial loans represent the predominant form of government aid. National-level investigations into small informal enterprises in India have identified structural constraints as the primary hindrance to the establishment of a robust support system for these enterprises (Das, 2007).

In response to these challenges and to bolster small enterprises, the Indian government has implemented credit guarantee schemes such as the Credit Guarantee Fund Scheme for Micro and Small Enterprises (CGTMSE, 2000), Pradhan Mantri Mudra Yojana (PMMY, 2015), and Start-Up India (2016). These schemes adopt a market-oriented approach to provide financing to small enterprises (Boocock & Shariff, 2005; Chandler, 2012; Riding et al.,

2007). However, the informal structure, lack of transparency, and limited bargaining power of UREs create potential impediments to their creditworthiness. These factors elevate the risks of market failure due to issues associated with adverse selection and moral hazards when UREs seek financial loans from commercial banks and non-banking institutions (Craig et al., 2009).

Banks often opt for higher fees and reduced exposure when dealing with UREs, compounding the problem of nonperforming assets (NPAs). In some cases, banks encourage small enterprises to opt for guaranteed loans instead of regular loans, as they are more profitable for the banks (De Rugy, 2007). Therefore, strengthening and streamlining credit guarantee schemes are imperative to alleviate financial constraints faced by small enterprises (Das, 2007).

Moreover, our analysis unveiled that forms of government assistance beyond financial loans, such as support for raw materials, training, and marketing, make up a negligible share of total assistance. Hence, it is advisable for the government to consider direct forms of assistance, including grants, subsidies, tax incentives, and training programmes, as these can prove to be efficient and cost-effective measures to stimulate the growth of UREs (Green, 2003; Dandapat et al., 2020; Dandapat et al., 2021).

The empirical analysis indicates that government assistance significantly influences the growth status of UREs. UREs receiving government assistance are more likely to experience expansion compared to those without such assistance. This finding aligns with research by Xiang and Worthington (2017), who also concluded that government assistance is effective in improving the performance of unorganized enterprises. They highlighted that firms receiving government guaranteed credit tend to have higher reliability, increasing their chances of obtaining non-government assistance in the future.

However, it is crucial to note that many government programmes for small enterprise development in India predominantly target registered enterprises. In India, the percentage of registered UREs is surprisingly low, with less than 40 percent of enterprises across the country being registered. A significant portion of these registered entities falls under local bodies such as panchayats and municipalities. The low rate of registration in India can be attributed to the absence of persistent official costs associated with registration, making the implicit cost of transitioning from an informal to a formal structure a deterrent for UREs seeking government benefits (De Soto, 1989; Sharma, 2014; Dandapat et al., 2020; Dandapat et al., 2021). Additionally, the need for assistance varies throughout the lifecycle stages of UREs (Singh & Wasdani, 2016).

This discussion underscores the need for a more inclusive and comprehensive approach to government assistance for UREs in India. Addressing the challenges of limited reach, structural constraints, and low registration rates is essential to unlock the full potential of these enterprises and promote their sustained growth and development in the dynamic retail landscape of India.

Conclusions and Policy Implications

UREs operating within India's informal structure play a pivotal role in the nation's distribution system and significantly contribute to its economic growth. However, the informality and opacity that often characterize these enterprises have led to a limited number of them benefiting from government assistance. Among the UREs in India that have accessed government support, those located in the southern region have secured the largest share, while the northeastern region lags behind. The prevalence of registered UREs in the southern region compared to other areas likely places it in a relatively advantageous position. Notably, Himachal Pradesh stands out as a high performer, demonstrating a commendable increase in the share of UREs receiving government assistance among major states.

Financial loans emerge as the most common form of government assistance, followed by subsidies. However, there is a pressing need to expand the provision of direct assistance, including training, marketing support, tax incentives, and more. This diverse range of support can facilitate the smoother operation of UREs, ultimately contributing to their growth and modernization. The study's analysis reveals that government assistance exerts a positive and significant impact on fostering the expansion of UREs. This underscores the vital role that government intervention can play in facilitating the development of UREs. Therefore, a key policy implication is the need to emphasize systematic bookkeeping and registration for UREs. This can help mitigate information asymmetry among enterprise owners regarding the perceived costs and benefits of registration under government authorities. Such measures can enable a significant proportion of informal traders to access governmental policies offering legislative, financial, and infrastructural support (Sharma, 2014).

Furthermore, this study contributes by unveiling the hitherto unexplored landscape of the Indian unorganized retail sector in relation to government assistance. It provides critical insights into the challenges and opportunities faced by UREs in India's dynamic retail landscape.

While this study sheds light on various facets, it is important to acknowledge its limitations. Future research endeavours should delve into understanding the reasons behind enterprises' reluctance to register with government authorities, despite the potential gains. Additionally, there is a need for comprehensive monitoring of the channels through which benefits are made accessible to primary units, with a focus on reducing regional disparities and ensuring equitable access to government support.

In light of the research findings and discussions, several key policy implications emerge, offering valuable insights into how government assistance can be harnessed to empower UREs in India and promote their sustainable growth and development.

Promote Registration of UREs: Implement policies and initiatives aimed at encouraging and facilitating the registration of UREs. Reducing the barriers to registration, including simplifying the process and minimizing associated costs, can incentivize more UREs to formalize their operations. Launch public awareness campaigns to inform URE owners about the benefits of formalization and registration. Highlight the advantages, such as access to government support, legislative protection, and financial opportunities.

Diversify Assistance: Expand the scope of government assistance beyond financial loans and subsidies. Consider introducing targeted programmes that offer training, marketing support, tax incentives, and other forms of direct assistance to UREs. This diversified approach can enhance the overall competitiveness and sustainability of these enterprises.

Regional Equity: Recognize and address regional disparities in the distribution of government assistance. Develop strategies to ensure that UREs in less advantaged regions receive equitable support, possibly through state-specific schemes tailored to their unique needs.

Strengthen Credit Guarantee Schemes: Strengthen and streamline credit guarantee schemes for small enterprises like the Credit Guarantee Fund Scheme for Micro and Small Enterprises (CGTMSE), the Pradhan Mantri MUDRA Yojana (PMMY), and Start-Up India. Ensuring the accessibility and efficiency of these schemes can help alleviate the financial constraints faced by UREs. Implement robust monitoring mechanisms to track the accessibility and distribution of government benefits to UREs. Ensuring that assistance reaches primary units without intermediaries can enhance the effectiveness and transparency of support programmes.

Enhance Financial Literacy: Launch initiatives to enhance financial literacy among URE owners and operators. Improved financial knowledge can empower them to make informed decisions about accessing and managing credit, potentially reducing the risks associated with government loans.

Evaluation and Feedback: Continuously evaluate the impact of government assistance programmes on UREs and solicit feedback from beneficiaries. Use this information to refine and improve the effectiveness of existing policies and initiatives.

Long-Term Sustainability: Develop strategies for the long-term sustainability of UREs, taking into account the changing dynamics of the retail sector. Encourage innovation, technology adoption, and the adoption of modern retail practices to ensure UREs remain competitive.

These policy suggestions aim to address the challenges faced by UREs in India while leveraging their significant potential for economic growth and job creation. By adopting a holistic and inclusive approach to government assistance, policymakers can foster an environment where UREs can thrive and contribute more substantially to the nation's retail industry and overall economic development.

References

Beck, T., Demirgüç-Kunt, A., & Maksimovic, V. (2008). Financing patterns around the world: Are small firms different?*Journal of Financial Economics*, 89(3), 467–487.

Beck, T., Demirgüç-Kunt, A. S. L. I., & Maksimovic, V. (2005). Financial and legal constraints to growth: Does firm size matter?*The Journal of Finance*, 60(1), 137–177.

Berger, A. N., & Udell, G. F. (2006). A more complete conceptual framework for SME finance. *Journal of Banking & Finance*, 30(11), 2945–2966.

Boocock, G., & Shariff, M. N. M. (2005). Measuring the effectiveness of credit guarantee schemes: Evidence from Malaysia. *International Small Business Journal*, 23(4), 427–454.

Chandler, V. (2012). The economic impact of the Canada Small Business Financing Program. *Small Business Economics*, 39, 253–264.

Craig, B. R., Jackson, W. E., & Thomson, J. B. (2009). The economic impact of the Small Business Administration's intervention in the small firm credit market: A review of the research literature. *Journal of Small Business Management*, 47(2), 221–231.

D'Andrea, G., Lopez-Aleman, B., & Stengel, A. (2006). Why small retailers endure in Latin America. *International Journal of Retail & Distribution Management*, 34(9), 661–673.

Dandapat, A., & Das, P. (2022). Role of microfinance to promote the growth of unorganized manufacturing enterprises in India: An analysis. In Ramesh Chnadra Das (eds.),*Microfinance to Combat Global Recession and Social Exclusion: An Empirical Investigation* (pp. 131–146). Singapore: Springer Nature Singapore.

Dandapat, A., Dasgupta, S., & Das, P. (2020). Growth status of unorganised food processing enterprises in India, *International Journal of Social Sciences*, 9(4), 291–299.

Dandapat, A., Dasgupta, S., & Das, P. (2021). Productivity of unorganized manufacturing enterprises in India, *Economic Affairs*, 66(1).DOI:10.46852/042 4-2513.1.2021.2

Dannhaeuser, N. (1980). The role of the neighborhood store in developing economies: The case of Dagupan City, Philippines. *The Journal of Developing Areas*, 14(2), 157–174.

Das, K. (2007). SMEs in India: Issues and possibilities in times of globalization. *Asian SMEs and Globalization*, 5, 69–97, ERIA Research Project Report.

De Rugy, V. (2007). The SBA's justification IOU. *Regulation*, 30, 26.

De Soto, H. (1989). *The Other Path* (p. 17133). New York: Harper & Row.

Dietrich, A. (2012). Explaining loan rate differentials between small and large companies: Evidence from Switzerland. *Small Business Economics*, 38, 481–494

Gandhi, M., & Chinnadorai, K. M. (2017). A Study on problems in unorganized retail with regards to customer and retailer perception. *International Journal of Engineering Development and Research*, 5(4), 928–932.

Green, A. (2003). *Credit Guarantee Schemes for Small Enterprises: An Effective Instrument to Promote Private Sector-Led Growth?* Vienna, Austria: UNIDO, Programme Development and Technical Cooperation Division.

Guiso, L., & Minetti, R. (2010). The structure of multiple credit relationships: Evidence from US firms. *Journal of Money, Credit and Banking*, 42(6), 1037–1071.

Guruswamy, M., et al. (2005). FDI in India's retail sector: More bad than good?*Economic and Political Weekly*, 40(7), 619–623.

Kalhan, A. (2007). Impact of malls on small shops and hawkers. *Economic and Political Weekly*, 42(22), 2063–2066.

Kon, Y., & Storey, D. J. (2003). A theory of discouraged borrowers. *Small Business Economics*, 21, 37–49.

Kotler, P. (1980). *Principles of marketing. Englewood Chiffs.* New Jersey: Prentice-Hall.

Lenartowicz, T., & Balasubramanian, S. (2009). Practices and performance of small retail stores in developing economies. *Journal of International Marketing*, 17(1), 58–90.

Liu, M. H., Margaritis, D., & Tourani-Rad, A. (2011). Asymmetric information and price competition in small business lending. *Journal of Banking & Finance*, 35(9), 2189–2196.

Mahajan, V., Banga, K., & Gunther, R. (2006). *The 86 Percent Solution*. Upper Saddle River, NJ: Wharton School Publishing.

Mehrotra, S., Gandhi, A., Saha, P., & Sahoo, B. K. (2013). Turnaround in India's employment story: Silver lining amidst joblessness and informalization?*Economic and Political Weekly*, 48, 87–96.

Mukherjee, A., & Goyal, T. M. (2012). Employment conditions in organized and unorganized retail: Implications for FDI policy in India. *Journal of Business and Retail Management Research*, 6(2), 26–37.

Nath, H. K. (2013). Foreign direct investment (FDI) in India's retail sector. *Journal Space and Culture, India*, 1, 1–12.

Peter, F., Adegbuyi, O., Olokundun, M., Peter, A. O., Amaihian, A. B., & Ibidunni, A. S. (2018). Government financial support and financial performance of SMEs. *Academy ofStrategic Management Journal*, 17, 1–10.

Riding, A., Madill, J., & Haines, G. (2007). Incrementality of SME loan guarantees. *Small Business Economics*, 29, 47–61.

Riemers, C. (1998). Functional relations in distribution channels and location patterns of the Dutch wholesale sector. *GeografiskaAnnaler: Series B, Human Geography*, 80(2), 83–100.

Roever, S. (2016). Informal trade meets informal governance: Street vendors and legal reform in India, South Africa, and Peru. *Cityscape*, 18(1), 27–46.

Sharma, S. (2014). Benefits of a registration policy for microenterprise performance in India. *Small Business Economics*, 42, 153–164.

Singh, C., & Wasdani, P. (2016). Finance for micro, small, and medium-sized enterprises in India: Sources and challenges. ADBI Working Paper581.

Sinha, P., Gokhale, S., and Rawal, S. (2015). Online retailing paired with Kirana – A formidable combination for emerging markets. *Customer Needs and Solutions*, 2, 317–324.

Vetrivel, V. (2017). Financial problems of unorganized retail sector. *InternationalJournal of Applied Research*, 3, 161–164.

Xiang, D., & Worthington, A. C. (2017). The impact of government financial assistance on the performance and financing of Australian SMEs. *Accounting Research Journal*, 30(4), 447–464.

15

POLICIES AND STRATEGIES FOR INSTITUTIONAL PARTICIPATORY GOVERNANCE AND ITS CROSS-COUNTRY EVIDENCE OF DEVELOPMENT

José G. Vargas-Hernández, Ramesh Chandra Das, and M. C. Omar C. Vargas-González

Introduction

Participatory governance is a perspective of democracy and sustainability in public policy with citizen participation. Participation is linked to governance concerning the policy process from being the elected representatives, experts, and bureaucratic to the inclusion of citizens and the recognition of experiential forms and expert knowledge. Participatory development and democracy approaches are variant initiatives in different contexts linked to policy and governance. Participatory governance is characterized by the creation of new institutions supported by participative policies and strategy approaches. Institutions include different actors, stakeholders, and representatives in the consultation, deliberation, and decision-making processes to analyze the conditions for participatory governance arrangements, the institutional designs and cultural cooperation development at all levels of policymaking, representing institutions that have already experienced in practice.

There are ongoing discussions and debates on public participation and creating methods and tools for participatory governance processes through the implementation of representative democracy in some contexts of institutional policymaking. Well-informed and knowledgeable participants in the debates become more technical in content and policy processes strategic adaption in a long-term orientation. The technocratic positivist approach to policy analysis is inherent to the orthodox concept of government. Science provides arguments for policy analysis advocacy, political disputes, and contra expertise (Jennings, 1987; Sclove, 1995). Participatory state-initiated governance arrangements articulate institutional forms for interactive policy analysis, decision-making, and agenda setting in which non-state actors

DOI: 10.4324/9781003530688-18

actively engage in formal political institutions (Rowe & Frewer, 2004). Participatory governance arrangements are instrumentally set in policy design and implementation (Papadopoulos & Warin, 2007: 446). Participatory governance arrangements and practices take place in the design and implementation of policies aimed at urban rehabilitation and regeneration, social inclusion, community development and safety, and so forth. At the core of the policy and strategy debates of institutional participatory governance are the issues and concerns of state formation, liberal democracy, public participation, civil society organizations, economic development, citizenship capabilities, social inclusion and equity, sustainable environment, etc., all of which may lead to the implementation of different types of development programs.

The theoretical studies of participatory governance have engaged in dialogue beyond their boundaries in open structures for cooperation and negotiations with other stakeholders, agencies, and public participation without considering the transaction cost and undermining policy strategic performance (Harter, 1982; Harmon, 1995; Roberts, 2002; Mee, 1997; Ansell, 2011). At the participatory policymaking level and strategy, participatory governance has been proved to be positive (Singleton, 2002; Innes & Booher, 2000; Freeman, 1997; Wondolleck & Yaffee, 2000; Gunningham, 2009; Kelly, 2004). The increasing public participatory democracy to become influential in policymaking must undergo political and strategic administrative reforms and changes that affect the functions' performance of citizens within the decision-making processes. The institutions of participatory governance may affect diverse economic, social, environmental sustainability, institutional, and policymaking environments. Consensus-based models are useful and praised for the mitigation of naturally occurring conflicts emerging during policy and strategy formulation and decision-making processes.

The neo-Tocquevillian role marks out contemporary governance policies. Regional institutional building and pluralistic policy and strategic approach are elements of the neo-functional multilevel governance model which differs from the inter-governmentalism perspective based on the nation's state. A multilevel governance construct can be termed cross-border governance (Hooper & Kramsch, 2004; Struver, 2004). Resources and capabilities are a factor of reform aimed to create the state's capacity to manage the participatory institutions and implement public policies and strategies. Institutional participatory governance may affect positive outcomes of public policies, democratic rights, deliberation, decision-making processes, liberal democracy, citizen learning, and social well-being. The nature of life politics issues often creates conflictive situations requiring adjustments and opening opportunities for participation at different levels. For example, conservation becomes possible through coordination and conservation policies and strategies at various levels and by creating opportunities for participation.

Policy Analysis

The meaning of institutional participatory governance convergences with public policies related to socio intercultural participation and development, etc. (Nagy, 2015; Sørensen, Kortbek, & Thobo Carlsen, 2016; Jancovich, 2011, 2015, 2017; Bonet and Négrier, 2018). Participatory governance as negotiated rule-making enhances the flow of information and promotes policy performance (Lubell, 2000) although its improvement has been questioned. The institutional ambiguity results empirically from the rules and norms shaping politics and policymaking regarding specific participatory governance issues considered problematic. The core of participatory governance is the inclusion of stakeholders in non-state policymaking, such as the popular participatory governance methods used of public meetings and advisory committees (Adams, 2004; Wang & Wart, 2007). The participatory governance methods used by some institutions in policymaking processes have generally been beneficial. Participatory governance institutions in the context of high demand for public resources and inserted in policymaking processes may be able to manage expectations even in the slow intensity of change. Policymaking in participatory governance institutions is a critical factor of contemporary democratic governance of institutions reshaping the state, democratic life, civil society, and social well-being.

Culture plays a crucial role in participatory governance and public policies. Institutional participatory governance is the foundation of sustainable values on natural and cultural resources initiatives shaped by democratization of public policies and strategic decisions aimed to further improve the institutional framework of responsibilities. The third wave of democratization introduces as innovation the voices of the citizens into the complexity of the policymaking processes. Participatory governance is articulated to cultural heritage and connected to institutions and cultural policies at the margin of governance. Cultural participation is a conceptual, operational, and interpretative foundation of cultural human rights based on institutional participatory governance policies such as the encouragement of social inclusive transformation. The emerging patterns of institutional transformation and participation in policymaking and politics are intimately related. Participation in policy analysis for participatory democracy attempts to consider the analytic processes and stimulate a plural debate.

The institutional analysis of the cultural policy orientation of participatory governance in new forms of cultural organization should respond from the bottom-up practices created and developed by citizens, communities social and nongovernmental organizations, private companies, etc. The development of organizational cultural resources as an active engagement in emerging practices is based on public and civil partnerships and institutional participatory governance from the perspectives of argument-based policy involving public institutions and authorities, community and civil society organizations, and other relevant actors and stakeholders.

The community driven development transforms decision and policymaking in local institutions for local participatory governance. Marginalized groups in local communities have not always had good representation in institutional participatory governance initiatives and programs, leading to policies that tend to privilege only the attending groups. Citizens engage in public concerns and issues getting involved in the formulation, selection, and oversight of policy. Policymaking with a focus on citizen involvement in accountability and transparency as the guiding principles to form the basis of programs should be implemented to prevent corruption cases and resources leakage. Institutional participatory governance is concerned with the exercise of citizens to have voice and vote allowed by the state-sanctioned institutional processes leading to resulting in the implementation of public policies that produce individual changes with an impact on the well-being of the citizen's lives. Civil society organizations and citizens actively engage in state-sanctioned policymaking formulation, deliberative and decision functions based on authority assigned and resources available. Mobilized citizens who attend meetings to deliberate and vote over resources and spending allocation policies make decisions for public policies and elect local and community representatives. The selected policies are implemented under the citizenship-based oversight organizations.

Collaborative participatory governance is an innovation in policymaking processes including the role of civil society (Baltà Portolés, 2017) in the innovation and implementation of public policies and programs. Public–civil partnerships and public–private partnerships require a dialogue for institutional participatory governance to include the condition to define common goals and agenda related to both individuals and communities and leading to new public policy development. Sudden events focusing on political and public policy issues and concerns in governmental agendas may lead to policy reforms and new institutional participatory governance arrangements shape decisions in specific policy domains (Busenberg, 2001). The level of public participation accepted to be effective can be achieved by the dialogue between citizens and other actors involved in participatory governance to strengthen opportunities in decision-making and policy analysis, design, and implementation. The participation of citizens is related to confidence in democracy to get involved in policymaking processes, cast the vote, and get a mandate to make budget decisions (Sveriges Kommuner och Landsting, SKL, 2009). Policymaking and activism are concerned about the specific contexts that better suit participatory governance to reframe the process of transformation, although there is a lack of knowledge about types of institutions given the limited resources available for institutional building. Policymakers and scholars sustain those institutional participatory institutions to improve democratic public life.

The interactive relationships of public policies manifested in the phenomena of participatory governance attempt to support the implementation of change through bottom-up initiatives that can create instrumental solutions for the formation (Hajer & Wagenaar, 2003: 13). The rules governing institutional participatory governance efforts must be created matching the policy situation. The participatory development principle in institutional governance policy aimed at the establishment of democracy models and sharing responsibility for common decision-making implies the notion of decentralization and de-etatization of power structures as structural reformation challenges (Sternfeld, 2013). A decentralized structure of governance provides an amount of power bringing local governance closer to the citizens (Alfaro, 2010), which may add more complexity and bureaucracy in decision and policymaking processes. Power and leadership exerting the control over institutional levers lead to political consensus and the integration of policy actions to be carried out by political coalitions.

In attempting to measure the normative and complexities of the institutional participatory governance program, must be considered the capabilities, the dynamics of civil society organizations, and reforms of the state, democracy issues of deliberation, interest mediation, representation, policy outcomes and social well-being. Public participation is a political matter and is the distribution of political power among the political and bureaucratic actors aimed to enable the capabilities of citizens in developing public engagement in accepting the rights regarding decision-making, negotiation, and policy formation processes. Participatory governance matters in terms of resources and capabilities of citizens, state reforms, civil society publics, representative democracy, and public policy. The new political spaces are in relation to formal governance arrangements to provide an official setting place of politics and policymaking described as political institutions of representative democracy when this one form is unable to cope with unruled societal problems.

Public participatory changes in public governance include provisions canalized through rising participatory debates in increased and strengthened representative democracy at various levels of decision-making and policy formation at various levels. Public debates can have a significant impact on institutional policies and arrangements with different results among the policy domains and countries. In some cases and issues, the result may be to rework regulatory approaches across several domains of life politics and the creation of the new government agency. Participatory governance institutions act as generators to link citizens to each other, involving them in policy networks, expanding the contacts, and developing bonds of solidarity and social capital (Alexander, 2006). Participatory governance institutions have a positive effect on the ability to mobilize civil social organizations in any community to develop constituency service access to new policy networks and create alliances. Political coalitions get involved in participatory practices supporting social actors and non-profit civil aimed to develop a city-wide inclusion policy.

Public participation of citizens in old and new formal and informal networked organizations and networks may provide improved access to policy formation and decision-making processes (Trägårdh & Vamstad, 2009). Politically elected representatives used to have a paternalist and elitist role in decision-making processes (Hertting & Klijn, 2018) resulting in passive public participation under the arguments of technical efficiency, pragmatic functionalism, and policy knowledge (Montin & Granberg, 2013). Other forms of participatory knowledge production are often related to specific interests and concern part of the implementation of conservation policies in cases where they only benefit a limited group of people instead of a broader group. The participatory governance mechanisms involve citizens in decision-making processes over the allocation of funding between local communities and the design of public policies, monitoring and evaluating public spending (Speer, 2012: 2379). The use of some mechanisms for developing and strengthening the public participation and citizenship influence in policy process and decision-making (Hertting & Klijn, 2018) lead to improve the complementary elements of representative democracy and more participative governance.

The institutional participatory governance model in the decision-making process ensures the preconditions of decentralization functions of the state and the participation principle. A process analysis includes diverse issues and aspects involved in public participation such us transparency, credibility, reliability, the execution of job description, and the needed political and citizenship positions during the participation in the decision-making processes. However, public participation is not limited to policymaking process. The trend of participatory governance regeneration should be a priority in urban areas with a tendency for an instrumental approach for short-term planning and consistency, design, formulation, and implementation of communication and consultation in participatory governance policy. The participatory governance reflects the involvement of the stakeholders in the design and implementation of public policies at all levels of governance (Sørensen, Kortbek, & Thobo-Carlsen, 2016). Institutional actors in policy communities of sustainable urban planning and renewal projects are concerned with participation in policymaking and implementation of urban initiatives undergoing consultation of social organizations and civil society.

Governance and participation are approaches of city governing including the inclusion model prevailing and the complementary practices contributing to the governability of the city in the presence of explicit and comprehensive policy. The inclusion of nonpolitical actors is framed by exogenous constraints, rules, pressures, institutional and governance arrangements concerning the urban and metropolitan governments, institutional resources, and cognitive, normative, and political pressures related to the promotion of inclusive policymaking at the different levels of government, transnational, supranational, international, national, regional, local, etc. Urban participatory governance process may support the interventions of the effectiveness in smart city as a living lab experiment based on the co-creation of a behavioral change aimed to strengthening the reciprocal trust between policymakers and citizens and adopting participatory practices (Castri, Veiga Simão, & Granato, 2020). Community decision and policymaking is related to citizens in actions of participatory practices, challenging the beliefs that links participatory practices and institutional development.

Competitiveness and growth in neo-liberal urban policies are radical by can be hybridized with social and environmental policies, concerns and issues opening the economic development policies to participatory governance with the inclusion of non-economic actors. The right created and invited places and spaces to present the problems, expose the arguments, discuss, make decisions and policies, and develop trust among all the actors and stakeholders should be the institutions aimed to enhance the participatory governance. New urban policies aimed at economic development make up political measures in competitiveness and innovation supported in the coexistence of social cohesion, growth, and solidarity farmed by the politics of development with the coexistence of participatory governance practices and including the consultation programs of urban renewal projects. Village assemblies do not necessarily lead to deliberation, decision, and policymaking processes to participatory governance and self-government to prepare development plans.

The most relevant actors involved in institutional participative governance are the citizens, civil society, nonprofit and nongovernmental organizations with initiatives of flexible forms of responding to public needs and issues, reshaping local policies, and contributing to local development. However, representatives of civil society, nongovernmental and social organizations are held more responsible, in some issues and concerns, that the citizens in general or government representatives questioning the power and mandate of regulations and public policies, changing their roles and functions from governing to regulating or monitoring and the issues of indemnity. The exercise competencies of low politics at regional and local levels have no legislative powers. Meanwhile, the government authorities with police powers are considered police powers.

Government representatives can formally use created participation spaces to have control over the lack of satisfaction and eventual resistance of civil society with policymaking decisions (Venter, 2006). In this situation, the government is becoming powerlessness questioning the degree of the mandate for the regulation and monitoring roles. Participation in governance decisions and policymaking has the purpose to obtain agreement from as many actors and stakeholders as possible, to overcome resistance and mitigate conflicts. Sometimes, government authorities are not prepared and willing to accept or tolerate criticism and response to a situation that may be spiraling out of control and challenged with the arising needs despite the knowledge and expertise of government officials. Institutional participatory governance processes present numerous problems and questions that are significant at local decision-making and autonomy levels in introducing appropriate principles, ruling mechanisms of participation, designing, and shaping public policies, representing, and sharing responsibilities as an appeal of democracy (Held, 2006: 261). A process analysis includes diverse issues and aspects involved in public participation such as transparency, credibility, reliability, the execution of job description, and the needed political and citizenship positions during the participation in the decision-making processes. However, public participation is not limited to policymaking process.

A model of local participatory governance may be based on the advice of experts creating committees made up of experts, volunteer residents, and professionals, who receive the mandate to develop policy and project proposals. Participatory actions involving the different sectors, are a response to the economic, socio-political, and environmental crisis, may be people-oriented local and regional policies. The model of participative governance framework based on shared ownership provides support for other institutional participative governance models that respond to the needs of local non-institutional and the development of new policy design and formation frameworks that ensures the long-term sustainability and adaptability of a new institutional participative governance format. Participation of people in regional cross border participatory governance happening in reference to participatory actions is framed by the inclusion of the different policy design, decision-making, and deliberation. Policy deliberation on new institutional and organizational participatory governance designs and new partnership configurations should endeavor but not endanger. The emerging decisions from public deliberation and representative participation governance processes to ensure integration and implementation into public policies aim to achieve substantive and sustainable goals and outcomes.

Some of these participatory governance forms are deliberative and included in the participatory arrangements with not tight regular processes of policies and representative institutions while others are more linked to policymaking in representative institutions (Hertting & Kugelberg, 2018: 1). Policymaking areas of institutions and governments that can make use of formal arrangements for participatory governance tend to increase, although it may be difficult to replace the spontaneous participation emerging from a plural society driven by the state participatory initiatives and exercises. It is more likely to happen during the regulation phases where the concerned publics have a relevant function.

More formal arrangements of participatory governance are aimed to democratize policy-and decision-making and recreation of trust in contested policy issues and areas within a broad context than other forms of political participation and participatory governance practices. The deliberative process expands the political and policy debates in the public sphere, with new forms of engagement, listening, and speaking affecting all the involved government officials and citizens exchanging information, learning, and arguing rather than politicians. A deliberative process to be effective, according to Carson et al. (2005), must have influence on decision and policymaking, be inclusive of diverse values and provide equal opportunity to participate and quality on deliberation, open access to information and dialogue, and frame issues an option to search common grounds. The citizens' involvement in public participative governance and representative democracy in policymaking is in the interest of both citizens and political representatives.

Good governance is transparent and includes public participation in design policies, decision-making, and evaluation of programs and projects. Participatory institutions and the public consisting of citizens mobilizing themselves around democratic values allow civil society organizations to participate in formal delivery and policymaking process and promote the adoption of state institutions to protect these new practices (Wampler & Avritzer, 2004). Polycentric institutional participatory governance focuses on multilevel analyses stemming from the subsidiary principle of democratic public policies, democratic values of socio intercultural diversity and openness, and the needs of local and regional inclusive communities. Conservation policies are characterized by competing imperatives and conflicts between multilevel governance and local implementation. Shifting from one-dimension conservation practices toward a more complex comprehensive approach may be more intrinsically linked to participatory forms of knowledge production with emphasis on ethnicization and trust in conservation policies.

Multilevel polity in empowering subsidiarity within regional policy is attractive for participatory actions that influence development at the cross border contexts. Regional policymaking in participatory governance should enhance regionalization and legitimacy of politics. The ability to influence decision and policymaking can be curtailed from external and internal spheres of participatory governance spaces due to political pressures and intimidation of participants. The implementation of a strategic agenda-setting on participatory deliberation policies designed from the bottom-up including citizenship at geographic territorial multilevel and happening at all socio-economic sectors. At multilevel implementation of institutional participatory governance framework created and adopted in different areas including the cultural policies to provide the foundations and guidelines for supporting and empowering either through top-down or bottom-up implementation of initiatives. Bottom-up and mixed cases of institutional participative governance addressing policy and political issues, officials of local governments are interested in creating new institutions.

The participatory initiatives transform local decision and policymaking aimed to empower the marginalized. Empowerment of local government officials, citizens, and activists may become plausible to produce public policy outcomes to gain support. Local administration units hold consultation, deliberation, decision, and policymaking open to the participation of all citizens. Local governments facilitate to citizens to make decisions and choices that have an impact on public policy outcomes, making necessary to modify the state's administrative structures. National policies may include additional measures, relating to individual inclusion in participatory governance development methods more evident in the form of support for development programs. Institutional participatory governance practices are recognized in comparative analyses between nations and regions considered as imagination and creating the new structure of public policy and decision-making in specific contexts including cultural polycentric and pluralism, creative autonomy, participation, and cooperation (Primorac & Obuljen Koržinek, 2016: 4). Participation and cooperation increase the direct relationships aimed to achieve effective and tangible policy outcomes (Ansell & Gash, 2008: 552). To treat the issue of pluralism can be used in several approaches to solve pluralism policy connected to the community through inclusion in institutional participatory governance development as a permanent dynamic process.

Participation may be reflected through the prism of the myth considered by the imperative of evidence-based policy to justify investments in institutional and organizational governance where the participatory decision-making must ensure the inclusion of those involved (Bevir & Rhodes, 2010 in Jancovich, 2017: 4). Independence and fragmentation between the institutional components of local-urban government considering the proximity for participation autonomy from regional and national governments may hamper the local implementation of the policy of inclusion influencing or constraining the inclusive initiatives.

Participatory governance has positive effects on policy performance, which externally may vary depending on the transaction costs. Transaction costs are related to internal and external factors that have effects not always positive of participatory governance on policy performance (Rigg & O'Mahony, 2013; Robertson & Choi, 2012). The institutional participatory governance methods vary in the positive effect of participatory governance and are limited by high-transaction-cost policy conditions. In the situation of increasing transaction costs, it is needed that agencies and human resources have more interactions using participatory governance methods the effects on policy performance may be negative. Participatory governance interventions and programs have spillover effects on social dynamics and local institutions such as meeting the citizens' demands for public deliberation and consultation getting involved and engaged in local decision and policymaking, as the example of the open budget. However, there is little evidence that some forms of participatory governance can transform decision and policymaking in local institutions.

Participatory governance is limited by higher transaction costs. In institutional participatory governance, transaction costs are more meaningful to policy conditions rather than political environments, but political environments are more significant in non-institutional participatory governance rather than transaction costs. No institutional participatory governance on policy performance even under low transaction costs is less positive that the institutional participatory governance. Participatory governance and advisory committee spending have positive effects on policy performance, although uncertain behavioral and environmental conditions lead to high transaction costs and the interaction variables between advisory committee spending and transaction-cost-related policy conditions are negative. Citizens have the responsibility to identify themselves and participate in decision and policymaking processes in all the environmental issues and concerns (Luger, 2004).

Lobby, hearings, issue salience, and investigations are transaction-cost-related policy conditions and the political environment variables are executive–legislative unified government, conflict, and liberalism. Political environments spend less than the advisory committees which tend to be institutional in policy communities. Agencies consider their political environments regarding the management of public meetings and related to transaction cost policy conditions. Public meetings are ineffective non-institutional participatory governance methods under low transaction costs policy conditions.

The effect of participatory governance decreases as transaction cost increases in lobbying, hearings, issue salience, and investigations. The positive effect of public meetings on policy performance tends to decrease as the transaction costs increase. Depending on transaction-cost-related policy conditions, public meetings and advisory committees have positive effects on policy performance. Participatory governance accentuates the effects of interactions to gain a better understanding of environments and improve policy performance (Paletta, 2012; Neshkova & Guo, 2012; Nicholson-Crotty & O'Toole, 2004). Participatory governance influences policy performance shaped by internal and external factors related to transaction costs. If the transaction costs are uncertain, the effect is less positive (Lee, 2016).

However, other studies have concluded that participatory governance does not necessarily improve policy performance (Doberstein, 2016; Gerlak, Heikkila, & Lubell, 2012; Choi, 2014) and its effect may vary depending on the methods used (Frieling, Lindenberg, & Stokman, 2014; Robertson &

Choi, 2012). This implies that participatory governance is not always related to policy performance (Marcus, Geffen, & Sexton, 2002) and varies in the relationship between internal and external factors and the transaction costs incurred in the transactions. Creation, development, and growth of new models of institutional participatory governance and innovative policies in institutions and organizations require an adjustment of existing legal frameworks aimed to ensure the design and implementation of more hybrid democratic policies. The design and implementation of new forms and types of institutional participatory governance requires more research, knowledge, and experiences in policy experiments based on the existing research and recommendations.

The new models of institutional participatory governance develop evolutionary steps in policy development and responses to enhance the values of democracy in society, decentralization, and local development. New models of participatory governance can be experimented based on expert advisory committees formed by volunteer residents, professionals, and experts aimed to develop policy proposals on sustainable issues and other actions. Experimenting with a new model of participative governance based on the work of advisory committees composed of volunteer residents, professionals, and experts committed to develop policy and project proposals with respect to concerns, actions, and issues such as the participatory budgeting model.

Implications in Designing and Implementing Strategies

A strategy aimed to ensure institutional participatory governance sustainability is the law codifications despite the disjunction between the formal law and the governing practices. The strategic objectives of participatory governance imply the notions of citizenship participation and engagement, involvement in decision-making and authority, and governance devolution. In participatory practices and initiatives, the actors bear interests and values oriented toward common goods and strategies of urban space exploitation and economic growth such as the associations, social movements, committees, individuals, and so forth are included in priorities.

Strategies of inclusive practices and initiatives have different meanings and natures in various forms of participation and governance into the inclusion of a governing process analyzed by the social and political sciences. Giving voice and facilitating participation to different identities and conflicting interests is a strategy pursued by explicit politics and policy of inclusion through complementary and coordinated political practices of participatory governance. Participation and voice of citizens translate into specific governance outcomes which may fall into overlapping policy categories, such as education, health environment, transportation, mobility, etc. The relationships between inclusion initiatives and strategies promote practices that may be in opposition or on intermediate positions in the continuum. There is empirical evidence of inclusive practices, strategies, and policies based on governance and participation shared in the participatory governance framework.

Issues of politics life have a broad impact leading to the loss of institutional trust on established practices in government regulations, and to experiment with new participatory strategies to regain trust through participation. Ethos and pathos as strategic rhetoric in classical Greek play a relevant role in participatory governance. Participation in the politics of life is an elaborated theoretical framework to be used against the background of social change processes and the emergence of strategies of new governance. The new governance arrangements as the act of governing are designed with non-state actors or individuals not being elected as representatives and individuals in civil service, participates in policy analysis or policymaking processes. Participation contributes to solve the contentious problems of governance through policies concerned with the dimensions of the politics of life under human control and limited to socio-political control. These dimensions of the politics of life are connected to normative, value, and moral factors, such as responsibility toward non-human nature and ozone in future generations. In these dimensions, the traditional mechanisms of governance may hamper policymaking in institutional experimentation.

The new forms of direct democracy tend to limit the power of political and party elites to increase the participation of excluded groups and allow them to get involved in deliberative and policymaking ongoing processes. The discourse and practice of deliberative democracy centered around the meaningful public participation needs and issues are valued for the potential and have influence to facilitate government decision and policymaking. The emerging new forms of participatory governance and development are promising new democratic solutions but bringing many challenges that may be not overcome with new policy statements from above, but the strategic design of institutional change, behavioral change, and capacity building. New forms of institutional participation in policymaking approached from a conventional perspective may fit the model of participation in the forms of citizen surveys and referendums.

Participatory governance in institutional designs is the practice of involving and consulting public members in the agenda setting, decision-making, and policy design activities of organizations and institutions that are responsible for policy analysis and development (Rowe & Frewer, 2004). Government institutions and agencies must design and implement the best strategy to reduce or absorb uncertainty in domains of life politics based on policies precautionary principle, considering that may be broader to include uncertainty about regulation and governance of benefits and risks of using the novel technology. Participatory governance arrangements are context-specific terms and features in learning, trust development, modes of governance, individual and collective responsibility, strategies, and concerns to cope with uncertainty, complexity, risk, value conflict, etc., as some of the most relevant issues of the effective and legitimate politics of life. Citizens make collective decisions and policymaking in more inclusive, democratic, and participative processes to be delegated to the community. The legitimation process of participatory governance extends to inclusive initiatives and practices within the various policy domains and issues. The implementation of participatory governance requires the strategic design of institutional change, behavioral change, and capacity building.

Public participation in institutional participatory governance is a strategy designed and implemented by policymakers in the face of crisis and uncertainty events aimed to build public support for regulatory means and measures. More open and flexible public participation leading to participatory governance combines a variety of approaches to give support to activities and practices strategically used in spontaneous and informal forums and participation to more formal participation among a variety of stakeholders and actors. A broad use of participatory approaches involves citizens and beneficiaries of projects and policies concerning decision and policymaking process in programming, implementation, and evaluation. Interconnections between participatory governance and cultural heritage as a strategic resource for sustainability through structured dialogue, social dimension, and synergy coordination among the actors and stakeholders involved in the procedures of heritage valorization of the interests. Multiple lanes for citizen engagement link community development, social organizations and movements, and political parties with local governance strategies, using a variety of participatory methods. Participatory methods and approaches have entered the government spheres to confront issues of policy and institutional changes. Citizens use different participatory strategies aimed to engage in local governance and create engagement spaces for direct civil society participation in decentralized powers of local governments.

Local governments can improve the public participation in policymaking by advancing social and political awareness of the meaning, methods, and tools (Montin and Granberg, 2013). Local government must be committed to develop and increase the opportunities for the public participation of citizens in influencing the decision and policymaking processes and adding elements of deliberative and representative democracy, leading to a functioning representative democracy, and adapted to participatory governance (Trägårdh, 2011). The engagement of citizens with government, but outside of participatory governance, requires strategic actions to be implemented to amplify their voices through advocacy, lobbying for policy change, monitoring, and performance. Poor participants engage in behaviors associated with strategies implemented by higher income citizens in more dynamic participatory institutions and contentious civil society.

Local community articulations of socio-political values based on heritage are strategic in local development underlining the need for sustainable development models of participative governance and management about the preservation and management of infrastructure and species. Institutional participatory governance is linked to local political environment programs designed to facilitate citizens the reshaping rights of local policy outcomes. Local governments can pressure the central normative government to implement inclusive methods in strategic planning, consultation procedures, and others. An institutional and formal process of negotiating and adapting strategies between local government officials and citizens is necessary to secure the outcomes.

Economic globalization processes have an impact on urban areas in different forms leading to their reactions by policymaking and strategies with different orientations (Savitch & Kantor, 2002; Jessop, 2002; Brenner & Theodore, 2002; d'Albergo & Lefèvre, 2007). Cities worldwide are framed by information and communication technologies to be considered as smart city strategies oriented by active people engaged in co-creative innovation in urban services (Castri, Veiga Simão, & Granato, 2020). The so-called government technologies have been developed to overcome the capacity deficit resulting from the imperfect information flows emerging from the policy target groups and the public policy actors (Mayntz & Scharpf, 1975; cf. Mayntz, 1980). The technology assessments have limited impacts due to the participatory practices which are more democratic oriented and practical like the policy practices toward the social basis for decision-making on science and technology and improvement of the technological design and other attempts of classification.

The mobilization strategy of the participatory governance of public services delivery model engages government service providers with demand side. Critiques of the government policies based on evidence of unequal and unfair tariffs for public services in which the government is responsible for financing and implementing them may resonate and find support with social and environmental movements. In such situations, there should be mutual respect between the two actors involved based on the political functions of the egalitarian and inclusive nature of participants with consideration of observations and opinions in the deliberation, decision, and policymaking processes and absence of coercion (Carson & Hartz-Karp, 2005).

With a new strategy for institutional development, regional and local participatory governance may remain elaborated and rated on the scale of urban planning and development areas based on priorities. Government officials and actors prefer to appear as pure or affected publics to engage publics in some specific policy areas. To build participatory governance are required to formulate and implement strategies considering the functioning of the states, regional and local conflicts and ethnic violence, dysfunctionalities in civil societies and communities with weak engagements. Any disease that affects humans strongly disrupts the institutional organization affecting the policy areas of public health and other fields organized in isolation from one another. The development of strategies for civil society engagement in economic arenas is a challenge.

The configuration analysis of the state must be able to assess the impact of state policies favoring and engaging citizens, more likely in post-conflict poor regions than in other environments where a well-functioning state has developed greater capacities to implement public policies with greater expectations for achievements. The effectiveness of the state is related to local governments that are likely to adopt public policies enhancing participatory institutions to meet the needs of citizens. However, if the states are becoming less effective, the participatory institutions should address the emerging policy problems. Strategies of participatory governance can be implemented at the regional level but have less influence at local and community levels. The participatory approach of dual power is implemented through strategies of partnership and cooperation between local governments and grassroots communities to contribute to public decision and policymaking.

The performative dimension refers to the strategic efforts to control interactions in the directions of desired outcomes and to a structuralist interpretation to hold personal participations (Burke, 1969) self-activated being involved in an occurrence and less involuntary made-to-be part of and self-motion (Sartori, 1987). Analysis of the assessment of public institutional participatory governance overlooking the political manifestation and participation in collaborative policymaking should be under scrutiny (Connick & Innes, 2003: 178). Assessing the institutional architecture of participatory governance to evaluate the inputs–outputs, policymaking should be interested in strategic participatory institutions to set the goals with strong or weak states and strong or weak societies. Policymakers, strategies, practitioners, and scholars learn from the adoption of participatory governance institutions. Policymakers, strategists, and scholars can develop evidence of participatory institutions that produce benefits related to the nature of participation, structural context, rules, forms, designs, and modalities of adoption.

Empirical Association between Participatory Governance and Human Development

For examining whether participatory governance has any association with human development as measured by the Human Development Index (HDI), the study goes for some statistical analysis. The data on participatory governance is obtained from the global data governance mapping (www.globaldatagovernancemapping.org) and the data on HDI are obtained from the United Nations Development Program (UNDP) for the year 2021 across three sets of countries from high, upper middle, and lower middle income groups, 10 from each leading to 30 countries in total. A high score on participatory governance (maximum score may be 100 and minimum score may be 0) means the country has good participatory governance and vice versa. To find a degree of association between participatory governance and HDI the product moment correlation coefficient is computed using the following formula:

$$r = \text{Covariance}(x,y) / \text{SD}(x) * \text{SD}(y)$$

where r is the correlation coefficient between two variables (x for participatory governance and y for HDI) and SD is the standard deviation. The statistical significance of 'r' is tested by the 't' statistic as:

$$t = r^* \sqrt{(n-2)} / \sqrt{(1-r^2)}$$

where n is the number of observations which is 30, and $n - 2$ is the degrees of freedom.

Table 15.1 gives the scenario of the three sets of countries in participatory governance and HDI. It is observed that the so-called high income countries are mostly with very high values of participatory governance and the countries from the lower middle income group are with very low scores in the same. Further, the HDI values of the former are greater than that of the latter. The average values (as given in the last row) show that the score for the high income group in participatory governance is 73.3, while it is 49.9 for the upper middle income group and 19.8 for the lower middle group. On the other hand, the average HDI scores are, respectively, 0.927, 0.78, and 0.637. Thus, there is the scenario of positive association between participatory governance and human development.

Figure 15.1 presents the scenario of the countries in participatory governance and HDI for the year 2021.

It is observed from the figure that the lower middle income group stays in the south-west zone and the high income group stays in the north-east zone leading us to conclude that there are positive associations between participatory governance and human development. The line joining the data in the scatter plot shows an upward trend which justifies the positive association. The product moment correlation coefficient between the two across all the 30 countries is computed to be 0.576 and the corresponding 't' value to be 3.73, which is large enough at 28 degrees of freedom to justify the positive association between participatory governance and human development.

Concluding Observations

According to the objective of this study and after a careful policy analysis based on the assumption leading to the effects of policies and strategies, it is concluded that the design and implementation are critical to developing an

TABLE 15.1 Status of Participatory Governance and Human Development of the Listed Countries

	High Income			Upper Middle Income			Lower Middle Income	
Country	Participatory Score	HDI	Country	Participatory Score	HDI	Country	Participatory Score	HDI
France	100	0.903	Russia	33	0.822	India	33	0.633
Germany	100	0.942	Turkye	33	0.838	Philippines	33	0.699
Italy	33	0.895	Argentina	67	0.842	Bangladesh	0	0.661
Japan	67	0.925	Brazil	67	0.754	Pakistan	33	0.544
Netherlands	33	0.941	Mexico	100	0.758	Ghana	33	0.632
Norway	33	0.961	China	33	0.768	Egypt	0	0.731
Spain	100	0.905	Indonesia	33	0.705	Nigeria	33	0.535
Sweden	67	0.947	Malaysia	33	0.803	Morocco	0	0.683
UK	100	0.929	Thailand	33	0.8	Vietnam	33	0.703
USA	100	0.921	South Africa	67	0.713	Tanzania	0	0.549
Average	73.3	0.9269	Average	49.9	0.7803	Average	19.8	0.637

Source: Computed by the authors

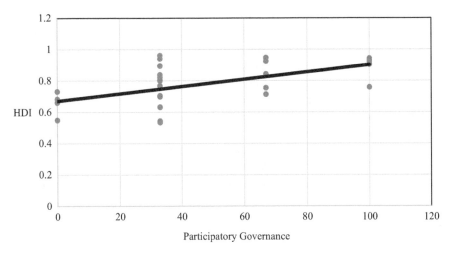

FIGURE 15.1   Combinations of participatory governance and HDI of the countries.

Source: Drawn by the authors.

institutional participatory governance framework. The trend of institutional participatory governance is a movement toward the decentralization of governmental structures and allowing the involvement of citizens in public affairs, decision-making and policymaking. Policy scholarly agendas can help to understand the potential of institutions of participatory governance to transform the economic, social, and sustainable environment in which they are embedded. The rules governing the participatory processes must match the policy issues adapting the rules to reflect community and local needs and demands.

Participatory initiatives contribute to policy change and inform policymaking of the realities and priorities of local people in making decisions leading to the overall development of the countries. The empirical evidence across the 30 countries in three different income groups has shown that participatory governance has positive association with the level of development as measured by the HDI score.

The internal organizational and administrative processes must be required to be reengineered to provide the information that policy experts, all participants, and ordinary citizens need to know to make decisions. The establishment of institutional participatory governance based on resources and strategic direction of development requires shaping the organizational structure considering that there are interests and the needs of citizens to incorporate new forms. Formal public consultation based on a strategic agenda should be implemented when less risky and costly approaches of participatory governance are not feasible and likely to fail. The inclusion of non-political actors in inclusive participatory governance must consider some subjective factors, goals, and strategies. The new governing arrangements supported by government officials require policy and political incentives and limited authority to promote investments for scarce resources. However, in participatory governance and public participation, there is not any preferred approach across many policy domains. The institutional governance arrangements support the structure of territorial governments and the political leadership as relevant factors of city-wide governing based on the authority and institutional resources needed for the implementation of the inclusion policy by the institutional local government. The territorial cooperation processes of participatory governance need to be developed by a facilitator with legal instruments in accordance with the political tools aimed to elaborate public policies at the different levels of government.

References

Adams, B. (2004). Public meetings and the democratic process. *Public Administration Review*, 64(1): 43–54.

Alexander, J. C. (2006). *The Civil Sphere*. New York: Oxford University Press.

Alfaro, D. (2010, April 19). *Montreal's Borough System*, Retrieved from http://meslin.wordpress.com/2010/04/19/boroughs/

Ansell, C. & Gash, A. (2008). Collaborative governance in theory and practice. *Journal of Public Administration Research and Theory*, 18(4): 543–571

Ansell, C. K. (2011). *Pragmatist Democracy: Evolutionary Learning as Public Philosophy*. New York: Oxford University Press.

Baltà P. J. (2017). Towards more collaborative cultural governance. In: *Reshaping Cultural Policies. Advancing Creativity for Development* (pp. 35–53). Paris: UNESCO. Available online at: http://unesdoc.unesco.org/images/0026/002605/260592e.pdf (2/2/2018)

Bevir, M. & Rhodes, R. A. W. (2010). *The State as Cultural Practice*. Oxford: OUP Oxford

Bonet, L. & Négrier, E. (2018) The participative turn in cultural policy: Paradigms, models, contexts. In: *Poetics* (Volume 66, pp. 64–73). doi: 10.1016/j.poetic.2018.02.006

Brenner, N. & Theodore, N. (2002). Cities and the geographies of actually existing neoliberalism. In: N. Brenner & N. Theodore (eds.), *Spaces of Neoliberalism. Urban Restructuring in North America and Western Europe*. Blackwell, Oxford. DOI: 10.1111/1467-8330.00246

Burke, K. (1969). *A Rhetoric of Motives*. California, USA: University of California Press.

Busenberg, G. J. (2001) Learning in organizations and public policy. *Journal of Public Policy*, 21(2): 173–189.

Carson, L. & Hartz-Karp, J. (2005). Adapting and combining deliberative designs: Juries, polls, and forums. In: Gastil J & Levine P (eds.), *The Deliberative Democracy Handbook: Strategies for Effective Civic Engagement in the Twenty-First Century* (Volume 2005, pp. 120–138). San Francisco: Jossey-Bass.

Carson, S. H., Peterson, J. B. & Higgins, D. M. (2005). Reliability, validity, and factor structure of the creative achievement questionnaire. *Creativity Research Journal*, 17(1): 37–50.

Castri, F. C. R., Veiga Simão, J., & Granato, P. (2020). Co-creating app-based policy measures for mobility behavior change: A trigger for novel governance practices at the urban level, *Sustainable Cities and Society*, 53: 2020. DOI: 10.1016/j.scs.2019.101911.

Choi, T. (2014). Revisiting the relevance of collaborative governance to Korean public administration. *Korean Journal of Policy Studies*, 29(2): 21–41.

Connick, S. & Innes, J. (2003) Outcomes of collaborative water policy making: Applying complexity thinking to evaluation. *Journal of Environmental Planning and Management*, 46(2): 177–197.

d'Albergo, E. & Lefèvre, Ch. (2007). Why cities are looking abroad and how they go about it. *Environment and Planning C: Government and Policy*, 25(3). DOI: 10.1068/c2503ed

Doberstein, C. (2016). Designing collaborative governance decision-making in search of a collaborative advantage. *Public Management Review*, 18(6): 819–841.

Freeman, J. (1997). Collaborative governance in the administrative state. *UCLA Law Review*, 1(1): 1–98.

Frieling, M. A., Lindenberg, S. M., & Stokman, F. N. (2014). Collaborative Communities through coproduction: Two case studies. *American Review of Public Administration*, 44 (1): 35–58.

Gerlak, A. K., Heikkila, T., & Lubell, M. (2012). The promise and performance of collaborative governance. In S. Kamieniecki & M. E. Kraft (eds.), *The Oxford Handbook of U.S. Environmental Policy* (pp. 413–434). New York: Oxford University Press.

Gunningham, N. (2009). The new collaborative environmental governance: The localization of regulation. *Journal of Law and Society*, 36(1): 145–166.

Hajer, M. A. & Wagenaar, H. (eds.). (2003) *Deliberative Policy Analysis: Understanding Governance in the Network Society* (Theories 238–239). Cambridge University Press.

Harmon, M. M. (1995). *Responsibility as Paradox: A Critique of Rational Discourse on Government*. Thousand Oaks, CA: Sage.

Harter, P. (1982). Negotiating regulations: A cure for the malaise. *Georgetown Law Journal*, 71(1): 1–118.

Held, D. (2006) *Models of Democracy*. Cambridge: Polity.

Hertting, N. & Klijn, E. H. (2018). Institutionalization of local participatory governance in France, the Netherlands, and Sweden: Three arguments reconsidered. In: N. Hertting & C. Kugelberg (eds.), *Local Participatory Governance and Representative Democracy*. New York and London: Routledge.

Hertting, N., & Kugelberg, C. (Eds.). (2018). *Local Participatory Governance and Representative Democracy: Institutional Dilemmas in European Cities* (1st ed.). Routledge. https://doi.org/10.4324/9781315471174

Hooper, B., & Kramsch, O. (Eds.). (2004). *Cross-Border Governance in the European Union* (1st ed.). Routledge. https://doi.org/10.4324/9780203563380

Innes, J. & Booher, D. (2000). *Public Participation in Planning. New Strategies for the 21st Century*. Berkeley: University of California, Institute of Urban and Regional Development.

Jancovich, L. (2011) Great art for everyone? Engagement and participation policy in the arts. *Cultural Trends*, 20(3–4): 272–279.

Jancovich, L. (2015) Breaking down the fourth wall in arts management: The implication of engaging users in decision-making. *International Journal of Arts Management*, 18(1): 14–28. Special Issue. Cultural Audiences and Populations: New Challenges for Creation and Appropriation.

Jancovich, L. (2017) The participation myth. *International Journal of Cultural Policy*, 23(1): 107–121.

Jennings, B (1987) Interpretation and the practice of policy analysis. In: F. Fischer & J. Forester (eds.), *Confronting Values and Policy Analysis: The Politics of Criteria*. Newbury Park, CA: SAGE Publications.

Jessop, B., (2002) Liberalism, neoliberalism and urban governance: A state-theoretical perspective. In: N. Brenner & N. Theodore (eds.), *Spaces of Neoliberalism. Urban Restructuring in North America and Western Europe*. Oxford: Blackwell Publishing. DOI: 10.1111/1467-8330.00250

Kelly, T. (2004). Unlocking the iron cage: Public administration in the deliberative democratic theory of Jürgen Habermas. *Administration and Society*, 36(1): 38–61.

Lee, J. (2016) Designed to succeed: Participatory governance, transaction cost, and policy performance. *Korean Journal of Policy Studies*, 31(2): 1–22.

Lubell, M. (2000). Cognitive conflict and consensus building in the national estuary program. *American Behavioral Scientist*, 44(4): 629–648.

Luger, M. (2004). Engineer, Ninham Shand; Author of Skuifraam Dam EIA. Interview on 18 May.

Marcus, A. A., Geffen, D. A., & Sexton, K. (2002). *Reinventing Environmental Regulation: Lessons from Project XL*. Washington DC: RFF Press.

Mayntz, R. (ed.). (1980). *Implementation Politischer Programme*. Koningstein: Athenäum.

Mayntz, R. & Scharpf, F. (1975). *Policy Making in the German Federal Bureaucracy*. Amsterdam: Elsevier.

Mee, S. (1997). Negotiated rulemaking and combined sewer overflows (CSOs): Consensus saves ossification? *Boston College Environmental Affairs Law Review*, 25(1): 213–245.

Montin, S. & Granberg, M. (2013). *Moderna Kommuner*. Stockholm: Liber.

Nagy, S. (2015) *Integration Through Culture? Participatory Governance in the European Capitals of Culture Programme*. Budapest: Central European University.

Neshkova, M. I., & Guo, H. (2012). Public participation and organizational performance: Evidence from state agencies. *Journal of Public Administration Research and Theory*, 22(2): 267–288.

Nicholson-Crotty, S., & O'Toole, L. J. (2004). Public management and organizational performance: The case of law enforcement agencies. *Journal of Public Administration Research and Theory*, 14(1): 1–18.

Paletta, A. (2012). Public governance and school performance. *Public Management Review*, 14(8): 1125–1151.

Papadopoulos, Y. & Warin, P. (2007). Are innovative, participatory, and deliberative procedures in policy making democratic and effective? *European Journal of Political Research*, 46. DOI: 10.1111/j.1475-6765.2007.00696.x

Primorac, J. & Obuljen Koržinek, N. (2016). *Compendium Cultural Policies and Trends in Europe. Country profile: Croatia*. Last profile update: July 2016. Council of Europe/ERICarts. Available online at: http://www.culturalpolicies.net/web/countries-profiles-download.php (2/2/2018).

Rigg, C., & O'Mahony, N. (2013). Frustrations in collaborative working. *Public Management Review*, 15(1): 83–108.

Roberts, N. C. (2002). Keeping public officials accountable through dialogue: Resolving the accountability paradox. *Public Administration Review*, 62(6): 658–669.

Robertson, P. J. & Choi, T. (2012). Deliberation, consensus, and stakeholder satisfaction, *Public Management Review*, 14(1): 83–103.

Rowe, G. & Frewer, L. J. (2004). Evaluating public-participation exercises: A research agenda. *Science, Technology, & Human Values*, 29(4): 512–556. DOI: 10.1177/0162243903259197

Sartori, G. (1987). *The Theory of Democracy Revisited*. Chatham, New Jersey: Chatham House.

Savitch, H. & Kantor, P. (2002). *Cities in the International Marketplace: The Political Economy of Urban Development in North America and in Western Europe*. Princeton: Princeton University Press.

Sclove, R. (1995). *Democracy and Technology*. London: The Guilford Press.

Singleton, S. (2002). Collaborative environmental planning in the American West: The good, the bad and the ugly. *Environmental Politics*, 11(3): 54–75.

Sørensen, A. S., Kortbek, H. B. & Thobo-Carlsen, M. (eds.). (2016) *Nordisk Kulturpolitisk* Tidsskrift. 19 (1), Available online at: https://www.idunn.no/nkt/2016/01 (8/3/2018).

Speer, (2012). Participatory governance reform: A good strategy for increasing government responsiveness and improving public services? *World Development*, 40(12): 2379–2398.

Sternfeld, N. (2013). *Playing by the Rules of the Game*. Helsinki: Department of Art, Aalto University. Available online at: https://cummastudies.files.wordpress.com/2013/08/cummapapers1_sternfeld1.pdf (5/2/2018).

Struver, A. (2004), Space Oddity: a thought experiment on European cross-border mobility. https://www.researchgate.net/publication/305149411_Space_Oddity'_a_thought_experiment_on_European_cross-border_mobility

Sveriges Kommuneroch Landsting, SKL. (2009). *Civilsamhället som utvecklingskraft. Positionspapper*. Stockholm: SKL.

Trägårdh, L. (2011) Rethinking the position of civil society in the Nordic social contract: Social trust and radical individualism. In: F. Wijkström & A. Zimmer (eds.), *Nordic Civil Society at a Cross-Roads*. Baden-Baden: Nomos.

Trägårdh, L. & Vamstad, J. (2009). *Att ge eller beskattas. Avdragsrätt för gåvor tillideella organisationer i Sverige och andra länder* (Volume 3, p. 239). Stockholm: Sektor.

Venter, D. (2006). *Chair, Berg Water Project Environmental Monitoring Committee*. Interview on 17 August.

Wampler, B. & Avritzer, L. (2004). Participatory publics: Civil society and new institutions in Democratic Brazil. *Comparative Politics*, 36(3): 291–312.

Wang, X. & Wart, M. W. (2007). When public participation in administration leads to trust: An empirical assessment of managers' perceptions. *Public Administration Review*, 67(2): 265–278.

Wondolleck, J. M. & S. L. Yaffee. (2000). *Making Collaboration Work: Lessons from Innovation in Natural Resource Management*. Washington, DC: Island Press.

INDEX

Pages in *italics* refer to figures and pages in **bold** refer to tables